Behavior Modification
in Applied Settings

Fourth Edition

Behavior Modification in Applied Settings

Fourth Edition

Alan E. Kazdin

Professor of Psychology
Yale University

Brooks/Cole Publishing Company
Pacific Grove, California

Brooks/Cole Publishing Company
A Division of Wadsworth, Inc.

Printed in the United States of America
10 9 8 7 6 5 4

Library of Congress Cataloging-in-Publication Data
Kazdin, Alan E.
    Behavior modification in applied settings.

    Bibliography: p.
    Includes indexes.
    1. Behavior modification. 2. Psychology, Applied.
I. Title.
BF637.B4K4   1989   153.8'5   88-30930
ISBN 0-534-11116-5

Sponsoring Editor: *Claire Verduin*
Editorial Assistant: *Gay Bond*
Production Editor: *Nancy L. Shammas*
Manuscript Editor: *Eugene Zucker*
Permissions Editor: *Carline Haga*
Cover Design: *Sharon L. Kinghan*
Art Coordinator: *Lisa Torri*
Typesetting: *TCSystems, Inc., Shippensburg, PA*
Cover Printing: *Phoenix Color Corporation, Long Island City, NY*
Printing and Binding: *R.R. Donnelley & Sons Company, Crawfordsville, IN*

*To Eve, Joann, Nicole, and Michelle—
past, present, and future sources of inspiration*

Preface

The purpose of this book is to provide an introduction to behavior modification techniques in applied settings. The major focus of the book is on the application of operant conditioning principles, the implementation of behavior modification techniques, and the measurement and evaluation of program effectiveness. The applications include a variety of settings, such as hospitals, institutions, schools, the home, day-care centers, businesses and industry, and communities, as well as outpatient applications for clients who come for treatment. Emphasizing the application of operant procedures permits details to be provided that would ordinarily be sacrificed in a cursory review of the entire domain of behavior modification. However, the focus on operant procedures is one of emphasis rather than one of exclusion. Because of their increased use in applied settings, procedures that rely on other conceptual views, such as social learning theory and cognitively based interpretations of behavior, are also discussed.

An enormous number of books on behavior modification have appeared. These books include both introductory manuals designed for such audiences as parents, teachers, or mental health workers and scholarly texts that present theoretical issues and review the field generally. There is an obvious hiatus between "how to do it" manuals and extensive scholarly reviews that de-emphasize applied research in behavior modification. Behavioral techniques in clinical and applied settings have been well studied, and recommendations for treatment can often be derived from research findings. Thus, a need exists for a text that integrates research and practice for audiences of diverse disciplines who wish to learn about behavior modification. In this book, I attempt to emphasize applied research and clinical intervention techniques and to achieve a balance not usually found in other texts.

Like the previous editions, this edition discusses and illustrates major techniques for altering behavior and the conditions that influence their effectiveness. It provides updated information regarding the effects and limitations of these techniques. The revisions have encompassed many substantive areas. For example, progress has been made in identifying techniques that promote the maintenance of behavior change and the transfer of behavior change to new settings once the behavioral program has been terminated; in developing self-control and cognitively based techniques for use in applied settings; and in extending interventions to many areas of everyday life. The updating consisted not only of providing contemporary examples but also of presenting new techniques, procedural variations, and research findings. Advances with many reinforcement and punishment techniques reflect creative practices that were not available, widely used, or carefully evaluated only a few years ago.

The fourth edition reflects several developments within the field. First, applications have been extended to many new areas since the previous editions were prepared. For example, there has been a proliferation of behavioral programs to treat and manage physical diseases such as cancer and diabetes, to treat and take care of elderly persons, to cope with child abuse and neglect, to enhance personal safety and productivity in business and industry, and to deal with community problems. Such programs are illustrated in this edition. Second, it reflects the increased attention that has been received by many issues within the field. One such issue is the extent to which behavioral programs can produce long-term changes in behavior; another is the large-scale extension of behavioral programs. To disseminate the benefits of intervention more widely, behavioral techniques have been extended to entire school systems and to the workplace in many businesses. The purpose of discussing current issues and advances is not only to chart the progress of the field but also to identify new ways of designing effective programs and evaluating their impact.

The overall organization of this edition is similar to that of the previous editions. In a few chapters, material was condensed; in others, the content was shifted, reorganized, or expanded to facilitate comprehension. The content of many sections has been expanded to reflect recent developments or new areas of emphasis within the field.

Chapters 1 and 2 place the behavior approach, broadly conceived, in historical context and detail the assumptions, characteristics, and principles that underlie applications of behavioral techniques. One of the most distinct characteristics of behavior modification is the careful assessment of behavior and the evaluation of treatment techniques. The methods of assessment and treatment evaluation are discussed (Chapters 3 and 4) because of their importance for designing effective treatments. Three chapters (5, 6, and 7) are devoted to positive and negative reinforcement, punishment, and extinction. Technique options, factors that dictate program effectiveness, issues, and limitations are discussed in each of these chapters. Special technique variations to enhance program effectiveness, self-control techniques, and cognitively based techniques are detailed in separate chapters (8, 9, and 10). Response maintenance and transfer of training, elaborated in Chapter 11, are areas in which considerable progress has been made in the last few years. Chapter 12 focuses on current applications of behavioral techniques and expands on the range of foci highlighted in previous chapters. It illustrates behavioral techniques in several areas, including the prevention and treatment of medical and psychological dysfunctions, personal safety at home and in business and industry, and applications in everyday life such as conserving energy, maintaining traffic safety, and obtaining employment. Large-scale studies and the long-term effects of interventions are also discussed. The final chapter (13) examines key characteristics that may account for the widespread applicability and effectiveness of behavioral techniques. It also evaluates the social, ethical, and legal issues raised by applying intervention techniques, limitations of the behavioral approach, and future directions.

Several teaching aids have been included with the text. Outlines at the beginning of each chapter help convey the content, the direction, and the key points that are to be covered. Suggested readings are provided at the end of each chapter to provide further discussion of conceptual, procedural, and practical issues in the development of behavioral programs. As in previous editions, a glossary is included at the end of the book to help review concepts introduced in the text.

Many people have contributed significantly to the completion of this book. Drs. Richard D. Tucker and Thomas R. Kratochwill provided extremely helpful critiques which influenced many facets of this edition. Prominent among those who aided the final product is Mary Dulgeroff, who typed and helped prepare the manuscript. Special appreciation is extended to my daughters, Nicole and Michelle. By unwittingly (but effectively) applying behavior change techniques to their parents on a daily basis, they have enhanced my comprehension of how those techniques work and what their beneficial and adverse side effects are. In particular, they have greatly helped me realize how much of human behavior I cherish but do not understand. I am quite grateful for the support of a Research Scientist Development Award (MH00353) and to the support of other projects related to assessment, diagnosis, treatment, and prevention of clinical dysfunction (MH35408, MH39642, MH39976, and MH40021) from the National Institute of Mental Health during the period in which this book was written.

Alan E. Kazdin

Contents

Chapter Six

Punishment   142

Types of Punishment: Presentation of Aversive Events.
Withdrawal of Positive Consequences. Punishing Consequences
Based on Effort. *Selecting Procedures to Suppress Behaviors.*
Factors that Influence the Effectiveness of Punishment: Delay
of Punishment. Schedule of Punishment. Source of
Reinforcement. Timing of Punishment in the Response
Sequence. Reinforcement of Alternative Responses. General
Comments. *Side Effects of Punishment:* Types of Effects.
Illustrations from Applied Settings. *Characteristics of the*
Punishment Process: Immediacy of Effects. Specificity of
Effects. Recovery after Punishment Withdrawal. *When and*
How to Use Punishment. Summary and Conclusion.

Chapter Seven

Extinction   174

Factors that Influence the Effectiveness of Extinction: Schedule
of Reinforcement. Other Variables Affecting Extinction.
Identifying the Reinforcer Maintaining Behavior. Controlling the
Source of Reinforcement. *Characteristics of the Extinction*
Process: Gradual Reduction in Behavior. Extinction Burst.
Spontaneous Recovery. Possible Side Effects. *Applications of*
Extinction. When and How to Use Extinction. Other
Applications of Extinction. Summary and Conclusion.

Chapter Eight

Special Technique Variations to Enhance Client
Performance   190

Enhancing Client Performance: Prompting. Shaping. Response
Priming. Reinforcer Sampling. Vicarious Processes.
Group-Based Programs: Group Contingencies. Team-Based
Contingencies. Consequence Sharing. Lotteries. Considerations
in Using Group-Based Programs. *Peer-Administered*
Contingencies: Illustrations. Considerations in Using
Peer-Administered Contingencies. *Summary and Conclusion.*

Introduction

Behavior modification is an approach to the assessment, evaluation, and alteration of behavior. The approach focuses on the treatment of clinical problems and on the development of adaptive functioning in everyday life. Although many people associate behavior modification with a specific form of treatment, in fact the approach embraces a large number of quite different *treatment techniques*. These techniques can be applied to many *different behaviors,* including such clinical problems as anxiety, depression, aggression, substance abuse, child and spouse abuse, sexual deviance and dysfunction, pain, and hypertension. In addition, behavior modification is often used to improve a variety of behaviors in everyday life. Developing healthy lifestyles (e.g., eating a well-balanced diet, exercising), altering child behavior in nonpunitive ways, and interacting more positively with one's spouse are examples of such applications.

The techniques of behavior modification have been applied to a broad range of *persons and populations,* including children, adolescents, and adults in such everyday settings as the home, school, and workplace and special populations such as psychiatric patients, prisoners, nursing home residents, and autistic children. Behavior modification includes many *different theories* about how clinical problems emerge and are maintained. These theories vary in their explanation of behavior and in the role they accord to the influence of processes within the individual (e.g., thoughts, beliefs, perceptions) or processes resulting from events in the environment (e.g., cues, feedback, and consequences that behavior produces). In short, behavior modification encompasses many treatments, clinical problems, populations, and conceptual views.

MAJOR CHARACTERISTICS

Because of the diversity of treatments and applications, a simple definition of behavior modification is difficult to provide. Yet several characteristics distinguish behavior modification as a unique approach treatment.

Primacy of Behavior

Within behavior modification, overt behavior plays a major part in the assessment and treatment of clinical dysfunction. Whenever possible, clinical problems are operationalized in terms of overt behavioral referents. Indeed, symptoms or groups of symptoms that go together (syndromes or disorders), such as fear and avoidance, autism, depression, hyperactivity, substance abuse, and sexual deviance, are conceptualized primarily as problems of behavior.

Although emphasis is placed on behavior, or what people do, this does not mean that problems are viewed solely in terms of overt actions. How people feel (affect) and think (cognition) are often central to the specific problems brought to treatment. For example, depressed persons often feel sad (affect), believe they cannot do anything right (cognition), and engage in few activities (behaviors) in their everyday lives. Although affect and cognition are important, behavioral treatments give primary attention to behavior as a means of dealing with the clinical problem. In the treatment process, a depressed patient may be encouraged to engage in specific activities involving interactions with others and in setting goals for accomplishing specific tasks at home or at work.

Increases in activity and completion of tasks are behaviors that have been found to alter depressive symptoms, including feelings and thoughts. Consequently, behavior modification often focuses on behavior both as an end in itself and as a means of changing affect and cognition.

Importance of Learning

An assumption of behavior modification is that behaviors of interest in the context of therapeutic, educational, social, and other settings can be altered by providing new learning experiences. Understandably, the approach has drawn heavily on learning theories and research in psychology. Using learning as a point of departure, behavioral treatments essentially provide special learning experiences to alter deviant or clinically maladaptive behavior and to increase adaptive behavior in everyday life.

It is important not to overstate the claim that new learning experiences can change behavior. Proponents of behavior modification do *not* necessarily adhere to the view that all behaviors are learned and can be changed through learning. Diverse biological, behavioral, social, cultural, and other factors influence behavior. The influences that control behavior are not fully understood. Thus, behaviors are often difficult to alter. In any given case, a particular behavior or client may not change at all. The key feature of the behavioral approach is recognition of the plasticity of behavior or the amenability of behavior to change when systematic learning experiences are provided. Whether providing new learning experiences will effectively alter behavior can only be determined by testing what changes occur. The assumption that learning experiences can alter behavior has proven to be extremely helpful in developing effective treatments.

Directive and Active Treatments

Behavior modification techniques usually rely on directive and active treatments. This means that clients who come for treatment are given specific directions for the procedures that they are to perform. This does not mean that clients are simply told what to do. Indeed, in most cases involving children, adolescents, and adults, the client plays an important role in developing the plan of action to change behavior. Behavioral techniques do not rely heavily on the therapeutic relationship or such therapeutic processes as talking about one's problems to relieve emotional distress or to develop insight. To be sure, these processes may have beneficial effects during the course of treatment. However, talking about one's problems is not viewed as the most effective way of producing behavior change. Rather, explicit training experiences are prescribed in treatment.

Actions or activities to help achieve desired changes are often carried out during treatment sessions. Often, too, such actions or activities are assigned to persons as "homework." Therapeutic change in behavior modification is conceptualized as *learning new behaviors* that are to be performed in everyday life. Specific and direct activities serve as the basis for developing these new behaviors.

Importance of Assessment and Evaluation

A central characteristic of behavior modification is a commitment to the assessment and evaluation of alternative treatments. The effects of treatment are evaluated empirically, by measuring the impact on the client or patient seen in treatment.[1] The evaluation of treatment involves several components.

First, the behaviors to be altered are carefully assessed. The assessment may consist of several ways of measuring the problem or desired behavior, including direct observation of how the person performs at school or at work, evaluations by significant others (parents, spouses, peers), and, of course, evaluations by the clients themselves. The assessment is central to identifying the extent and nature of the problem.

Second, the goals and the means for reaching them are usually well specified. Before treatment, the therapist conducts a careful evaluation to identify what the problem is, how the client and others are affected by it, and the circumstances under which it emerges. Once the problem has been carefully identified and assessed, the procedures and the goals toward which they will be directed can be specified. Explicit formulation of the procedures and goals is an important characteristic of behavior modification.

Third, the effects of treatment are assessed to determine whether the desired outcomes have been obtained. In research, behavior modification places major emphasis on measuring outcome and evaluating treatment in controlled studies to decide whether alternative treatments are effective and which treatments are more effective than others. The emphasis on research to investigate treatment has been a hallmark of the approach. Evaluation is also very important in clinical work with individual clients. In this context, evaluation refers to measuring the specific behaviors of interest and thus to monitoring the progress that the client makes during the course of treatment. Such evaluation may be accomplished by having the patient complete various questionnaires about the severity of specific symptoms or by having the patient keep a record or diary of activities. For example, a patient who abuses alcohol may rate, on a daily or weekly basis, the extent to which drinking or the urge to drink was a problem. Also, a relative (e.g., spouse) who lives with the client may keep records of the number of drinks that the client actually consumes.

Ideally, of course, the information (data) obtained during treatment reveals that the client is improving and that treatment is working. However, one of the most useful features of the evaluation is that one can identify when treatment is not working. The therapist can use this information to alter treatment and, if necessary, to try different techniques. In general, evaluation of progress in treatment is facilitated by having clearly specified goals and procedures.

Use of Persons in Everyday Life

Behavioral techniques are often carried out outside the therapist's office. Applications are often conducted at home, at school, in various institutional settings (psychiatric hospitals, prisons), in business and industry, and in the community. Persons responsible for the care, management, and education of the clients, such as parents, teachers, relatives, spouses, roommates, peers, supervisors, and colleagues, are often utilized to help with the behavior change program. These persons are occasionally referred to as *paraprofessionals* because they work along with professionals in achieving therapeutic change.

Paraprofessionals who are in frequent contact with the client can observe the client's behaviors in the actual situations in which they are performed, so they are in the best position to focus on behavior as it is actually occurring. In applications with children, for example, parents, teachers, and peers are often trained in behavior change techniques. Because these persons are in direct contact with the client at home and at school, they are likely to be in a better position than the therapist to change behaviors of interest (e.g., tantrums, oppositional behavior, completion of homework). Paraprofessionals can often identify these behaviors when they occur and can often immediately provide consequences intended to develop more adaptive behaviors.

Case Illustration

The above characteristics of the behavioral approach are quite broad. Breadth and perhaps ambiguity are required to encompass the many techniques that behavior modification embraces and the many behaviors and clinical problems toward which those techniques are directed. An illustration will convey more concretely how some of the behavioral approach characteristics are manifested in actual practice.

Consider the case of Arlene, a 35-year-old woman who suffered from agoraphobia (fear of open spaces). Persons with agoraphobia often remain at home as much as possible. When they leave home, they experience high levels of anxiety, which is reflected in agitation, worry, arousal, sweating, and in general great discomfort. Anticipation of leaving home and going to public places may increase their anxiety and their belief that they will lose control, faint, and even become insane in the presence of others. It is not clear how agoraphobia develops, though many theories have been advanced. Even though the causes of the problem are not known, effective behavioral treatments have been developed. For the behavior therapist, the task of treatment is to provide new learning experiences that will eliminate anxiety and help the patient function adequately in a variety of everyday situations.

Before treatment began, the therapist interviewed Arlene for approximately two hours to discuss exactly what she considered to be the problem. The therapist asked about the times she felt anxious, about the range of the circumstances in which anxiety emerged, and about how this anxiety interfered with her everyday life. In addition, Arlene completed a questionnaire that asked about a number of problems, including anxiety, depression, sleep disturbance, and uncontrollable thoughts and urges. The purpose of the questionnaire was to assess the full range of problems that she may have experienced. Arlene's problems focused on anxiety when she left her house or thought about doing so. She rigidly structured her daily activities to accommodate her anxiety. For example, to avoid going to a store on her own, she ordered the delivery of groceries or paid a neighbor's teenage boy for picking them up.

After the evaluation, the therapist explained what the treatment was and how it would be used to overcome anxiety. For Arlene, the techniques of *graduated exposure* and *relaxation training* were used. She was introduced (exposed) to a variety of situations outside her home. The situations were introduced on a graduated basis. At first, situations were introduced that were not too demanding or threatening and the therapist was present. As Arlene progressed, more difficult situations were introduced and the therapist was absent.

Before Arlene began specific tasks, she was trained to engage in deep muscle relaxation. The purpose was to provide her with a technique for remaining relaxed when she felt that anxiety might develop. Developing the ability to relax deeply usually requires only a few sessions. Relaxation was developed by having Arlene first close her eyes and remain quiet. The therapist then instructed her to focus attention on various groups of muscles (e.g., lower arm, upper arm, neck and shoulders). She alternately tensed and relaxed muscle groups encompassing the major skeletal muscles in response to the therapist's instructions. In this way, Arlene learned how to use the release from tensing the muscles as a way of achieving a relaxed state in those muscle groups. As she completed the tensing and relaxing cycle for each of several muscle groups, she became deeply relaxed. After a few sessions, she became relaxed relatively quickly with little or no assistance from the therapist.

After Arlene learned how to relax, treatment continued with a series of behavioral tasks. At first, she was required to take a short walk with the therapist near her home, so that the location would be familiar and probably not very anxiety provoking. If she became anxious, the therapist helped her to relax. The brief walks, the presence of the therapist, and the use of relaxation decreased the likelihood that high levels of anxiety would emerge. Within two sessions, a significant reduction of anxiety was evident on these brief walks.

In further sessions with the therapist, Arlene was exposed to additional situations, including walking to various stores, driving in a car to a restaurant and a shopping mall, riding a bus, and other tasks related to situations that she found anxiety provoking. She was also given "homework" assignments— activities to carry out on her own. The first assignment was to visit a friend who lived a few houses away from her. Arlene and her friend spoke on the phone for extended periods each day. The assignment was to visit the friend and talk to her for at least 30 minutes on at least two separate days during the week. The friend, who was well aware of the problem, was eager to help and did so by having Arlene over for coffee. After three visits, Arlene felt better about leaving her home. She was then assigned to go to a store with her friend and to walk to a mailbox (two blocks away from her home) by herself. After further practice trials with the therapist and further homework assignments, Arlene reported very little anxiety about being out of the house, going out on errands alone, or being in crowds.

Throughout the course of treatment, Arlene's progress was systematically evaluated. Arlene kept a daily diary regarding her behavior and anxiety. In it, she recorded each trip she took, how long she was out of the house for the trip, and how much anxiety she felt, as rated on a scale from 1 (perfectly relaxed) to 10 (extremely uncomfortable and anxious). At the beginning of treatment, Arlene made few entries in the diary. At that time, she left home only when absolutely necessary—about twice a week. On these occasions, her trips were brief (usually less than 30 minutes) and were rated with very high levels of anxiety (9 or 10 on the rating scale). After many sessions and after homework assignments had been in effect for some time, she left home 15–20 times per week (going out to visit a neighbor, walking to a store, driving to a shopping mall). Most of the trips lasted well over an hour. Arlene's anxiety decreased, as reflected in ratings of 3 and 4 on the scale. Eventually, her anxiety for all the outings decreased to 2, 3, or 4 and she stated that being out of the house and in public places did not bother her. Over the course of treatment, the information provided by the diary was useful in deciding when to proceed to more difficult tasks and whether the treatment was achieving its goals.

In Arlene's case, treatment progressed relatively quickly. Within 10 weeks, her ratings indicated that she was not bothered at all by being out of the house. She engaged in more social activities, including going out evenings with her friend and a group of new friends. In addition, within four months after treatment ended, she obtained a full-time job in a department store. Thus, by her own report and information about her activities, therapy apparently achieved its goals.

General Comments

Several features of the behavioral approach can be seen in the case of Arlene and her treatment. The focus on behavior, the use of active treatments to reduce anxiety, applications in everyday situations, and involvement of others in treatment are primary examples. Perhaps less dramatically illustrated but even more important was the effort to evaluate Arlene's progress. The central question is whether the treatment is achieving the desired ends. The data gathered about Arlene's progress were obtained to address this question.

Although the general characteristics of behavior modification have been conveyed by key points noted previously and by the case illustration, the story is incomplete. Behavior modification includes different views and techniques of treatment. To convey these different traditions within the field, it is useful to highlight the historical foundations of behavior modification and the emergence of behavior modification as a contemporary approach to treatment.

FOUNDATIONS OF BEHAVIOR MODIFICATION

Many paths led to the emergence of contemporary behavior modification (see Kazdin, 1978). Although these paths cannot be examined in detail here, a few are especially noteworthy.

Experimental Animal Research

Classical Conditioning.   Behavior modification can be traced to laboratory research in physiology in the 1800s and 1900s. Among the many influences, the work of the Russian physiologist Ivan P. Pavlov (1849–1936) is particularly significant. Pavlov studied digestion, especially how reflex responses were influenced by substances placed in the digestive system. He stimulated various portions of an animal's digestive system with food or food powder and observed the physiological reactions. As part of his studies, he found that gastric secretions were stimulated when animals—in this case dogs—merely saw the food or heard the preparation of the food. This was significant because it suggested that digestive processes could be stimulated even without direct physical stimulation. Pavlov thought that this resulted from the animal's experience in the laboratory (i.e., learning). He shifted his research to study how connections were made between various environmental stimuli (sights and sounds) and reflex reactions such as salivation in response to food.

The type of learning that Pavlov studied has been referred to as *classical or respondent conditioning*. Classical conditioning is concerned with stimuli that evoke responses. Certain stimuli in one's environment (such as noise, shock, light, and the taste of food) *elicit* reflex responses. These responses are referred to as *respondents* or unconditioned responses. Respondents are frequently viewed as involuntary or automatic responses that are not under control of the individual. Examples of respondents include a startle reaction in response to loud noise, salivation in response to the presence of food in one's mouth, pupil constriction in response to bright light, or flexion of a muscle in response to pain. The connection between the unconditioned stimulus and the response is automatic (i.e., not learned). However, reflex behavior sometimes occurs in response to a stimulus that does not automatically elicit the response.

Through classical conditioning, a neutral stimulus (that is, a stimulus that does not elicit a particular reflex) can be made to elicit a reflex response. In a simple arrangement to achieve this, the neutral stimulus (referred to as a conditioned stimulus) is paired with a stimulus that elicits a reflex response (an unconditioned stimulus). If the conditioned stimulus is consistently paired with an unconditioned stimulus, the conditioned stimulus alone can elicit the response (referred to as a conditioned response). The process whereby new stimuli gain the power to elicit respondent behavior is called classical or respondent conditioning. This is not a mechanical process in which merely pairing stimuli automatically leads to their connection. Learning the relation between stimuli depends on a variety of factors that help or hinder the association and determine whether the neutral stimuli elicit the unconditioned response (see Rescorla, 1988).

Pavlov's work was significant because of both his specific findings and his methods of investigation. His findings suggested one way in which behaviors could be learned. The concepts of conditioning from his laboratory work were extended to explain virtually all learning, including such broad areas as the learning of language, the acquisition of knowledge, and the development of deviant and maladaptive behavior (e.g., alcoholism). It is clear today that the concepts were overextended, because they did not give accurate or complete accounts of these areas. Also, more recent research has shown that conditioning itself is more complex than originally thought (e.g., certain kinds of connections are more easily learned than others, and pairing stimuli does not automatically lead to learning). However, Pavlov's significant contribution was his scientifically and learning-based explanation of behavior. His clear demonstration of the process of learning under well-controlled conditions helped foster more elaborate studies of different kinds of learning.

Another significant feature of Pavlov's work was the method of his experiments. Pavlov used precise methods that permitted careful observation and quantification of what he was studying. For example, in some of his studies, drops of saliva were counted to measure the conditioned reflex. His meticulous laboratory notes and his rigorous methods helped greatly to advance a scientific approach toward the study of behavior. Because his methods were described so clearly, they could be used by others. Also, the *Zeitgeist* fostered application of the scientific approach to diverse areas of inquiry. Pavlov seemed to exemplify scientific values and hence served as a model to others. His receipt of the Nobel Prize (1904) in physiology for his research on digestion increased the visibility of his work and adoption of his methods.

Operant Conditioning.   While Pavlov was conducting his experiments, a type of learning that did not involve reflex responses was under investigation. Investigators were evaluating the impact of different consequences on the development of new behaviors (see Kazdin, 1978). Along these lines, the work of Edward L. Thorndike (1874–1949) is noteworthy. Thorndike was concerned with the learning of new behaviors, rather than with establishing new connections of reflex behavior. Among his many animal experiments, the most well known are his puzzle-box experiments with cats.

Thorndike placed a hungry cat in a box and recorded how long it took the cat to escape by moving a barrier. A small piece of food placed outside the box provided the cat with an incentive for learning to escape. The cat immediately attempted to escape by exploring diverse solutions in a trial-and-error fashion. Eventually, the cat removed the barrier and consumed the food. The cat was then placed in the box again. With repeated trials, Thorndike found that it took less and less time for the cat to escape. Eventually, as soon as the cat was placed in the box, it removed the barrier, escaped, and ate the food. Thorndike plotted the time it took the cat to escape over repeated trials and reported a learning curve. This curve reflected the fact that the animal took less and less time to perform the behavior.

From many similar experiments and observations, Thorndike formulated laws or principles of behavior. The most significant of these was the *Law of Effect*, which states that consequences that follow behavior help learning. The rewards (e.g., food for the cat after escape) provided consequences that increased learning of the behavior. Thorndike's emphasis on the consequences of behavior was a significant preview of subsequent developments in laboratory and applied research.

B. F. Skinner (1904–   ) was influenced by Pavlov and Thorndike and also conducted a number of animal laboratory studies. Like Thorndike, Skinner explored the impact of various consequences on behavior. He helped clarify learning that resulted from consequences and its differences from the respondent conditioning studied by Pavlov. He noted that many behaviors are *emitted* spontaneously and are controlled primarily by their consequences. He referred to such behaviors as *operants* because they were responses that operated (had some influence) on the environment. Operant behaviors are strengthened (increased) or weakened (decreased) as a function of the events that follow them. Most of the behaviors performed in everyday life are operants. They are not reflex responses (respondents) controlled by eliciting stimuli. Operant behaviors include reading, walking, working, talking, nodding one's head, smiling, and other freely emitted responses. Operants are distinguished by virtue of being controlled (influenced) by their consequences. The process of learning operant behaviors is referred to as *operant conditioning*.

Several types of consequences and principles were developed to explain how operant behaviors could be developed and altered. The major relations that were investigated can be seen in Table 1–1, which summarizes the basic principles of operant conditioning. These principles provide general statements about the relations between behaviors and environmental events. Investigations of these principles began with laboratory animals (e.g., rats, pigeons) engaging in simple responses (e.g., pressing a lever) under highly controlled

TABLE 1-1   Summary of Basic Principles of Operant Conditioning

Principle	Characteristic Procedure and Its Effect on Behavior
Reinforcement	Presentation or removal of an event after a response that increases the frequency of the response.
Punishment	Presentation or removal of an event after a response that decreases the frequency of the response.
Extinction	No longer presenting a reinforcing event after a response that decreases the frequency of the previously reinforced response.
Stimulus control and discrimination training	Reinforcing the response in the presence of one stimulus but not in the presence of another. This procedure increases the frequency of the response in the presence of the former stimulus and decreases the frequency of the response in the presence of the latter stimulus.

conditions. Current applications of the general principles bear very little resemblance to these experimental beginnings.

As with Pavlov's work, the significance of Skinner's work stemmed from the approach toward the study of behavior. Skinner's method included a focus on overt behavior, assessment of the frequency of behavior over extended periods, and the study of one or a few organisms at a time. His goal was to identify the variables that influenced behavior by careful and intensive study of one or two subjects. Because of their contemporary influence on behavior modification, we will return to the principles of operant conditioning and the method of study developed by Skinner.

Behaviorism in America

The late 1800s and early 1900s reflect a broader orientation of which significant contributors such as Pavlov and Thorndike, and later Skinner, were a part. Increased interest in the scientific method was evident in diverse areas of work. Research on infrahuman species was particularly important at the time. This was due in part to the influence of Darwin, whose *Origin of Species by Means of Natural Selection* (1859) and *The Descent of Man* (1871) had suggested the continuity of species and the relevance of animal behavior.

Psychological research in America was greatly influenced not only by the specific contributions of Pavlov and his contemporaries but also by the larger movement toward more objective methods of studying behavior. In America, John B. Watson (1878–1958) crystallized a movement in psychology that is referred to as *behaviorism*. Watson was interested in animal psychology and in applying methods from animal research to the study of human behavior. He criticized psychology because of its use of subjective methods such as introspection (e.g., asking people to report on their private experience) to study mental phenomena (e.g., thoughts and feelings). This method of study, Watson contended, was neither objective nor scientific.

Watson was greatly influenced by the work of Pavlov and his contemporaries and transplanted concepts and methods of conditioning to American psychology. He argued for a new "behaviorist" approach in psychology. His position, as reflected, for example, in *Psychology from the Standpoint of a Behaviorist* (1919), greatly influenced the shape of psychology. He accorded learning a critical role in many areas. In fact, he suggested that learning could entirely shape human behavior. In addition, he used conditioning as the basis for explaining virtually all behavior that was acquired as part of development. Watson's purpose was to win support for the view that the concepts of conditioning and scientific methods could be applied to the study of behavior. Many of his specific statements about human behavior and its development were extreme and went well beyond what was known at the time. Behavior modification had not yet emerged formally. Watson's major contribution was that of moving psychology toward the scientific study of behavior.

EMERGENCE OF BEHAVIOR MODIFICATION

The emergence of behavior modification as an approach to treatment and clinical work can be considered from at least two interrelated perspectives. One of these perspectives concerns the extension of the concepts of conditioning and scientific methods to clinical work. The second perspective concerns the prevalent theoretical orientation toward abnormal behavior and its treatment at the time that behavior modification was developing. Considerable dissatisfaction with the prevalent approaches to clinical problems and with alternative psychotherapy techniques helped spawn behavior modification.

Clinical Extensions

Respondent and operant conditioning were used increasingly as a basis for conceptualizing personality, psychotherapy, and behavior change. Also, concepts of respondent and operant conditioning were used to develop new techniques for treating adults and children for a host of psychological and behavioral problems. A few illustrations will convey important steps that led to contemporary work.

Respondent Conditioning.   A historically significant attempt to show the importance of respondent conditioning was provided by Watson and Rayner (1920), who conditioned a fear reaction in an 11-month-old boy named Albert. Prior to the study, the investigators noted that a loud noise (unconditioned stimulus) produced a startle and fear reaction (unconditioned response) in Albert. In contrast, Albert freely played with a white rat without any adverse reaction. The investigators wished to determine whether the startle reaction could be conditioned to the presence of the white rat. To condition the startle reaction, the presence of the white rat (neutral or conditioned stimulus) was immediately followed by the noise. Whenever Albert reached out and touched the rat, the noise sounded and Albert was startled. Over a period of one week, the presence of the rat and the noise were paired only seven times. Finally, when the rat was presented without the noise, Albert fell over and cried. The conditioned stimulus elicited the fear response (conditioned response). Moreover, the fear generalized to other objects that Albert had not been afraid of previously (e.g., a rabbit, a dog, a Santa Claus mask, a sealskin coat, and cotton wool). This suggested that fears could be acquired through respondent conditioning. Of course, it is difficult to say whether fears evident in everyday experience are in fact acquired through respondent conditioning, because one rarely has access to an individual at the time that fears develop. Other evidence suggests that fears may be acquired for objects with which the individual has had no direct personal contact (Marks, 1987). Independently of how fears are actually learned, respondent conditioning may be useful in ameliorating fears because the power of conditioned stimuli to elicit fear reactions can be altered.

Another early extension of respondent conditioning was in the treatment of enuresis (bed-wetting). Enuresis can be conceptualized as a failure of certain stimuli (bladder cues) to elicit a response (waking) so that the individual can get up and urinate appropriately. To condition waking to the bladder cues (distension), a stimulus that elicits waking is required. O. H. Mowrer and W. M. Mowrer (1938) devised an apparatus to classically condition waking to the cues that precede urination while the child is asleep. The apparatus includes a liquid-sensitive pad that is placed in the child's bed. As soon as the child urinates, a circuit is closed and an alarm is activated. The alarm serves as an unconditioned stimulus that eventually elicits waking prior to urination and the sounding of the alarm. The procedure results in control of urination and permits the individual to sleep through the night without urination. This procedure, an effective technique for dealing with enuresis, was actually available prior to the 1930s. Historically, its reemergence was significant because the procedure was couched in terms of classical conditioning.

A more contemporary extension of classical conditioning to clinical work was made by Joseph Wolpe (1958), who developed a classical conditioning procedure for the treatment of anxiety. Wolpe, a physician working in South Africa, conducted experiments investigating anxiety and avoidance reactions in laboratory animals (cats). He investigated a phenomenon referred to as *experimental neurosis*—an experimentally induced state in which animals show agitation, disruption of behavior, and other signs that resemble anxiety in humans. Experimental neuroses had been studied for some time, beginning in Pavlov's laboratory. Wolpe's special contribution was to develop a procedure for overcoming anxiety in the cats he studied and then to extend the method to the treatment of humans with anxiety disorders.

After anxiety had been developed, Wolpe gradually exposed the cats to situations that elicited anxiety. When the cats were exposed to the situation (room) in which anxiety had been developed, they showed severe signs of anxiety and would not engage in any other behaviors. Wolpe then exposed the cats to cues (other rooms) that only resembled the original situation. With less avoidance and agitation due to a reduced dose of anxiety-provoking stimuli, he encouraged them to engage in other responses such as eating. He reasoned that exposure to a series of anxiety-provoking situations while engaging in competing responses would gradually overcome the anxiety. Continuation of this procedure eventually eliminated the anxiety of the cats.

An especially significant step was Wolpe's use of the information he derived from experiments with cats to develop a technique for treating human anxiety. Wolpe developed *systematic desensitization,* a treatment in which humans were exposed in real life or in imagination to situations that provoked anxiety. They were exposed in a graduated series of stimuli. To overcome anxiety, Wolpe trained clients to become deeply relaxed so that exposure to mild representations of the anxiety-provoking situation would cause very little anxiety. Over time, the clients were exposed to or imagined situations that provoked greater anxiety and relaxation would overcome that anxiety. Eventually, the clients responded without anxiety to the situations that originally provoked anxiety.

The procedure was conceptualized from the standpoint of classical conditioning. Certain cues or stimuli in the environment elicit anxiety or fear. The fear can be altered by conditioning an alternative response (relaxation) that is incompatible with fear. As relaxation becomes associated with the imagined scenes, the capacity of the stimuli to elicit fear is eliminated. Altering the valence of the capacity of stimuli to elicit reactions adheres closely to the respondent conditioning paradigm.

Wolpe (1958) reported the use of this technique in various forms with over 200 patients. He claimed that the treatment had been effective. Case studies are not acceptable scientifically because the basis for the change cannot be determined. Yet Wolpe's technique and claims eventually stimulated a great deal of research on the effects of systematic desensitization. From a broader perspective, Wolpe's work was quickly assimilated because of other influences, such as his reliance on animal laboratory methods, his use of learning concepts, and his concerns over objective bases of developing treatments.

The above illustrations are among the well-known extensions of respondent conditioning to clinical problems. Many other behavioral techniques derived from classical conditioning have been used to alter a variety of behaviors, including excessive eating, the drinking of alcohol, cigarette smoking, and deviant sexual behavior (Kazdin, 1978; O'Leary & Wilson, 1987). Such procedures alter the valence of events by pairing them with real or imagined stimuli.

Operant Conditioning.   The control that rewarding consequences exerted over behavior was not a new insight identified by laboratory research on operant conditioning. However, laboratory research on the lawful effects of rewarding consequences on behavior was eventually extended from infrahuman species to humans (Lindsley, 1956, 1960). Some of the early laboratory work seemed to have clinical relevance. For example, laboratory studies were conducted with hospitalized psychotic patients who performed on various apparatus daily to earn small rewards (e.g., money, pictures). The purpose was to examine response patterns under various arrangements of rewarding consequences. The results showed that the response patterns of psychiatric patients differed from the patterns that had been evident in "normal" adults. Also, performance on the laboratory apparatus was often interrupted by pauses in which psychotic symptoms (e.g., vocal hallucinatory behaviors) could be observed. These observations suggested that the operant conditioning paradigm might be an objective way to study psychotic behavior. Perhaps of even greater significance was the finding that responding to laboratory tasks appeared to result in a reduction of symptoms (e.g., staring into space) both in the laboratory and on the hospital ward (King, Armitage, & Tilton, 1960; Lindsley, 1960). This clearly suggested that symptoms might be altered in important ways by increases in operant responding.

Laboratory extensions of operant conditioning were made to study the behavior of many populations, such as mentally retarded children and autistic children. In most of the studies, the goals were merely to use operant conditioning laboratory methods to investigate how special populations responded. Operant conditioning methods were soon extended to human behavior outside the laboratory. Quite simple demonstrations suggested that important behaviors might be greatly influenced by environmental consequences.

Several demonstrations were completed in the 1960s to examine the extent to which consequence could influence the behavior of hospitalized psychiatric patients. One of these demonstrations involved a depressed patient who complained of sleeping difficulties and reported pains in her back, chest, head, and shoulders (Ayllon & Haughton, 1964). Medical evaluation revealed no physical problems to account for these difficulties. It appeared that these bodily (somatic) complaints might be influenced by their consequences, namely the reactions of staff to her complaints. Observations were made to record the daily frequency of the patient's complaints for several days. After these observations (referred to as *baseline*), staff were told to change the way they reacted to the patient. Specifically, staff were instructed to ignore complaints rather than to provide the usual consolation, sympathy, and attention that they had given. Perhaps attention had served as a reward (reinforcer) for the behavior, leading to its high levels; if so, cessation of the attention would reduce the behavior. Observations of complaints continued. After several days, staff were told to revert to their previous ways of responding to the patient's complaints. If staff attention was really influencing the complaints, one would expect the complaints to increase again. After several days of this, staff were finally told to withdraw their attention.

The effects of altering consequences for somatic complaints can be seen in Figure 1–1. The frequency of complaints is evident during baseline (staff behaving as usual), extinction (staff ignoring complaints), reinforcement (staff

FIGURE 1–1

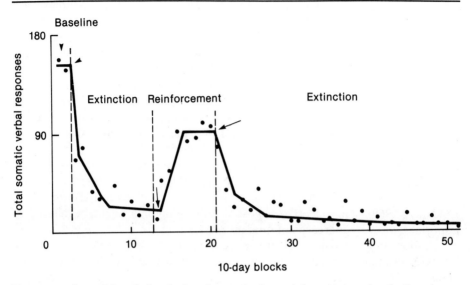

Frequency of complaints during the baseline, extinction, reinforcement, and extinction phases. During baseline, staff behaved as usual. During the reinforcement phase, they provided attention when the patient complained. During the extinction phases, staff ignored the patient's complaints.

SOURCE: Reprinted with permission from *Behaviour Research and Therapy, 2,* 87–97. Ayllon, T., & Haughton, E. Modification of symptomatic verbal behaviour of mental patients. Copyright 1964, Pergamon Press Inc.

attention for complaints), and extinction (ignoring as before). The frequency of complaints changed dramatically as staff behavior changed. These results suggested that attention and consequences from others can greatly influence patient behavior.

These demonstrations and many others like them indicated that human behavior in applied settings could be altered by changing the consequences. The idea of using consequences to change behavior was not new: numerous examples of rewarding and punishing consequences for behavior could be found throughout civilization. What was new was the application of such consequences under a variety of special conditions and with careful assessment of behavior. The early extensions of operant conditioning principles to human behavior merely began an area of research. The present book illustrates the breadth and range of applications resulting from the extension of operant conditioning principles and approaches.

In passing, a unique extension of operant conditioning is worth noting. Skinner's work (1938) was primarily restricted to animal laboratory demonstrations, the significance of which was acknowledged. Soon after that work was well under way and had made important progress, he began extending the principles of operant conditioning well beyond the laboratory. Skinner (1953) made major conceptual leaps by discussing the relevance of operant conditioning to everyday life, including education, government, business, religion, psychotherapy, and social interaction in general. He wrote a well-known and still popular novel about a utopian society (*Walden Two*) in which the principles of operant conditioning served as the basis for structuring the community (Skinner, 1948). These extrapolations went way beyond what was known from laboratory research. It was not really clear that operant conditioning principles could be readily applied to complex human behavior and could alter socially significant behaviors. However, these extrapolations drew attention to Skinner's findings and methods and posed important challenges to those interested in applying operant conditioning principles to clinical ends.

Traditional Approaches Toward Deviant Behavior

The development of laboratory research and the scientific study of behavior were significant ingredients underlying the development of behavior modification. No less significant was the emerging dissatisfaction with traditional approaches to clinical problems. Behavior modification represents a significant departure from traditional conceptualizations of personality and behavior that dominated mental health–related fields such as clinical psychology, psychiatry, social work, counseling, education, and rehabilitation.

Intrapsychic Approaches.   Traditionally, personality had been viewed by many theorists as an assortment of psychological forces inside the individual (Hall & Lindzey, 1978). Although these forces vary depending on specific theories of personality, they generally consist of such psychological factors as drives, impulses, needs, motives, conflicts, and traits. The traditional approach to understanding behavior, both abnormal and normal, can be referred to as *intrapsychic* because psychological forces within the individual are accorded the crucial role. "Normal" behavior generally represents a socially acceptable expresssion of intrapsychic forces. On the other hand, "abnormal" behavior reflects disordered personality development or psychological processes.

Many intrapsychic theories have been proposed to account for personality. Certainly, the most influential intrapsychic theory of personality is *psychoanalysis,* proposed by Sigmund Freud (1856–1939). Freud explained virtually all behaviors by referring to manifestations of unconscious personality processes. In his view, understanding behavior required a careful scrutiny of personality to determine the meaning of behavior, that is, what motives behavior represents. He regarded the psychological processes and motives behind behavior as existing in the individual. The Freudian view is frequently referred to as a *psychodynamic* view. Dynamic refers to a branch of mechanics (in physics) in which phenomena are explained by referring to energy forces and their relation to motion and change in physical matter. Freud's dynamic view of personality describes behavior in terms of psychological energies, or motivating forces, drives, and impulses, and their interrelations. It traces growth and psychological development to psychological impulses and their expression at various stages early in the child's development. It holds that diverse behaviors can be traced to the expression of a few psychological forces.

According to the psychoanalytic view, normal behavior develops from the expression of impulses, wishes, and desires in socially appropriate ways and abnormal behavior develops from the disruption of the normal unfolding, expression, and gratification of drives and needs. Psychological drives can become blocked or can fail to find expression in socially appropriate ways. Drives and unresolved conflicts may, however, find expression in psychological symptoms or aberrant behaviors.

Psychoanalytic theory provided several important contributions to the understanding of behavior. First, it advanced the notion that behavior is *determined*. This means that behavior, whether deviant or normal, is not random but can be traced to psychological causes. For example, Freud suggested that abnormal behaviors, habits, dreams, slips of the tongue, and indeed all facets of behavior could be traced to intrapsychic processes formed early in child development. Second, psychoanalytic theory stimulated other theories on the psychological bases of behavior. Many of Freud's disciples began to develop their own intrapsychic theories; others developed theories that completely challenged the basic tenets of psychoanalysis. Third, psychoanalytic theory stimulated the development of psychological forms of treatment. If psychological forces caused emotional disturbance, treatments were needed to alter those forces. Psychoanalytic treatment began as a method of uncovering and resolving intrapsychic processes that were assumed to underlie behavior. The primary method of treatment was talking with a therapist and working through various impulses, conflicts, defenses, and unresolved childhood experiences. Many variations of psychotherapy also emerged that relied on talk as the primary medium of change.

Intrapsychic approaches to clinical problems generated a number of psychotherapy techniques. Various forms of psychotherapy have been applied to help people resolve the underlying causes presumed to account for their distress and abnormal behavior. Treatments based on intrapsychic views tend to focus on bringing to light underlying feelings, motives, and thoughts that are considered responsible for behavior. The primary agents for change are talk, expression of feelings, and the development of a close relationship with the therapist. Clients are encouraged to understand their own motives and to express thwarted feelings. Psychotherapy based on the intrapsychic approaches has been applied to many clinical disorders, including psychoses, depression, anxiety, obsessions and compulsions, alcohol and drug abuse, and antisocial behavior.

Dissatisfaction.   As noted previously, the emergence of behavior modification was facilitated by expressions of dissatisfaction with traditional notions related to assessment, diagnosis, and treatment of deviant behavior. The intrapsychic approach to personality and behavior grew from the disease approach of medicine in the late 1800s and early 1900s. Successes in identifying causes of many diseases furthered a more general approach of looking for underlying causes of symptoms. Freud, himself a physician, advanced a disease-type view in his model of psychoanalysis. An intrapsychic view suggests that psychological symptoms (deviant behavior) owe their origin to underlying dysfunction (personality conflicts). The dominance of the disease orientation in clinical work is reflected in such terms as mental *illness*, mental *health*, and mental *patients* and in references to persons who receive treatment as having *symptoms* or being *cured*.

Criticisms of intrapsychic approaches, especially psychoanalysis, increased in the 1950s and 1960s. The criticisms focused on difficulties in empirically verifying many of the claims of psychoanalysis, inconsistencies within psychoanalytic theory and in the therapeutic procedures derived from psychoanalytic theory, the neglect of social and cultural influences on behavior, and the lack of empirical support (see Kazdin, 1978; Salter, 1952; Stuart, 1970). Perhaps most significant was the fact that psychoanalytic views did not seem to be based on research or easily subjected to scientific inquiry. With behaviorism on the increase, there was a need for and strong interest in approaches that were more amenable to scientific research.

Psychoanalytic theory has evolved considerably over the years, and major additions and reformulations have since given greater attention to the influence of external events and social experiences on behavior. However, the general position of orthodox psychoanalysis has been that underlying drives, impulses, and conflicts are the primary determinants of behavior. It is this view that has exerted a major impact on the conceptualization of abnormal behavior.

It was not merely the intrapsychic view or the general approach of psychoanalysis that was subjected to criticism. Considerable dissatisfaction was also voiced over the focus on intrapsychic processes that characterized the traditional forms of psychotherapy. In the early 1900s, psychoanalysis and psychoanalytically oriented psychotherapy dominated clinical practice. In the 1940s and 1950s, many researchers began to question and criticize the effects of these techniques. In 1952, Hans Eysenck published a paper that expressed dissatisfaction with traditional treatments. He reviewed contemporary research and claimed that the evidence did not support the efficacy of psychotherapy. He noted that providing psychotherapy seemed to be no more effective than simply leaving people alone (no treatment). Eysenck's paper and subsequent revisions in the 1960s yielded a simple conclusion, namely that traditional forms of treatment had not been shown to work. His evaluation of the available research and his overall conclusion were very actively debated.

Eysenck had also suggested that learning-based treatments were more effective than traditional forms of treatment. At that time, there was no clear evidence that provided a strong basis for this claim. Yet the claim helped polarize the field of psychotherapy in different ways. To those interested in traditional psychotherapy, Eysenck's papers served as a challenge to conduct the research needed to determine whether, or to show that, the treatments were really effective. To those dissatisfied with the traditional approaches, Eysenck's work helped point the way to learning-based approaches.

Over the last 20 years, a tremendous amount of research has emerged on the effects of psychotherapy (Garfield & Bergin, 1986). The findings cannot be easily summarized since they vary among the different types of treatment and among the different clinical problems to which those types of treatment are applied. Generally, large-scale evaluations have suggested that psychotherapy often leads to positive changes in behavior (Brown, 1987). In contrast to Eysenck's claim, it has been found that treatment is usually significantly better than no treatment. But over 400 different current forms of psychotherapy have been identified for adults (Karasu, 1985) and well over 200 have been identified for children and adolescents (Kazdin, 1988), and the fact remains that very few of these forms have been studied. Consequently, the effectiveness of most types of treatment remains unknown.

CONTEMPORARY BEHAVIOR MODIFICATION

Contemporary behavior modification represents a convergence of different theories and influences into a heterogeneous movement. The central characteristics that unite the movement pertain primarily to an orientation toward treatment, a focus on behavior, an emphasis on learning, and assessment and evaluation. Two central themes evident in the animal research and early extensions of concepts from the laboratory to clinical populations pertain to the importance of learning and the careful assessment of behavior.

Current Theory in Behavior Modification

Learning continues to occupy a central role in contemporary behavior modification. Three types of learning are considered important in developing and altering behavior. Classical (or respondent) conditioning and operant conditioning have been discussed previously. A third type of learning that has been important is referred to as *observational (vicarious) learning* or *modeling*. Observational learning occurs when an individual observes another person (referred to as a *model*) engage in a particular behavior. The observer sees the model perform the behavior but does not engage in overt responses himself or receive any consequences. The observer learns the behavior merely by watching a model.

To clarify modeling effects, it is important to distinguish *learning* from *performance*. The requirement for learning through modeling is observation of a model. The modeled response is assumed to be acquired by the observer through cognitive or covert coding of the events observed (Bandura, 1977). However, whether a learned response is actually performed may depend on the consequences of the response or on the incentives associated with the response.

The importance of response consequences in dictating performance was demonstrated several years ago (Bandura, 1965). Children observed a film in which an adult modeled aggressive responses (hitting and kicking a large doll). For some children, the model's aggression was rewarded; for others, it was punished; and for still others, it met with no consequences. When the children were given the opportunity to perform the aggressive responses, those who had observed the aggression punished displayed less aggression than did those who had observed the aggression rewarded or ignored. To determine whether all of the children had learned the aggressive responses, an incentive was given to them for performing those responses. There were then no differences in aggressive responses among the three groups. Apparently, all of the groups had learned the aggressive responses, but the consequences to the model and the observer determined whether those responses would be performed. The extent to which modeling stimuli influence performance also depends on other factors, such as the similarity of the model to the observer; the prestige, status, and expertise of the model; and the number of models observed. As a general rule, imitation of a model by an observer is greater when the model is similar to the observer, more prestigious, and higher in status and expertise than the observer and when several models perform the same behavior.

A frequently cited example of modeling in the history of behavior modification was reported by Jones (1924). In this example, a young boy named Peter, who was afraid of a rabbit and several other furry objects (e.g., a fur coat, a feather, cotton wool), was placed in a play situation in which three other children and a rabbit were present. The other children, selected because they were unafraid of rabbits, interacted with the rabbit in a nonanxious fashion. Peter touched the rabbit immediately after observing others touch it. Other procedures were employed to overcome Peter's fear, such as associating the rabbit with the presence of food, so the precise contribution of modeling in reducing the fear is uncertain.

Modeling has been used in behavior modification to alter a variety of behaviors (see Rosenthal & Bandura, 1978). In many therapeutic applications, problems such as fear or lack of social skills have been treated effectively with both children and adults. In most applications of modeling, it is utilized along with other behavioral procedures. For example, in applications of operant conditioning techniques, modeling often plays a major role in conveying to the client exactly what the desired responses are. Yet it is supplemented with other techniques such as feedback and positive reinforcement.

Social Learning Theory: An Integration of Learning Concepts

Each type of learning has been developed largely on its own by means of extensive laboratory research, often with infrahuman subjects. Obviously, however, clinical problems that are evident in human behavior represent much more complex phenomena than the behaviors studied in animal research in laboratory settings. Animal research often does not reflect the complexity of processes that appear to be involved in human behavior such as language and thought.

Several authors have provided theories of behavior that attempt to integrate aspects of different learning paradigms and to take cognitive processes into account (e.g., Bandura, 1977; Rotter, 1954; Staats, 1975). For example, Bandura has developed a social learning theory that encompasses various types of learning and the wide range of influences that each type entails. Thus, social learning approaches utilize elements of classical, operant, and observational learning to explain behavior. They integrate events in the environment and, to a much greater extent, cognitions (thoughts, beliefs, perceptions) about environmental events into a general framework that depends on different learning experiences. Social learning approaches emphasize the multiple types of influences on behavior that occur in the context of social development and provide a framework from which behavior in general can be explained. The advantage of social learning approaches is that they can account for a broad range of behaviors to a greater extent than accounts based on simplistic applications of one type of learning rather than another.

In behavioral treatment, knowledge of the different types of learning is essential. In understanding how behavior develops and how it can be altered, the concepts from various types of learning need to be integrated. Social learning provides an integrated conceptual approach to understanding clinical problems and their treatment.

Even when concepts from one area of learning are relied on for a particular purpose, other types of learning are relevant as well. For example, behavior modification programs in applied settings such as the home, school, hospital, and institution rely heavily on operant conditioning techniques. Nonetheless, knowledge of other types of learning is important in implementing operant techniques. For example, an operant program in a classroom setting may increase a student's desirable behavior (e.g., working on assignments) by following such behavior with a favorable consequence or event (e.g., praise from the teacher). Yet modeling and respondent conditioning as well as operant conditioning may be operative in the situation. Students other than the one who is praised may increase in desirable behavior because of modeling influences (i.e., observing their peers) (Kazdin, 1979a). Classical conditioning may also be involved in the control of classroom behavior. For example, if a teacher shouts at a student (unconditioned stimulus), a startle reaction (unconditioned response) may occur. The teacher's close proximity to the child (conditioned stimulus) may, through repeated association with shouting, eventually elicit anxiety and arousal (conditioned response). Of course, if the teacher's proximity to the child elicits anxiety, this may detract from the teacher's reinforcing properties. As is obvious by now, a behavioral approach draws heavily on the psychology of learning to explain how behavior develops, is maintained, and is altered.

APPLIED BEHAVIOR ANALYSIS

Most of the behaviors of concern in applied settings and everyday life can be conceptualized as operants. Clients engage or fail to engage in behaviors that might be altered by consequences. Operants that can be altered by the application of techniques derived from operant conditioning include speech in children; academic, self-care, or social skills in mentally retarded persons; regular exercise; adherence to medical regimens; and the deviant behaviors of many patient samples.

The extension of operant conditioning principles and methods of studying human behavior to clinically and socially important human behaviors has become an area of research within behavior modification. The principles of operant conditioning, previously noted in Table 1–1, refer to the relations between events in the environment and changes in behavior. The principles, such as positive reinforcement and extinction, are simple, and indeed, many consider it simplistic to extend them to explain the complexities of human behavior. However, the issue is the extent to which those principles can be used to develop effective interventions for significant clinical and social problems. That issue can be decided only by examining the research itself, as covered in subsequent chapters.

The current approach to behavior change in applied settings is more than an extension of specific principles. Behavior analysis is an experimental approach for studying behavior in the laboratory in which the behavior of one or a few individuals is assessed over time to monitor the changes due to various interventions. The extension of experimental methods to applied settings generated a new area of research referred to as *applied behavior analysis* (Baer, Wolf, & Risley, 1968). Various characteristics of applied behavior analysis are highlighted in Table 1–2. The special focus of applied behavior analysis is on clinically or socially relevant behaviors in such areas as psychological and psychiatric disorders, education, rehabilitation, medicine, business, and industry.[2]

TABLE 1–2   Characteristics of Applied Behavior Analysis

Characteristics
· Focus on behaviors of applied (social or clinical) significance.
· Search for marked intervention effects that make a clear difference to the everyday functioning of the individual.
· Focus on overt behaviors.
· Focus on the behaviors of one or a small number of individuals over time.
· Assessment of behavior through direct observation, as in counting the frequency of responses.
· Assessment continuously over time for extended periods (hours, days, weeks).
· Use of environmental (and observable) events to influence the frequency of behavior.
· Evaluation and demonstration of the factors (e.g., events) that are responsible for behavior change.

Applied behavior analysis, unlike other areas within behavior modification, is often referred to as *radical* behaviorism. It is considered radical because its focus is exclusively on overt behavior, rather than subjective states (affect) and thoughts (cognition). The focus of applied behavior analysis can be clarified by noting other conceptual views within behavior modification.

Current conceptual views within behavior modification can generally be cast as mediational or nonmediational. *Nonmediational views* focus on direct connections between environmental and situational events and behaviors. The consequences that follow behavior serve as one major category of environmental events. For example, praise for a job well done can increase performance at home, at school, or at work through the principle of positive reinforcement. The consequences in nonmediational views refer primarily to events in the environment, such as praise from others. Operant conditioning and its extensions to behavior reflect a nonmediational view.

In contrast, *mediational views* emphasize the cognitive underpinnings of behavior. These underpinnings, such as perceptions, plans, attributions, expectations, and beliefs, are considered in mediational views to play a central role in behavior. According to mediational views, environmental events can influence behavior, but the person processes these events through his or her beliefs and attributions. Thus, cognitive processes imbue an event with meaning and help determine its impact. The influence of perceptions and beliefs on behavior is obvious in everyday life. For example, the way in which we behave in response to a glance from another person on the street or on a bus depends on whether we *perceive* the glance as threatening or friendly.

The dominant view within behavior modification is social learning theory, which recognizes the importance of both cognitive and environmental influences and their interaction. A broad social learning view is a useful way of considering multiple influences on behavior and of incorporating research from many areas. Applied behavior analysis has been criticized for not addressing the full range of the influences that may account for behavior. However, the goal of applied behavior analysis has not been to develop a broad theory of behavior. The overall questions of applied behavior analysis concern the extent to which principles developed in laboratory research can be useful in developing effective treatment, education, and rehabilitation programs and the extent to which human behavior can be altered in significant ways to improve functioning in everday life. Those questions can be answered empirically, that is, by seeing what can be accomplished by applying the principles. The present book elaborates the principles and the techniques that derive from them and illustrates applications that address the overall questions of applied behavior analysis.

NOTES

1. The term *client* will be used throughout the text to refer to the person for whom the intervention is provided. The reference is a convenient way to encompass different persons (e.g., psychiatric patients, children and adults in therapy, students, employ-

ees in a factory). Historically, the term has also been important as a substitute for the term *psychiatric patient*. This has been an issue because the term *patient* reflects the medical orientation toward deviant behavior to which proponents of behavior modification have objected.

2. Research in applied behavior analysis is published in many journals in psychology, education, rehabilitation, community work, and other areas. However, the *Journal of Applied Behavior Analysis* is devoted exclusively to this type of research.

FOR FURTHER READING

Baer, D. M., Wolf, M. M., & Risley, T. R. (1968). Some current dimensions of applied behavior analysis. *Journal of Applied Behavior Analysis, 1,* 91–97.

Catania, A. C. (1984). *Learning* (2nd ed.). Englewood Cliffs, NJ: Prentice-Hall.

Kazdin, A. E. (1978). *History of behavior modification: Experimental foundations of contemporary research.* Baltimore: University Park Press.

O'Leary, K. D., & Wilson, G. T. (1987). *Behavior therapy: Application and outcome* (2nd ed.). Englewood Cliffs, NJ: Prentice-Hall.

Skinner, B. F. (1953). *Science and human behavior.* New York: Macmillan.

Chapter Two

Principles of Operant Conditioning

In the previous chapter, three kinds of learning—classical conditioning, operant conditioning, and observational learning—were discussed. Although all three types of learning are evident in behavior modification, programs in applied settings such as the classroom, hospitals, institutions, and the home—and even in society at large—rely heavily on the principles of operant conditioning. The present chapter briefly explains the basic principles.[1] Later chapters elaborate the major principles and the various procedures that have been developed from them.

CONTINGENCIES: THE ABC'S OF BEHAVIOR

The principles of operant conditioning describe the relationship between behavior and the environmental events (antecedents and consequences) that influence behavior. This relationship, referred to as a *contingency*, includes three components: antecedent events (A), behaviors (B), and consequent events (C). The notion of a contingency is important not only for understanding behavior but also for developing programs to change behavior. Antecedent events refer to stimuli before the behavior, such as instructions, gestures, or looks from others. Behaviors refer to the acts themselves (i.e., some response that the individual performs). Consequences refer to events that follow behavior. Table 2–1 illustrates the three components of a contingency with simple examples from everyday life.

Developing effective programs depends on understanding the types of antecedent events and consequences that influence behavior. In most programs, emphasis is placed on the *consequences* that follow behavior. One of the most basic requirements of using consequences effectively pertains to how they are applied to behavior. For a consequence to alter a particular behavior, it must be dependent or *contingent upon* the occurrence of that behavior. Stated another way, *behavior change occurs when certain consequences are contingent upon performance.* A consequence is contingent when it is delivered only after the target behavior has been performed and is otherwise not available. When a consequence is not contingent upon behavior, this means that it is delivered independently of what the person is doing. The noncontingent delivery of consequences ordinarily does not result in systematic changes in a preselected target behavior, because the consequences do not consistently follow that behavior.

For example, if a psychiatric patient receives attention (the consequence) from an attendant on the ward each time he or she speaks, the attention is considered to be contingent upon speech. On the other hand, the patient may receive attention every so often from an attendant independently of what he or she is doing. In that case, attention is delivered noncontingently. To increase speaking, attention should be contingent upon instances of speaking. In everyday life, many consequences are contingent upon our behavior. Wages

TABLE 2–1 Three Components of a Contingency and Illustrations from Everyday Life

	Component	
Antecedent	Behavior	Consequences
Telephone rings	Answer phone	Voice of person at the other end
Wave from a friend	Approach friend	Visiting and chatting
Parent instruction for the child to clean his room	Child picks up toys	Praise and allowance
Warning not to eat spoiled food	Eating the food	Nausea and vomiting

are contingent upon working, grades are contingent upon studying for exams, and health is contingent to some extent upon the care with which we treat ourselves.

The notion of contingency is important because behavioral techniques alter behavior by modifying the contingencies that influence behavior. The principles of operant conditioning refer to different kinds of contingent relationships between behavior and the events that follow behavior. The major principles are reinforcement, punishment, and extinction.

REINFORCEMENT

The *principle of reinforcement* refers to an increase in the frequency of a response when that response is immediately followed by certain consequences. The consequence that follows behavior must be contingent upon behavior. A contingent event that increases the frequency of behavior is referred to as a *reinforcer*. Positive and negative reinforcers constitute the two kinds of events that can be used to increase the frequency of a response (Skinner, 1953). *Positive reinforcers* are events presented after a response has been performed that increase the frequency of the behavior they follow. *Negative reinforcers* (which will also be referred to as *aversive events* or *aversive stimuli*) are events removed after a response has been performed that increase the behavior preceding their removal.

Positive Reinforcement

Positive reinforcement refers to an increase in the frequency of a response that is followed by a favorable event (positive reinforcer). In everyday language, such positive or favorable events are frequently referred to as *rewards*. However, it is desirable to distinguish the term *positive reinforcement* from the term *reward*. A positive reinforcer is defined by its effect on behavior. If an event follows a behavior and the frequency of that behavior increases, the event is a positive reinforcer. Conversely, any event that does not increase the behavior it follows is not a positive reinforcer. An increase in the frequency or probability of the preceding behavior is the defining characteristic of a positive reinforcer. In contrast, rewards are defined merely as something that is given or received in return for doing something. Rewards such as prizes, sums of money, and vacations are usually highly valued, but they do not necessarily increase the probability of the behaviors they follow. The distinction between rewards and reinforcers may seem subtle, but it plays an exceedingly important part in the development of an effective treatment program.

Many rewards or events that a person evaluates favorably when queried may serve as reinforcers. However, the reinforcing value of an event cannot be known on the basis of a person's verbal statements alone. A person may be unaware of or not consider as rewards many events that are reinforcers. For example, verbal reprimands (e.g., "Stop that!") and physical restraint have occasionally served as positive reinforcers (e.g., Favell, McGimsey, & Jones, 1978; Madsen, Becker, Thomas, Koser, & Plager, 1970). Yet it is unlikely that anyone would ever refer to these consequences as rewards. Hence, a reward is not synonymous with a positive reinforcer. Whether an event is a positive reinforcer has to be determined empirically. Does the frequency of a particular behavior increase when the event immediately follows the behavior? Only if the behavior increases is the event a positive reinforcer.

Examples of positive reinforcement in everyday life would seem to be abundant. However, rarely does anyone actually measure whether a favorable event that followed a behavior increases the frequency of that behavior. Nevertheless, it is useful to mention some everyday situations that probably exemplify positive reinforcement. Studying for an exam is probably reinforced if a student receives an A. Studying reinforced by an excellent grade is likely to increase in the future. Alternatively, if a child whines or complains before going to bed and is then allowed by his or her parents to stay up longer, the frequency of whining before bedtime may increase. Letting the child stay up is likely to be a positive reinforcer. Winning money at a slot machine usually increases the frequency of putting money into the machine and pulling the lever. Money is a powerful reinforcer that increases performance of a variety of behaviors.

Types of Positive Reinforcers

Positive reinforcers include any events that, when presented, increase the frequency of the behavior they follow. There are two categories of positive reinforcers, namely *primary,* or *unconditioned,* and *secondary,* or *conditioned,* reinforcers. Events that serve as primary reinforcers acquire their reinforcing value without special training. Food and water are examples of primary reinforcers. Primary reinforcers may not be reinforcing all of the time. Food will not serve as a reinforcer to someone who has just finished a large meal. When food does serve as a reinforcer, however, its value is automatic (unlearned) and does not depend on a previous association with any other reinforcers.

Many events that control behavior are secondary, or conditioned, reinforcers. Conditioned reinforcers, which include events such as praise, grades, money, and completion of a goal, have acquired reinforcing value through learning. Conditioned reinforcers are not automatically reinforcing. Stimuli or events that were once neutral in value may acquire reinforcing properties by being paired with events that are already reinforcing (either primary reinforcers or other conditioned reinforcers). If a neutral stimulus is repeatedly presented prior to or along with a reinforcing stimulus, the neutral stimulus becomes a reinforcer. For example, praise may not be reinforcing for some individuals. To establish praise as a reinforcer, it must be paired with an event that is reinforcing, such as food or money. When a behavior is performed, the individual's behavior is praised and reinforced with food. After several pairings of the food with praise, the praise alone serves as a reinforcer and can be used to increase the frequency of other responses (Lancioni, 1982).

Some conditioned reinforcers are paired with more than one primary or conditioned reinforcer. When a conditioned reinforcer is paired with *many* other reinforcers, it is referred to as a *generalized conditioned reinforcer*. Generalized conditioned reinforcers are extremely effective in altering behaviors because they have been paired with a variety of events. Money is an example of a generalized conditioned reinforcer. It is a *conditioned* reinforcer because its reinforcing value is acquired through learning. It is a *generalized* reinforcer because a variety of reinforcing events contribute to its value. Additional examples of generalized conditioned reinforcers include attention, approval, and affection from others (Skinner, 1953). These are generalized reinforcers because their occurrence is often associated with a variety of other events that are themselves reinforcing. For example, attention from someone may be followed by physical contact, praise, smiles, affection, or delivery of tangible rewards (such as food) and other events.

In behavior modification programs, generalized reinforcers in the form of tokens are used frequently (Kazdin, 1977a). The tokens may consist of poker chips, coins, tickets, stars, points, or check marks. Tokens serve as generalized reinforcers because, like money, they can be exchanged for many other events that are reinforcing. For example, in a psychiatric hospital, tokens may be delivered to patients for attending group activities, grooming and bathing, and other behaviors. The tokens may be exchanged for snacks, cigarettes, and such privileges as watching television and attending social events. The potency of tokens derives from the reinforcers that back up their value. The events that tokens can purchase are referred to as *back-up reinforcers*. Generalized conditioned reinforcers, such as money or tokens, are usually more powerful than any single reinforcer because they can purchase many different back-up reinforcers.

In identifying positive reinforcers, it is important to keep two considerations in mind. First, an event (e.g., praise, candy, or a pat on the back) may be a positive reinforcer for one person but not for another. Although some events have wide generality in serving as reinforcers (e.g., food or money), others may not (e.g., sour candy). Second, an event may be a reinforcer for one person under some circumstances or at some times but not under other circumstances or at other times. These considerations require careful evaluation of what is reinforcing for a given individual. Because of cultural norms and the common experiences of many people, some suggestions may be given as to events that probably serve as reinforcers. However, there is no guarantee that a particular event will be reinforcing.

The Premack Principle

The reinforcing events referred to above include *stimuli* or specific events such as praise, smiles, food, or money that are presented after a response. However, reinforcers are not limited to the stimuli presented to a client.

Allowing an individual to engage in certain *responses* can be used as a reinforcer. Premack (1965) noted that when an individual is given the opportunity to select among various responses, behaviors performed with a relatively high frequency can reinforce behaviors performed with a relatively low frequency. If the opportunity to perform a more probable response is made contingent upon performance of a less probable response, the frequency of the latter should increase. On the basis of laboratory research, the *Premack principle* has been formulated to reflect this relation: *Of any pair of responses or activities in which an individual engages, the more frequent one will reinforce the less frequent one.* Stated more simply, a higher-probability behavior can reinforce a lower-probability behavior.

To determine what behaviors are high or low in frequency requires observing the behaviors that a person performs when given the opportunity to engage in behavior without restraints (e.g., what someone does when given free time at home, at school, on the weekends). A behavior observed to occur more frequently can be used to follow and reinforce a lower-frequency behavior (e.g., studying, engaging in chores). For example, for many children, playing with friends is performed at a higher frequency than is practicing a musical instrument. If the higher-frequency behavior (playing with friends) is made contingent upon the lower-frequency (playing the instrument), the lower-probability behavior will increase.

Although the Premack principle is effective as a basis for identifying reinforcers, it is not entirely clear why it works. One explanation, referred to as the *response deprivation hypothesis,* suggests that the effectiveness of making one response contingent upon another has to do with setting up a deprivation condition (Timberlake & Allison, 1974). Stated simply, the individual is deprived of opportunities to perform the desired (high-probability) behavior when that behavior is contingent upon completing some other response (low-probability behavior). Performance of the target response increases to overcome the decreased rate (deprivation) of the preferred response. The importance of response deprivation has been corroborated in laboratory and applied work (Konarski, Johnson, Crowell, & Whitman, 1981).

For applied purposes, the Premack principle is useful for expanding the range of reinforcers that can be used to alter behavior. Behaviors or activities that individuals appear to engage in during opportunities for free time, or self-reported preferences about what clients like to do, have been used to reinforce behavior in many applications. Of course, frequently performed behaviors or highly preferred activities may not serve as reinforcers. Yet a number of demonstrations attest to the utility of various activities as reinforcers.

An example of the use of the Premack principle to increase the activity of schizophrenic patients was reported by Mitchell and Stoffelmayr (1973). The patients frequently sat or paced in the ward. To increase their activity, the investigators wished to develop work at a task (stripping coil from wires). The two behaviors of interest were inactivity or sitting (higher-probability behavior) and work (lower-probability behavior). To increase work, sitting was made contingent upon doing some work. The investigators set a criterion for completing work before the clients earned the opportunity to sit down. Gradually, they increased the amount of work required to earn the opportunity to sit. The results showed a marked increase in work behavior when it was followed by sitting.

Numerous relatively frequent behaviors that an individual performs—for example, going on trips, being with friends, engaging in certain activities, hobbies, or privileges—can serve as reinforcers for other behaviors. The Premack principle requires that the target response be of a lower probability than the behavior that will reinforce it. Of course, in everyday life, high-probability behaviors often *precede* rather than follow low-probability behaviors. For example, students may study (low-probability behavior for many students) after going out with their friends (high-probability behavior). Spouses may complete yard work (low-probability behavior) after watching a football game (high-probability behavior). In such cases, the low-probability behavior is not likely to increase in frequency unless the sequence of the behaviors is reversed. Performing the high-probability behavior before performing the low-probability behavior amounts to the noncontingent delivery of reinforcers.

Negative Reinforcement

Negative reinforcement refers to an increase in the frequency of a response by removing an aversive event immediately after the response has been performed. Removal of an aversive event or a negative reinforcer is contingent upon a response. An event is a *negative reinforcer* only if its removal after a response increases performance of that response (Skinner, 1953). Events that appear to be annoying, undesirable, or unpleasant are not necessarily negatively reinforcing. The qualifications made in the discussion of positive reinforcers hold for negative reinforcers as well. An undesirable event may serve as an aversive event for one individual but not for another. Also, an event may be a negative reinforcer for an individual at one time but not at another time. A negative reinforcer, like a positive reinforcer, is defined solely by its effect on behavior.

It is important to note that *reinforcement (positive or negative) always refers to an increase in behavior.* Negative reinforcement requires an ongoing aversive event that can be removed or terminated after a specific response has been performed. The aversive event is "just there" or present in the environment. Once this event is present, then some behavior may stop or end it. That behavior is negatively reinforced. For example, if a young neighbor constantly turns on very loud music, this music is likely to be an aversive event to another neighbor who is not of the same generation (e.g., over 40 years old). The bothered neighbor has an ongoing aversive event, so a critical condition for negative reinforcement is present. To terminate the event, the neighbor screams, "Stop that _____ music, or I will call the _____ police." Assume for a moment that this behavior (screaming, swearing, and making a threat) stops the noise. The behavior has been negatively reinforced, because it was followed by elimination of the aversive event. Thus, the likelihood of future screaming, swearing, and threatening has been increased.

Other examples of negative reinforcement abound in everyday life. Taking medicine to relieve a headache may be negatively reinforced by the termination of pain. Similarly, nagging by a parent may increase room cleaning by a child. The aversive event (parental nagging) is terminated by performing the behavior. Strictly speaking, negative reinforcement occurs in the above examples only if the behavior that terminates the undesirable state increases.

Interesting combinations of positive and negative reinforcement that may foster socially undesirable behavior occur in social interaction (Patterson, 1982). In social interaction, the response of one individual is sometimes negatively reinforced because it terminates an aversive behavior initiated by another individual. At the same time, the aversive behavior of the other individual may be positively reinforced. For example, if parents pick up a young child who is whining, whining is, for the parents, an aversive event that is terminated after they respond. Picking up the child is negatively reinforced by a cessation of whining. However, the child's whining may be positively reinforced because he or she receives parental attention contingent upon this behavior. Positive and negative reinforcement in social interaction also occur when the victim of an aggressive act (e.g., physical assault) complies with the wishes of the aggressor (e.g., by giving up his wallet) in order to terminate an aversive situation. Unfortunately, the act of compliance positively reinforces the aggressor, increasing the probability of future aggression by the aggressor.

Negative reinforcement requires presentation to the individual of some aversive event, such as shock, noise, or isolation, that can be removed or reduced immediately after he or she responds. Because of the undesirability of using aversive stimuli, negative reinforcement is used infrequently in programs designed to alter behavior. Also, several less objectionable and more positive procedures are readily available.

As with positive reinforcers there are two types of negative reinforcers, primary and secondary. Intense stimuli, such as shock or loud noise, that impinge on the sensory receptors of an organism serve as primary negative reinforcers. Their aversive properties are not learned. In contrast, secondary, or conditioned, aversive events become aversive by being paired with events that are already aversive. For example, disapproving facial expressions or saying the word *no* can serve as aversive events after being paired with events that are already aversive (e.g., Dorsey, Iwata, Ong, & McSween, 1980).

Escape and Avoidance

Negative reinforcement occurs whenever an individual *escapes* from an aversive event. Escape from aversive events is negatively reinforcing. However, *avoidance* of aversive events is negatively reinforcing too. For example, one avoids eating rancid food, walking though an intersection with oncoming cars, and leaving the house without an umbrella on a rainy day. Avoidance occurs *before* the aversive event takes place (e.g., becoming sick from rancid food, being injured by a car, getting wet from rain). The avoidance response prevents the aversive event from occurring. Since no aversive events seem to have occurred, how are avoidance behaviors maintained?

Avoidance learning is an area in which classical and operant conditioning are operative. Avoidance behavior is sometimes learned by pairing a neutral stimulus (conditioned stimulus) with an unconditioned aversive event (unconditioned stimulus). For example, a frown (conditioned stimulus) from a parent may precede corporal punishment (unconditioned stimulus) of a child. Corporal punishment may elicit crying and escape from the situation (unconditioned response). The child learns to *escape* from the situation when the adult frowns and thereby *avoids* corporal punishment. The sight of the frowning parent elicits crying and escape. Avoidance of unconditioned aversive events is actually escape from conditioned aversive events. Thus, classical conditioning may initiate avoidance behavior. Operant conditioning is also involved in avoidance behavior. Behaviors that reduce or terminate an aversive event are negatively reinforced. The escape from the conditioned aversive event (e.g., frown) is negatively reinforced because it terminates the event. To reiterate, the conditioned aversive event elicits an escape response (classical conditioning) that is negatively reinforced (operant conditioning).

Operant conditioning is involved in yet another way in avoidance learning. A conditioned aversive event serves as a cue signaling that particular consequences will follow. The presence of the conditioned aversive stimulus signals that a certain response (escape) will be reinforced. A variety of cues control avoidance behavior in everyday life. Indeed, most avoidance behavior appears to be learned from verbal cues (warnings) by others, rather than from direct experience with unconditioned aversive stimuli. For example, a sign saying "Danger" or "Beware of Dog" signals that certain consequences (e.g., physical harm) are likely to occur if a particular response (e.g., trespassing) is performed. The escape response made after reading the sign is not *elicited*, as are reflex responses. The sign merely acts as a cue that consequences of a particular sort are likely to follow alternative courses of action. An individual does not have to experience physical harm to learn to avoid particular situations. In examples from everyday experience, avoidance behavior is under the control of antecedent stimuli (e.g., screeching car brakes, threats, and traffic signals) signaling that a particular event is likely to follow. Traditionally, both respondent and operant conditioning have been considered to influence avoidance learning. Yet the processes by which avoidance behavior is developed, maintained, and eliminated are not completely understood (see Catania, 1984; Hineline, 1977).

PUNISHMENT

Punishment is the presentation of an aversive event or the removal of a positive event following a response, which decreases the frequency of that response. This definition is somewhat different from the everyday use of the term. As ordinarily defined, punishment refers to a penalty imposed for performing a particular act. The technical definition includes an additional requirement, namely that the frequency of the response is decreased (Azrin & Holz, 1966). Because of the negative connotations frequently associated with punishment, it is important to dispel some stereotypical notions that do not apply to the technical definition of punishment. Punishment does not necessarily entail pain or physical coercion.[2] In addition, it is not a means of retribution or payment for misbehaving. Punishment is sometimes employed in everyday life independently of its effects on subsequent behavior. For example, misbehaving children are "taught a lesson" by undergoing a sacrifice of some kind. Similarly, criminals may receive penalties that do not necessarily decrease the frequency of their criminal acts. *Punishment in the technical sense is defined solely by the effect on behavior.* In this sense, punishment is operative only if the frequency of a response is reduced. Similarly, a punishing event is defined by its suppressive effect on the behavior that it follows. As will become evident in later chapters, a variety of events that suppress behavior depart from ordinary practices that are termed punishment in everyday life.

There are two types of punishment. In the first type, an aversive event is *presented* after a response. The numerous everyday examples of this type of punishment include being reprimanded or slapped after engaging in some behavior. Similarly, being burned after touching a hot stove involves the presentation of an aversive stimulus after a response. The second type of punishment is the *removal* of a positive event after a response. Examples include losing privileges after staying out late, losing money for misbehaving, being isolated from others, and having one's driver's license revoked. In this type of punishment, some positive event is taken away after a response has been performed.

Punishment and negative reinforcement are often confused even though they are very different. *The key difference is that reinforcement, whether negative or positive, always refers to procedures that increase a response, whereas punishment always refers to procedures that decrease a response.* In negative reinforcement, an aversive event is *removed* after a response; in punishment, an aversive consequence *follows* a response.

Figure 2–1 provides a simple way of distinguishing the operations involved in reinforcement and punishment, depicting two operations that can occur after a response has been performed. An event can be presented to, or removed from, the client after a response (left side of the figure). The figure also shows two types of events that may be presented or removed, namely positive and aversive events. The four combinations forming the different cells depict the principles of positive reinforcement (Cell I), negative reinforcement (Cell IV), and the two types of punishment (Cells II and III).

EXTINCTION

An important principle of operant conditioning is not represented in Figure 2–1. This principle does not involve presenting or withdrawing events in the usual sense. Rather, it refers to no longer following behavior with an event that was previously delivered.

FIGURE 2–1

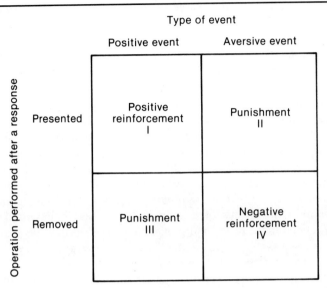

Illustration of principles of operant conditioning based on whether positive or aversive events are presented or removed after a response has been performed. The figure provides a simple way to convey the major principles of operant conditioning, but the simplicity of the figure has a price. In fact, a more technical discussion of the principles would quickly reveal inaccuracies in the figure. For example, the figure implies that a particular event that can negatively reinforce behavior can also be used to suppress (punish) some other response that it follows. Although this is usually true, many exceptions exist. It is not necessarily the case that the same event whose removal negatively reinforces a behavior will suppress a behavior when it is presented, or vice versa (Azrin & Holz, 1966). Hence, in the present text, the term *aversive stimulus,* or *aversive event,* will be used to refer to any event that may be negatively reinforcing and/or punishing. In general, the principles of operant conditioning refer to more complex relationships than are depicted here (see Morse & Kelleher, 1977). Interestingly, behavior modification programs tend to rely on the simple versions of the principles discussed here.

Behaviors that are reinforced increase in frequency. However, a behavior that is no longer reinforced decreases in frequency. During extinction, a response that was previously reinforced is no longer reinforced. *Extinction refers to the cessation of reinforcement of a response.* Nonreinforcement of a response results in its eventual reduction or elimination. It is important to keep this procedure distinct from punishment. In extinction, *no consequence* follows the response; an event is neither taken away nor presented. In punishment, some aversive event follows a response or some positive event is taken away. In everyday life, extinction usually takes the form of ignoring a behavior that was previously reinforced with attention. A mother may ignore her child when the child whines. A teacher may ignore children who talk without raising their hands. A therapist or counselor may ignore certain self-defeating statements made by the client. In each of these examples, the reinforcer (e.g., attention, approval, or sympathy) previously given for the response is no longer presented.

As an example, extinction was used as part of a program to change several feminine sex-typed behaviors of a five-year-old boy named Kraig (Rekers & Lovaas, 1974). Kraig continually engaged in traditionally female-typed behaviors such as dressing in women's clothes, playing with dolls and cosmetics, and mimicking feminine gestures and mannerisms. He avoided all male-typed activities. Treatment was implemented because of the social difficulties that cross-gender activities may create for a child and also because such behaviors are often precursors to later sexual deviance such as transvestism (cross dressing) and transsexualism (opposite-sex-role identity). At the clinic, the mother and child were placed in a room where the child had the opportunity to play with what were traditionally regarded as female-typed objects (e.g., dolls, cosmetics, women's clothes) or male-typed objects (e.g., cars, boats, guns). The mother was instructed to ignore any play with female-typed objects by simply reading a book that she brought into the room. The purpose was to *extinguish* play with female-typed objects by withholding attention. The mother was also instructed to reinforce play with male-typed objects. The mother was instructed to provide attention, smiles, and praise whenever Kraig played with these objects. Thus, extinction was combined with positive reinforcement. The program was also carried out at home, where Kraig received token reinforcement for many gender-appropriate behaviors. Interestingly, the program led to a dramatic increase in masculine behaviors and a dramatic decrease in feminine behaviors. These treatment effects were maintained when Kraig was checked 26 months after treatment.[3]

In everyday life, extinction may contribute to behavioral problems as well as ameliorate them. Often, desirable behavior is accidentally extinguished. For example, parents sometimes ignore their children when the children are playing quietly and provide abundant attention when the children are noisy. This may extinguish quiet play while positively reinforcing noisy play. Merely altering parental attention so that it follows appropriate play is often sufficient to develop appropriate behavior and to extinguish inappropriate behavior.

Cessation of attention is not the only example of extinction. For example, putting money into vending machines (a response) will cease if the reinforcer (e.g., cigarettes, food, or drink) is not forthcoming; turning on a radio will cease if the radio no longer provides sound; and attempting to start a car will cease if the car does not start. In each of these examples, the consequences that maintain the behavior are no longer forthcoming. The absence of reinforcing consequences reduces the behavior. Extinction can be used as a technique to reduce or eliminate behavior. However, the events that reinforce behavior must be identified so that they can be prevented from occurring after the response.

SHAPING AND CHAINING

Frequently, the development of new behavior cannot be achieved by reinforcing the response when it occurs. In many cases, the response may never occur. The desired behavior may be so complex that the elements making up the response are not in the repertoire of the individual. For example, developing the use of words requires, among other things, the use of sounds, syllables, and their combinations. *In shaping, the terminal or goal behavior is achieved by reinforcing small steps or approximations toward the final response rather than reinforcing the final response itself.* Responses are reinforced that either resemble the final response or include components of that response. By reinforcing *successive approximations* of the final response, it is gradually achieved. Responses increasingly similar to the final goal are reinforced, and they increase; responses dissimilar to the final goal are not reinforced, and they extinguish.

Shaping, along with other procedures, is used to develop the use of language in children. Responses that approach the final goal are reinforced. Responses that do not approach that goal are extinguished. For example, when parents are trying to develop use of the words *mommy* or *daddy* in an infant, they usually reinforce any approximation (e.g., *ma* or *da-da*) by smiling, hugging, and praising effusively. At the same time, but usually without thinking about it, they do not attend to (extinguish) sounds that are not close to the words they wish (e.g., *goo, milk*). Over time, the parents reinforce sounds and syllables that come closer to the words *mommy* and *daddy*.

An obvious example of shaping is training animals to perform various tricks. If the animal trainer waited until the tricks were performed (e.g., jumping through a burning hoop) to administer a reinforcer, it is unlikely that reinforcement would ever occur. Animals normally do not perform such behavior. By shaping the response, however, the trainer can readily achieve the terminal goal. First, food (positive reinforcement) might be delivered for running toward the trainer. As that response becomes consistent, the trainer might reinforce running up to him when he is holding a hoop. Other steps closer to the final goal would be reinforced in sequence, including walking through the hoop on the ground, jumping through it when it is partially on fire, and finally, jumping through it when the hoop is completely on fire. Eventually, the terminal response will be performed with a high frequency, whereas the responses or steps developed along the way will have been extinguished.

As an example, shaping was used to develop appropriate speech in Alice, a 15-year-old mentally retarded girl who was severely withdrawn (Jackson & Wallace, 1974). At first, her speech was almost completely inaudible. A reinforcement program was used to shape progressively louder speech while she read various words in experimental sessions with a trainer. A microphone that she wore was used to detect the volume of her speech. At the beginning of training, only slight increases in voice volume were required. When the desired volume was registered through the microphone, a token was automatically delivered. The tokens could be used for various items that Alice desired, such as a photo album and beauty aids. When Alice's voice consistently met the volume required to earn tokens, the requirement was increased slightly. She gradually developed louder and louder speech until her voice volume was equal to that of her peers.

Shaping requires reinforcing behaviors already in the repertoire of the individual that resemble or approximate the final goal. As the initial approximation is performed consistently, the criterion for reinforcement is altered slightly so that the response to be reinforced resembles the final goal more closely than does the previous response. Through reinforcement of responses that approach the final goal and extinction of responses that do not, the terminal response is developed. In the above example, shaping was used to increase voice volume. Training began with the existing response and gradually increased volume over time. Reinforcing successive approximations is used in an identical fashion to develop new behaviors that have never been performed by the client, such as feeding, walking, and dressing.

Most behaviors consist of a sequence of several responses. A sequence of responses is referred to as a *chain*. The component parts of a chain usually represent individual responses already in the repertoire of the individual. Yet the chain represents a combination of the individual responses ordered in a particular sequence. For example, one behavioral chain that illustrates the ordering of component responses is "getting dressed." Getting dressed is a set of behaviors often trained among severely mentally retarded children. A sequence of behaviors can be identified, though this may vary depending on the specific skills of the individual. For example, the sequence may include such behaviors as taking clothes out of the drawer, placing them on a bed, putting on a shirt, and so on for other articles of clothing. Putting on individual articles of clothing also consists of a chain of behaviors. Putting on a shirt can be divided into several constituent behaviors such as pulling the shirt (e.g., turtleneck) over one's head, putting one's arms through the sleeves, pulling the shirt down, tucking the shirt in, and so on. These examples reflect chains of behavior because they comprise many individual responses that are linked together in a specific order.

There are many sequences or behavioral chains in everyday life. It is often the case that long sequences of behavior are performed, even though the reinforcer comes only at the very end of the chain. For example, dieting, mastering a musical instrument, preparing for athletic competition, studying for an advanced degree, and writing a book all require a series of intermediate responses before the final reinforcing event is achieved. The major question is, What maintains all of the intermediate responses that precede attaining the final goal? The answer requires explaining the factors that link the response components of a chain.

To begin with, it is important to note that an event immediately preceding reinforcement becomes a signal for reinforcement. An event that signals that behavior will be reinforced is referred to as a *discriminative stimulus* (S^D). An

S^D sets the occasion for behavior: it increases the probability that a previously reinforced behavior will occur. However, an S^D not only signals reinforcement but eventually becomes a reinforcer itself. The frequent pairing of an S^D and the reinforcer gives the S^D reinforcing properties of its own. This procedure was mentioned earlier in the discussion of conditioned reinforcement. The discriminative stimulus properties of events that precede reinforcement and the reinforcing properties of these events when they are frequently paired with reinforcers are important in explaining how chains of responses are maintained.

Consider the chain of responses involved in completing a painting. The sequence may include an indefinite number of components, beginning perhaps with purchasing paints and canvases, sketching drafts of the painting on scratch paper, drawing an outline on the canvas itself, actually painting the canvas, and finally seeing the finished product. The first response (purchasing the materials) is quite far removed from completion of the painting. Assume for a moment that seeing the final product (or for those more materially oriented, selling the painting) is the final reinforcer. Only the final response near the reinforcer— placing the final strokes of paint—are followed by the reinforcing consequences (seeing the finished product). This final response is directly reinforced with seeing the finished product. Recall that any event that precedes reinforcement becomes an S^D for reinforcement. In this chain of responses, the last response performed (painting the final strokes) becomes an S^D for reinforcement, since the response signals that reinforcement will follow. Yet the pairing of an S^D with the reinforcer (seeing the product) eventually results in the S^D becoming a reinforcer as well as a discriminative stimulus. Hence, the response preceding direct reinforcement has become an S^D for subsequent reinforcement and a reinforcer in its own right. It serves as a reinforcer for the previous link in the chain of responses. The response (putting strokes on the canvas) becomes a reinforcer for the previous behavior (sketching the canvas). Since sketching the canvas now precedes reinforcement, it too becomes an S^D. As with other responses, the pairing of the S^D with reinforcement results in the S^D becoming a reinforcer. The process continues in a backward direction so that each response in the chain becomes an S^D for the next response in the chain and serves as a reinforcer for the prior response in the chain.

Although the sequence appears to be maintained by a single reinforcer at the end of the chain of responses (seeing the finished product), the links in the chain are assumed to take on conditioned reinforcement value. To accomplish this, building response chains requires training from the last response in the sequence that precedes direct reinforcement back to the first response. Because the last response in the sequence is paired immediately and directly with the reinforcer, it is most easily established as a conditioned reinforcer that can maintain other responses. Also, the shorter the delay between a response and reinforcement, the greater the effect of reinforcement. The last response in the chain is immediately reinforced and is more likely to be performed frequently.

General Comments.   The differences between shaping and chaining and between the conditions that dictate their use may be unclear. Generally, both shaping and chaining may be used to develop new behaviors. With each technique, discriminative stimuli (e.g., instructions, gestures) and direct reinforcement (e.g., praise) may be provided for the desired behavior. In some circumstances, shaping can be distinguished by focusing on a series of steps that finally lead to the desired behavior. In contrast, chaining is often used to develop a sequence of separate behaviors. The final goal may be a sequence of several different responses, as in dressing oneself.

Certainly, the major difference is that chaining proceeds in a backward direction beginning with the last response and building prior behaviors, whereas shaping works in a forward direction. Moreover, the goal in shaping is to develop a terminal response. The behaviors along the way toward the goal are usually not evident when shaping has been completed. In chaining, however, individual behaviors developed early in training are still evident when training has been completed.

In spite of the differences between shaping and chaining, the relative utility of the procedures in applied settings has not been evaluated empirically. Sequences of behaviors (chains) can be developed by shaping and using cues and reinforcement for the performance of behaviors in a particular sequence. Thus, in many situations either chaining or shaping may be used. For example, toilet training of children consists of a series of responses that follow in sequence: walking to a bathroom, lowering pants, positioning oneself in front of or on the toilet, and so on. Following completion of the entire chain, praise for proper elimination can serve as reinforcement. Although chaining can be used to develop this sequence of responses, shaping is also effective (Azrin & Foxx, 1971; Mahoney, Van Wagenen, & Meyerson, 1971).

In light of current research, it is not clear when chaining or shaping should be selected. For some individuals, however, cues normally used in shaping (e.g., instructions) may exert little influence on behavior, so that the behaviors in a sequence of responses are not consistently performed. Chaining might be particularly useful in such cases because each behavior in the chain becomes a cue for the next response to be performed. Moreover, the conditioned reinforcement provided by each response in the chain facilitates performance of the correct order of responses. Shaping is well suited to developing a chain of several responses, especially when cues such as instructions are effective in initiating the early behaviors in the chain. Even so, the notion of a behavioral chain is very important because many behaviors that are trained are long sequences of individual behaviors.

PROMPTING AND FADING

Developing a behavior is facilitated by using cues, instructions, gestures, directions, examples, and models to initiate a response. *Prompts are events that help initiate a response.* They come before a response has been performed and are designed to facilitate its performance. When a prompt results in the response, the response can be reinforced. Without the prompt, the response might occur infrequently or not at all. Prompts serve as antecedent events (e.g., instructions, gestures) that help generate the desired response.

Behavior can be prompted in different ways, such as *guiding* the behavior of a person physically (e.g., holding a child's arm to assist him in placing a spoon in his mouth), *instructing* the person to do something, *pointing* to the person to do something (e.g., come inside the house), and *having the person observe* another person (a model) perform a behavior (e.g., having the person watch someone else play a game). Prompts play a major role in shaping. Developing a terminal response using reinforcement alone may be tedious and time consuming. Assisting a person in beginning the response can enable the person to make more rapid approximations to the final response.

For example, a recent investigation focused on teaching a job skill to profoundly retarded adult women (Schepis, Reid, & Fitzgerald, 1987). The women could comply only with simple requests and engaged in aggressive and self-injurious behavior. The goal was to train a job skill that consisted of preparing envelopes for mailing, including stamping a return address on the envelopes. To train the task, different kinds of prompts were used. Verbal instructions (verbal prompt) were provided to explain the sequence of behaviors; modeling (visual prompt) was provided if the individual did not show the requisite behaviors; finally, the individual was aided by guiding her through the task with physical assistance (physical prompt). These prompts were designed to increase the likelihood of correct performance of the behaviors, so that reinforcement (in this case praise) could be provided. While a response is being shaped, prompts may be used frequently to facilitate performance of the terminal response.

Although prompts are cues that initiate behavior, they often take on the value of events (consequences) that follow them. Thus, if the prompted behavior is consistently reinforced, the prompt may become an S^D for reinforcement. For example, if a parent tells a child to return home from school early and the child is praised when he does this, the instruction (prompt) becomes an S^D. Instructions signal that reinforcement is likely when certain behaviors are performed. Eventually, instructions alone are likely to be followed by the behavior. In general, when a prompt consistently precedes reinforcement of a response, the prompt becomes an S^D and can effectively control behavior.

Prompts can become aversive if they are associated with punishing consequences. For example, parents may constantly remind (prompt) their teenage son or daughter to clean his or her room, to practice playing a musical instrument, or to do homework. These prompts become aversive because they are cues for other aversive events (e.g., threats, loss of privileges and reprimands at home, poor grades at school). It takes little time for such prompts to become aversive in their own right. A child may try to terminate the aversive prompts by completing the prompted behavior, leaving the room, or shouting at the parent. In behavior modification programs, prompts are typically used to initiate behavior, so that it can be positively reinforced. Once reinforcement can be provided, the behavior can be maintained by the reinforcing consequences.

Usually, the ultimate goal is to obtain the terminal response in the absence of prompts. Although prompts may be required early in training, they can be withdrawn gradually or faded as training progresses. *Fading refers to the gradual removal of a prompt.* If a prompt is removed abruptly early in training, the response may no longer be performed. But if the response is performed consistently with a prompt, the prompt can be progressively reduced and finally omitted. For example, teaching a person how to serve in tennis or how to play the piano may include reminders (prompts) regarding how to hold the racket or how to place his or her fingers on the keys. As the person begins to perform these behaviors, the prompt can be provided less frequently. The correct behaviors are reinforced without reminders and soon do not need to be prompted at all or only very rarely.

For example, in the study mentioned previously, prompts were used to train a specific set of behaviors with mentally retarded women (Schepis et al., 1987). Over the course of training and as the behaviors were performed correctly, trainers began to fade the prompts. The number of prompts was decreased over time, and more intrusive (physical) prompts were decreased or eliminated. The terminal goal of the project was to develop the behavior so that it could be performed independently (i.e., without prompts). This goal was facilitated by introducing prompts to develop the behavior and by gradually fading and eliminating the prompts and reinforcing independent performance.

The achievement of behavior without prompts requires fading and reinforcing the responses in the absence of prompts. It is not always necessary to remove all prompts. For example, it is important to train individuals to respond in the presence of certain prompts, such as instruction, that exert control over a variety of behaviors in everyday life.

DISCRIMINATION AND STIMULUS CONTROL

Operant behavior is influenced by the consequences that follow behavior. However, antecedent events also control behavior. Prompts represent a group of controlling events (e.g., instructions, physical guidance, models, and reminders) that precede and facilitate performance. Yet other antecedent stimuli come to exert control over behavior. In some situations (or in the presence of certain stimuli), a response may be reinforced; in other situations (in the presence of other stimuli), the same response may not be reinforced.

Differential reinforcement refers to reinforcing a response in the presence of one stimulus and not reinforcing the same response in the presence of another stimulus. When a response is consistently reinforced in the presence of a particular stimulus and consistently not reinforced in the presence of another stimulus, each stimulus signals the consequences that are likely to follow. As mentioned earlier, a stimulus whose presence has been associated with reinforcement is referred to as an S^D. A stimulus whose presence has been associated with nonreinforcement is referred to as an S^Δ (S delta). The eventual effect of differential reinforcement is that the reinforced response is likely to occur in the presence of the S^D but unlikely to occur in the presence of the S^Δ. When an individual responds differently in the presence of different stimuli, he or she has made a *discrimination*. When responses are differentially controlled by antecedent stimuli, behavior is considered to be under *stimulus control*.

Instances of stimulus control pervade everyday life. For example, the sound of a doorbell signals that a certain behavior (opening the door) is likely to be reinforced (by seeing someone). Specifically, the sound of the bell has frequently been associated with the presence of visitors at the door (the reinforcer). The ring of the bell (S^D) increases the likelihood that the door will be opened. In the absence of the ring (S^Δ), the probability of opening the door for a visitor is very low. The rings of a doorbell, telephone, alarm, and kitchen timer all serve as discriminative stimuli (S^D) and signal that certain responses are likely to be reinforced. Hence, the probability of the responses is increased.

Stimulus control is also evident in the selection and consumption of foods. For example, the color and smell of foods (e.g., an orange that has turned blue, milk that smells sour) influence the likelihood that we will eat them. Characteristics of the foods are cues for particular consequences (e.g., flavor, nausea) and exert stimulus control over our eating. In recognition of this point, natural foods (e.g., fruit) or products (e.g., leather) often have artificial colors and fragrances added to them to increase the likelihood of their purchase. Stimulus control is also important in social interaction. For example, a smile or wink from someone is likely to occasion a social response on our part (e.g., initiation of conversation). Whereas a smile serves as an S^D (signals that reinforcement is likely to follow our social response), a frown serves as an S^Δ (signals that reinforcement is not likely to follow our social response).

The notion of stimulus control is exceedingly important in behavior modification. In many programs, the goal is to alter the relation between behavior and the stimulus conditions in which the behavior occurs. Some behavior problems stem from a failure of certain stimuli to control behavior, though such control would be desirable. For example, children who do not follow instructions given by their parents illustrate a lack of stimulus control. The instructions do not exert influence over the children's behavior. The goal of a behavior modification program is to increase responsiveness to instructions. Other behavioral problems occur when certain behaviors are under the control of antecedent stimuli when such control is undesirable. For example, the eating behavior of obese individuals is often controlled by the mere sight of food (among other stimuli), rather then hunger. Treatment of overeating focuses on reducing the control that the sight of food has on eating.

Stimulus control is always operative in behavior modification programs. Such programs are conducted in particular settings (e.g., the home) and are administered by particular individuals (e.g., parents). Insofar as certain client behaviors are reinforced or punished in the presence of certain environmental cues or of particular individuals and not in the presence of other stimuli, those behaviors will be under stimulus control. In the presence of the cues associated with the behavior modification program, the client will behave in a particular fashion. In situations lacking those cues, the client's behavior is likely to change because the contingencies may be different.

A familiar example of stimulus control that may arise in a behavior modification program pertains to the behavior of students when the teacher is in rather than out of the classroom. As most of us might recall from our elementary school years, the amount of disruptive behavior often varied depending on whether the teacher was in the room enforcing the rules of the classroom. Once the stimulus (teacher) associated with the reinforcing or punishing consequences was no longer present, behavior often deteriorated. Indeed, the stimulus control that individuals such as parents and teachers exert over behavior often creates a problem in behavior modification. The children may perform the responses in the presence of parents or teachers but not in their absence. Special contingency arrangements are often needed to ensure that the desired behaviors transfer to new people, situations, and places.

The control that different stimuli exert over behavior explains why behavior is often situation specific. Individuals may behave one way in a given situation or in the presence of a particular person and differently in another situation or in the presence of another person. Because different reinforcement contingencies operate in different circumstances, individuals can discriminate among stimuli that are likely to be followed by reinforcement.

People in everyday life are quite familiar with the concepts of differential reinforcement and stimulus control, though these terms, of course, are not used. For example, children behave differently in the presence of their mothers than in the presence of their fathers in part because of the different reinforcement contingencies that operate. Children often know which parent to ask in making specific requests because the likelihood of reinforcement (affirmative answer) differs between parents on various issues. Similarly, children often behave quite differently at home and at school. Such differences in behavior may lead to perplexed parents and teachers who argue that the child is "not really like that." Yet the child's behavior may vary considerably as a function of different reinforcement contingencies at home and at school.

The significance of differential reinforcement and stimulus control is difficult to convey in everyday examples because many events are operative that obscure the factors controlling behavior. The impact of differential reinforcement and its role in leading to differences in behavior are illustrated clearly in a study completed several years ago (Redd & Birnbrauer, 1969). In this study, two adults working at different times provided mentally retarded children with food (candy, ice cream, or sips of cola) and praise for performing a specified response (e.g., playing cooperatively with another child). When the first adult was with one child, reinforcement was administered for the cooperative response (contingent delivery of praise). When the second adult was with the same child, reinforcement was delivered independently of his actual behavior (noncontingent delivery of praise). Overall, each adult administered the same amount of the available reinforcers. In a short period, the adults exerted stimulus control over the behavior of the children. The presence of the adult who was associated with the contingent delivery of praise led to cooperative play, whereas the presence of the adult who was associated with the noncontingent delivery of praise did not. The children discriminated among the different contingencies associated with each of the adults. Thus, adults can serve as discriminative stimuli for reinforcement. Children respond differentially to different adults, depending on the behaviors that each of the adults reinforces. Similarly, in everyday life, children often engage in different behaviors in front of each of their parents in part because of the different behaviors that each parent has reinforced.

People make discriminations across a variety of situations for most behaviors. For example, eating habits probably vary depending on whether one is at home or in a restaurant. Even more subtle discriminations are made. Eating behavior may differ depending on whether one is in an expensive or a fast-food restaurant. Also, people behave differently in the presence of their coworkers than in the presence of their boss. Numerous other variations in behavior are evident because of differences in situations and in the contingencies associated with them.

GENERALIZATION

The effect of reinforcement on behavior may either extend beyond the conditions in which training has taken place or extend to behaviors other than those included in the program. The ways in which the effects of the program may extend beyond the contingency are referred to as *generalization*.

Stimulus Generalization

Behavior occurs in specific situations. A response repeatedly reinforced in the presence of a particular situation is likely to be repeated in that situation. However, situations and stimuli often share common properties. The control exerted by a given stimulus is shared by other stimuli that are similar or share common properties (Skinner, 1953). A behavior may be performed in new situations similar to the situation in which reinforcement occurred. Stimulus generalization occurs if a response reinforced in one situation or setting also increases in other settings (even though it is not reinforced in the other settings). *Stimulus generalization refers to the generalization or transfer of a response to situations other than those in which training takes place.*

Generalization is the opposite of discrimination. When an individual discriminates in the performance of a response, this means that the response fails to generalize across situations. Alternatively, when a response generalizes across situations, the individual fails to discriminate in his or her performance of that response.

Figure 2–2 illustrates stimulus generalization. S_1 refers to the *stimulus condition,* or the situation in which the response is reinforced. R_1 refers to the *response,* or the behavior that is reinforced. The figure shows that the trained response (R_1) is performed across a variety of stimuli or situations (S_2, S_3, S_4, S_5). The degree of stimulus generalization is a function of the similarity of new stimuli (or situations) to the stimulus under which the response was trained. Of course, over a long period of time, a response may not generalize across situations because the individual discriminates that the response is reinforced in one situation but not in others.

Examples of stimulus generalization are frequent in everyday experience. For example, a child may talk about certain topics in the presence of his family because talking about those topics is reinforced (e.g., discussed freely, attended to) among family members. The child may also discuss the same topics in the presence of company. In that case, the child's behavior (talking about certain topics) has generalized across situations. Parents may show considerable embarrassment when children freely discuss family secrets or embarrassing personal topics (e.g., how one's father puts on his toupee or how a parent looks in the shower). Generalization is also readily apparent when a child responds to a teacher in a fashion similar to the fashion in which he or she responds to a parent (e.g., in the expression of affection). To the extent that a child sees parents and teachers as similar, the stimulus control exerted by parents will be shared by the teacher. Because the antecedent events (ap-

FIGURE 2–2

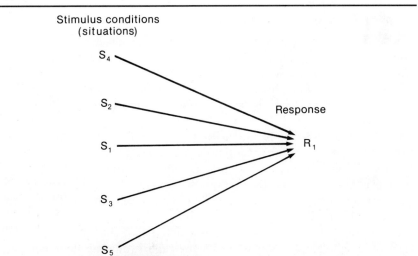

Stimulus generalization: A response (R_1) reinforced in one situation (S_1) generalizes to other, similar situations (S_2, S_3, S_4, S_5).

proaches by the adult, expressions of affection) and the consequent events (hugs, kisses) are different for the child in relation to teachers and parents, the child quickly learns a discrimination. Consequently, expressions of affection are more likely in the presence of parents (S^D) than of teachers (S^Δ).

An example of generalization across situations and stimulus conditions was reported in a program for a 21-year-old hospitalized schizophrenic patient (Fichter, Wallace, Liberman, & Davis, 1976). The patient was very withdrawn and spoke inaudibly when he did speak. Also, he spoke very briefly and engaged in inappropriate hand gestures, such as tapping his face with his fingers, biting his fingers, and rocking with his hands between his thighs. Treatment consisted of prompting louder and longer speech and appropriate use of hands and arms (e.g., placing them on the armrests of a chair) while he interacted socially with a staff member. The prompting procedure was conducted in the hospital. After the patient was discharged, however, observations were also conducted in the residential care home where he lived and in the day-treatment center where he spent his days. The observations revealed that the improvements achieved in the hospital extended to these other settings, even though the prompts were never used there. Thus, behavior *generalized* to new staff members, new settings, and across new topics of conversation that were not included in training.

Stimulus generalization represents an exceedingly important issue in behavior modification. Invariably, training takes place in a restricted setting such as a classroom, a home, a hospital ward, and/or an institution. It is desirable that behaviors developed in these settings generalize or transfer to other settings.

Response Generalization

Another type of generalization involves responses rather than stimulus conditions. Altering one response can inadvertently influence other responses. For example, if a person is praised for smiling, the frequency, not only of smiling, but also of laughing and talking might increase. *The reinforcement of a response increases the probability of other responses that are similar* (Skinner, 1953). This is referred to as response generalization. To the extent that a nonreinforced response is similar to one that is reinforced, the probability of the nonreinforced response increases. Response generalization is depicted in Figure 2–3, where S_1 refers to the stimulus condition in which training of a response takes place and R_1 refers to the response that is reinforced. Although only one response is trained in the situation, a variety of similar responses (R_2, R_3, R_4, R_5) may also be performed.

Altering one behavior is often associated with changes in other behaviors as well. For example, according to one report, altering noncompliance (not completing the requests of adults) in four children also decreased such inappropriate behaviors as aggression (e.g., pushing, hitting, biting), disruption (e.g., whining, crying, screaming), property destruction (e.g., pushing, kicking

FIGURE 2–3

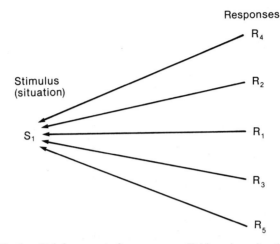

Responses

R₄

Stimulus
(situation)

R₂

S₁

R₁

R₃

R₅

Response generalization: Reinforcement of one response (R₁) in a given situation (S₁) may result in an increase of other, similar responses (R₂, R₃, R₄, R₅).

furniture, pounding on or throwing objects), and placing inedible objects in their mouths (Parrish, Cataldo, Kolko, Neef, & Egel, 1986). Alternative procedures, based primarily on variations of positive reinforcement, effectively increased compliance among these children. Interestingly, when their compliance increased, their aggression, disruption, and other inappropriate behaviors decreased, even though there had been no specific focus on these other behaviors.

The notion of response generalization is often used to explain changes in responses other than the target response. Technically, the term *response generalization* may not be accurate for two reasons. First, responses that are not supposed to be focused on may inadvertently receive reinforcing consequences. For example, a child praised for studying in class may improve in reading even though reading may not have been the response to which the reinforcing consequences were directed. Although this may be spoken of as generalization, it may reflect the direct operation of reinforcement and not be generalization at all. When a child is praised for paying attention, he or she may be reading on some of the occasions that reinforcement is delivered. Thus, it is difficult to speak of response generalization, because the behavior was directly reinforced.

There is a second, slightly more complex reason that response generalization may not accurately account for the many changes that occur with treatment. Response generalization refers to changes in behaviors that are similar to the target behavior. Yet research has shown many examples in which change in one behavior has consistent effects on other behaviors that appear to have no direct relation or resemblance to the target behavior. For example, in one study, the excessive talking of a seven-year-old boy was altered by withdrawing teacher attention (Sajwaj, Twardosz, & Burke, 1972). Other behaviors changed as well; for example, the boy's conversation and cooperative play with his peers increased and his use of "girls'" toys during free play decreased. These behaviors had no clear relation to the target focus and could not be accounted for by changes in teacher attention to them. It is unclear why the other behaviors changed, because only excessive verbalizations with the teacher were altered. Similarly, other studies have shown that changing one behavior may result in changes in behaviors bearing no obvious relation to that behavior (see Kazdin, 1982a; Wahler, Berland, & Coe, 1979).

The reasons that various responses change when treatment focuses on a particular behavior are unclear. Wahler (1975) has carefully observed children over extended periods in the home and at school and has found that individuals often have clusters of behavior (i.e., groups of specific behaviors that consistently go together). For example, for one child, engaging in self-stimulation, socially interacting with adults, complying with adult instructions, and other behaviors tended to go together. Treatment that focused on one behavior that was part of the cluster altered other behaviors as well. The spread of treatment effects to those behaviors could not be explained by the similarity of the behaviors.

The tendency of responses to change together or as a cluster has been referred to as *response covariation*. The responses co-vary (are correlated and change together). A number of studies have demonstrated that behaviors cluster and that altering one of the behaviors in a cluster alters other behaviors as well. The spread of the effects of altering a behavior in a cluster can be predicted by knowing what other behaviors are in the cluster. However, the phenomenon of response covariation has received relatively little attention and will require further investigation before it is fully understood.

In behavior modification, the concepts of stimulus and response generalization are ordinarily used to denote that changes occur across various stimulus conditions (situations or settings) or across responses. In fact, however, there is rarely any evidence that the spread of treatment effects across stimulus or response dimensions is actually based on the *similarity* of the stimuli or responses to those used in training. Technically, therefore, the terms *stimulus* and *response generalization* are often used incorrectly. However, the technical difficulties in using these terms do not detract from the importance of the spread of treatment effects across stimulus conditions or behaviors during the course of treatment.

CONCLUSION

The principles outlined in this chapter provide the basis for most of the operant conditioning programs in applied settings. The principles may seem overwhelming at first because of the many different terms that were introduced. Yet these principles describe basic relationships between events and behavior and account for diverse treatment interventions. The complexity of the programs used in behavior modification cannot be conveyed by a mere statement of the principles. Each principle requires elaboration because a number of factors determine its effective application. In later chapters, principles that have been widely employed in a variety of settings will receive detailed attention.

NOTES

1. Discussion of the principles introduces several new terms. To aid the reader, major terms and their definitions are italicized when they are first introduced. Also, a glossary at the end of the book provides a summary definition of the major terms that arise in this chapter and throughout the text.
2. As Skinner (1974) has noted, the word *pain* traces to Latin and Greek. The Latin word from which it was derived refers to punishment, which explains in part why the two notions are inextricably bound in language and thought.
3. Altering the sex-role behaviors of children has raised many controversial issues about whether the definition of appropriate behaviors should be based on traditional values, whether treatment of the children was warranted, and whether the long-term goals of heterosexual adjustment were appropriate or necessarily facilitated by treatment (see Nordyke, Baer, Etzel, & LeBlanc, 1977; Winkler, 1977). Issues raised in the selection of behaviors for intervention will be discussed further in Chapter 13.

FOR FURTHER READING

Cooper, J. O., Heron, T. E., & Heward, W. L. (1987). *Applied behavior analysis.* Columbus, OH: Merrill.

Domjan, M., & Burkhard, B. (1986). *The principles of learning and behavior* (2nd ed.). Pacific Grove, CA: Brooks/Cole.

Millenson, J. R., & Leslie, J. C. (1979). *Principles of behavior analysis* (2nd ed.). New York: Macmillan.

Panyan, M. (1980). *How to use shaping.* Austin, TX: Pro-Ed.

Sulzer-Azaroff, B., & Mayer, G. R. (1977). *Applying behavior analysis procedures with children and youth.* New York: Holt, Rinehart & Winston.

Chapter Three

How to Identify, Define, and Assess Behavior

Many behavior modification techniques have been developed from the principles of operant conditioning discussed in the previous chapter. Most of the following chapters elaborate and illustrate these principles as they are applied in treatment, rehabilitation, educational, and community settings. But before behavior modification techniques are described, a few critical topics need to be elaborated. A behavior modification program is not begun merely by choosing a particular technique and trying it out on a client. The success of behavior modification has resulted not only from the specific techniques that are used but also from the ways in which behaviors are measured and intervention programs are evaluated. Successful treatment depends on carefully identifying, defining, and measuring behaviors. If behaviors are carefully identified and defined, then consequences contingent upon their performance can be applied. If behaviors can be consistently observed, one can evaluate whether the behavior modification program is leading to change. If the program is not working, the intervention can be modified until behavioral change is obtained. This chapter and the next consider requirements for measuring behavior, evaluating whether behavior change has occurred, and determining whether the behavior modification program was responsible for the change. These topics are important for understanding how to implement various behavioral techniques and for deciding whether treatment has or has not produced the desired change.

IDENTIFYING THE GOAL OF THE PROGRAM

Implementation of a behavior modification program requires clearly stating the goal of the program and carefully describing the behaviors that are to be developed. Although the program's goal is to change some behavior, the change is not made simply by focusing on that behavior alone. It is also important to specify the contingencies, including the environmental conditions associated with the behavior and the conditions that will be used to achieve behavior change. The environmental conditions include the antecedent and consequent events that influence behavior.

Many behavioral problems stem from a failure to perform behaviors in the presence of particular antecedent events. Such failures are considered to reflect a lack of appropriate stimulus control. For example, a child may complete schoolwork when he or she should be looking at the board, reciting, or playing at recess. The teacher may constantly remind the child to put his or her materials away or to pay attention. Yet the child's behavior is not controlled by these instructions (antecedent events). Training may focus on instructing the child to engage in some behavior and on reinforcing compliance.

Similarly, parents may wish to train their children not to talk to strangers who offer them candy or ask them to enter their cars. Parents do not want children to act suspiciously toward some of the new adults they meet (e.g., new teachers at school, distant relatives they have not seen previously, parents of their friends). The goal requires training children to act cautiously only in special circumstances that may be dangerous. Thus, the antecedent events and situational cues become essential for deciding what behaviors are to be performed. For all behavioral programs, one can ask a basic question: Under what circumstances or in the presence of what cues should the target behavior be performed? Ultimately, the program will focus on developing specific behaviors in the presence of certain cues and not in the absence of those cues.

In some cases, the initial goal of the program may be to develop the responsiveness of individuals to certain consequent events. These individuals usually do not respond to events that play a major role in social interaction, such as attention, physical contact, praise, or mild disapproval. For example, autistic children, who show pervasive deficits in language and social behavior, are often unresponsive to events that are reinforcing for most children (Schreibman, 1988). Similarly, delinquents and conduct problem children in the home are often unresponsive to praise (Herbert et al., 1973). In such cases, contingencies are devised to alter the value of such stimuli as physical contact or praise from an adult. In these programs, neutral stimuli (e.g., statements of approval) are paired with reinforcing events (e.g., food and termination of an aversive event). Eventually, the previously neutral stimuli serve as positive reinforcers. Once the events have been established as reinforcers, they can be used to develop specific behaviors.

The main goal of a program is to alter or develop a particular behavior referred to as the *target behavior*. If the target behavior is performed too infrequently or not at all, it should be increased; if the target behavior is performed too frequently, it should be decreased. The goal of changing behavior applies to a particular stimulus condition (e.g., the home, the classroom, certain times of the day, or the presence of particular individuals). Thus, both the behavior and the situation in which it is or is not to be performed must be identified.

DEFINING THE TARGET BEHAVIOR

Identification of the target behavior may appear to be a relatively simple task. In a given setting (e.g., the home, school, or workplace), there is general agreement as to the "problems" of the clients whose behaviors need to be changed and as to the general goals of the program. Global or general statements of behavioral problems are usually inadequate for actually beginning a behavior modification program. For example, it is insufficient to select as the goal alteration of aggressiveness, learning deficits, speech, social skills, depression, psychotic symptoms, self-esteem, and similar concepts. Traits, summary labels, and personality characteristics are too general to be of much use. Moreover, definitions of the behaviors that make up such general labels may be idiosyncratic among different behavior change agents (parents, teachers, or hospital staff). The target behaviors have to be defined explicitly so that they can actually be observed, measured, and agreed upon by individuals administering the program.

As a general rule, a response definition should meet three criteria: objectivity, clarity, and completeness (Hawkins & Dobes, 1975). To be *objective,* the definition should refer to observable characteristics of behavior or environmental events. Definitions should not refer to inner states of the individual, such as aggressiveness or emotional disturbance. To be *clear,* the definition should be so unambiguous that it can be read, repeated, and paraphrased by observers. Reading the definition should provide a sufficient basis for beginning actual observations. To be *complete,* the definition must delineate the boundary conditions so that the responses to be included and excluded can be enumerated.

Developing a complete definition often creates the greatest difficulty because decision rules are needed to specify how behavior should be scored. If the range of responses included in the definition is not described carefully, observers have to infer whether such a response has occurred. For example, a simple greeting response such as waving one's hand to greet someone may serve as the target behavior. In most instances, when a person's hand is fully extended and moving back and forth, there would be no difficulty in agreeing that the person was waving. However, ambiguous instances may require judgments on the part of observers. A child might move his or her hand once (rather than back and forth) while the arm is not extended, or a child may not move his or her arm at all but simply move all of the fingers on one hand up and down (in the way that infants often learn to say good-bye). These responses are instances of waving in everyday life, because we can often see others reciprocate with similar greetings. For assessment purposes, the response definition must specify how these and related variations of waving should be scored.

Behavior modification programs have reported clear behavioral definitions that were developed from global and imprecise terms. For example, in one program conducted in the home, the focus was on bickering among the children (Christophersen, Arnold, Hill, & Quilitch, 1972). Bickering was defined as verbal arguments louder than the normal speaking voice between any two children or among all three children. In another program, the focus was on reducing the frequency of talking to oneself for a hospitalized schizophrenic patient (Wong et al., 1987). Self-talk was defined as any vocalization not directed at another person but excluding sounds associated with physiological functions (e.g., coughing). These examples illustrate how clear behavioral definitions can be derived from general terms that may have diverse meanings to different individuals.

Before developing a definition that is objective, clear, and complete, it is useful to observe the client informally. Descriptive notes of what behaviors occur and which events are associated with their occurrence may be useful in generating specific response definitions. For example, if a psychiatric patient is labeled as being withdrawn, it is essential to observe the patient's behavior on the ward and to identify the specific behaviors that have led to the use of the label. The specific behaviors rather than the global concept become the object of change. A useful preliminary exercise, before embarking on a behavior modification program, is to select various concepts and trait labels used in everyday language and to provide alternative behavioral definitions for each of them. Athough the definition of the target response may differ across behavior modification programs, even for two individuals who are referred to as aggressive, practice in specifying target behaviors is valuable.

ASSESSMENT

Target Behaviors

When behavior has been defined in precise terms, assessment can begin. Assessment of behavior is essential for at least two reasons. First, assessment determines the extent to which the target behavior is performed. Assessment reflects the frequency of occurrence of the target behavior prior to the program. The rate of preprogram behavior is referred to as the *baseline* or *operant rate*. Second, assessment is required to reflect behavior change after the program is begun. Because the major purpose of the program is to alter behavior, behavior during the program must be compared with behavior during baseline. Careful assessment throughout the program is essential.

It may be tempting to rely on human judgment or general impressions, rather than objective assessment, to evaluate the extent to which behavior is performed or whether change has occurred with treatment. Yet human judgment may greatly distort the actual rate of behavior. For example, such behaviors as tantrums may be so intense that parents or teachers may recall them as occurring very often even when they are relatively infrequent. In contrast, some children have so many tantrums that their parents have become accustomed to a high rate and perceive tantrums as being less frequent than they really are. Judgment may also be inadequate to evaluate whether behavior change has occurred. Human judgment sometimes does not correspond to the actual records of overt behavior. Indeed, parents, teachers, and institutional staff may judge behavior as improving when there is no change or even when the behavior has become worse (Kazdin, 1973a; Schnelle, 1974). Judgments about behavior can be influenced by many factors other than the behavior itself. For example, in clinic settings, parents (usually mothers) are asked to evaluate the behavior of their children. Parent evaluations are influenced not only by the child's level of deviant behavior but also by such factors as the psychological state of the parent. Parents who are more depressed or anxious or who are experiencing marital discord and stress in the home tend to rate their children as more deviant (e.g., Forehand, Lautenschlager, Faust, & Graziano, 1986; Mash & Johnson, 1983).

Direct observations are designed to reveal more directly than global impressions or ratings the level or amount of the target behavior and the degree of behavior change. Observing behavior has its own obstacles, sources of bias, and pitfalls. For example, direct observation of behavior is not entirely free from human judgment. Typically, observers or persons within the environment must record (judge) the occurrence of behavior, and many extraneous factors can influence the results. However, overt behavior is a direct measure of how well or poorly a behavior change program is working and provides a very useful basis for making decisions about the intervention and about whether changes in the program are needed.

Stimulus Events

Recording the occurrence of the target behavior excludes a great deal of important information that may be useful in designing a behavior modification program. Various antecedent and consequent events are likely to be associated with the performance of the target behavior. In most applied settings, social stimuli or interactions with others constitute a major category of the events that influence client behavior. For example, parents and teachers may provide verbal statements (e.g., instructions or praise), gestures (e.g., physical contact, motions, or nonverbal directives), and expressions (e.g., smiles or frowns) that exert control over behavior. These stimuli may precede (e.g., instructions) or follow (e.g., praise) a particular target behavior.

In any given setting, it is useful to obtain descriptive notes to record the events that immediately precede or follow behavior. Antecedent and consequent events associated with the target behavior may generate hypotheses about which events control behavior and thereby can be used to alter behavior. These hypotheses can be tested directly by altering the events to determine their influence on behavior. For example, informal observation may indicate that the target behavior is performed at a particular time during the day, before a specific event, or in the presence of some other person. These clues, if borne out by careful assessment, may provide insights about stimulus conditions that exert control over the target behavior.

Observing the consequences that ordinarily follow behavior is exceedingly important. If an undesirable behavior is performed consistently, some environmental event is likely to be maintaining it. Conversely, if a desirable behavior is not performed consistently, certain environmental events (i.e., positive reinforcers) may not be following it. In a behavior modification program, it is important to assess the consequences that follow behavior. In the majority of programs, the consequences that follow the target response are altered in some way. To ensure that those consequences are delivered in a particular fashion (e.g., contingently and with a high frequency), they must be assessed. If they are not assessed, there is no systematic way to determine whether they were altered as intended.

STRATEGIES OF ASSESSMENT

Assessment of overt behavior can be accomplished in different ways. In most behavior modification programs, behaviors are assessed on the basis of discrete occurrences of the response or on the amount of time that the response occurs. However, several variations and different types of measures are available.

Frequency Measures

Frequency counts simply require tallying the number of times the target behavior occurs in a given period of time. A frequency measure is particularly useful when the target response is *discrete* and when it takes a *relatively constant amount of time* each time it is performed. A discrete response has a clearly delineated beginning and end, so that separate instances of the response can be counted. The performance of the behavior should take a relatively constant amount of time, so that the units counted are approximately equal. Ongoing behaviors such as smiling, sitting in one's seat, lying down, and talking are difficult to record simply by counting because each response may occur for a different amount of time. For example, if a person talks to a peer for 15 seconds and to another peer for 30 minutes, these might be counted as two instances of talking. However, a great deal of information is lost by simply counting instances of talking, because they differ in duration.

Frequency measures have been used for a variety of discrete behaviors. For example, in a program for an autistic child, frequency measures were used to assess the number of times that the child engaged in social responses such as saying hello or sharing a toy or object with someone and the number of times that she engaged in self-stimulatory behaviors such as rocking or repetitive pulling of her clothing (Russo & Koegel, 1977). With hospitalized psychiatric patients, one program assessed the frequency with which patients engaged in intolerable acts (such as assaulting someone or setting fires) and social behaviors (such as initiating conversation or responding to someone else) (Frederiksen, Jenkins, Foy, & Eisler, 1976). Additional discrete behaviors can be readily assessed with frequency counts, including the number of cigarettes smoked, the number of times a person attends an activity or hits another person, the number of objects thrown, the number of times homework is turned in, the number of times medication was taken, and so on.

Frequency measures require merely noting the instances in which behavior occurs. Usually there is an additional requirement that behavior be observed for a constant amount of time. Of course, if behavior is observed for 20 minutes on one day and 30 minutes on another day, the frequencies are not directly comparable. However, the *rate of response* each day can be determined by dividing the frequency of the responses by the number of minutes observed each day. This measure will yield frequency per minute, or rate of response, which is comparable for different durations of observations.

A frequency measure has several desirable features for use in applied settings. First, frequency is relatively simple to score. Keeping a tally of behavior is usually all that is required. Moreover, counting devices are available, such as a golf counter worn as a wristwatch to facilitate recording. Second, frequency measures readily reflect changes over time. The number of times that a response occurs is sensitive to change resulting from alterations in contingencies. Since the principles of operant conditioning refer to changes in the frequency of a response, it is desirable to observe the response frequency or rate directly. Third, and related to the above, frequency expresses the *amount* of behavior performed, which is usually of concern to individuals in applied settings. The goal of most programs is to increase or decrease the number of times that a certain behavior occurs. Frequency provides a direct measure of the amount of behavior.

Discrete Categorization

Often it is very useful to classify responses into discrete categories such as correct-incorrect, performed–not performed, or appropriate-inappropriate. In many ways, discrete categorization is like a frequency measure because it is used for behaviors that have a clear beginning and end and a constant duration. But there are at least two important differences. With a frequency measure, performances of a particular behavior are tallied. The focus is on a single response. Also, the number of times that the behavior may occur is theoretically unlimited. For example, one child hitting another may be measured by frequency counts. How many times the behavior (hitting) may occur has no real limit. Discrete categorization is used to measure whether several different behaviors have occurred. There are only a limited number of opportunities to perform the response.

For example, discrete categorization might be used to measure how messy a college student's roommate is. A checklist can be devised that lists several behaviors, such as putting one's shoes in the closet, removing underwear from the kitchen table, putting dishes in the sink, and putting food in the refrigerator. Each morning, each behavior on the checklist could be categorized as performed or not performed. The total number of behaviors or steps that have been performed correctly constitutes the measure.

Discrete categories have been used in many behavior modification programs. For example, in one project, mentally retarded and physically handicapped young adults were trained to ride the bus in the community (Neef, Iwata, & Page, 1978). Several behaviors related to finding, boarding, and leaving the bus were included in a checklist and classified as performed correctly or incorrectly. The effect of training was evaluated on the number of steps performed correctly. In a camp setting, the cabin-cleaning behaviors of emotionally disturbed boys were evaluated using discrete categorization (Peacock, Lyman, & Rickard, 1978). To evaluate the effects of the program, such tasks as placing coats on hooks, making beds, having no objects on the bed, and putting toothbrushing materials away were categorized as completed or not.

Discrete categorization is very easy to use because it requires listing a number of behaviors and checking off whether they were performed. The behaviors may consist of several steps that all relate to the completion of a task, such as dressing or grooming behaviors in children. Behavior can be evaluated by noting whether or how many steps are performed (e.g., removing a shirt from the drawer, putting one arm through, then the other arm, and pulling it over one's head). On the other hand, the behaviors need not be related to one another, so that performance of one behavior may not have anything to do with performance of another one. For example, room-cleaning behaviors are not necessarily related; performing one behavior correctly (making one's bed) may be unrelated to performing another behavior (cleaning up dishes). Discrete categorization can yield convenient summary scores as reflected in the total number of the desired behaviors performed or the percentage of correct responses (calculated by forming a ratio of occurred or performed responses to total possible responses and multiplying by 100). A familiar example is correct responses on an examination, which can be expressed as either a total number or a percentage. Overall, discrete categorization is a very flexible method of observation that allows assessment of all sorts of behaviors independently of whether they are necessarily related to one another.

Number of Persons

Occasionally, the effectiveness of behavioral programs is evaluated on the basis of the number of persons who perform a response. The measure is used in group situations such as a classroom or a psychiatric hospital or in society at large. In such cases, the purpose is to increase the overall performance of a particular behavior, such as completing homework, coming to an activity on time, or driving a car safely. Once the desired behavior has been defined, the observations record how many participants in the group have performed the response. As with frequency and categorization measures, the observations require classifying the response as having occurred or not having occurred. But here the number of *individuals* are counted rather than the number of times that an individual performs the response.

Several programs have evaluated the impact of treatment on the number of people who are affected. For example, one program focused on mildly mentally retarded women in a halfway house who tended to be very inactive (Johnson & Bailey, 1977). A reinforcement program that increased participation in various leisure activities (e.g., painting, playing games, working on puzzles, rugmaking) was evaluated by the number of participants who performed these activities. In another program, the investigators were interested in reducing speeding among highway drivers (Van Houten, Nau, & Marini, 1980). To record speeding, a radar unit was placed unobtrusively along the highway. A feedback system visible to drivers was evaluated by measuring the percentage of drivers who exceeded the speed limit. Another program was designed to improve seat belt use among elementary school children (Sowers-Hoag, Thyer, & Bailey, 1987). The effects were evaluated by recording the percentage of the children who used their seat belts when picked up by their parents at the end of the day.

Knowing the number of people who perform a response is very useful when the explicit goal of the program is to increase performance in a large group of subjects. Consistent with this overall goal is developing behaviors in an institution and even in society at large. Increasing the number of people who exercise, give to charity, or seek treatment when early stages of serious diseases are apparent and decreasing the number of people who smoke, overeat, and commit crimes are important goals of this kind that behavioral interventions have addressed.

Many programs do not provide information about the performance of particular individuals. The number of people who perform a response may be increased in an institution or in society at large. However, the performance of any particular individual may be sporadic or very low. One really does not know whether a particular individual has been affected. This information may or may not be important, depending on the goals of the program.

Interval Recording

A frequent strategy for measuring behavior in applied settings is based on units of time rather than discrete response units. Behavior is recorded during short periods of time falling within the entire time that it is performed. The two most frequently used methods of time-based measurement are interval recording and response duration.

With interval recording, behavior is observed for a *single block of time*, such as 30 or 60 minutes once per day. A block of time is divided into a series of short intervals (e.g., each interval may equal 10 or 15 seconds). During each interval, the target behavior is scored as having occurred or not having occurred. If a discrete behavior, such as hitting someone, occurs one or more times in a single interval, the response is scored as having occurred. Several response occurrences within an interval are not counted separately. If the behavior is ongoing with an unclear beginning or end (such as talking, playing, and sitting) or occurs for a long period of time, it is scored during each of the intervals in which it is occurring.

Behavior modification programs in classroom settings frequently use interval recording to score whether students are paying attention, sitting in their seats, and working quietly. The behavior of an individual student may be observed for 10-second intervals over a 20-minute observational period. For each interval, an observer records whether the child was working quietly in his or her seat. If the child remains in his seat and works for a long period of time, many intervals will be scored for attentive behavior. If the child leaves his seat (without permission) or stops working, inattentive behavior will be scored. During some intervals, a child may be in his seat for half of the time and out of his seat for the remaining time. Because the interval has to be scored for *either* attentive or inattentive behavior, a rule for scoring behavior in such instances has to be devised. Often, getting out of the seat will be counted as inattentive behavior and will nullify the portion of attentive behavior within the interval.

Interval recording for a single block of time has been used in many programs beyond the classroom setting. For example, one program focused on several inappropriate behaviors (e.g., roughhousing, touching objects, playing with merchandise) that children performed while they accompanied their parents during shopping (Clark et al., 1977, Exp. 3). Observers followed the family in the store to record whether the inappropriate behaviors occurred during consecutive 15-second intervals. Interval assessment was also used in a program designed to reduce self-injurious behavior (biting one's own hand, arm, or shoulder and scratching oneself) in a way that caused bodily damage to two profoundly retarded adolescents (Pace, Iwata, Edwards, & McCosh, 1986). Observations in the hospital were conducted daily in an individual therapy room and a group therapy room. In each setting, an observer recorded whether any self-injurious behavior occurred during each of several 10-second intervals.

Interval scoring of behavior is facilitated by a scoring sheet on which intervals are represented across time (see Figure 3–1). In Figure 3–1, each number across the top denotes a time interval. During each interval, a + or 0 is circled or checked to denote whether the behavior has occurred for the subject. The basic sheet can be expanded to include many subjects and intervals, as shown in Figure 3–2. For example, each student in a classroom or each patient on a ward can be observed for a large number of intervals. The first person would be observed for the first interval (e.g., 15 seconds). After that person's behavior has been recorded, the second person would be observed. This would be continued until each person has been observed for one interval (down the left column in Figure 3–2). The order would then be repeated until each person had been observed for another interval, and so on for the remaining intervals. Often more than one behavior is scored during an interval, so that the presence of several behaviors will be judged during each interval. To accomplish this, a data sheet may include many symbols in each interval block so that various behaviors can be coded. A letter or symbol is checked or circled for the different categories of behavior that occur during the interval.

In using an interval scoring method, an observer looks at the client during the interval. When one interval is over, the observer records whether the behavior occurred. If an observer is recording several behaviors during an interval, a few seconds may be needed to record all of the behaviors that were

FIGURE 3–1

				Intervals					
1	2	3	4	5	6	7	8	9	10
+ 0	+ 0	+ 0	+ 0	+ 0	+ 0	+ 0	+ 0	+ 0	+ 0

Circle appropriate symbol in each interval.
+ = behavior occurred during interval
0 = behavior did not occur during interval

Example of interval scoring sheet for one individual.

FIGURE 3–2

		Intervals								
	1	2	3	4	5	6	7	8	9	10
1	+ 0	+ 0	+ 0	+ 0	+ 0	+ 0	+ 0	+ 0	+ 0	+ 0
2	+ 0	+ 0	+ 0	+ 0	+ 0	+ 0	+ 0	+ 0	+ 0	+ 0
3	+ 0	+ 0	+ 0	+ 0	+ 0	+ 0	+ 0	+ 0	+ 0	+ 0
4	+ 0	+ 0	+ 0	+ 0	+ 0	+ 0	+ 0	+ 0	+ 0	+ 0
5	+ 0	+ 0	+ 0	+ 0	+ 0	+ 0	+ 0	+ 0	+ 0	+ 0
6	+ 0	+ 0	+ 0	+ 0	+ 0	+ 0	+ 0	+ 0	+ 0	+ 0
7	+ 0	+ 0	+ 0	+ 0	+ 0	+ 0	+ 0	+ 0	+ 0	+ 0

Individuals (row labels at left)

Example of interval scoring sheet for many individuals.

observed during that interval. If the observer records a behavior as soon as it occurs (before the interval is over), he or she might miss other behaviors that occurred while the first behavior was being scored. Hence, many investigators use interval scoring procedures that allow time for recording after each interval of observation.

A variation of interval recording is referred to as *time sampling*. This variation uses the interval method, but the observations are conducted for brief periods *at different times* rather than in a single block of time. For example, with the time-sampling method, a child might be observed for 10-second intervals, but these intervals might be spread out over a full day.

As an illustration, psychiatric patients participating in a hospital reinforcement program were evaluated with time-sampling procedures (Paul & Lentz, 1977). Each hour, an observer looked at a patient for a two-second interval. At the end of the interval, the observer recorded the presence or absence of several behaviors related to social interaction, activities, self-care, and other responses. The procedure was continued throughout the day, sampling one interval at a time. The advantage of time sampling is that the observations represent performance over the entire day. Of course, in many settings, such as the home or the classroom, it is more convenient to complete observations in a single observation session.

There are significant features of interval recording that make it one of the most widely adopted strategies in applied settings. First, interval assessment can record virtually any behavior. Whether a response is discrete and does not vary in duration or is continuous or sporadic, it can be classified as occurring or not occurring during any time period. Second, the observations resulting from interval recording can be easily converted into a percentage. The number of intervals during which the response is scored as having occurred can be divided by the total number of intervals observed. This ratio multiplied by 100 yields the percentage of the intervals in which the response has been performed. For example, if social responses are scored as having occurred in 20 of the 40 intervals that were observed, the percentage of the intervals of social behavior is 50 percent (20/40 × 100). A percentage is easily communicated to others by noting that a certain behavior occurs a specific percentage of time (intervals). Whenever there is doubt as to what assessment strategy should be adopted, an interval approach is always applicable and can be readily employed.

Duration

Another time-based method of observation is *duration,* or the amount of time that the response is performed. This method is particularly useful for ongoing responses that are continuous, rather than discrete acts or responses of extremely short duration. Programs that attempt to increase or decrease the length of time that a response is performed might profit from a duration method.

Duration has been used in fewer studies than have interval observations. As an example, one investigation trained two severely withdrawn children to engage in social interaction with other children (Whitman, Mercurio, & Caponigri, 1970). Interaction was measured by simply recording the amount of time that children were in contact with each other. Duration was also used to measure the suspicious and accusing statements that an elderly male stroke victim directed toward his wife (Green, Linsk, & Pinkston, 1986). His wife's use of praise for appropriate verbalizations was effective in decreasing the amount of time each day in which her husband engaged in such statements.

Another measure based on duration is not how long the response is performed but rather how long it takes for the client to begin the response. The amount of time that elapses between a cue and the response is referred to as *latency.* Many programs have used response latency to evaluate treatment. For example, in one report, adults (ages 60 or over) who suffered insomnia received treatment based on stimulus control procedures (Puder, Lacks, Bertelson, & Storandt, 1983). Treatment consisted of having clients associate drowsiness with going to bed. Sleep-incompatible behaviors (e.g., worrying, eating, watching TV) were to be performed in a room other than the bedroom. Gradually, the consistent association of the bedroom with sleeping helped clients get to sleep better. The effectiveness of treatment was reflected in the reduced latency in going to sleep after going to bed.

Assessment of response duration or latency is a fairly simple matter: one starts and stops a stopwatch or notes the time when the response begins and ends. However, the onset and termination of the response must be carefully defined. If these conditions have not been met, duration and latency are extremely difficult to employ. For example, a child in a tantrum may cry continuously for several minutes, whimper for short periods, stop all noise for a few seconds, and begin intense crying again. In recording the duration of the tantrum, a decision is required to handle changes in the intensity of the behavior (e.g., crying to whimpering) and pauses (e.g., periods of silence) so that these are consistently recorded as part of the response or as a different (e.g., nontantrum) response.

The use of response duration is generally restricted to situations in which the length of the time that a behavior is performed is a major concern. In most behavior modification programs, the goal is to increase or decrease the frequency of a response rather than its duration. There are notable exceptions, of course. For example, it is desirable to increase the length of the time that students study or that persons practice a skill they wish to learn (e.g., playing an instrument, speaking a foreign language). However, because interval measures are widely used and readily adaptable to virtually all responses, they are often selected as a measure over duration. The number or proportion of the intervals in which study behavior occurs reflects changes in study time, since interval recording is based on time.

Other Strategies

One of the above methods of assessment is generally used in behavioral programs. Occasionally, other measures are used because they provide direct measures of behavior that are of obvious importance. For example, behavior modification programs for obesity or cigarette smoking have evaluated intervention effects by simply recording client weight in pounds or the number of cigarettes smoked. In other programs, the specific behavior may lend itself to a measure unique to the investigation. For example, interventions designed to conserve energy can monitor gas or electric meters at home or look at a car's odometer to record whether home or car use of energy has changed. In applications to medical problems such as hypertension or diabetes, specific measures such as blood pressure or the glucose concentration in the patient's urine have been used to evaluate behavioral treatment programs.

Selection of an Assessment Strategy

In most situations, the investigators use an assessment procedure based on frequency, interval, or one of the other methods mentioned above. Some behaviors, such as the number of profane words used or the number of toileting or eating responses, lend themselves well to frequency counts or categorization because they are discrete; others, such as reading, working, or sitting, lend themselves well to interval recording; and still others, such as time spent in studying, crying, or exercising, lend themselves well to duration. Target behaviors can usually be assessed in more than one way, so there is no single strategy that must be adopted. For example, an investigator working in an institution for delinquents may wish to record the aggressive behavior of a particular adolescent. Hitting others (e.g., making physical contact with another individual with a closed fist) may be the response of interest. What assessment strategy should be used?

Aggressive behavior might be measured with a *frequency* count by having an observer record how many times the youth hit others during a certain period each day. Each hit would count as one response. The behavior might also be observed using *interval recording*. A block of time such as 30 minutes could be set aside for observation. The 30 minutes could be divided into 10-second intervals. For each of these intervals, the observer would record whether any hitting had occurred. Perhaps time sampling might be used. Each hour during the day, the youth could be observed for a 15-minute period, for which the presence or absence of aggressive behavior would be recorded. This interval method has the advantage of sampling behavior over the entire day.

A *duration* measure might be used. It may be difficult to time the duration of hitting because instances of hitting are too brief to clock unless there is a series of hits (as in a fight). Recording the amount of time from the beginning of each day until the first aggressive response might be easier. This *latency* measure records the time without hitting. Presumably, if a program decreased aggressive behavior, the amount of time from the beginning of the day until the first aggressive response would increase.

Although many different measures can be used in a given program, the measure finally selected may be dictated by the purpose of the program. Different measures sometimes reflect slightly different goals. For example, consider two behavioral programs that focused on increasing toothbrushing, a seemingly simple response that could be assessed in many different ways. One of the programs observed the *number of individuals* in a boys' summer camp who brushed their teeth (Lattal, 1969). The boys knew how to brush their teeth, and an incentive system increased their performance of the response. In the other program, the clients were mentally retarded residents at a state hospital (Horner & Keilitz, 1975). The residents were unable to brush their teeth at the beginning of the program, so the many behaviors involved in toothbrushing were developed. *Discrete categorization* was used to assess toothbrushing; each component step of the behavior (wetting the brush, removing the cap, applying the toothpaste, and so on) was scored as performed or not performed. The percentage of steps correctly completed measured the effects of training. Although both of these investigations assessed toothbrushing, the different methods reflect different goals, namely getting children who can brush to do so or training the response in mentally retarded residents who did not know how to perform it.

CONDUCTING OBSERVATIONS

Issues and Problems in Sampling Behavior

The purpose of assessment is to sample the extent to which behavior is performed over the total period of time that behavior change is desired. Performance fluctuates over time on a given day and across days and weeks. It is important to determine the level of behavior without allowing the fluctuations to misrepresent the overall rate. If behavior were unvarying in its level over each hour and each day, any sample of that behavior (e.g., one hour) would be representative of behavior at all other times. However, behavior is rarely performed at a consistent rate. (The only time there is such complete consistency is when the behavior is never performed and the rate is zero.) Thus, to obtain a representative sample, assessment must be carried out over an extended period of time.

Three decisions need to be made regarding the observations that are required. First, the *number of times* that data will be collected must be decided. When possible, it is desirable to observe behavior each day or during each session (e.g., in a classroom) that the target behavior may occur. The frequency of observation depends on such factors as the variation of behavior over time, the availability of observers, and scheduling exigencies in the treatment setting. If the target behavior is very stable from one day to the next, daily assessment becomes less essential than if the target behavior fluctuates radically. As a general rule, behavior should be observed on as many occasions as possible, and preferably daily.

A second decision to be made before beginning assessment is the *length of time* set aside for a given observation period. The guiding general rule is that behavior should be observed for a period of time that will yield data representative of typical performance over the entire period of interest. For example, if it is desirable to alter behavior in the classroom, observational data should reflect performance over a relatively long period (e.g., one hour) or for several short periods throughout the day, rather than just a few minutes during a brief block of time.

For some behavioral problems or in some settings, the target behavior may occur only during a specific period of the day. For example, child behaviors at home, such as getting dressed for school, completing chores, or going to bed without a tantrum, all occur at brief and specific times during the day. Thus, long periods of observation are not always necessary to assess the target behavior.

For practical reasons, it is usually unfeasible to observe behavior over an extended period or over several shorter periods throughout the day. In such instances, behavior might be observed for a single block of time during the period in which behavior change is most obviously required. An initial assessment at different times over a few days can determine which periods require the greatest attention. Subsequently, assessment can focus on those periods.

A third decision related to the length of the time that behavior is observed is *when the observations are conducted*. Observations using frequency, interval, or duration methods can record behavior in a block of time in a single day or at different times throughout the day. The advantage of sampling behavior at various times over the entire day is that the observed behavior is more likely to be representative of behavior over different time periods.

If interval assessment is used, in addition to the above decisions, the duration of the interval has to be decided. Although observations may be made for 30 minutes or one hour each day, the length of the intervals within that period must be decided. If behavior occurs at a high rate or is an ongoing response, relatively short intervals are recommended (e.g., 10 or 15 seconds). Longer intervals (such as 60 seconds) would exclude much of the responding, because the interval is recorded for the presence or absence of only one response. If the behavior occurs 20 times during one 60-second interval, the interval is scored on the occurrence of the first response and the behavior cannot be scored again until the next interval. Thus, a great deal of behavior goes unrecorded. As a result of a behavior modification program, behavior may change from 20 times to 10 times per 60-second interval. However, this change will not be reflected in the data because the interval will continue to be scored merely for the presence or absence of the response.

There are several considerations that dictate the duration of intervals. First, interval duration should be relatively short (e.g., 10 or 15 seconds) for discrete behaviors that occur frequently. Second, very short intervals (e.g., five or fewer seconds) are sometimes difficult to score reliably because observers have difficulty in synchronizing observations. The interval is so short that it is not clear in which interval the behavior was performed. Third, the length of the interval may be less important when behavior is continuous (e.g., reading or watching television) than when it is discrete, because shorter or longer intervals are not likely to exclude "instances" of behavior. Many studies have used 10-second intervals, whereas others have reported intervals of one or a few minutes. Because there are no fixed rules for interval length, a wide range of durations has been employed.

Conditions Under Which Observations Are Obtained

Observations are usually completed by placing one or more observers in a position to see the client. Occasionally, the observer may be out of sight, such as behind a one-way mirror in an observation booth adjacent to a classroom or a hospital ward. At other times, observations may be taken from videotapes, so the observer is not present in the situation. In most studies, however, observers and clients are in the same situation, such as the home, the ward, or the classroom.

If the client is aware of the observer's presence, the assessment procedure is said to be *obtrusive*. A potential problem with obtrusive assessment is that the client's behavior may be affected by knowing that observations are being made. Assessment is *reactive* if the observer's presence alters the client's behavior. Several investigations have shown that the presence of an observer may alter the behaviors of the persons who are observed (see Haynes & Horn, 1982; Kazdin, 1982b). But in most cases, the effects are temporary if they occur at all. For example, a wife may observe the amount of time that her husband engages in communication. (Insufficient communication is a spouse complaint that frequently emerges in marital therapy.) Once the husband is aware of the observation focus and procedure, the amount of his communication may temporarily increase. However, that increase is not likely to continue as the husband adapts to the novelty of the observations. Without new antecedents or consequences for the behavior, long-term behavior change would not be expected.

In situations where external observers enter into a situation to collect observations (e.g., enter a classroom to record child behavior), reactivity can be minimized by avoiding interactions between the observer and the persons being observed. Thus, in the classroom, an observer would avoid behavior that might maintain the children's interest, such as eye contact, smiles, and conversation. To minimize reactivity by helping the clients to adapt to the novelty of the new person, many investigators place the observer into the situation on several occasions before actual assessment begins.

Another consideration in observing behavior pertains to the observers themselves. It is important not to inform observers that the intervention is having the intended effects. Telling observers that improvements in performance are expected and then providing them with praise when their data sheets confirm this expectation can lead to biased observations (O'Leary, Kent, & Kanowitz, 1975). Of course, observers are likely to develop their own expectations when they see treatment implemented or detect the investigator's expectations. For example, when a reinforcement program is used with a hyperactive child, it is not difficult to conclude what everyone is expecting. Yet even when observers expect behavior change, their observations may not reflect the expected change (Kent, O'Leary, Diament, & Dietz, 1974).

Another issue important in conducting observations pertains to the definitions of behaviors that observers use. In some programs, many observers are used. When these observers are first trained to record behavior, they may adhere to the same definition of behavior. Once they master the definition, it is often assumed that they continue to apply the same definition and to record behavior accurately. However, evidence suggests that observers "drift" or gradually depart from the original definition over time (Kent, Kanowitz, O'Leary, & Cheiken, 1977; Kent et al., 1974). For example, if observers record talking out in a class of students, their criteria for scoring the behavior may gradually change over time from the criteria of the original definition. They may score whispers or brief vocalizations differently over time, and their threshold to score the behavior may change.

To ensure that observers adhere to consistent definitions over time, many programs conduct periodic retraining. Observers may meet as a group, rate behavior in a situation or from videotapes, and receive feedback on the accuracy of the observations. The feedback conveys the extent to which observers correctly invoke the definitions for scoring behavior and helps reduce drift from the original behavioral codes (DeMaster, Reid, & Twentyman, 1977). Other recommendations have been provided for handling problems arising from reactive assessment, observer expectancies, and observer drift (Kazdin, 1977b; Kent & Foster, 1977).

Reliability of Assessment

Need for Reliability.   It is important for individuals who observe the target behavior to agree on the occurrence of the response. Interobserver agreement, often referred to as *reliability* of assessment, is important for three major reasons.[1] First, assessment is useful only when it can be achieved with some consistency. For example, if frequency counts differ greatly depending on who is counting, it will be difficult to know what the client's actual performance is. The client may be scored as performing a response frequently on some days and infrequently on other days as a function of who scores behavior, rather than of differences in actual client performance. Inconsistent measurement introduces variation in the data that adds to the variation stemming from normal fluctuations in client performance. If measurement variation is large, there may appear to be no systematic pattern to the behavior. If a behavior modification program is implemented, it may be difficult to determine whether behavior is changing, because the data are highly variable as a function of inconsistent recording. Stable patterns of behavior are required to reflect behavior change. Hence, reliable recording is essential.

Second, assessing agreement is important because it minimizes or circumvents the biases of any individual observer. If a single observer records the target behavior, any recorded change in behavior may result from a change over time in the observer's definition of the target behavior, rather than in the actual behavior of the client. The observer may become lenient or stringent over time. For example, the observer may expect and perceive improvement in the target behavior, even though no improvement actually occurs. If two or more observers are used, one can see whether the pattern in the data varies as a function of who completes the observations. Agreement between observers provides a check on the consistency of their recording of behavior.

Finally, assessing agreement is important because agreement reflects whether the target behavior is well defined. If observers readily agree on the occurrence of the behavior, it will be easier for the persons who eventually carry out the program to agree on the behaviors and to apply the intervention (e.g., reinforcing consequences) contingently.

Conducting Checks on Agreement.   To ensure that the behavior is agreed upon, reliability checks need to be made before baseline data are gathered. A few days of prebaseline observation are generally useful to finalize the rules for observing behavior and to handle instances in which it is not clear whether the target behavior has occurred. Once baseline begins, it is advisable to continue reliability checks intermittently throughout the program to ensure that behavior is consistently observed. If such checks are made only at the inception of the program, observers may over time become increasingly lax in their scoring or drift away from the definitions that they should be using. Hence, observers may become less reliable over time.

Agreement has to achieve an acceptable level before baseline observations are begun and has to maintain that level throughout the project. Although no single criterion for acceptable agreement has been set, convention dictates that agreement be between 80 and 100 percent. Interobserver agreement lower than 80 percent suggests that a moderate amount of error occurs in recording. Obtaining low agreement before a program is begun is no reason to be discouraged. In many instances, low agreement signals that the response definition should be more carefully specified. It is desirable to find this out early, so that the response definition can be clarified for those who administer the program as well as those who observe behavior.

How the reliability checks are conducted may influence the level of interobserver agreement. Hence, in addition to specifying the level of agreement, it is important to ensure that this level is determined under carefully conducted conditions. A major factor that may influence interobserver agreement is whether observers know that their agreement is being checked. When observers are aware that this is being done, they tend to show higher agreement than when they are led to believe that their agreement is not under scrutiny (e.g., Kent et al., 1974, 1977). Also, knowing that agreement is being assessed may even influence the behaviors that observers record. In some studies, observers have recorded less disruptive behavior when they were aware that their agreement was being checked than when they were not aware that this was being done (Romanczyk, Kent, Diament, & O'Leary, 1973).

It is important to make the conditions of assessment similar on both assessed and unassessed days. It may be useful to convey the impression that all observations are being checked, so that the data obtained on checked days will not differ from the data obtained on unchecked days. Because observers tend to be more accurate when they believe that their agreement is being assessed, keeping them aware and informed of frequent reliability checks may be advantageous even on days in which no checks are made (Taplin & Reid, 1973).

In general, assessment of agreement should be structured so as to minimize the possibility of bias in judging how well observers agree with each other. First, observers should work independently, without access to each other's recording sheets. If observers communicate with each other or look at each other's recording sheets, their agreement may be inflated because they are influencing each other. Second, observers should be supervised during a reliability check. Supervision ensures that the observations are independent, particularly if observers are aware of the supervision. Third, observers should be unaware of the contingencies to alter client behavior and when those contingencies are implemented, if it is possible to hide this information. If this is not possible, it may be useful to bring in an observer to check reliability who is unfamiliar with the program and thus less likely to present biased data. Finally, observers should not compute their own interobserver agreement. Observers left on their own to assess how well they are agreeing with each other tend to calculate higher reliability estimates than those calculated by an experimenter (Kent et al., 1974). If the above conditions can be met or closely approximated, the interpretation of interobserver agreement is likely to reflect the clarity of the behavioral codes and the extent to which observers agree in their behavioral definitions.

Estimating Agreement.   Interobserver agreement provides an estimate of how consistently behavior is observed and scored. The procedures for estimating agreement differ somewhat depending on the assessment method used. The procedures that estimate agreement for frequency and interval methods are highlighted here because they can readily be adapted to the other assessment procedures.[2]

Agreement for frequency measures requires that two observers simultaneously, but independently, count the target response during the time set aside for observation. At the end of the observation period, the frequencies obtained by the observers are compared. The major interest is whether the observers record the target behavior with equal frequency. A percentage of agreement can be formed to measure the degree to which two observers agree in their final counts.

It is likely that no two observers will agree perfectly in their recorded frequencies. To determine the percentage of agreement, a fraction is formed from the frequency obtained by each observer. *Interobserver agreement is determined by dividing the smaller frequency by the larger frequency and multiplying by 100.* For example, in the home, parents may count the number of times that a child spills food on the floor during a meal. During a reliability check, both parents independently count food spills. By the end of the meal, one parent has counted 20 instances of spilling, whereas the other parent has counted 18 instances. To form a percentage of agreement, the smaller number (18) is divided by the larger number (20) and the quotient is multiplied by 100. Agreement for this observation period was 90 percent (18/20 × 100).

Interpretation of this percentage must be made cautiously. The figure indicates that the observers agree on the total frequency of the behavior with a 10 percent (100 percent minus 90 percent) margin of error. This does not mean that the observers agree 90 percent of the time. Although one observer recorded 18 responses and the other recorded 20 responses, there is no way of knowing whether they recorded the *same* responses. Thus, reliability reflects agreement on the total number of responses, rather than agreement in any specific instance. A potential disadvantage in using a frequency measure is that when the behavior is not carefully defined, a high percentage of agreement for frequency data may still conceal a substantial amount of disagreement.

Calculation of agreement is different when an interval method of assessment is used. Interobserver agreement is usually computed on the basis of the proportion of intervals in which two observers agree on the occurrence of a target response. An agreement is scored if both observers record the occurrence of behavior in the same interval. A disagreement is scored when one observer scores a behavior in an interval and the other does not. For example, in a reliability check made between two observers independently recording the aggressive behavior of a child in an elementary school classroom, both observers are required to observe the child at the same time. Each observer records behaviors for several intervals. During each interval that the child is observed, the observer marks the occurrence or nonoccurrence of aggressive behavior. When the observers finish recording, reliability can be calculated.

Interobserver agreement is determined by dividing the number of intervals in which both observers mark the behavior as occurring (agreements) by the number of agreements plus the number of intervals in which one observer scored the behavior and the other did not (disagreements) and multiplying by 100. For example, if two observers recorded behavior for 50 10-second intervals and both observers agreed on the occurrence of the behavior in 20 intervals and disagreed in 5 intervals, overall agreement would be $20/(20 + 5) \times 100$, or 80 percent.

Although the observers recorded behavior for 50 intervals, not all of the intervals are used to calculate reliability. An interval is counted only if at least one observer recorded the *occurrence* of the target behavior. Excluding intervals in which neither observer recorded the target behavior is based on the following reasoning. If these intervals were counted, they would be considered agreements because both observers "agree" that the response did not occur. Yet in observing behavior, many intervals may be marked without the occurrence of the target behavior. If these were included as agreements, the reliability estimate would be inflated beyond the level obtained when occurrences alone are counted as agreements. To avoid this increase, most investigators restrict agreements to response occurrence intervals.

The above formula for estimating interobserver agreement for interval assessment is very commonly used. Yet many investigators have questioned its adequacy. The main concern is whether agreement should be restricted to intervals for which both observers record an occurrence of the behavior or should also include intervals for which both observers record a nonoccurrence. In one sense, both of these situations indicate that the observers were in agreement for a particular interval. The issue is important because the estimate of reliability depends on the frequency of the client's behavior and on whether occurrence and/or nonoccurrence agreements are included in the formula. If the client performs the target behavior relatively frequently or infrequently, observers are likely to have a high proportion of agreements on occurrences or nonoccurrences, respectively. Hence, the estimate of reliability may differ greatly depending on what is counted as an agreement between observers. Several investigators have discussed the problem of deciding what should be counted as an agreement and have suggested additional formulas for possible ways of using both occurrence and nonoccurrence intervals (see Kazdin, 1982c).

SUMMARY AND CONCLUSION

Before beginning a behavior modification program, the target behavior has to be identified and carefully defined. The definition should ensure that few inferences need to be made by observers who assess behavior or by those who will ultimately be responsible for providing consequences to alter behavior. Several methods of assessment are available, including frequency counts, discrete categorization, the number of clients who perform the response, interval assessment, and response duration.

Once the assessment strategy has been selected, it is essential to evaluate the extent to which observers agree when scoring the response. Interobserver agreement or reliability of assessment is evaluated while observers record the response independently. The formula for estimating reliability depends on the assessment method. Also, the interpretation of reliability estimates depends on the conditions under which evaluation of reliability is conducted. Observers often slightly alter the definitions of the behavior they invoke over the course of a program. Periodic retraining and constant reliability assessment help ensure that observations reflect the client's actual performance. Assessment of the target behavior provides an important step that needs to be resolved adequately before contingencies to alter client performance are implemented.

NOTES

1. Among terms, *interobserver agreement* more accurately reflects the issue of interest in applied behavior analysis. *Reliability* is a much broader term in psychological assessment and reflects a number of different characteristics of measurement, most of which have been used in the context of developing and evaluating questionnaires and various inventories. However, the term *reliability* continues to be used as interchangeable with the term *interobserver agreement* in published studies of behavioral programs. Hence, the convention is continued here.
2. The methods of estimating agreement between and among observers extend beyond the material provided here. For a more technical discussion of these methods and how they are used, other sources should be consulted (Hartmann, 1977; Kazdin, 1982c).

FOR FURTHER READING

Barrett, B. H., Johnston, J. M., & Pennypacker, H. S. (1986). Behavior: Its units, dimensions, and measurement. In R. O. Nelson & S. C. Hayes (Eds.), *Conceptual foundations of behavioral assessment* (pp. 156–200). New York: Guilford.

Hawkins, R. P. (1986). Selection of target behaviors. In R. O. Nelson & S. C. Hayes (Eds.), *Conceptual foundations of behavioral assessment* (pp. 331–385). New York: Guilford.

Kazdin, A. E. (1985). Selection of target behaviors: The relationship of the treatment focus to clinical dysfunction. *Behavioral Assessment, 7,* 33–47.

Chapter Four

How to Evaluate a Behavior Modification Program

Assessment of behavior change is essential in behavior modification. Assessment may reveal that behavior has changed, but it does *not* show what caused the change. Proponents of behavior modification are extremely interested in determining the cause of behavior change. Once the cause is clear, our knowledge about the factors that influence behavior is increased. Also, if treatment can be shown to be responsible for change, it can be applied to the same person in the future and to clients in other settings, with increased confidence that behavior will change in the new applications as well.

In many cases, the person who conducts the program may be interested only in changing behavior and not in isolating the cause of the change. Yet even in such a case, it may be important to identify what was responsible for behavior change. For example, a program may be carried out by a parent to reduce the fighting of two children at home. After fighting has been assessed (baseline), a program may be implemented (e.g., praising the children for playing cooperatively). Once this has been done, assessment may reveal that the behavior has changed. Did the praise cause the behavior change? Perhaps the change occurred because one of the children was no longer physically ill when the program began and was therefore less irritable and less likely to get into fights. Or perhaps other events (in addition to praising the children) for one or both of the children—such as a new friend in the neighborhood, new after-school activities, or changes in the behavior of the children's peers or parents—contributed to the change. All of these explanations can be ruled out to determine whether delivery of praise was responsible for the change.

The cause of behavior change can be demonstrated in different ways. The person who designs the program must plan the situation so that the specific contribution of the program to behavior change can be demonstrated. The plan of the program used to demonstrate what accounted for behavior change is referred to as the *experimental design*. Different experimental designs can be used to show that the program, rather than extraneous events, altered behavior. These designs are usually referred to as *single-case experimental designs*. Although such designs can be used with large groups of individuals, their unique characteristic is that they can be used with individual cases (one patient, student, etc.).[1]

REVERSAL OR ABAB DESIGN

The reversal design shows the effect of the behavior modification program by alternately presenting and removing the program over time. The purpose of the design is to demonstrate a *functional relationship* between the target behavior and the experimental condition (program). A functional relationship is demonstrated when altering the experimental condition or contingency systematically changes behavior. Behavior is shown to be a *function* of the environmental events that produced change.

In a reversal design, behavior is assessed to obtain the baseline rate of performance before implementing specific contingencies. The baseline period or phase (referred to as the *A phase*) is continued until the rate of the response appears to be stable or until it is evident that the response does not improve over time. A stable rate of behavior duing baseline serves as a basis for evaluating subsequent change. Baseline provides an estimate of what behavior would be in the future if the program were not introduced. After behavior stabilizes and follows a consistent pattern (several days are usually sufficient), the experimental phase is begun. During the experimental phase, the intervention (e.g., reinforcement, punishment, extinction, or some combination of procedures) is implemented. The experimental phase (referred to as the *B phase*) is continued until behavior reaches a stable level or diverges from the level predicted by the baseline rate.

Figure 4–1 provides a hypothetical example of observations of some desirable behavior plotted over several days. Although the behavior fluctuates during baseline, there is a reasonably stable pattern or a fairly narrow range within which the behavior occurs. During the experimental phase (e.g., reinforcement of the target behavior), there is an increase in performance. Up to this point in the program, the *change* in behavior is evident. However, the *cause* of the change is unclear. Because the change in behavior coincides with implementation of the program, it is likely that the program accounts for the change. However, one cannot be sure.

After behavior attains a stable level, the experimental condition is withdrawn and the baseline condition (A phase) is reinstated. During the baseline condition, of course, no program or intervention is used to control behavior. A return to baseline conditions is called a *reversal* phase because the experimental condition is withdrawn and behavior usually reverses (i.e., returns to or near the level of the original baseline). The purpose of the reversal phase is to

FIGURE 4–1

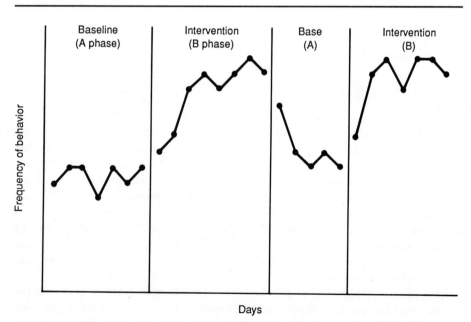

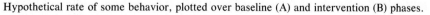

Hypothetical rate of some behavior, plotted over baseline (A) and intervention (B) phases.

determine whether performance would have remained unchanged (relative to baseline) had the program not been introduced. In Figure 4–1, the second A phase shows this reversal of behavior toward baseline. When behavior reverts to or near baseline levels, the experimental phase (B phase) is reinstated. If the intervention is responsible for the change, behavior should change again in the second experimental or B phase.

Changes in A and B conditions from one phase to another are not made until performance during a given phase is stable or is clearly different from performance during the previous phase. When changes are evident after the pattern of performance is clear within a phase, the results are easy to interpret. The pattern in Figure 4–1 suggests that the intervention was responsible for change. The reason is that whenever the intervention was in effect (B phases), behavior improved; whenever there was no intervention (A phases), behavior remained at a stable but lower rate. It is possible that something other than the intervention caused the change. However, the intervention is the most plausible cause.

The design is referred to as a reversal design because phases in the design are reversed to demonstrate the effect of the program. The design is also referred to as an ABAB design because A and B phases are alternated. If performance changes in the experimental phase relative to baseline, reverts to baseline or near baseline levels during the second baseline phase, and again changes in the final experimental phase, this provides a clear demonstration of the effectiveness of the experimental condition.

Examples of reversal designs are abundant. One program clearly illustrating the design focused on the aggressive behavior of elementary school children (Murphy, Hutchison, & Bailey, 1983). The children were 344 first and second graders who played outside before school began. The purpose of the study was to develop and evaluate an intervention to reduce the relatively high rates of aggressive behavior (e.g., striking, slapping, tripping, kicking, pushing, or punching others) on the playground. During baseline, the children were observed for 12 days to assess the number of aggressive behaviors during the 20-minute period before school began. The intervention, which included several components, began after baseline. The major component was organized game activities, including rope jumping and foot races supervised by playground aides. Aides led these activities, which structured the play of the children. Aides were also instructed to praise appropriate play behavior (reinforcement) and to use a mild punishment procedure (placing disruptive children on a bench for two minutes for particularly unruly behavior). The intervention was discontinued after seven days in a reversal phase to see whether the program was responsible for behavior change. Finally, the intervention was reinstated. The results are presented in Figure 4–2. The figure shows that the number of aggressive incidents during each intervention phase decreased relative to the baseline and reversal phases. This demonstrated that behavior improved only when nonverbal approval increased. From the changes in behavior that occurred when the experimental condition was presented,

FIGURE 4–2

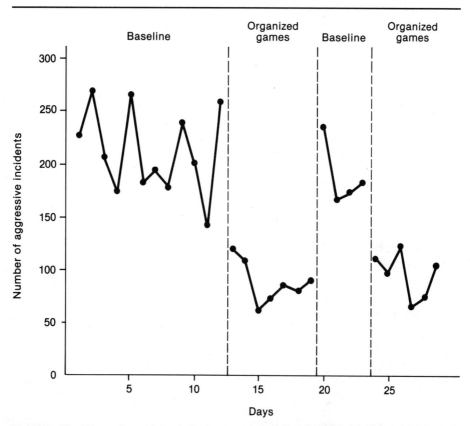

Number of incidents of aggressive behavior recorded on the playground before school started. Baseline—no intervention. Intervention—organized activities, praise, and time-out. Reversal—return to baseline conditions. Intervention—return to the activities, praise, and time-out procedures.

SOURCE: Murphy, H. A., Hutchison, J. M., & Bailey, J. S. (1983). Behavioral school psychology goes outdoors: The effect of organized games on playground aggression. *Journal of Applied Behavior Analysis, 16,* 29–36. Copyright 1983 by the Society for the Experimental Analysis of Behavior, Inc.

withdrawn, and re-presented, it could be concluded that other influences probably did not account for the results.

The reversal design requires that the experimental condition be presented and temporarily withdrawn at some point in time. There are variations of this basic design. Sometimes it is undesirable to begin with a baseline phase because some immediate intervention is urgently required. For example, if fighting among delinquents were frequent and intense in a given setting, it might be undesirable to begin with a baseline period, because some immediate therapeutic intervention is needed. In other situations, it might also be reasonable to forgo the baseline phase. For example, in some cases, target behaviors such as exercising, completing homework, or saving money have not been performed at all or their rates are exceedingly low, so that baseline may not be the first phase of the program. In instances where baseline is not employed initially, a BABA design might be used. This is a reversal design that begins with the experimental phase (B) and continues with baseline or reversal (A) phases.[2]

Reversal Phase

The requirement for the reversal design is that the contingency be altered during the reversal phase to determine whether behavior is controlled by the experimental intervention.

Withdrawal of the Intervention.   The most commonly used alternative in the reversal phase is withdrawal of the intervention. This usually restores the conditions to how they were during baseline. Thus, if praise or attention were systematically applied to increase the activity of a nursing home resident or to increase the paying attention of a student in class, these would be withdrawn during reversal phase. Understandably, behavior would be likely to revert to baseline levels if the intervention were withdrawn.

Noncontingent Reinforcement.   Another alternative during the reversal phase is *noncontingent delivery of the reinforcer*. Essentially, this refers to delivery of the consequences independently of behavior. This strategy is selected to show that it is not the event per se (e.g., praise) that results in behavior change but rather the relationship of the event to behavior. For example, Twardosz and Baer (1973) trained two severely retarded adolescent boys to ask questions. The boys received praise and tokens for asking questions in experimental sessions in which speech was developed. After behavior change was demonstrated, the boys were given noncontingent reinforcement, receiving tokens and praise at the beginning of the session rather than after asking questions. They did not have to perform the response to earn the reinforcers. As expected, noncontingent reinforcement led to a reversal of behavior toward baseline levels.

The potent effects that reinforcement often shows in applied programs come from the contingent application of consequences for specific behaviors. If reinforcing consequences are provided noncontingently, this means that they are given unsystematically and independently of the behaviors performed. Sometimes the noncontingent consequences might accidentally follow the desired behaviors, but other times they do not. At best, noncontingent reinforcement amounts to intermittently reinforcing the desired behavior, which will not develop behavior very well. Although this could lead to change, the change will be weak relative to the application of contingent consequences (Kazdin, 1973a; Lindsay & Stoffelmayr, 1976). Noncontingent delivery of reinforcement is suitable for reversal phases, but it should not be confused with the effective application of reinforcement to alter behavior.

Reinforcing Other Behaviors.   Another variation of the reversal phase is to continue contingent reinforcement. However, the contingency is altered so that the reinforcer is delivered for every behavior *except* the one that was reinforced during the experimental phase. The procedure for administering reinforcement for all behaviors except a specific response is called *differential reinforcement of other behavior* (or DRO schedule). During a reversal phase using a DRO schedule, all behaviors would be reinforced except the one that was reinforced during the experimental phase. For example, in the classroom setting, praise on a DRO schedule might be delivered whenever children were not studying. This strategy is selected to illustrate that the specific contingency is required for behavior change.

For example, Rowbury, Baer, and Baer (1976) provided behavior problem preschool children with praise and tokens that could be exchanged for play time. Reinforcers were given for *completing* various preacademic tasks that involved fitting puzzle pieces and matching forms. During a DRO phase, tokens were given for just sitting down or for starting the task rather than for completing it. In short, behaviors other than completing the task were rewarded. Under the DRO schedule, each child completed fewer tasks than he or she had completed during the intervention.

The DRO schedule is different from the previous variation of the reversal phase, in which reinforcement was delivered independently of behavior. During a DRO phase, reinforcement is contingent on behaviors—but on behaviors different from the one reinforced during the experimental phase. The reason for using a DRO strategy in the reversal phase is to rapidly show the effect of the contingency. Behavior reverses more quickly when other behavior is reinforced directly than when noncontingent reinforcement is administered, even though both are suitable for use in reversal phases (Goetz, Holmberg, & LeBlanc, 1975). Whether a reversal phase employs a return to baseline, noncontingent presentation of the event, or a DRO schedule, the purpose is to show that altering the contingency changes behavior.

Problems and Considerations in Using a Reversal Design

A reversal design requires that behavior revert to baseline or near baseline rates at some point to demonstrate that behavior change was caused by an alteration of the contingencies. Significant problems related to the reversibility of behavior are associated with this design. Sometimes when a program is withdrawn and a reversal phase is implemented, behavior does not return to the baseline rate of performance. When this happens, it is not clear whether the experimental condition or some other event led to initial behavior change.

In punishment programs, for example, behavior occasionally does not return to baseline levels after the program is withdrawn. In one report, electric shock was used in a desperate effort to decrease the coughing of a 14-year-old boy who had not responded to medical treatment or to attempts to ignore coughing (Creer, Chai, & Hoffman, 1977). The cough was so disruptive and distracting to others that the boy was expelled from school until his cough could be controlled. Treatment consisted of applying a mild electric shock to the boy's forearm. After only one shock, the coughing was completely eliminated. The boy returned to school and did not suffer episodes of coughing for up to $2\frac{1}{2}$ years after treatment. Stopping the punishment after one shock amounts to a reversal phase. Fortunately for the boy, cessation of the shock did not lead to a return of the behavior. It is highly likely that treatment accounted for the change, especially given the history of the behavior and the rapidity of the change. Without such dramatic and rapid effects, it is generally difficult to attribute behavior change to treatment if no reversal in behavior occurs when treatment is withdrawn.

In other situations, a reversal design should not be used because behavior would not be expected to reverse. Once certain behaviors have been developed or altered, they may be maintained by favorable consequences that result directly from their performance. For example, if an "aggressive" child is praised by a teacher, improvement in behavior may lead to enduring changes in the child's environment. Peers in the child's environment may be more socially responsive because the previously aggressive child can play nicely with others. Even if there were a reversal phase (removal of teacher praise), attention from the child's peers might maintain the desirable behavior. A reversal of behavior may be difficult to achieve in situations in which the behavior is maintained by naturally occurring environmental events that are not directly manipulated by the teacher, parent, therapist, or investigator.

The most important practical consideration in using the reversal design is that even if it is possible to demonstrate a reversal of behavior, it is usually *undesirable* to do so. For example, autistic and mentally retarded children sometimes severely injure themselves by banging their heads for extended periods of time. If a program decreased this behavior, it would be undesirable to show that headbanging returns in a reversal phase. The behavior is often dangerous. Clearly, once decreases were obtained, it would be undesirable to have the children revert to baseline levels. Even when behavior is not dangerous, making it worse after gains have been made is usually undesirable. Behavioral programs are designed to focus on behaviors that are clinically or socially important to clients and those with whom they interact. Once improvements have been made, it is difficult to justify a reversal phase, even if only for a short period.

Finally, ethical issues obviously arise when a reversal phase is implemented. A reversal phase is essentially designed to make the client's behavior worse in some way. Whether behavior should be made worse and when such a goal would be justified are difficult issues to resolve. In a given clinical situation, the consequences of making the client worse need to be weighed carefully for the client and for those in contact with the client. In fact, when reversal phases are used, they tend to be relatively brief—even for only one or a few days. Yet the problems of reversing behavior may still arise. Fortunately, other designs are available to demonstrate the effects of the program without using a reversal of conditions.

MULTIPLE-BASELINE DESIGNS

Multiple-baseline designs do *not* rely on a reversal of conditions or phases to show the effect of the behavior modification program. Rather, the effect of the contingency is demonstrated by showing that behavior change is associated with its introduction at different points in time. One of three types of multiple-baseline designs is generally used, depending on whether data are collected across behaviors, individuals, or situations.

Multiple-Baseline Across Behaviors

In this version of the multiple-baseline design, baseline data are collected across *two or more behaviors* of a given individual or group of individuals. After each baseline has reached a stable rate, the experimental condition is implemented for only one of the behaviors while baseline conditions are continued for the other behavior(s). The initial behavior subjected to the experimental condition is expected to change, and the other behaviors are expected to remain at baseline levels. When rates are stable for all behaviors, the second behavior is included in the contingency. This procedure is continued until all of the behaviors for which baseline data were gathered are included in the contingency. Ideally, each behavior changes only as it is included in the experimental contingency and not before. Control of the specific experimental contingency is demonstrated when each of the behavior changes has been associated with its introduction. The multiple-baseline design across behaviors is useful when an individual or group has a number of behaviors that are to be changed.

A multiple-baseline design across behaviors was nicely illustrated in a project designed to develop social interaction skills among four elementary school children (Bornstein, Bellack, & Hersen, 1977). The children were considered by their teachers to be excessively shy, passive, unassertive, and conforming. Training developed skills that enabled the children to communicate more effectively and, in general, to be more assertive. The children were deficient in specific behaviors such as making eye contact with others while speaking, speaking too softly, and not making requests. Individual behaviors were changed in a multiple-baseline design across behaviors for each child.

Baseline observations of behavior were obtained as a child behaved in role-playing situations in which he or she acted out various social situations with two other people. The child responded verbally to the other people in several everyday situations such as talking in class, playing in a game at school, and borrowing objects from peers. After baseline, training was implemented to develop each of the specific behaviors. Training consisted of prompting the child to make a response in situations that the child acted out, providing feedback about the response and how it might be improved, modeling of the response by the trainer, and having the child engage in continued practice to improve the response.

The results for Jane, an eight-year-old girl, are presented in Figure 4–3. The three trained behaviors were improving eye contact, increasing loudness of speech, and increasing the number of requests that the child made of other people. The behavior graphed at the bottom of the figure, which represented an overall rating of Jane's assertiveness, was never focused on directly. Presumably, if the other behaviors were changed, the child's overall assertiveness

FIGURE 4–3

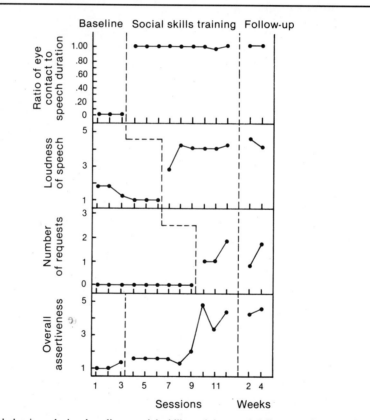

Jane's social behaviors during baseline, social skills training, and follow-up phases, with the intervention (training) program introduced for each of the behaviors in a multiple-baseline design.

SOURCE: Bornstein, M. T., Bellack, A. S., & Hersen, M. (1977). Social-skills training for unassertive children: A multiple-baseline analysis. *Journal of Applied Behavior Analysis, 10,* 183–195. Copyright 1977 by the Society for the Experimental Analysis of Behavior, Inc.

ratings would improve. Each behavior changed as it was included in training. The results were maintained when Jane was observed two and four weeks after treatment.

The requirements of the multiple-baseline design were clearly met in this report. If all of the behaviors had changed when only the first one was included in the contingency, it would have been unclear whether the contingency caused the change. In that case, an extraneous event might have influenced all of the behaviors simultaneously. The specific effects obtained in this report strongly suggest the influence of training on each behavior.

Multiple-Baseline Across Individuals

In this design, baseline data are collected for a particular behavior across *two or more individuals*. After the behavior of each individual has reached a stable rate, the experimental condition is implemented for only one of the individuals while baseline conditions are continued for the other(s). The behavior of the individual exposed to the experimental condition should change, whereas the behavior of the other individual(s) should not. When behavior stabilizes for all of the individuals, the contingency is extended to another individual. This procedure is continued until all of the individuals for whom baseline data were collected are included in the contingency. As with other multiple-baseline designs, no reversal of the experimental condition (e.g., return to baseline or DRO) is required to demonstrate that the contingency was responsible for behavior change. The multiple-baseline design across individuals is useful when a given behavior is to be altered across a number of clients in a group.

A multiple-baseline design across individuals was used in a study designed to train emergency fire safety skills in third-grade children (Jones, Kazdin, & Haney, 1981a). The target behaviors, identified from fire safety materials and by firefighters, consisted of complex sequences of responses that varied based on where the fire was in the home, whether there was smoke, whether doors on rooms on the path to escape were hot, and other factors. Safe escape from fires at home was trained by setting up a simulated bedroom at school in which the training was actually carried out. Instructions about safety, modeling of correct responses, practice, feedback, and praise for correct responses were used in training. The program was introduced in a multiple-baseline design across five children. Baseline data were obtained for each child before the intervention was introduced. Data indicated that none of the children could perform the correct escape behaviors in a way that would ensure safety. The intervention was introduced to the first child while baseline data continued to be gathered for the other children. At different points in time, training was introduced to the second, third, and other children. As is evident in Figure 4–4, the behavior of each child changed when training was introduced. Other events that might have influenced the behavior, such as practice escaping without training or know-

FIGURE 4–4

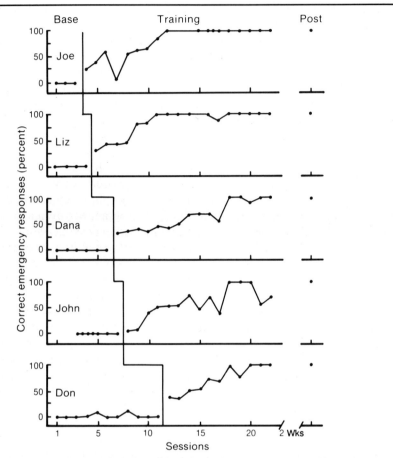

Correct emergency escape responses. Baseline—no intervention was implemented. Training—implementation of the training program. Postcheck—assessment two weeks after training was completed to see whether the skills were maintained. (Missing data points for John during baseline resulted from his starting late. Extra sessions were given during baseline to provide several data points during this phase.)

SOURCE: Jones, R. T., Kazdin, A. E., & Haney, J. I. (1981a). Social validation and training of emergency fire safety skills for potential injury prevention and life-saving. *Journal of Applied Behavior Analysis, 14,* 249–260. Copyright 1981 by the Society for the Experimental Analysis of Behavior, Inc.

ledge that safety and escape from fires were the focus, could not easily explain the change. The results strongly argue for the role of training as the crucial event in developing the behavior.

Multiple-Baseline Across Situations, Settings, or Time

In this design, baseline data on a given behavior for an individual or a group are collected *across two or more situations* (e.g., at home and at school). After behavior has stabilized in each of the situations, the experimental contingency is implemented in the first situation. The baseline phase is continued for behavior in the other situation(s). Eventually, the contingency is extended to behavior in the next situation while baseline data continue to be gathered in the remaining situations. The contingency is extended to each situation until all of the situations have been included. The specific effect of the contingency is shown if behavior changes in a particular situation only when the contingency is introduced. The multiple-baseline design across situations is useful when an individual or a group performs or fails to perform a behavior across different situations or at different times within a given situation.

A multiple-baseline design across situations was used to evaluate treatment for a severely withdrawn boy who was enrolled in a special school for emotionally disturbed and handicapped children (Kandel, Ayllon, & Rosenbaum, 1977). The boy, named Bobby, was diagnosed as autistic and suffering from brain dysfunction. At school, he was always physically isolated, talked to himself, and spent his free playtime alone. A program was designed to improve his social interaction during the two separate free-play situations at school. The situations included activity on the playground and juice time, when the children assembled each day in a courtyard outside class.

Baseline data on the occurrences of social interaction with peers were gathered in each situation. On the final day of baseline, the investigators encouraged other children to interact with Bobby, which proved very upsetting to him and was not pursued further. The treatment after baseline consisted of training the child directly in the situation with his peers, an intervention referred to as *systematic exposure*. Treatment began on the playground, where the trainer modeled appropriate social interaction for Bobby and then brought two other children to interact with him. The two children also encouraged him to participate in additional activities on the playground and helped keep him from leaving the activities. Toys were used as the focus of some of the interactions in training sessions. Also, rewards (candy) were given to the two children who helped with training. The exposure procedure was first implemented on the playground, then extended in the same fashion to the other free-play period.

The training program was evaluated in a multiple-baseline design across the two settings. As is evident in Figure 4–5, social interaction improved in each setting as soon as training was introduced. The marked and rapid changes make the effects of the intervention very clear. Follow-up, conducted three weeks later when the program was no longer in effect, showed that the behaviors were maintained. The nine-month follow-up (upper portion of figure) was conducted after Bobby had been attending a regular school where his behavior during free time was observed. Apparently, he maintained high levels of social interaction in the regular school.

When a particular behavior needs to be altered in two or more situations, the multiple-baseline design across situations or settings is especially useful. The intervention is first implemented in one situation, and then, if effective, it is gradually extended to other situations. The intervention is extended until all of the situations in which baseline data were gathered are included.

FIGURE 4–5

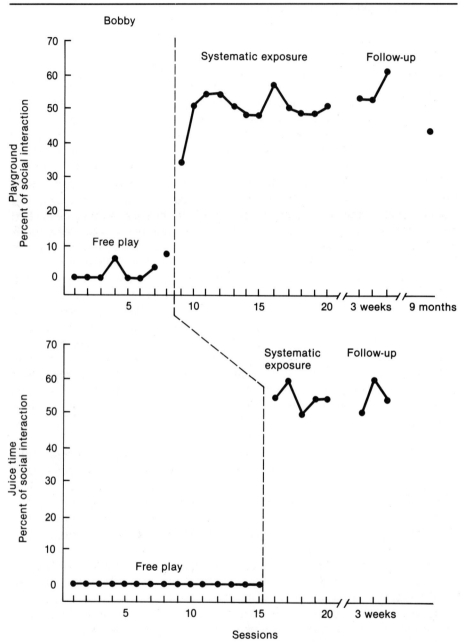

Bobby's social interaction on the playground and in the courtyard at juice time, the two settings in which the intervention was introduced.

SOURCE: Reprinted with permission from *Journal of Behavior Therapy and Experimental Psychiatry, 8*, 71–81. Kandel, H. J., Ayllon, T., & Rosenbaum, M. S. Flooding or systematic exposure in the treatment of extreme social withdrawal in children. Copyright 1977, Pergamon Press Inc.

Problems and Considerations in Using Multiple-Baseline Designs

Multiple-baseline designs demonstrate the effects of contingencies without using a reversal phase. With such designs, there is no need to return to baseline conditions and temporarily lose the gains made during the behavior modification program. Hence, these designs should be used when a reversal in behavior would be undesirable or unexpected. The designs require that there be two or more observable behaviors, individuals, or situations.

There are possible problems with multiple-baseline designs that should be mentioned. In the multiple-baseline design across behaviors, a clear demonstration of the effect of the contingency depends on showing that behavior changes *only* when the contingency is introduced. If a behavior changes before the contingency for that behavior is introduced (i.e., during baseline), it is unclear whether the contingency is responsible for change. If changing the first behavior also changes the second behavior before the second behavior is included in the contingency, the specific effect of the contingency on behavior is unclear. Studies report that altering one behavior of an individual occasionally results in changes in behaviors not included in the contingency (Kazdin, 1973b; Marholin & Steinman, 1977; Parrish, Cataldo, Kolko, Neef, & Egel, 1986). In situations where generalization across responses or response covariation occurs, a multiple-baseline design across behavior would not show the causal effect of the contingencies. There are analogous problems in the multiple-baseline designs across individuals or across situations. In these designs, changes in the behavior of one individual may alter the behavior of other individuals for whom baseline conditions are still in effect, or changes in behavior in one situation may be associated with changes in other situations even though the program has not been introduced in these situations (see Kazdin, 1982c).

In spite of the potential problems in demonstrating the specific effect of the contingencies in multiple-baseline designs, these designs are usually quite useful in demonstrating the relationship between a behavior and an experimental contingency. The problem appears to occur infrequently. But if it appears likely that altering one behavior (or behavior of one individual, or behavior in one situation) can produce generalized effects, a multiple-baseline design might be avoided.

An important consideration in using a multiple-baseline design is deciding how many baselines will be needed. Two baselines are a minimum, but more are usually desirable. As a general rule, the more baselines across which the effect of the intervention is demonstrated, the more convincing is the demonstration of a causal relationship. Whether an investigation provides a convincing demonstration across a given set of baselines depends on such factors as the duration of the baselines, the presence of trends or excessive variability during baseline, the rapidity of behavior change after the intervention, and the magnitude of behavior change. Usually two or three baselines are enough if the baseline data are stable and the intervention produces marked effects. Because it is difficult to predict the magnitude of behavior change and the stability of behavior within phases, it is often safer to choose a minimum of three baselines.

CHANGING-CRITERION DESIGN

The effect of a contingency can be demonstrated without using a reversal or multiple-baseline design. The changing-criterion design demonstrates the effect of the contingency by showing that behavior matches a criterion that is set for reinforcement or punishment (Hartmann & Hall, 1976). As the criterion is repeatedly changed, behavior increases or decreases to match the criterion.

The changing-criterion design begins with a baseline period of observation. After baseline, the experimental contingency is introduced so that a certain level of performance is required to earn reinforcement. For example, the behavior may have to be performed a certain number of times per day to earn the reinforcer. When performance consistently meets or surpasses that criterion over a few days, the criterion is made more stringent. The criterion is repeatedly changed in a gradual fashion until the goal is achieved. The effect of the contingency is demonstrated if the behavior appears to match the criterion repeatedly as that criterion is changed.

Foxx and Rubinoff (1979) used a changing-criterion design to evaluate a program to decrease caffeine consumption in three adults. Caffeine consumed in large quantities has been associated with a variety of symptoms ranging in severity from general irritability and gastrointestinal disturbances to cardiovascular disorders and cancer. The intervention consisted of having the participants deposit money ($20) at the beginning of the program and return a small portion of the money if caffeine consumption fell below the criterion set for a given day. The participants signed a contract that specified how they would earn back or lose the money. Each of the participants recorded daily caffeine consumption on the basis of a list of beverages that provided their caffeine equivalence (in milligrams).

The effects of the program for one of the participants, a female schoolteacher, are illustrated in Figure 4–6. During baseline, her daily average caffeine consumption was 1,000 milligrams (equal to approximately eight cups of brewed coffee). When the intervention began, she was required to reduce her daily consumption by about 100 milligrams less than baseline. When her performance was consistently below the criterion (solid line), the criterion was reduced further by about 100 milligrams. This change in the criterion continued over separate subphases. In each subphase, she earned money back only if her caffeine consumption fell at or below the criterion. The figure shows that her performance consistently fell below the criterion. Assessment 10 months after the end of the program indicated that she maintained her low rate of caffeine consumption.

FIGURE 4–6

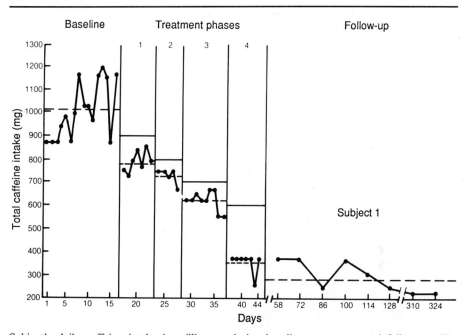

Subject's daily caffeine intake in milligrams during baseline, treatment, and follow-up. The criterion level for each treatment phase was 102 milligrams of caffeine less than that of the previous treatment phase. Solid horizontal lines indicate the criterion level for each phase. Broken horizontal lines indicate the mean for each condition.

SOURCE: Foxx, R. M., & Rubinoff, A. (1979). Behavioral treatment of caffeinism: Reducing excessive coffee drinking. *Journal of Applied Behavior Analysis, 12,* 335–344. Copyright 1979 by the Society for the Experimental Analysis of Behavior, Inc.

Problems and Considerations in Using a Changing-Criterion Design

The changing-criterion design is especially well suited to responses that are shaped gradually rather than acquired in one or a few trials. If performance shows a marked improvement or attainment of the final goal when the criterion is not set at that level, the relationship between the intervention and behavior change is unclear. To show that alteration of the criterion accounts for changes in behavior, the rate of behavior has to be such that it allows several changes to be made in the criterion before the terminal goal is achieved. Thus, a behavior to be decreased may need to be performed at a high rate so that several changes can be made in reaching the terminal level. A behavior to be increased may need to have a potential number that is high enough to permit several criterion levels.

The changing-criterion design is less satisfactory than reversal and multiple-baseline designs in ruling out the influence of extraneous events that might account for behavior change. Even if a behavior matches a criterion, the behavior may be changing as a function of some other event in the person's life that led to a directional change (i.e., a decrease or an increase) in the behavior over time. A clear relationship is demonstrated only when performance matches the criterion very closely.

The design can be strengthened by making bidirectional changes in the criterion during the intervention phase. Rather than simply making the criterion increasingly stringent, it can be made more stringent at some points and slightly less stringent at others. This does not mean that a reversal (return to baseline) phase is implemented. Instead, the criterion could be shifted to a previous criterion level. If behavior improves as the criterion is made more stringent and stops improving or decreases as the criterion is made less stringent for a brief period, it is extremely unlikely that extraneous events could account for the results.

SIMULTANEOUS- (OR ALTERNATING-) TREATMENT DESIGN

The simultaneous- or alternating-treatment design examines the effects of different interventions, each of which is implemented during the same phase. The design is especially useful when the investigator is interested in determining which among two or more experimental conditions is more or most effective (Barlow & Hayes, 1979; Kazdin & Hartmann, 1978).

The design begins with baseline observation of a response. After baseline, two or more interventions are implemented to alter the response. The different interventions are administered during the same phase but under varied and alternating stimulus conditions. For example, two interventions could be compared by implementing both of them on the same day but at different periods (morning and afternoon). The different interventions are *balanced* across all of the conditions so that their effects can be separated from those conditions until the response stabilizes under the separate interventions. If the response stabilizes at different levels during the intervention phase, the interventions differ in effectiveness. Once the differential effectiveness of the interventions has been demonstrated, a phase may be implemented in which the more (or most) effective intervention is given under all of the conditions (e.g., each period).

A simultaneous-treatment design was used to evaluate different interventions designed to reduce the frequency of stereotyped repetitive movements among hospitalized mentally retarded children (Ollendick, Shapiro, & Barrett, 1981). Three children, ages seven to eight years old, exhibited stereotypical behaviors such as repetitive hand gestures and hair twirling. Observations of each child were made in a classroom setting while the child performed various visual-motor tasks (e.g., puzzles). The behavior of the child was observed each day for three sessions, after which the intervention phase was implemented.

During the intervention phase, three conditions were compared—two active interventions and a continuation of baseline conditions. One of the treatment procedures consisted of physically restraining the child's hands on the table for 30 seconds, so that he or she could not perform the repetitive behaviors. The second treatment procedure consisted of physically guiding the child to engage in the appropriate use of the task materials. Instead of merely restraining the child, this procedure was designed to develop appropriate alternative behaviors that the child could perform with the hands. The final condition during the intervention phase was a continuation of baseline. Physical restraint, positive practice, and continuation of baseline were implemented each day across three time periods.

Figure 4–7 illustrates the results for a child who engaged in hand-posturing gestures. As is evident from the first intervention phase, both physical restraint and positive practice led to reductions in performance; positive practice was more effective. The extent of the reduction is especially clear in light of the continuation of baseline as a third condition during the intervention phase. When baseline (no-treatment) conditions were in effect during the intervention phase, performance remained at the approximate level of the original baseline phase. In the final phase, positive practice was applied to all of the daily time periods. Positive practice, which had proven to be the most effective condition

FIGURE 4–7

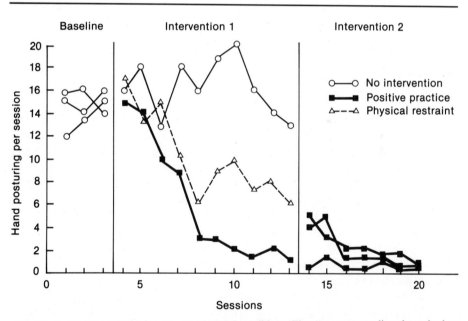

Stereotypical hand posturing across experimental conditions. The three separate lines in each phase represent the three separate time periods of each session. Only in the initial intervention phase (Intervention 1) were the three separate conditions in effect. In the second intervention phase (Intervention 2), positive practice was in effect for all three periods.

SOURCE: Ollendick, T. H., Shapiro, E. S., & Barrett, R. P. (1981). Reducing stereotypic behaviors: An analysis of treatment procedures using an alternating-treatments design. *Behavior Therapy, 12*, 570–577. Copyright 1981 by the Association for Advancement of Behavior Therapy. Reprinted by permission of the publisher and the author.

in the previous phase, also led to dramatic reductions in performance when it was implemented across all of the time periods. Thus, the strength of this intervention is especially clear from the design.

Problems and Considerations in Using a Simultaneous-Treatment Design

The main feature of the simultaneous-treatment design is that it permits comparison of different interventions implemented in a single treatment phase for a given client. The design addresses the very practical question of which among alternative treatments is the most effective for a particular client. In practice, the design may be difficult to implement if more than two or three conditions are compared. As the number of treatments increases, it becomes increasingly difficult to ensure that each treatment is administered among each of the conditions. For instance, in the previous example, it would be difficult to balance three or four treatments so that they are given an equal number of times during each of the two observation periods. Balancing the different treatments becomes especially difficult if the treatments are administered at different time periods and by different staff (e.g., Kazdin, 1977c). A large number of days are needed to ensure that each treatment is given under all the combinations of the conditions of administration.

A few other restrictions of the simultaneous-treatment design should be kept in mind. For example, the design depends on showing that a given behavior changes in response to changes in treatment on a given day. It is important that there be no carryover effect from one intervention to another. For example, it may be difficult to compare drug and behavioral treatments in a simultaneous-treatment design because the influence of the drug may still be present when the behavioral treatment is implemented. Also, the behavior selected for the design must be able to change rapidly. The response must occur frequently enough during the observation periods to reflect change for each intervention and, if the interventions have different effects, a differential amount of change across interventions. Despite the potential obstacles in practice, the design has been quite useful in identifying variations of reinforcement and punishment (e.g., Kazdin & Geesey, 1977; Singh, Watson, & Winton, 1986). Once the more or most effective intervention has been identified for a given client, it can be implemented in all of the time periods to maximize its impact on the client.

CONTROL-GROUP DESIGN

The control-group design is another way to demonstrate the effect of an experimental contingency. A variety of control-group designs are suitable for applied settings (Cook & Campbell, 1979; Kazdin, 1980a). The basic design requires at least two groups, of which one receives the intervention (the experimental group) and the other does not (the control group). To determine whether the experimental contingency was effective, the rates of the target behavior in the experimental and control groups are compared. For example, a reinforcement program might be conducted in one school classroom but not in another. Immediately before and after the program, the behavior of all the students in both classrooms is assessed. To determine whether the program was effective, the performance averages of the groups are compared at the end of the program. If these averages are different, this suggests that the program was responsible for the change.

To be sure that any difference between the two groups is due to the program, the groups must be similar to begin with. The best procedure to control for systematic differences between groups before implementation of the program is to assign subjects *randomly* to each of the groups. If subjects are not randomly assigned to groups, the likelihood is greater that the groups will be different in their performance of the target behavior before the program has been implemented and will differentially change in the target behavior over time for some reason other than the effect of the program.

O'Brien and Azrin (1972) used a control-group design to evaluate the effects of a program to train mentally retarded adults to eat appropriately. The residents seldom used utensils, spilled food on themselves, and displayed grossly improper table manners, such as stealing food from others and eating food that had been spilled on the floor. The residents were randomly assigned to one of two groups that received either training or no training. Training consisted of individually meeting with a resident and providing the resident with praise for correct eating behaviors and reprimands (saying the word *no*) and time out from reinforcement for inappropriate eating behaviors. Also, instructions and manual guidance (physical prompts) were given to help the residents perform the desired responses. No-training residents, of course, did not receive the special training program to develop specific eating behaviors.

The program was evaluated by observing the eating behavior of both groups of residents immediately before training (pretest) and immediately after training (posttest), when each resident was observed while eating alone. Two weeks later, a follow-up meal was observed in which residents ate in a group situation. The results of the program, presented in Figure 4–8, were evaluated with statistical tests that showed significantly greater improvement for the training group. The effects of the program are also clear from the figure, which shows a much higher level of inappropriate eating for the no-training group.

In some cases, control-group and single-case designs are combined. For example, one investigation evaluated the effects of reinforcement on the punctuality of workers in an industrial setting (Hermann, deMontes, Dominguez, Montes, & Hopkins, 1973). Of 12 persons who were frequently tardy for work, 6 were assigned to a treatment group and the other 6 to a control group. The treatment group received slips of paper for coming to work on time. These could be exchanged for small amounts of money at the end of the week. The control group received no treatment.

The program was administered to the treatment group in a reversal design.

FIGURE 4–8

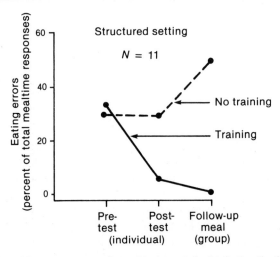

The percentage of mealtime responses performed improperly by institutionalized mental retardates.

SOURCE: O'Brien, F. & Azrin, N. H. (1972). Developing proper mealtime behaviors of the institutionalized retarded. *Journal of Applied Behavior Analysis, 5,* 389–399. Copyright 1972 by the Society for the Experimental Analysis of Behavior, Inc.

As shown in the lower panel of Figure 4–9, tardiness decreased when the program was introduced and it approached baseline levels when the program was withdrawn. This demonstration would have been quite sufficient with the treatment group alone, given the pattern of the results over the different phases. However, the control group provided additional information. With the control group as a basis for comparison, the magnitude of improvement due to the reinforcement program could be estimated. The level of performance of the untreated group may differ from the return-to-baseline rates evident in the treatment group because of the alteration of reinforcement and no-reinforcement phases. In fact, one can see from the figure's upper panel that without a program the control group became slightly worse over time. Thus, the control group provided useful information about the likely changes over time without an intervention.

Problems and Considerations in Using a Control-Group Design

The control-group design has not been employed as extensively as single-case designs in behavior modification programs in applied settings. The major reason is that the control-group design focuses on the behavior of groups rather than on the behavior of individuals. When the control-group study has been completed, the average frequency of behavior of individuals in the control group is compared with the average frequency of behavior of individuals in the

FIGURE 4–9

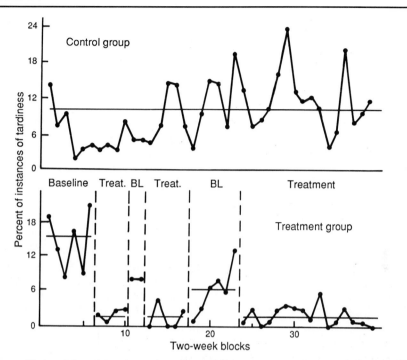

Tardiness of industrial workers. Control group—no intervention throughout the study. Treatment group—baseline (BL), in which no intervention was implemented and treatment, in which money was contingent upon punctuality. Horizontal lines represent the means for each condition.

SOURCE: Hermann, J. A., deMontes, A. I., Dominguez, B., Montes, F., & Hopkins, B. L. (1973). Effects of bonuses for punctuality on the tardiness of industrial workers. *Journal of Applied Behavior Analysis, 6,* 563–570. Copyright 1973 by the Society for the Experimental Analysis of Behavior, Inc.

experimental group. The focus on averages hides the behavior of individuals. Thus, the average performance of a group may change even if only a few individuals in the group have been affected by the program. Behavior modification programs in applied settings have usually been concerned with achieving relatively large changes in the behavior of individuals in such settings as the home, hospitals, classrooms, and institutions. In recent years, more applications have been evaluated in settings such as the community at large, where the focus has often been on large groups rather than on individuals (see Chapter 12). In such instances, control-group designs alone or combined with single-case designs have been used more frequently.

Another reason why the control-group design has not been used frequently in applied settings is that group studies usually do not measure behavior continually throughout the program. Behavior may be measured before and immediately after the program. In a behavior modification program, it is important to assess behavior continuously, such as every day or almost every day, so that the investigator knows how well the program is progressing while it is in effect. Continual observation may reveal that the program is not working very well. Because the observations are made while the program is in effect, the program can be changed immediately. If behavior is assessed only at the end of the program, as is usually the case in a control-group design, it is too late to alter a program that has not attained the desired changes.

The control-group design is often used in many areas of behavior modification research, especially to evaluate outpatient treatment for such problems as anxiety, obesity, marital discord, and excessive alcohol consumption. However, evaluations of behavior change techniques based on operant conditioning principles have relied more heavily on the single-case designs highlighted here. Of course, the particular type of design selected depends on such factors as the purpose of treatment and the questions of interest to the investigator rather than on the types of techniques that are used.

For many questions, a control group can provide valuable information that is difficult to obtain with single-case designs (Kazdin, 1980c). For example, comparing the effectiveness of different experimental programs is readily accomplished by using different groups of clients who receive the different treatments. Although the simultaneous-treatment design can compare treatments for the individual client, large-scale demonstrations across many clients and many treatments are restricted to control-group designs. In addition, when the effects of different treatments for different types of persons (e.g., younger versus older, men versus women) or different types of clinical problems (e.g., depression versus aggression, social interaction versus instruction following) are being evaluated, control-group designs are particularly useful. A large number of clients may be needed to show a systematic and different pattern of results for different types of persons.

EVALUATING CHANGE

In each of the single-case designs, the degree of behavior change is evaluated by comparing performance during baseline with performance during the experimental phase. A major issue is the degree of change needed to provide a convincing demonstration that behavior has improved. The decision that change has occurred is important both in the execution of the design and in the evaluation of the overall effects of treatment. For example, in the reversal design, the experimental condition may be withdrawn, altered, or reinstated at different points based on evidence that behavior has changed or failed to change. To decide whether alterations should be made in the phases and, more important, whether the client has improved sufficiently, behavior change must be evaluated.

Deciding whether Behavior Has Reliably Changed

In many instances in single-case research, behavior change is dramatic. Indeed, the usual purpose of the intervention is to obtain strong treatment effects. If these are obtained, they are usually quite evident from visual inspection, that is, from merely looking at the graphs to evaluate whether the change was reliable (see Kazdin, 1982c; Parsonson & Baer, 1978). In practice, a few guidelines are used to help decide whether behavior change has occurred and whether behavior has changed systematically from baseline. These guidelines are based on evaluating graphs on which performance is plotted across phases.

The first guideline is to see whether the *level of behavior during the experimental or intervention phase overlaps with the level of performance during baseline*. During the program, the data points may not even approach the data points obtained during baseline. Figure 4–10 (upper panel) shows such a data pattern. When there is *no overlap* of performance in the baseline and intervention phases, there would be general agreement that behavior change has occurred.

A second guideline for assessing the reliability of behavior change is to see whether there are *changes in the trend (slope) of the data*. For example, behavior may show a clear trend toward improvement during the intervention. Figure 4–10 (middle panel) shows such a pattern, with behavior decreasing during baseline and increasing during the intervention phase. If the data continued to be collected, the trend would be expected to change as the intervention was withdrawn and eventually reinstated.

Another guideline for evaluating behavior change is to see whether the *mean (arithmetic average) level of performance during the intervention phase differs from the average level of performance during baseline*. The mean may show a change even if only a slight change in behavior is evident. Figure 4–10 (bottom panel) shows a change in mean performance from one phase to the next. A change in means across phases may be difficult to evaluate, depending, of course, on the degree of change. Also, if it is not obvious that a change has taken place, this probably indicates that a more potent intervention is needed to help the client in relation to the target goals of the program. As a general rule, evidence that the means have changed across phases, when the other criteria regarding overlap and trend have not been met, provides only a tenuous demonstration of the reliable effects of the program.[3]

Change of Applied or Clinical Significance

Demonstrating that a reliable or genuine change has occurred is important but by itself does not address the question of whether the change is important. A major criterion for evaluating change is the *applied or clinical significance* of the effects of treatment. The effects produced by the intervention should be large enough to be of practical value. Also, the help of individuals in constant contact with the patient, resident, or client who was in the program is needed to evaluate whether an important change was obtained (Wolf, 1978).

It is not enough to demonstrate that behavior change occurred, because the change may be too weak to be of any practical value. For example, treatment may reduce the frequency with which an autistic child hits himself in the head from 100 times per hour to 50 times per hour. Change has been achieved, but a much larger change is needed. Self-injurious behavior is maladaptive and potentially dangerous, and it needs to be eliminated.

FIGURE 4–10

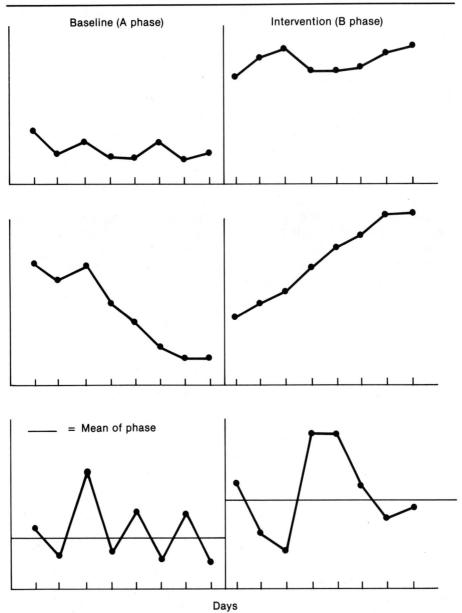

Hypothetical illustration of patterns of data that help in deciding whether a systematic change has occurred from baseline (A) to the intervention (B) phase. These patterns are shown: nonoverlapping data in separate phases (upper panel), changes in the trend—the slope of the lines representing data in each phase (middle panel), and changes in mean (average) performance in separate phases (lower panel).

Evaluating whether behavior change is of applied significance is referred to as *social validation* (Kazdin, 1977d; Wolf, 1978). Social validation consists of different methods for determining whether the amount of change is very important. One procedure compares the level of the client's behavior after treatment with that of his or her peers or others who are considered to be functioning adequately in their environment. For example, Walker and Hops (1976) developed appropriate classroom behaviors (such as working on assignments and following instructions) in primary-grade students in a special education classroom. Prior to participating in a reinforcement program, the students were markedly lower in their appropriate behavior than were their nondisruptive peers. When the program was completed and the children were placed in regular classrooms, their appropriate behavior was up to the level of their nondisruptive peers. These results suggest that the changes in behavior were clinically important, because the children were brought up to the level of peers who had not been identified as behavior problems. Several other programs have evaluated the extent of the change achieved in treatment by comparing the clients' level of behavior with that of people who were not considered to have problem behavior in the area focused in treatment.[4]

Another method of evaluating the importance of behavior change is to have the level of behavior judged by people who interact with the client or who are in a special position to do so by virtue of their expertise. It is possible that the program changed behavior but that the improvements are not clear to persons such as parents, teachers, colleagues, employers, or peers in everyday life. If clinically significant changes have taken place, this should be obvious to persons who are in a position to judge these changes.

For example, socially appropriate conversational skills were developed in a program for delinquent girls (Maloney et al., 1976). The girls received rewards for answering questions and for engaging in appropriate nonverbal behaviors, such as looking at the person. Conversational skills were observed and shown to change. Persons not involved in the program but with whom the girls might normally interact were asked to evaluate their conversational skills. Specifically, a social worker, probation officer, teacher, counselor, and student rated videotapes and segments of the girls' conversations. These judges, not knowing which tapes were from before and after training, could discern the girls' more appropriate social interaction. Thus, training produced a change that could be seen by other persons.

In general, applied operant programs seek treatment effects that clearly improve the level of the client's functioning in everyday situations. Showing that behavior change brings the client up to normative levels of functioning and that other persons with whom the client interacts can clearly detect change are two methods of evaluating whether the goals have been attained. In many cases, there are no fixed standards that can be used as criteria of whether performance is optimal after training. Thus, it is not always easy to evaluate whether persons monitor their diet, engage in exercise, use seat belts, and engage in a host of other personal and community-relevant behaviors. The goal in many cases is to develop specific behaviors that may never have been performed before or may have been performed infrequently. In such cases, the significance of the behavior (e.g., increase in exercise, reduction in smoking) may make the change of obvious import.

SUMMARY AND CONCLUSION

This chapter discussed experimental designs that are used to evaluate the effects of intervention programs. Assessment of behavior can evaluate whether change occurs when treatment is provided. But in addition to assessment, experimental designs are needed to determine whether the treatment was responsible for the change. Different designs are available, including the reversal (or ABAB) design, multiple-baseline design, changing-criterion design, simultaneous-treatment design, and control-group design. Although each of these designs can demonstrate a relationship between the intervention and behavior change, selection of the design may be determined by the population and behaviors of interest, demands of the clinical situation, the purposes of the intervention, and various advantages and disadvantages of specific designs. Independently of the design selected, the purpose of treatment is to achieve marked changes in behavior. Behavior change is usually evaluated by visually inspecting the graphed results to assess whether treatment was consistently associated with marked changes or by differences in trends across phases. The importance of behavior change may be evaluated by comparing the client's behavior with that of others whose behavior already appears to be at a satisfactory level of performance. Also, persons who interact with the client can be asked to evaluate the client's behavior to see whether the changes are detectable in everyday life.

In general, the methods of assessing and evaluating behavioral programs, as discussed in this and the previous chapter, provide tools that are essential for designing effective treatments. Identifying techniques to change behavior and obtaining clinically important effects depend on measuring the extent of the client's behavior prior to the intervention, seeing whether or how much change is obtained with the intervention, making adjustments in the intervention accordingly, and determining whether the intervention is responsible for change. Now that these important features have been discussed, we can turn to the many behavior change techniques that have been developed and identified in this fashion.

NOTES

1. For a detailed discussion of various single-case designs that are used to evaluate behavioral programs and of the rationale underlying their use, other sources can be consulted (Kazdin, 1982c).
2. Many other versions of the ABAB design have been used (Barlow & Hersen, 1984; Kazdin, 1982c). For example, several treatments may be used in an $AB_1B_2B_3AB_3$

design. The different treatments ($B_1B_2B_3$) may be needed if the first one did not work or did not work well enough to attain the desired level of change. Even when many interventions are used, the demonstration is a reversal design if it meets the basic requirement—evaluating the effect of the intervention(s) by implementing a phase that is intended to reverse behavior in the direction of the original baseline.

3. Several statistical techniques have been proposed to evaluate the effects of treatment in single-case designs (see Kazdin, 1982c). The use of statistical techniques has been controversial. Some investigators have suggested that developing an effective technology of behavior change requires that very strong treatment effects should be sought. Visually inspecting graphed results allows one to see only extremely strong treatment effects. In contrast, statistical analysis may identify intervention effects that are generally weak but meet a statistical criterion of significance. Visual inspection is still the primary criterion for evaluating programs using single-case designs. However, use of statistical analyses has increased in recent years.

4. The topics of social validation and the magnitude of treatment effects will be taken up again in Chapter 13, where the social context of behavioral interventions is discussed in more detail.

FOR FURTHER READING

Barlow, D. H., & Hersen, M. (1984). *Single-case experimental designs: Strategies for studying behavior change* (2nd ed.). New York: Pergamon.

Kazdin, A. E. (1982). *Single-case research designs: Methods for clinical and applied settings*. New York: Oxford University Press.

Chapter Five

Positive and Negative Reinforcement

Various populations in treatment, education, and rehabilitation settings are often identified for special intervention because of their behavioral deficits or their lack of appropriate skills. For example, autistic and mentally retarded children often lack a variety of appropriate personal, social, and intellectual skills. Other individuals are identified for intervention because of disruptive and deviant behaviors but may also lack such skills. For example, delinquents may engage in aggressive behaviors whose elimination will not ensure the performance of socially appropriate behaviors. Such behaviors need to be developed. Still other individuals whose behavior is identified as problematic may possess appropriate skills but perform them under conditions different from those in which they should be performed in everyday life. For example, a "hyperactive" child may "know" how to sit down but may rarely do so in a classroom setting. In society at large, increases may be desirable in a number of adaptive behaviors such as eating nutritious foods, preventing illness and injury, driving safely, and working productively at a job. These are not problem behaviors of special populations, but behaviors whose increase can improve life for the individual.

In the above cases, low-frequency behaviors have to be increased, new behaviors have to be established, or behaviors have to be developed in new situations. Because these goals entail developing or increasing behavior, reinforcement techniques are appropriate. Moreover, even in cases where the primary intent is to eliminate undesirable behaviors, reinforcement can play a major role. Reinforcement can develop socially appropriate behaviors that replace the undesirable behaviors. The present chapter considers positive and negative reinforcement. Greater attention is given to positive reinforcement because it plays a central role in almost all behavioral interventions in applied settings.

POSITIVE REINFORCEMENT

Positive reinforcement refers to an increase in the frequency of a response following the presentation of a positive reinforcer. Whether a particular event is a positive reinforcer is defined by its effects on behavior. If response frequency increases when followed by the event, it is a positive reinforcer. Defining a reinforcer by effects on behavior appears to be circular. However, the effectiveness of a reinforcer need not be limited to a particular behavior in a single situation. A reinforcer effective in altering one response in one situation may be effective in altering other behaviors in other situations as well. In addition, the Premack principle, discussed earlier, provides a way to assess whether an event is a reinforcer independently of the effects on behavior. Reinforcing consequences are the behaviors in a person's repertoire that have a relatively high probability.

Basic Requirements for Effective Application

Reinforcement programs consist of applying consequences to behavior. For reinforcement delivery to be effective, several basic conditions need to be met. These conditions are extremely significant because they determine the extent to which behavior will change or, indeed, whether behavior will change at all.

Contingent Application of Consequences.   The most fundamental condition for the effective application of a reinforcer is that the reinforcer be contingent on behavior. This means that the reinforcer is provided only if the desired response is performed. If the reinforcer is not provided contingently, behavior is not likely to change. Technically, noncontingent application of the reinforcer would not constitute reinforcement.

The contingent application of reinforcers is not necessarily an all-or-none matter. For example, when reinforcement is described to parents, teachers, and others who wish to implement behavioral programs, they often state that they have already used reinforcement, and with little or no success. However, reinforcement is usually carried out haphazardly in everyday situations. It is delivered contingently on some occasions and noncontingently on other occasions.

The differences between contingent and noncontingent reinforcement are dramatic and clear. Contingent reinforcement usually leads to marked behavior change; noncontingent reinforcement leads to little or no change; and reinforcement administered contingently on some occasions but not on others leads to performance somewhere in the middle (Baer & Wolf, 1970; Kazdin, 1973a; Redd & Birnbrauer, 1969). One might ask how noncontingent reinforcement can lead to any change in behavior. The reason is that noncontingent reinforcement accidentally follows the desired behavior on some occasions and hence constitutes weak and intermittent reinforcement for the behavior. Nevertheless, when the goal is to change behavior, noncontingent reinforcement should be avoided.

Delay of Reinforcement.   The effectiveness of reinforcement depends on the delay between the behavior and the delivery of reinforcing consequences (e.g., food, praise, points). Responses in close proximity to reinforcement are learned better than responses remote from reinforcement (Domjan & Burkhard, 1986). Thus, to maximize the effect of reinforcement, a reinforcer should be delivered *immediately* after the target response. If this is not done, a response different from the target response may be performed during the intervening period. If that happens, the intervening response will be immediately reinforced, whereas the target response will be reinforced after a delay. For example, children are often praised (or punished) for a behavior long after the behavior has been performed. If a child straightens up his or her room, a parent would do well to provide praise immediately. If praise is postponed until the end of the day, a variety of intervening responses may occur (including, perhaps, messing up the room). Similarly, in classroom settings, children are often told how "good" they are when they are on the verge of becoming restless or disruptive. The teacher may say that the class was well behaved in the morning and that she hopes it will remain well behaved. Such praise will be minimally effective because of the delay in delivering it.

Immediate reinforcement is especially important when the target response is being developed. After a response has been performed consistently, the amount of time between the response and reinforcement can be increased without a decrement in performance. For example, in classroom settings, students sometimes receive points or candy daily while high rates of academic behavior develop. However, after such behavior has stabilized, the reinforcers can be delivered every other day or every few days without a deleterious effect on performance. If a program begins with delayed reinforcement, behavior may not change at all or may change less rapidly than it would if reinforcement were immediate. After a behavior has been well developed, it is desirable to change from immediate to delayed reinforcement so that the behavior is not dependent on immediate consequences. A great many consequences in everyday life (accomplishments, wages, grades, and fame) follow long after a series of responses has been completed.

Magnitude or Amount of Reinforcement. The amount of reinforcement delivered for a response also determines the extent to which the response will be performed. The greater the amount of the reinforcer delivered for a response, the more frequent the response will be. The amount of the reinforcer can usually be specified in such terms as quantity of food, number of points, or amount of money.

Although the magnitude of reinforcement is directly related to performance, there are limits to this relationship. An unlimited amount of reinforcement does not necessarily maintain a high rate of performance. A reinforcer loses its effect when it is given in excessive amounts. This phenomenon is referred to as *satiation*. Hence, the effect of increasing reinforcement is limited by the point at which the individual becomes satiated. Satiation is especially evident with primary reinforcers such as food, water, and sex. In excessive amounts, each of these reinforcers quickly loses its reinforcing properties and may even become aversive. Of course, satiation of primary reinforcers is temporary; they regain their reinforcing value as deprivation increases. Secondary, or conditioned, reinforcers, such as praise, attention, and tokens, are also subject to satiation (Gewirtz & Baer, 1958; Winkler, 1971), but to a lesser extent than primary reinforcers.

The effect of the amount of a reinforcer on behavior depends on the satiation and deprivation states of the individual with respect to that reinforcer. An event (e.g., money) is not likely to be very effective as a reinforcer if an individual has unlimited access to it. If an individual is partially deprived of an event, a smaller amount of a reinforcer is needed to change behavior. In most everyday situations, people do not have unlimited access to reinforcing events (e.g., free time in a classroom situation or time with friends for children at home), and thus they normally undergo various mild forms of deprivation. This means that a variety of events can be effective as reinforcers without introducing deprivation.

Quality or Type of Reinforcer. The quality of a reinforcer, unlike the amount of a reinforcer, is not usually specifiable in physical terms (Domjan &

Burkhard, 1986) but is usually determined by the preference of the client. Reinforcers that are highly preferred lead to greater performance than those that are less preferred. For a given client, it is usually not difficult to specify highly preferred activities. Behaviors engaged in frequently provide a helpful indication of highly preferred reinforcers. However, preference for a particular reinforcer may change over time. Yet, certain types of reinforcers, elaborated later, tend to result in higher performance than others and to determine the extent of behavior change. For example, token reinforcement is often more effective than praise in altering behavior, and both of these are usually more effective than feedback.

Schedule of Reinforcement.   *Schedule of reinforcement refers to the rule denoting how many or which specific responses will be reinforced.* Reinforcers are always administered according to some schedule. In the simplest schedule, a response is reinforced each time it occurs. This schedule is referred to as *continuous reinforcement.* For example, to train a child to follow instructions, reinforcement can be given each time the child responds appropriately. On the other hand, reinforcement may be delivered after only some of the appropriate responses. This is referred to as *intermittent reinforcement.*

There are important differences between continuous and intermittent reinforcement while the behaviors are being reinforced and after reinforcement has been withdrawn. During the acquisition or reinforcement phase, a behavior developed with continuous reinforcement is performed at a higher rate than a behavior developed with intermittent reinforcement. Thus, while a behavior is developing, a continuous or "generous" schedule of reinforcement should be used. However, the advantage of continuous reinforcement is compensated after the reinforcement ceases. In extinction, behaviors that were continuously reinforced diminish at a much more rapid rate than do behaviors that were reinforced intermittently.

The difference between responses developed with continuous reinforcement and responses developed with intermittent reinforcement is apparent in examples from everyday experience. A familiar response that is reinforced every time is depositing coins in a vending machine and pressing the lever or button. Barring mechanical failure, the response is followed by the reinforcer (e.g., cigarettes, candy) almost every time. Once reinforcement no longer occurs, this response (depositing coins) follows a pattern identical to that of continuous reinforcement. As soon as the reinforcer (i.e., the product) is no longer delivered, extinction is almost immediate. If a vending machine does not deliver the reinforcer, few individuals will repeatedly put coins into it unless there is some evidence that it has been repaired. *For behaviors previously developed with continous reinforcement, extinction is rapid.*

A similar response—putting coins into a machine and pulling a lever— might be maintained by intermittent reinforcement, as in the case of slot machines. Sometimes putting money into a slot machine is reinforced (with money); many other times it is not. If money were no longer delivered (i.e., extinction), the response would continue to be performed at a high rate before extinguishing. It is difficult to discriminate when extinction begins on a highly intermittent schedule of reinforcement. The resistance of a response to extinction depends on how intermittent or *thin* the reinforcement schedule is. *Resistance to extinction is greater if very few responses are reinforced than if many responses are reinforced.*

The advantage of continuous reinforcement is that performance occurs at a high level while behavior is reinforced. The advantage of intermittent reinforcement is that resistance to extinction is greater when reinforcement is discontinued. Both advantages can be obtained by developing behavior with continuous reinforcement until a high rate of behavior has been well established and then, to ensure response maintenance, changing the schedule to intermittent reinforcement and making it increasingly intermittent.

Another advantage of intermittent reinforcement is its efficient use of available reinforcers. Intermittent reinforcement allows delivery of a few reinforcers for a large number of responses. Moreover, if reinforcers are administered only a few times, satiation is less likely to occur. For example, with intermittent food reinforcement, the client is not likely to become full quickly and thus temporarily unresponsive to food. A further advantage of intermittent reinforcement is that it requires less time for administering reinforcers than does continuous reinforcement.

Intermittent reinforcement can be scheduled in many ways (Catania, 1984), only a few of which will be considered here. Two simple types of reinforcement schedules can be distinguished. Reinforcement can be contingent upon the emission of a certain *number of responses*. This is referred to as a *ratio schedule* because the schedule specifies the ratio of the total number of responses to the one that is reinforced. Reinforcement can also be contingent upon the *amount of time* that passes. This is referred to as an *interval schedule*. With a ratio schedule, the amount of time that passes before the subject performs the response is irrelevant. The behavior of the subject controls the frequency of reinforcement. With an interval schedule, the number of responses performed is irrelevant as long as one response is performed after the prescribed amount of time has elapsed. The frequency of reinforcement is partially determined by the clock.

In both ratio and interval schedules of reinforcement, the requirement for reinforcement can be *fixed,* so that it is the same requirement every time. On the other hand, the requirement can be *variable,* so that it is different from time to time. Four simple schedules of reinforcement will be discussed: fixed ratio (FR), variable ratio (VR), fixed interval (FI), and variable interval (VI).

A *fixed-ratio schedule* requires that an unvarying number of responses be performed before a response is reinforced. The number following FR specifies which response will be reinforced. For example, FR : 1 specifies that only one response is required for the reinforcer to be delivered. (FR : 1 is also called continuous reinforcement, because every response is reinforced.) FR : 10 denotes that every 10th response is reinforced.

Performance under fixed-ratio schedules differs to some extent depending on whether the ratios are small or large. Characteristically, there is a temporary pause in responding after reinforcement is delivered, and then a rapid rise in response rate until the ratio is completed and reinforcement is again delivered. The pause after responding is a function of the ratio, with large ratios (when few responses are reinforced) producing longer pauses. Once the responses resume, reinforcement is maximized by performing all of the responses as quickly as possible. Examples of an FR schedule include any instance in which the reinforcer is delivered for a certain number of responses. For example, the behavior of factory workers who are paid according to how much they produce is reinforced on an FR schedule (commonly referred to as piecework). For every certain number of responses (products produced), the reinforcer (money) is earned. If several responses are required for reinforcement, there may be a temporary pause (no production) immediately after reinforcement.

A *variable-ratio schedule* specifies that reinforcement is to occur after a certain number of responses. However, that number *varies* unpredictably from occasion to occasion. On the average, a certain number of responses are performed before reinforcement is delivered. The number following VR specifies the average number of responses required for reinforcement. For example, VR : 5 indicates that, on the average, five responses are to be performed before the reinforcer is delivered. The second response may be reinforced on some occasions whereas the eighth response may be reinforced on other occasions. A different number of responses may be required each time. Across all occasions, however, reinforcement is delivered on the average of the number specified (e.g., five in the VR : 5 schedule). Of course, the number one cannot be used in a VR schedule, because using that number would be equivalent to reinforcing every response, which is a continuous reinforcement or FR : 1 schedule.

Performance under VR schedules is consistently high. The pauses after responding in FR schedules can be virtually eliminated with a VR schedule unless the average ratio is very long. Immediately after a response is reinforced, the subject begins to respond because the next reinforcer may follow only a few responses. Performance continues at a high rate until reinforcement is delivered, and immediately resumes again. Behavior previously maintained under a VR schedule extinguishes more slowly than behavior previously maintained under an FR schedule, particularly if the variable schedule requires many responses for reinforcement. Performance is relatively persistent and consistent following a VR schedule. Thus, VR schedules are highly suited to forestalling extinction. Before reinforcement is withdrawn, the ratio can gradually be made very *thin* by increasing the number of responses required for reinforcement.

Examples of VR schedules are abundant in everyday experience. The behavior of a fisherman is controlled, in part, by VR reinforcement. A fish (reinforcer) is not caught every time a line is tossed into the water (response). The response is reinforced only some of the time, and the variable nature of the schedule ensures that extinction will not take place rapidly. Slot machines, mentioned earlier, represent a dramatic application of VR schedules. Since any response can be reinforced, the person playing the slot machine usually performs at a consistently high rate. His or her performance is unlikely to extinguish for long periods of time.

A *fixed-interval schedule* requires that an interval of time (usually expressed in minutes) pass before the reinforcer is available. The first response that occurs after the interval passes is reinforced. In such a schedule, of course, the interval is unvarying. For example, in an FI : 1 schedule, the first response after one minute passes is reinforced. An *interval schedule* requires that only one response be performed after the prescribed interval has elapsed. While this efficiency in responding rarely occurs, the characteristics of responses to FI schedules are distinct. Following reinforcement, there is usually a pronounced pause, during which responses are performed. This does not interfere with receiving reinforcement, because a response before the appropriate time elapses is never reinforced. Only if the pause is longer than the fixed interval will the subject postpone reinforcement. FI schedules lead to less consistent rates of responding than do FR schedules because nonresponding immediately after reinforcement during an FI schedule does not postpone reinforcement, as it does with an FR schedule.

An example of an FI response pattern in everyday experience is looking to see whether one's mail has arrived. For most individuals, mail delivery is once a day, with (fairly) fixed periods of time (24 hours) before deliveries. The response (looking for mail in the mailbox) is reinforced (finding mail) daily. Immediately after reinforcement, there is no longer a response. One does not resume looking for mail again until the next day, when the 24-hour interval is almost complete. Looking for mail then increases until reinforcement is obtained, at which time the pause after reinforcement is again evident.

A *variable-interval* schedule specifies the *average length* of the intervals required for reinforcement. For example, a VI : 10 schedule denotes that, on the average, 10 minutes must elapse before a response is reinforced. On any given occasion, the interval may be more or less than 10 minutes. The reinforcer is delivered for the first response *after* the interval elapses. The studying behavior of students follows a pattern characteristic of a VI schedule if the instructor gives "pop quizzes." The interval between quizzes is unpredictable and varies from quiz to quiz. Studying tends to be relatively consistent under such a schedule. In general, responding tends to be higher under VI schedules than under FI schedules.

As already mentioned, it is desirable to reinforce continuously at the beginning of a behavior change program. In practice, it may be impossible to closely observe behavior constantly to ensure that every instance of the target behavior is reinforced. However, an almost continuous or rich schedule can be used initially before changing to increasingly intermittent schedules.

In selecting an intermittent schedule, both the characteristic response pattern of the schedule and practical exigencies should be considered. Although fixed schedules may be convenient to administer, the characteristic response pattern under such schedules includes pauses or lapses in performance of the reinforced behavior. For example, in a psychiatric hospital, ward attendants may reinforce behavior on an FI schedule. At the end of the timed periods (e.g., 30 minutes), staff may administer reinforcers (praise, tokens) to patients who behaved "appropriately." However, it is very likely that the desired performance of the patients will be high near the end of the interval, with pauses immediately after reinforcement. Variable schedules can reduce inconsistency in performance. Interval schedules tend to be easily administered, but client performance is usually higher under ratio schedules. Under ratio schedules, high rates of responding speed up the delivery of reinforcement. Apart from their influence on the development of behavior, reinforcement schedules have important implications for the maintenance of behavior (see Chapter 11).

TYPES OF REINFORCERS

The above discussion suggests that the effects of reinforcement can be maximized by reinforcing behavior immediately with a potent reinforcer that is delivered on a continuous (rich) reinforcement schedule. As behavior develops, reinforcement should be increasingly intermittent and delayed. An obviously important task is selecting a potent reinforcer. Different types of reinforcers vary in their effects on behavior and in their ease of administration in applied settings.

Food and Other Consumables

Food qualifies as a primary reinforcer because its reinforcing value is unlearned. Of course, food preferences are learned, which make some foods more reinforcing than others and some foods not reinforcing at all unless the individual has been deprived of all food. Because food is a primary reinforcer, it is very powerful. Studies have occasionally used food as a reinforcer, including cereal, candy, crackers, cookies, soft drinks, and ice cream.

Nonfood consumables have also been used as reinforcers. For example, cigarettes and gum may be strong reinforcers for some individuals. Because they are not primary reinforcers, their appeal does not extend to as many individuals as does food. Although the reinforcing properties of nonfood consumables are learned, eventually the reinforcing power of these consumables resembles that of primary reinforcers. Deprivation of these consumables may build up in a fashion analogous to that of food. In any case, when nonfood consumables are reinforcers, they tend to be very effective.

Because food is a primary reinforcer, its effects should apply widely among different client populations. However, food is not used very frequently in applied settings. The major reason is that food is not ordinarily present at or a part of the everyday situations in which behavioral interventions are applied.

Early applications of behavior modification and applications with institutional-ized populations have occasionally reported the use of food.

An interesting use of food as a reinforcer was reported with hospitalized physically handicapped children 1–3½ years of age (Riordan, Iwata, Finney, Wohl, & Stanley, 1984). These children also suffered from food refusal or high food selectivity. They would not eat enough food, would spit out food fed to them, or would eat a limited range of foods that were not sufficient in vitamins or minerals. During mealtime, several different foods were fed to the children (presented one bite at a time) to identify the foods that they ate and preferred. The preferred foods were used as a reinforcer for eating a bite of other foods. For example, one of the children preferred dry cereal and graham crackers. These were used as reinforcers. When the child ate a bite of some other food (fruit, vegetable, meat, or starch), the preferred food was immediately de-livered. At first, the preferred food was presented with the target food for a few bites; then the preferred food was delivered immediately after a bite of a target food. After several trials, the preferred food (reinforcer) was administered only intermittently. The use of preferred food increased the bites and consumption of a broader range of nutritionally balanced food.

Important Considerations in Using Food and Other Consumables.   The effectiveness of food and other consumables depends heavily on the depriva-tion state of the individual. If the individual is not at least partially deprived, food may be a weak reinforcer. Investigators sometimes use food reinforce-ment prior to mealtime or during mealtime itself. A difficulty with food as a reinforcer is that its reinforcement value may decline rather quickly. Even if the individual is hungry before training, as training proceeds on a given day, hunger and the reinforcing value of food may decline.

The effectiveness of food reinforcement depends on the type of food used. Specific foods used in a given program may not be reinforcing for particular individuals. For example, although ice cream may serve as a reinforcer for most children, the flavor will influence its reinforcing properties for many individuals. When a single food or consumable is relied on, the possibility exists that the event will not be effective with a number of people. Moreover, the preferences of a given individual change from time to time, so a single food or other consumable may have short-lived reinforcing properties.

There are potential problems in the administration of food reinforcers. The delivery and consumption of food after a response sometimes interrupt ongoing behavior. For example, if a special education classroom teacher distributed candy to her students while they were working attentively on an assignment, they might be distracted momentarily from the task. Also, the consumption of the reinforcer may temporarily distract the students.

Moreover, it may be difficult to dispense food and other consumables immediately because they are cumbersome. The setting in which food is used dictates the ease with which a particular type of food can be dispensed. Parents at home and staff in some institutions may be able to dispense food readily, depending on the type of food and on the ease of carrying a supply (e.g., small candies). However, in everyday life, parents, teachers, peers, employers, and others cannot easily carry food or other consumables with them all of the time for use as reinforcers.

A related problem is that food is not easily administered to several individuals in a group immediately after behavior has been performed. Because its administration to several individuals takes some time (e.g., selecting the quantity of food or passing a piece to each individual), food is not particularly well suited to group situations in which everyone receives reinforcers. Many programs using food have been conducted on an individual basis rather than in groups.

Finally, ethical and legal considerations may restrict the use of food and other consumables. These reinforcers are most effective when clients are deprived. However, deprivation of food is ethically objectionable, and also violates the legal rights of clients. Hence, food deprivation is not a viable treatment alternative. When food is used as a reinforcer, clients cannot be deprived of the food they would normally receive. Thus, the food and consumables used as reinforcers are often given over and above the food normally available to clients. Because clients normally have access to food, the extra food used as a reinforcer may be less potent than it would be if they were deprived. In part because of concern for the ethical and legal rights of clients and in part because of the availability of alternative reinforcers, food and other consumables are not the most frequently used reinforcers in applied settings.

Food and other consumables are used in situations where other events such as approval are not effective. For example, in institutions for severely and profoundly mentally retarded persons, food reinforcement is used to develop such behaviors as feeding oneself or using sounds, words, or gestures to communicate. In these applications, other reinforcers are often not available. Perhaps as important, food is useful in establishing the reinforcing properties of other events, such as praise, feedback, attention, smiles, and physical contact. Programs using food and other consumables invariably pair the delivery of the reinforcer with praise and other social events, so that these latter events can be used to change behavior.

Social Reinforcers

Social reinforcers such as verbal praise, attention, physical contact (including affectionate or approving touches, pats, and hand holding), and facial expressions (including smiles, eye contact, nods of approval, and winks) are conditioned reinforcers. Numerous studies have shown that attention or praise from a parent, teacher, or peer exerts considerable control over behavior.

For example, in one program, praise was used to alter the behavior of a 13-year-old boy named Tom in a seventh-grade classroom (Kirby & Shields, 1972). Tom was of average intelligence but was doing poorly on his class assignments, particularly the arithmetic assignments. Also, he rarely paid attention to the lesson and constantly had to be reminded to work. Praise was used to improve his performance on arithmetic assignments. Each day in class, after he completed the arithmetic assignment, he was praised for correct answers on his arithmetic worksheet. At first, every couple of responses was praised; but the number of correct problems required for praise was gradually increased. The praise consisted merely of saying "Good work," "Excellent job," and similar things. Figure 5–1 (upper portion) shows the improvements in

FIGURE 5–1

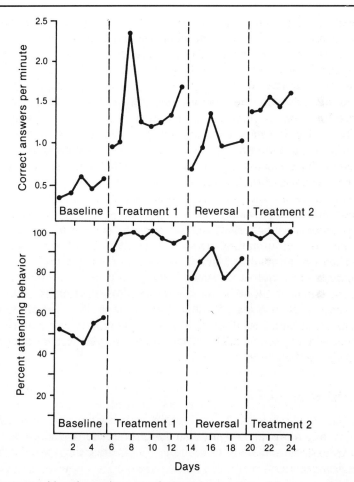

Number of correct arithmetic answers per minute and percentage of times scored as attending behavior as a function of baseline and treatment conditions.

SOURCE: Kirby, F. D., & Shields, F. (1972). Modification of arithmetic response rate and attending behavior in a seventh-grade student. *Journal of Applied Behavior Analysis, 5,* 79–84. Copyright 1972 by the Society for the Experimental Analysis of Behavior, Inc.

Tom's rate of correct answers per minute in the treatment phases of ABAB design. The lower portion shows that his attentive behavior also improved even though it was not focused on directly.

A number of other investigations have shown that reinforcing academic performance not only improves the specific target behaviors but also increases classroom attentiveness and reduces disruptive behavior (Ruggles & LeBlanc, 1982). In most classroom studies, teacher attention consists primarily of verbal praise supplemented with facial expressions and physical contact. However, nonverbal teacher attention alone (consisting of smiles, physical contact, and approving nods contingent upon appropriate behavior) also improves classroom deportment (Kazdin & Klock, 1973).

Important Considerations in Using Social Reinforcers.   Social consequences have a variety of advantages as reinforcers. First, they are easily administered in everyday life and in a large number of situations. Providing praise takes little time, so there is no delay in praising a number of individuals immediately. Indeed, praise can be delivered to a group as a whole, as in a classroom.

Second, praise need not disrupt the behavior that is reinforced. A person can be praised or receive a pat on the back while continuing to engage in appropriate behavior. Third, praise is a generalized conditioned reinforcer because it has been paired with many reinforcing events. As mentioned earlier, conditioned reinforcers are less subject to satiation than are food and other consumable items. Fourth, attention and praise are "naturally occurring" reinforcers employed in everyday life. Some reinforcers (such as food and other consumables) do not normally follow desirable behavior such as paying attention in a classroom, interacting socially with others, or working on a job. In contrast, social reinforcers such as attention from others or credit for a job well done often follow socially adaptive behaviors. Finally, because social reinforcers in everyday life may continue to follow those behaviors developed with social reinforcers in a treatment or training program, these behaviors may be more readily maintained outside the program setting than behaviors developed with other reinforcers.

Before embarking on a program employing social reinforcement, it is important to bear a few considerations in mind. Praise, approval, and physical contact are not reinforcing for everyone. Indeed, for some individuals, praise may even be aversive (Walker, Hops, & Greenwood, 1981). Because social events (praise, approval, and physical contact) are employed in everyday life, it is important to establish them as reinforcers by pairing them with events that are already reinforcers.

High-Probability Behaviors

When persons are given the opportunity to engage in various behaviors, they will select certain activities with a higher frequency than they select other activities. Activities selected with a higher frequency can often serve as reinforcers for activities selected with a lower frequency. As a practical guide, allowing persons to engage in preferred activities and to earn various privileges can reinforce behavior. Laboratory research has attempted to identify higher-frequency behaviors by observing performance or by depriving animals of certain sorts of activities and thereby making such activities more likely in the future. In clinical applications, higher-probability behaviors are often inferred from the client's expressed verbal preferences or from seeing what the client actually does in his or her free time.

High-probability behaviors have been used effectively in several applied programs. For example, Allen and Iwata (1980) increased the extent to which mentally retarded adults engaged in daily exercise as part of their rehabilitation program. During baseline, opportunities and prompts were provided to encourage these clients to exercise (e.g., knee bends, sit-ups) and to play games involving physical activity (e.g., various ball games). Playing games, the more frequent activity, was used to reinforce exercising. A group contingency was implemented in which everyone had to complete a minimum number of exercises before the games could be played. Exercising (lower-probability behavior) increased in frequency when playing games (higher-probability behavior) was contingent upon this behavior.

Important Considerations in Using High-Probability Behaviors. High-probability behaviors offer distinct advantages as reinforcers. In most settings, activities are privileges that are readily available. For example, in the home, access to television, peers, or the family automobile is likely to be associated with high-probability behaviors, depending on the person's age. At school, access to recess, free time, games, and entertaining reading materials may serve a similar function. In hospital and rehabilitation facilities, engaging in special recreational events or access to more desirable living quarters can also be used. In short, activities, and privileges that can be made contingent upon performance are usually available in any setting. Hence, extra reinforcers (e.g., candy or money) need not be introduced into the setting.

There are limitations in using high-probability behaviors as reinforcing events. First, access to an activity cannot always immediately follow low-probability behavior. For example, in a classroom setting, access to recess or games cannot readily be used to reinforce behavior immediately. Such access may need to be delayed, so that the reinforcing activity (e.g., games) does not interrupt the task (e.g., writing a story). After the lower-probability behavior has been established, access to the higher-probability behavior can usually be delayed to a more convenient time without loss of the behavior. Also, intermediate rewards such as praise or a token (exchangeable for the activity) can help bridge the delay between behavior and the reinforcing activity, so that some reinforcement is provided immediately. Thus, the child can be told by the parent that because a specific behavior (playing cooperatively with a sibling) was "Great!" (praise), he or she can stay up 15 minutes extra at bedtime. The praise is delivered immediately, an important condition for effective reinforcement delivery. The praise may in fact be sufficient to develop the behavior at a high rate. However, the extra bedtime privilege may well add to the effectiveness by introducing an important reinforcer.

Second, providing an activity is sometimes an all-or-none enterprise, so that it is either earned or not earned. This can limit flexibility in administering the reinforcer. For example, in institutions for psychiatric patients or delinquents, access to overnight passes and trips to a nearby town are sometimes used as reinforcing activities. These activities cannot be parceled out so that "portions" of them are earned. They have to be given in their entirety or not at all. If a client's behavior comes very near but does not quite meet the performance criterion for reinforcement a decision has to be made whether to provide the reinforcer. One solution is to shape behavior by initially setting low criteria for earning the activity. Gradually, the criteria for earning the reinforcer are increased. Another solution is to incorporate many privileges and activities into the contingency system. Different behaviors or varying degrees of a given behavior can then be reinforced with different privileges or with a choice among privileges.

Third, relying on one or two activities as reinforcers runs the risk that some individuals may not find them reinforcing. Since preferences for activities may be idiosyncratic, different activities need to be available. One alternative is to provide free time as the reinforcer, so that individuals can choose from a variety of activities.

A final consideration in using activities and privileges is that in many institutions activities must be freely available to the clients. Activities that might be made contingent upon performance are delivered independently of the client's performance. For example, it is required by law that many activities (e.g., opportunities for exercise, socialization) be provided noncontingently to ensure that institutionalized persons such as psychiatric patients, delinquents, and mentally retarded children and adults are not deprived of basic human rights. Hence, the person who develops a behavior change program has to provide special activities over and above those offered as part of routine care.

Feedback

Providing information about how a person has performed can serve as a reinforcer. Such feedback is a conditioned reinforcer because it is usually associated with the delivery of other reinforcing events. Feedback is implicit in the delivery of any reinforcer because it indicates which responses those who provide reinforcement regard as appropriate or desirable. Thus, when reinforcers such as food, praise, activities, or points are provided, a client receives feedback on how well he or she is doing. However, feedback can be employed independently of explicit approval or other reinforcers. Individuals can be informed of their behavior or of the extent to which their behavior has changed. Feedback refers to *knowledge of results* of one's performance and does not necessarily include additional events that may be reinforcing in their own right.

In one project, feedback was used to control the speeding of drivers on a highway entering a residential area (Van Houten, Nau, & Marini, 1980). Speeding was measured by a radar unit concealed in a litter can near the highway. After baseline observations, feedback was provided in the form of a conspicuous road sign that indicated the percentage of drivers not speeding on the previous day and the best percentage record obtained to date. The speed limit was 50 kilometers (31 miles) per hour. However, the police felt that 66 kilometers (41 miles) per hour was still safe, so this speed was used to define whether someone was speeding. The effects of feedback (posting the percentage of drivers who sped) are illustrated in Figure 5–2. The figure shows that speeding was reduced each time the feedback system was in effect. During the 26-week follow-up period, when the feedback system was used on a weekly rather than a daily basis (on a randomly chosen day each week), the effects of the program were maintained. Interestingly, during the feedback phase, a 57 percent reduction in the number of accidents was also noted compared to the two-year period before feedback had been implemented.

Feedback has also been used to train juvenile diabetics (aged 10 to 16 years) to measure the glucose content of urine (Epstein, Figueroa, Farkas, & Beck, 1981). Accurate assessment is essential to control diabetes. Diabetics assess their glucose levels several times a day and make important decisions about diet and exercise to maintain acceptable levels of serum glucose. The testing procedure is complex; it requires mixing urine with water and a reactive agent and interpreting glucose levels from what may be subtle variations in the color of the solution. When diabetics who had difficulty in assessing and

FIGURE 5–2

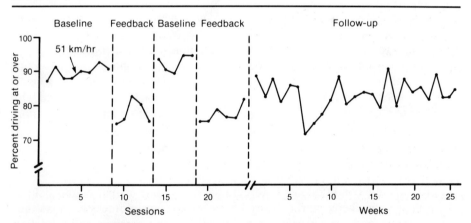

Percentage of motorists driving above the speed limit (50 km/hr or 31 mph) across baseline and feedback conditions. During the follow-up phase, the feedback procedure was conducted on a weekly basis rather than on a daily basis.

SOURCE: Van Houten, R., Nau, P., & Marini, Z. (1980). An analysis of public posting in reducing speeding behavior on an urban highway. *Journal of Applied Behavior Analysis, 13,* 383–395. Copyright 1980 by the Society for the Experimental Analysis of Behavior, Inc.

controlling their glucose levels were given feedback on their accuracy in interpreting the results of glucose tests, their accuracy increased from 36 percent to 72 percent. A comparison group that received practice without feedback failed to improve.

An important area involving feedback is *biofeedback*. Biofeedback consists of providing information to people about various physiological processes such as blood pressure, heart rate, muscle tension, and brain waves. Immediate information is provided to help clients learn to control various bodily processes. Biofeedback represents an important area of research in its own right and will be discussed later (Chapter 9).

Important Considerations in Using Feedback.   Because of the ease with which feedback can be applied, it has been employed with a variety of client populations and in a variety of settings. Feedback can be readily employed when there is an explicit performance criterion, such as academic achievement or work productivity. In other situations, various criteria can be set, such as cigarettes smoked, calories consumed, or days of exercise. Daily feedback can convey how well the client is doing in relation to the criterion set. Evidence suggests that specifying a criterion for performance is essential (Locke, Cartledge, & Koeppel, 1968). Without such a criterion, at least an implicit one, the desired level of performance may be unclear.

An extremely important consideration in using feedback is that its effects are often equivocal. Although feedback has often been effective, it has been ineffective or only moderately effective in several applications (e.g., Hall et al., 1972; Kazdin, 1973c; Van Houten, Hill, & Parsons, 1975). Feedback is usually less effective alone than in combination with other reinforcers such as praise or tokens. Hence, feedback is one of the less potent methods of altering behavior.

Programs based on feedback are often easier to implement than other reinforcement programs, such as token economies. Also, people who implement a feedback program may be more favorably disposed to delivering feedback alone than to providing extrinsic reinforcers. For these reasons, it may be useful to begin with a program based on feedback, perhaps paired with praise, and then to resort to a more potent source of reinforcement and a more complex program if the desired goals have not been achieved.

Tokens

Tokens are conditioned reinforcers such as poker chips, coins, tickets, stars, points, or check marks. They are generalized reinforcers because they can be exchanged for a variety of reinforcing events referred to as *back-up reinforcers*. A reinforcement system based on tokens is referred to as a *token economy*. In a token economy, tokens function in the same way that money does in national economic systems. Earned tokens are used to purchase back-up reinforcers, including various goods and services. The back-up reinforcers usually include food and other consumables, activities, and privileges. The rate at which tokens can be exchanged for back-up reinforcers must be specified, so that it is clear how many tokens are required to purchase various reinforcers. The target behaviors are made explicit, as in most programs, along with the number of tokens that are administered for their performance.

The tokens need to be established as conditioned reinforcers, because they have no reinforcing properties in their own right. For some populations, it is sufficient to explain that they can be exchanged for various goods. After the explanation, the tokens take on a value that is maintained by the actual exchange of tokens for other reinforcers. For individuals whose behavior is not controlled by instructions about the value of tokens, the tokens can be given noncontingently a few times. Immediately after they have been delivered, they can be exchanged or traded for a back-up reinforcer.

Token economies have been used extensively in special education, remedial, and "normal" classrooms. For example, a token economy was used to improve the behavior of 15 first-grade students whose academic and social behaviors were considered severe enough to interfere with their promotion into a regular second-grade classroom (Breyer & Allen, 1975). The program was directed at eliminating disruptive behavior (e.g., hitting peers) and improving appropriate on-task behavior (e.g., working on assignments, responding appropriately to the teacher). After baseline, the program began by having the teacher praise appropriate behavior and ignore inappropriate behavior. Although praise improved student performance, additional gains were needed. Hence, token reinforcement was used in which the students received points at various intervals depending on how well they were working. They exchanged the points for prizes ranging in value from $0.05 to $1.50 at a "good-study store" in class. The effects of the program, illustrated in Figure 5–3, show rather clearly that the token system greatly improved on-task behavior.

Token economies in classroom settings have led to benefits other than improved classroom behavior. Applications in elementary and secondary school settings have improved classroom performance in reading, writing, composition, and arithmetic. Improvements in these skills have also been evidenced in performance on standardized achievement tests and grades and in reductions in suspensions and expulsions from school (e.g., Bushell, 1978; Heaton & Safer, 1982).

Token economics have been used extensively in psychiatric hospitals. For example, in one of the most carefully evaluated programs, patients received tokens (colored plastic strips) for such behaviors as attending activities on the ward, group meetings, and therapy sessions and for grooming, making one's bed, showering, engaging in appropriate mealtime behaviors, and socially interacting (Paul & Lentz, 1977). Tokens could be exchanged for a variety of backup events such as purchasing cosmetics, candy, cigarettes, and clothing; renting chairs or bedside stands for one's room; ordering items from a mail-order catalog; using a piano, record player, or radio; spending time in a lounge; watching television; and having a private room and sleeping late. As

FIGURE 5–3

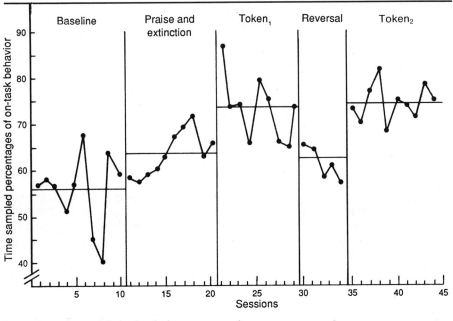

Percentage of on-task behavior during treatment phases.

SOURCE: Breyer, N. L., & Allen, G. J. (1975). Effects of implementing a token economy on teacher attending behavior. *Journal of Applied Behavior Analysis, 8,* 373–380. Copyright 1975 by the Society for the Experimental Analysis of Behavior, Inc.

patients improved in the ward, they advanced to higher levels within the program, in which more reinforcers were available and higher criteria were set for performance. Patients could "buy" themselves off the system by doing well and carried a "credit card" that allowed them free access to all of the available reinforcers as long as their performance was up to standards. The program was very successful in reducing bizarre behaviors, improving social interaction and communication skills, and developing participation in activities. The gains were reflected in the number of patients discharged and in their adjustment in the community from 1½ to 5 years after termination of the program.

A well-known program based on a token economy has been used to rehabilitate predelinquent youths who have committed various offenses (e.g., theft, fighting, school truancy, and academic failure) (Fixsen, Phillips, Phillips, & Wolf, 1976). The program was conducted at a home-style cottage setting, called Achievement Place, managed by two houseparents. Behaviors that earned points included watching the news, reading newspapers, keeping oneself neat and clean, performing chores around the house, and receiving good grades at school. Points could be lost for poor grades, aggressive talk (making threats), violation of rules, lying, stealing, lateness, fighting, and other disruptive behaviors. Points were used to purchase such privileges as staying up late, going downtown, watching TV, using tools, riding one's bicycle, and receiving an allowance. Interestingly, the boys participated actively in running the program by supervising one another's work, recording their own behavior, and developing and enforcing rules among their peers. The program has been shown to alter a variety of behaviors (e.g., social interaction, completion of homework, and performance of chores) in the home setting. Youths participating in the program committed fewer criminal offenses in the community and had fewer contacts with police than did delinquents placed on probation or in settings where the program was not in effect (Kirigin, Braukmann, Atwater, & Wolf, 1982; Kirigin, Wolf, Braukmann, Fixsen, & Phillips, 1979).

Token economies have been used as part of treatment for a number of medical problems. For example, a token system was used to help an 82-year-old patient who had suffered a massive heart attack (Dapcich-Miura & Hovell, 1979). After leaving the hospital, he was instructed to increase his physical activity gradually, to eat foods high in potassium (e.g., orange juice and bananas), and to take medication.[1] However, the patient rarely walked and neglected his diet and medication. A token reinforcement program was devised that provided him with poker chips each time he walked around the block, drank orange juice, or took his medication. The program was conducted by his granddaughter, with whom he lived. The patient could save the poker chips and exchange them for selecting the dinner menu at home or for going out to dinner at a restaurant of his choice. As shown in Figure 5–4, the token program was introduced for one behavior at a time in a multiple-baseline design. Improvements were obtained for each behavior as a function of token reinforcement. A temporary withdrawal of the program (second baseline) shows further how crucial the token system was in sustaining adherence to the medical regimen.

Token economies have been used with a variety of populations other than those illustrated here, including the mentally retarded, prisoners, geriatric or nursing-home residents, alcoholics and drug addicts, and outpatient children and adults (see Kazdin, 1977a). Similarly, the various settings in which token economies have been applied include the home, schools, institutions, hospitals, day-care centers, nursing homes, and business and industry. Also, as discussed in a later chapter, applications of reinforcement techniques to social problems have frequently relied on token economies to alter behavior in everyday life.

Important Considerations in Using Tokens. Tokens offer advantages over other reinforcers. First, tokens are potent reinforcers and can often develop behaviors at a higher level than that developed by other conditioned reinforcers such as praise, approval, and feedback. Thus, it is often useful to begin with a token reinforcement program to obtain high levels of performance. After performance is consistently high, it can be maintained with praise, which is more easily administered. Second, tokens bridge the delay between the target response and back-up reinforcement. If a reinforcer other than tokens (e.g., an activity) cannot be delivered immediately after the target response has been performed, tokens can be delivered instead and used to purchase a

FIGURE 5–4

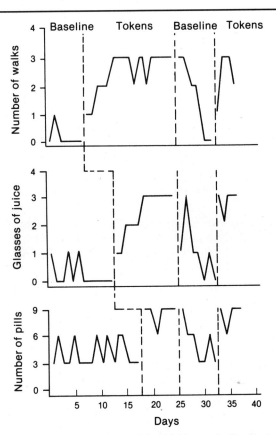

Number of adherence behaviors (walking, orange juice drinking, and pill taking) per day under baseline and token reinforcement conditions. The upper graph shows how many walks were taken; the middle graph shows how many glasses of orange juice were consumed; and the lower graph shows how many pills were taken.

SOURCE: Dapcich-Miura, E., & Hovell, M. F. (1979). Contingency management of adherence to a complex medical regimen in an elderly heart patient. *Behavior Therapy, 10,* 193–201. Copyright 1979 by the Association for Advancement of Behavior Therapy. Reprinted by permission of the publisher and the author.

back-up reinforcer later. Third, because tokens are backed up by a variety of reinforcers, they are less subject to satiation than other reinforcers. If a client is no longer interested in one or two back-up reinforcers, usually there are many other reinforcers that are of value to the client. Fourth, tokens can be easily administered without interrupting the target response. Tokens do not require consumption (as do such reinforcers as food) or the performance of behaviors that may interrupt the target response (e.g., participating in a special activity). Fifth, tokens permit administering a single reinforcer (tokens) to individuals who ordinarily have different reinforcer preferences. Those preferences can be exercised in the exchange of back-up reinforcers. Hence, with tokens, there is less likelihood that the reinforcers will be of value to only a few of the individuals in the setting. Finally, tokens permit parceling out other reinforcers (e.g., activities) that have to be earned in an all-or-none fashion. Tokens can be earned toward the purchase of a large or valuable back-up reinforcer.

There are potential disadvantages in employing tokens. In some programs, back-up reinforcers extraneous to the setting are introduced. For example, in a classroom program, tokens may be backed up with food. A potential problem is removing the token system after behavioral gains have been made and transferring the control of behavior to naturally occurring events such as privileges and activities. Food is not normally presented in a class and eventually needs to be eliminated. Of course, in a token economy, back-up reinforcers normally unavailable in the setting need not be introduced. Tokens can be used to purchase access to ordinary privileges, activities, and other events. Introducing tokens may itself be disadvantageous. Tokens (except for such tokens as money and grades) constitute a reinforcing event not available in most settings. Because the delivery of tokens is clearly associated with reinforcement of desirable behavior, they may exert stimulus control over that behavior. Clients learn that the presence of tokens signals that desirable behavior may decline. However, specific procedures are available to withdraw token reinforcement programs without a loss of behavioral gains (see Chapter 11).

Another possible disadvantage of tokens is that individuals in token economies may obtain them in unauthorized ways. For example, clients may steal tokens from each other. If tokens can be obtained without performing the target responses, their effect on behavior will diminish. To combat the stealing of tokens, they can be individually coded so that they differ for each individual.

General Comments

The variety of reinforcers provides a great deal of flexibility in devising reinforcement programs. At the very minimum, praise, activities, and privileges can be used in virtually any setting. The use of consumables may be limited by restrictions of the setting. For example, food may be too difficult to administer in a large group. Although tokens are usually the most powerful positive reinforcer in applied settings, they may not be needed in most settings. Praise, privileges, and feedback may be very effective. A token economy is somewhat more difficult to implement than other reinforcement programs (e.g., it requires delivering tokens plus back-up reinforcers and keeping track of token earnings), and it introduces problems (e.g., stealing or hoarding tokens, withdrawing tokens from the setting) that may not occur with other programs. Hence, in some applications, tokens may be introduced only if more easily implemented reinforcers have not been effective. On the other hand, token programs are used from the beginning in many cases because they provide a clear way of organizing the relationships among several target behaviors and different types of reinforcers.

The discussion of types of reinforcers should not imply that the various types of reinforcers have to be used independently. A program that incorporates a variety of reinforcers, such as a token economy, is likely to be more effective than one that uses only a few reinforcers. More than one type of reinforcer should be used for an additional reason. Programs using activities, feedback, consumables, or tokens should pair these events with praise and attention. Developing responsiveness to social reinforcers is important because social consequences are likely to be the major source of reinforcement once the client functions outside the treatment setting.

CONTINGENCY CONTRACTS

Often reinforcement contingencies are designed in the form of behavioral contracts between individuals who wish behavior to change (e.g., parents, teachers, hospital attendants) and clients whose behavior is to be changed (students, children, patients). An actual contract is signed by both parties indicating that they agree to the terms. *The contract specifies the relationship between behaviors and their consequences.* Specifically, the contract specifies the reinforcers desired by the client and the behavior desired by the individual who wishes behavior change. Any of the reinforcers discussed previously, as well as idiosyncratic rewards, may be specified in the contract.

Ideally, contingency contracts contain five elements (Stuart, 1971). First, they detail what each party expects to gain. For example, parents may want a child to complete his or her work or attend school regularly. The child may want free time with friends, extra allowance, and other reinforcers. Second, the stipulated behaviors of the client are readily observable. If parents cannot determine whether a responsibility has been met, they cannot grant a privilege. Thus, some behaviors may not be readily incorporated into a contingency contract. For example, parents often cannot easily monitor whether an adolescent visits certain friends, so it would not be advisable to include a stipulation regarding such visits in the contract. Third, contingency contracts provide sanctions for a failure to meet their terms. The aversive consequences for not meeting the contract terms are systematic and planned in advance (i.e., agreed to by all parties), not arbitrary and after the fact. Fourth, contingency contracts include a bonus clause that reinforces consistent compliance with their terms. Bonuses (extra privilege, activity, or extension of curfew limit) can be used to reinforce consistent performance over an extended period. For someone whose behavior was recently developed, bonuses for consistent performance may be especially important. Fifth, contingency contracts provide a means of monitoring the rate of positive reinforcement given and received. The records inform each party when reinforcement is to occur and provide constant feedback. Moreover, the records may cue individuals to make favorable comments about desirable behavior when earning of the back-up reinforcer is about to occur.

Contingency contracts need not be elaborate or complex. A sample contingency contract is illustrated in Figure 5–5. This contract was used to

FIGURE 5–5

Date

Contract no.

Mrs. Harris will initial a smiley card for Andrew each time he does one of the following:

1. Comes into school, hangs up his wraps, and takes his seat without arguing or fighting with another child.
2. Eats his lunch and has his noon recess without arguing or fighting with another child.
3. Clears his desk, gets his wraps, and goes to the bus without arguing or fighting with another child.

When Andrew has received 15 signatures from Mrs. Harris and has had his cards signed by one of his parents, he may choose one of the following rewards:

> Read a story to someone.
> Be first in line for lunch.
> Pass out supplies.
> Get notes from the office.
> Bring a treat from home for the class.
> Go to the library for free reading.
> Choose a book for Mrs. Harris to read to the class.
> Choose a friend for a math game.
> Bring a carrot for Chopper and get a chance to hold him.
> Be a student helper in math for 30 minutes.

I, Andrew, agree to the terms of the above agreement.

I, the classroom teacher, agree to provide Andrew with the reinforcers specified above if Andrew keeps his part of the agreement. I also agree *not* to provide Andrew with any of the above reinforcers during the term of the contract if he does not earn the necessary signatures.

I, Andrew's parent, agree to sign each card that Andrew brings home, to post the cards where Andrew can see them, and to help Andrew keep track of the number of signatures he has earned. Andrew can earn 15 minutes of extra "stay up" time by bringing home 3 signatures.

WE UNDERSTAND THAT THIS IS NOT A LEGALLY BINDING CONTRACT, BUT RATHER A FIRM COMMITMENT OF GOOD WILL AMONG PARTIES WHO CARE ABOUT EACH OTHER.

Sample contingency contract.

SOURCE: Bristol, M. M. (1976). Control of physical aggression through school- and home-based reinforcement. In J. D. Krumboltz & C. E. Thoresen (Eds.), *Counseling methods,* 180–186. Holt, Rinehart & Winston.

alter the behavior of an eight-year-old, second-grade boy named Andrew, who constantly fought at school (Bristol, 1976). The program involved the teacher, parents, and Andrew. Each morning, Andrew received a card with a smiling face on it. In the morning, after lunch, and at the end of the day (as specified in the contract), the teacher signed the card if he had not engaged in fighting. The teacher's signatures served as points that could be accumulated toward the purchase of a reward, also specified in the contract. The parents provided Andrew with praise, posted the cards in a conspicuous place, and gave extra rewards (staying up 15 minutes later at bedtime) for the signatures he received. As shown in Figure 5–6, Andrew averaged about nine fights per week before entering into the contingency contract and fewer fights while the contract was in effect. When the contract procedure was withdrawn, the number of fights increased. In the final phase, when the contract was reinstated, there were at first fewer fights, and for the last three weeks of the program, there were none. A report obtained seven months after the end of the program indicated that Andrew was doing well without any special assistance.

Another sample contingency contract is illustrated in Figure 5–7. This contract represents one of several that were used to alter the behavior of

FIGURE 5–6

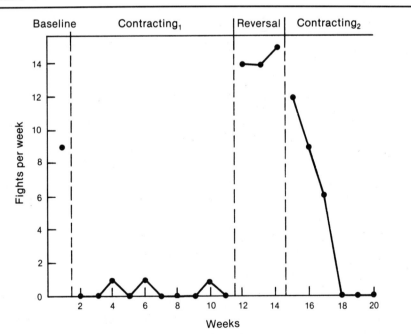

Weekly summary of the total number of fights occurring out of a possible maximum of 15.

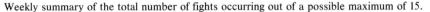

SOURCE: Bristol, M. M. (1976).Control of physical aggression through school- and home-based reinforcement. In J. D. Krumboltz & C. E. Thoresen (Eds.), *Counseling methods,* 180–186. Holt, Rinehart & Winston.

FIGURE 5–7

Effective dates: From _____6/2/89_____   to _____7/28/89_____

We, the undersigned parties, agree to perform the following behaviors:

John agrees to:

1. Take his medication as prescribed.

2. Attend his hospital work assignment daily (as an outpatient volunteer).

3. Refrain from smoking cigarettes in his bedroom.

4. Before visiting his sister and brother-in-law, call and ask permission to visit.

Mr. & Mrs. Harris agree to:

1. Give John a package of cigarettes each morning after breakfast.

2. Give John $10 per week spending money (on Saturday morning).

3. Stop nagging John about how much he smokes.

4. Allow John to visit his sister's home once a month on a Sunday, from 2:00 p.m. to 8:30 p.m.

Bonus: If John follows clause 4 (above) for four weeks, he may move from his present room to a single room in the front of the house.

Penalty: If there are more than 10 infractions of the house rules against smoking in bedrooms, John will lose his smoking privileges entirely.

_____
(Foster home resident)

_____
(Foster parent)

_____
(Foster parent)

_____
(Behavioral counselor)

This contract will be reviewed one week from date of agreement.

Sample contingency contract.

SOURCE: Upper, D., Lochman, J. E., & Aveni, C. A. (1977). Using contingency contracting to modify the problematic behaviors of foster home residents. *Behavior Modification, 1,* 405–416. Copyright 1977 by D. Upper, J. E. Lochman, and C. A. Aveni. Reprinted by permission of Sage Publications, Inc.

psychiatric patients who moved from a hospital to a foster home. A foster home is usually a sheltered living environment for former patients that a married couple manages. The facility allows former patients to live in a relatively nondemanding situation while functioning in the community. In this program, contracting was used to help foster parents (the couple who managed the facility) alter problematic behavior of the residents (Upper, Lochman, & Aveni, 1977). Individual contracts such as the one in Figure 5–7 were devised for each resident. A variety of behaviors were altered, such as refusing to eat meals, go to one's job, or take medication; threatening assaults on others;

frequently complaining; or making irrational comments (e.g., expressing suspiciousness, claiming to hear voices or to see strange objects). Residents completed a questionnaire to identify various events (watching television, drinking beer in the home, going to dances, spending time with a foster parent, going to movies) that might serve as positive reinforcers. Contingency contracting significantly reduced the frequency of problem behaviors. On the other hand, former patients who had not entered into contingency contracts tended to get worse over time.

Contingency contracts have been used successfully to alter a variety of problems, such as overeating, alcohol and drug abuse, cigarette smoking, problem behaviors of delinquents, academic and disruptive behavior of elementary school children, and studying in college students. Various authors have described procedures for developing contingency contracts that can be applied to a wide range of problems and have illustrated additional applications (see DeRisi & Butz, 1975; O'Banion & Whaley, 1981).

Advantages of Using Contingency Contracts

Contingency contracts have several distinct advantages. First, the performance of clients may be better if they are allowed to have some input into designing or implementing a program than if a program is imposed on them. Even if the program is not more effective, active participation by the clients is likely to make the program more acceptable to them (Kazdin, 1980b). Second, the contingencies specified in a contract are less likely to be aversive to the client. The client can negotiate the consequences and the requirements for reinforcement. If the system is minimally aversive, the client is less likely to attempt to escape from the contingencies or from those who administer them. Third, contingency contracts are usually flexible in that participants can renegotiate their terms. The reinforcers delivered for particular responses can be adjusted, response requirements can be increased, and so on. Fourth, the contract makes the contingencies explicit. The specification of the contingencies serves as rules or instructions for the client on how to behave and defines the consequences that will follow behavior. Although explicit instructions alone may not produce durable changes in performance, they often increase the effectiveness of reinforcement (e.g., Resick, Forehand, & Peed, 1974). Fifth, contingency contracts are particularly useful in structuring the relationship between persons whose interactions may be maladaptive. For example, when compared to the families of "normal" children, the families of delinquent and behavior-problem children engage in a lower rate of positive social exchanges and inadequately reinforce socially appropriate behavior (Patterson, 1982; Stuart, 1971). Contingency contracts make explicit the requirements for delivering positive consequences and increase the likelihood that reinforcement for the desired behaviors will actually be provided. Putting the contingencies in writing makes it easier to monitor whether they are carried out in the desired fashion.

Contingency contracts have been used frequently. However, research has not carefully examined how they should be devised to make them maximally effective or acceptable to clients. The importance of specifying a contingent relationship between behavior and consequences has been demonstrated, but other characteristics of contingency contracts, such as the number of reinforcers and the use of bonuses, have had unclear effects (e.g., Spring, Sipich, Trimble, & Goechner, 1978; Stuart & Lott, 1972). Although little work has been done to provide clear guidelines on how contingency contracts should be constructed to achieve maximal effects, their use to structure reinforcement programs is to be strongly encouraged.

REINFORCEMENT TECHNIQUES TO REDUCE UNDESIRABLE RESPONSES

In many situations, the major goal of the reinforcement program is to reduce undesirable behavior. Because reinforcement is a technique for increasing behavior, people often believe that employing it to decrease behavior is inappropriate. Hence, punishment and extinction, discussed in the next chapters, are used because they decrease response frequency directly. However, undesirable target responses can be decreased or eliminated by reinforcement. Indeed, reinforcement techniques for suppressing behavior are available (Deitz & Repp, 1973; Poling & Ryan, 1982).

Reinforcement of Other Behavior

One way to decrease undesirable behavior is to provide reinforcement when the client engages in any behavior other than the target response. *Differential reinforcement of other behavior* (DRO) consists of providing the reinforcing consequences of all responses *except* for the undesirable behavior of interest. The effect of this schedule is to decrease the target behavior. For example, Lowitz and Suib (1978) reduced the frequency with which an eight-year-old girl sucked her thumb. The intervention was required in part because of the dental problems that resulted from the constant sucking. A DRO schedule was used in which the child received pennies during special training sessions for each one-minute interval in which thumb-sucking did *not* occur. Within five sessions, thumb-sucking was virtually eliminated. The program was successfully extended to the home with a token system for non-thumb-sucking. The behavior was eliminated, and evaluation one year later showed that the effects were maintained.

In another application, DRO was used with an adult psychiatric patient with seizure activity (Burgio & Tice, 1985). The purpose was to evaluate whether seizures could be controlled by behavioral intervention rather than the more commonly used anticonvulsive medication. A program was devised in which the patient could earn a walk outside the hospital with a staff member at the end of a 24-hour period with no seizures. An ABAB design showed that seizures systematically declined when reinforcement was provided for other (nonseizure) behavior.

A DRO schedule provides reinforcement for *not* engaging in a behavior. The reinforcer is delivered as long as the client is not performing the undesired response. Thus, when the reinforcer is delivered, the person may be doing virtually anything except the target behavior. For example, a DRO schedule to eliminate a child's hitting of his peers would provide reinforcement for periods of nonaggression. The child may earn the reinforcer even when he is sitting alone and not interacting. It might be useful to provide reinforcement for positive behaviors (e.g., playing cooperatively with others), rather than for just not engaging in the undesirable response.

Reinforcement of Incompatible or Alternative Behaviors

Reinforcement of the nonoccurrence of a response or any other behavior (DRO) is useful when there are very high rates of the undesired target behavior and one wishes to provide reinforcement anytime the response is not evident. For example, if an autistic child is hitting himself at high rates, reinforcement might be delivered whenever this behavior does not occur. In most situations, it is useful to identify specific positive behaviors that are reinforced. These behaviors are selected because they directly or indirectly interfere with performance of the undesired behavior. Usually specific positive behaviors in the setting (e.g., working at one's desk at school, completing a chore at home) can be identified that the behavior change agent wishes to develop. Two differential reinforcement schedules are suited to this purpose.

In one of these schedules, reinforcement is provided for behaviors *directly incompatible* with the undesired response. An incompatible behavior is any behavior that directly interferes and cannot be performed with the undesired behavior. The incompatible behavior is often the direct *opposite* of the undesired behavior. Increasing the frequency of an incompatible behavior decreases the undesired behavior. This procedure, sometimes referred to as the *differential reinforcement of incompatible behavior* (DRI), focuses on reinforcing behaviors that are incompatible or compete with the undesired behavior.

Usually it is quite easy to select an incompatible response that can be reinforced. For example, if a child fights with siblings at home, reinforcement can be delivered for such behaviors as playing games cooperatively. If an institutionalized patient has violent outbursts and tantrums, reinforcement can be delivered for talking and sitting quietly and for calmly interacting with peers, which are incompatible with the undesired responses.

The effects of reinforcing a behavior incompatible with the undesired response were demonstrated in a program developed for a girl named Jane who had a high rate of self-injurious behavior (Nunes, Murphy, & Ruprecht, 1977, Exp. 2). Jane frequently slapped her face, hit her ears with her fists, and slammed her arms against the table when seated. The intervention was carried out in the classroom of a state hospital. To reduce self-injury, the reinforcer was provided when Jane used her hands to work on a puzzle rather than to hit herself. That behavior was incompatible with self-hitting. The reinforcer consisted of providing praise and turning on a back massager while she was engaging in the desired behaviors. If any self-injurious behavior occurred, the massager was turned off for 15 seconds. The effects of the program on self-injurious behavior are evident from Figure 5–8. Reinforcement of incompatible behavior systematically reduced self-injury, as shown in an ABAB design.

It is not always possible or necessary to identify a behavior that is physically incompatible with an undesired behavior that one wishes to decrease. A host of positive behaviors that serve as alternatives to the undesired behavior might be reinforced. These alternatives are behaviors whose performance decreases the likelihood that the undesired behavior will occur. Increasing the frequency of alternative behaviors, whether or not they are incompatible with the undesired behavior, decreases the undesired behavior. This

FIGURE 5–8

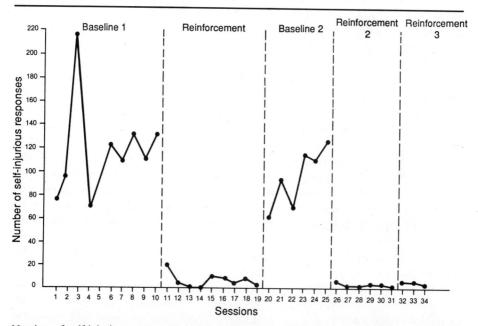

Number of self-injurious responses during each session exhibited by Jane across experimental conditions. In the first two reinforcement phases, the reinforcer was praise and a back massager. In the third reinforcement phase, a different reinforcer was used. The teacher put Jane on her lap and bounced her gently instead of using the massager.

SOURCE: Nunes, D. L., Murphy, R. J., & Ruprecht, M. L. (1977). Reducing self-injurious behavior of severely retarded individuals through withdrawal-of-reinforcement procedures. *Behavior Modification, 1,* 499–516. Copyright 1977 by D. L. Nunes, R. J. Murphy, and M. L. Ruprecht. Reprinted by permission of Sage Publications, Inc.

procedure is referred to as the *differential reinforcement of alternative behavior* (DRA).

Because of the many alternatives that are available, examples of DRA are somewhat easier to identify than examples of DRI. To suppress fighting among siblings, as noted above, playing cooperatively could be reinforced. Playing cooperatively is incompatible with fighting and constitutes a DRI. Other alternative behaviors could be reinforced, such as watching television together or completing a chore together. Neither of these behaviors is necessarily incompatible with fighting, yet their reinforcement is likely to decrease the frequency of fighting. These responses are part of a general class of behaviors that might, in casual terms, be referred to as "getting along." More opportunities for positive reinforcement are made available by identifying many alternative behaviors rather than only the alternative behaviors that are physically incompatible with the undesired response.

As an illustration, in one program, an adolescent, mentally retarded student spoke out excessively in class (Deitz, Repp, & Deitz, 1976). A DRI schedule reinforcing an incompatible response (being quiet) could have been used here. However, merely being quiet does not mean that the student is developing the behaviors that are important in a classroom setting. Given the goal of the setting, a DRA schedule was used in which reinforcement was provided for working on academic tasks. This response is not incompatible with talking out, because a person can do both. Yet if one is working at a task, the chances are that he or she is not talking. In this program, reinforcement of working at a task decreased talking out.

As may be evident, DRI and DRA are closely related. Actually, DRA refers to reinforcing any alternative positive responses that decrease the likelihood that the undesired behavior will be performed. DRI is a subtype of DRA in which the alternative behavior is one that is incompatible with the undesired response. In practice and in working with parents, teachers, and others, it is useful to develop a DRA schedule where a few specific alternative behaviors are identified as the target responses. These positive alternative responses may compete directly with the undesired behavior or simply decrease the likelihood that it will be performed.

Reinforcement of incompatible or alternative behaviors has been used effectively in many programs (Deitz & Repp, 1973). For example, the behaviors of hyperactive children in the classroom and at home have been altered using reinforcement techniques. Hyperactive behaviors include disturbing others excessively, blurting out statements, being out of one's seat, speaking rapidly, running around the room, not complying with the requests of parents or teachers, and generally engaging in very high levels of inappropriate activity. Rather than punish these behaviors, many programs have been designed to reinforce alternative behaviors (e.g., Ayllon, Layman, & Kandel, 1975; Shafto & Sulzbacher, 1977). Typically, programs of this kind provide tokens, praise, and consumable rewards (e.g., food) for such behaviors as correct responses on academic tasks, remaining in one's seat to work on specific tasks, and engaging in more restrained and quieter types of activity. Such programs have reduced hyperactive behaviors and increased the performance of on-task and academic behaviors.

Reinforcement of Low Response Rates

Another reinforcement technique for suppressing behavior is to provide reinforcing consequences for reductions in the frequency of the undesired behavior or for increases in the time in which that behavior does *not* occur. These procedures, referred to as *differential reinforcement of low rates of responding* (DRL), can effectively suppress behavior (see Deitz, 1977).

In one variation of a DRL schedule, the client receives reinforcing consequences for showing a *reduction in the frequency of target behavior*. For example, Deitz (1977, Exp. 2) decreased the inappropriate talking out of an educable mentally retarded male adolescent who attended a special education class. After baseline observations of talking out, the teacher told the student that if he emitted three or fewer "talk-outs" during a 55-minute period, she would spend extra time working with him. The youth would receive the reinforcing consequence only if he showed a low rate of disruptive behavior. This DRL contingency was evaluated in an ABAB design. The results, shown in Figure 5–9, demonstrate that talking out decreased whenever the DRL contingency was in effect.

The DRL schedule can completely eliminate a behavior by making the requirements for reinforcement increasingly stringent. A client may be allowed a certain number of instances of the undesired behavior within a given period to earn the reinforcer, and in order to eliminate the behavior, this number may be decreased over time (Deitz & Repp, 1973). Alternatively, a client may receive reinforcing consequences for going longer and longer periods without performing the undesired behavior. For example, in separate programs, reinforcement has increased the amount of elapsed time between one response and the next to reduce stereotypical behaviors and rapid eating (e.g., Lennox, Miltenberger, & Donnelly, 1987; Singh, Dawson, & Manning, 1981). In several other variations, reinforcement for performance of a few or no instances of the response has effectively suppressed behavior (Deitz & Repp, 1973; Poling & Ryan, 1982).

Advantages of Using Positive Reinforcement

Reinforcement techniques using the schedules discussed previously have reduced or eliminated a wide range of undesirable and maladaptive behaviors in children and adults. The procedures appear to be at least as effective as various punishment procedures in their capacity to decrease undesirable behaviors. Although punishment and extinction can decrease behavior, these procedures do not train people in socially appropriate alternative behaviors. Even if punishment or extinction is used, its effects can be greatly enhanced by incorporating reinforcement for appropriate behavior into the program. Also,

FIGURE 5–9

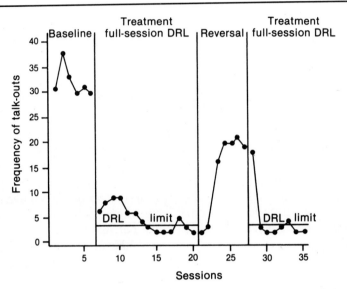

The frequency of talk-outs per 55-minute session of an educable mentally retarded male. During treatment, if the client emitted three or fewer talk-outs per session, the teacher spent 15 minutes working with him.

SOURCE: Reprinted with permission from *Behaviour Research and Therapy, 15,* 103–111. Deitz, S. M. An analysis of programming DRL schedules in educational settings. Copyright 1977, Pergamon Press, Inc.

many ethical concerns and negative client reactions raised by punishment procedures are largely circumvented if the program is based on positive reinforcement. Given these benefits, reinforcement techniques should be used whenever the goal is to decrease behavior.

NEGATIVE REINFORCEMENT

Negative reinforcement can also be used to develop behavior. A behavior is increased or strengthened through negative reinforcement when it results in *escape* from or *avoidance* of an aversive event. Escape occurs when the individual comes in contact with the aversive event and the appropriate behavior eliminates the event. Many behaviors in everyday life are maintained by negative reinforcement through escape. For example, leaving the house to escape from an argument with one's roommate or spouse, turning off an alarm to escape from a loud noise, screaming to quiet noisy neighbors, and taking medicine to alleviate pain all represent escape.

Avoidance behavior allows the individual to prevent or indefinitely postpone contact with an aversive event. As mentioned in Chapter 2, avoidance learning may develop after an individual learns to escape an aversive event. Through classical conditioning, a previously neutral event acquires the capacity to elicit escape behavior. The escape behavior is automatically reinforced by terminating the conditioned aversive event. Thus, avoidance involves classical and operant conditioning. Avoidance refers to escape from a conditioned aversive event.

Most avoidance behavior is acquired without direct experience with the aversive event. Verbal cues from other individuals instruct us that certain consequences are to be avoided. The cues are discriminative stimuli indicating that certain untoward consequences may follow if we behave in a particular way. Examples of avoidance based on verbal cues are present in everyday experience. For example, one can avoid personal harm by responding to the threat of an impending flood. Avoidance of the flood is escape from or elimination of the threat. Behavior that reduces the threat is strengthened through negative reinforcement. Other examples of negative reinforcement through avoidance are parking one's car in a particular place to avoid a traffic fine, wearing a coat to avoid a chill, drinking alcohol sparingly to avoid a driving mishap, and leaving a sinking ship to avoid drowning.

Negative reinforcement, in the form of escape from an aversive event, has not been widely used in applied settings for various reasons. First, negative reinforcement requires an ongoing aversive event (shock, noise) that can be terminated when the desired target behavior occurs. This means that the aversive event must be delivered frequently before reinforcement can occur. The use of aversive events is ethically indefensible if positive events (through positive reinforcement) have not been attempted first. Because there are many types of positive reinforcement programs (token economies, contingency contracts), there is rarely a need to employ negative reinforcement. Second, the use of aversive events often produces undesirable side effects. Shock, physical restraint, reprimands, isolation, and other aversive consequences lead the client to escape from the situation, to avoid the persons who administer these events, and even to aggress against them. These side effects can be avoided by relying on positive reinforcement. Third, negative reinforcement is often difficult to administer. The aversive stimulus must be carefully controlled, so that it can be terminated immediately after the appropriate behavior occurs. Usually this requires carefully monitoring behavior, often with certain apparatus. For these reasons, it is no surprise that negative reinforcement has been used quite sparingly.

Yet negative reinforcement has been used in some cases (Iwata, 1987). For example, negative reinforcement was used to increase conversation among psychiatric patients during their group therapy sessions (Heckel, Wiggins, & Salzberg, 1962). After the group had been silent for more than one minute, a loud noise sounded through a speaker hidden in the air-conditioning vent of the room. The noise continued until one patient broke the silence. Hence, the desired response (talking) terminated the aversive event (noise). Using this negative reinforcement contingency increased patient conversation dramatically. This example is a historically early application of negative reinforcement.

No doubt, the problem would be approached quite differently in contemporary research. It is likely that to increase conversation, prompts (initiations of conversations, reminders of appropriate behaviors) and positive reinforcement (praise, tokens) would be used to develop patient conversation. Using reinforcement and shaping, the desired behaviors could be readily developed without any aversive events.

In another application, negative reinforcement was used to alter behaviors of a socially withdrawn psychiatric patient (Fichter, Wallace, Liberman, & Davis, 1976). The goal was to increase the volume and duration of the patient's speech, because he spoke inaudibly and only for very brief periods. Also, the patient used his hands in a ritualistic and self-stimulatory fashion by repetitively tapping or biting his fingers. Nagging was used as the aversive event. During conversations with the staff, the patient was constantly reminded to speak louder or for longer periods. If the patient did not comply within a brief period (three seconds), the reminder was repeated. If the desired behavior occurred, the request to perform the behavior was not given. From the patient's standpoint, the appropriate behavior (e.g., louder and longer speech) avoided further nagging. Positive reinforcement was not provided; rather, avoidance of the aversive event was the basis for changing behavior. The results demonstrated that each of the behaviors that staff nagged the client to perform increased with this avoidance contingency.

This study is especially interesting because of the experimental evaluation of nagging, a familiar technique for anyone who has ever been a child or parent. However, on the basis of this single application, it would not be appropriate to conclude that nagging would be effective in a variety of circumstances. Nagging (perhaps like a threat) may lose its aversive properties and effectiveness over time if there are no additional consequences for failing to perform the response. Also, clients might simply avoid the people who nag, precisely in the way that children often avoid their nagging parents.

In the above examples, it is quite likely that positive reinforcement would have been effective in achieving the desired ends. Positive reinforcement has many variations, and they are usually effective. Consequently, negative reinforcement is a technique that should probably be employed as a last resort. There are possible exceptions that warrant consideration. In some situations, an aversive event is presented to the client as part of a punishment program. If punishment (presentation of an aversive event after behavior) is to be used, it is more effective if it is combined with reinforcement than if it is presented alone. Negative reinforcement can increase adaptive behavior and thereby increase the efficacy of punishment.

For example, Hobbs and Forehand (1975) compared two variations of time-out to decrease the frequency with which children did not comply with their mothers' requests. When a child did not comply, time-out was used. The mother simply left the room and removed the toys the child was playing with. This is a punishment procedure. For half of the children, time-out was over at the end of a brief period. For others, time-out ended only after they were not disruptive for 15 seconds. For this latter group, the aversive event (time-out) was terminated by appropriate behavior. Hence, appropriate behavior was negatively reinforced. The results showed that negative reinforcement plus time-out was more effective than time out alone in decreasing noncompliant and disruptive behavior.

Occasionally, negative reinforcement is combined with positive reinforcement. Here too, negative reinforcement might be considered if there is an aversive event inherent in the situation, as in the above application of time-out. For example, a recent application focused on children who were highly disruptive during their visits to the dentist (Allen & Stokes, 1987). Behaviors such as kicking, screaming, hitting, and noncompliance interfered with restorative dental treatment. It was assumed that the treatment procedure itself (i.e., remaining in the dental chair, having a drill turned on) was aversive. In special practice sessions immediately before dental treatment, the children were individually instructed that they could practice being "big helpers," which meant sitting quietly. The behavior (sitting quietly) was negatively reinforced by terminating the procedure. For example, when the child sat quietly for only three seconds, the aversive event (e.g., having the drill on) was quickly terminated. This is an example of negative reinforcement. This response (sitting quietly) was gradually extended (shaping) to six minutes. Positive reinforcement was also used; it consisted of praise and stickers for increased cooperative behavior. The effect of the combined negative and positive reinforcement contingency markedly reduced disruptive behavior and permitted completion of the dental session.

Negative reinforcement has occasionally been applied as part of therapy techniques to alter such behaviors as excessive alcohol consumption, overeating, and sexual deviance, including transvestism and fetishism. For example, one form of treatment for alcoholics that involves punishment and negative reinforcement requires the client to ingest the drug disulfiram (Antabuse). If the client drinks alcohol less than 24 hours after ingesting the drug, intense nausea results. Nausea can be *avoided* by not consuming alcohol. Of course, the client can also avoid the aversive contingency by failing to take the drug.

Evaluation of Negative Reinforcement

A major restriction in using negative reinforcement is the risk of undesirable side effects. One such side effect is trying to escape or avoid the behavior change program and those associated with it. It is easy to see how this could happen. If parents, teachers, or supervisors administer aversive events (and not positive ones as well), they become aversive. Escape from such persons by leaving home, the classroom, or changing jobs is negatively reinforced. Programs based on positive reinforcement do not foster this type of escape and avoidance behavior.

From the standpoint of designing a behavior modification program, aversive stimuli should be avoided or minimized. When they are used, emphasis should be placed on positive reinforcement for desirable behavior. In many applications of negative reinforcement, strong aversive stimuli are required because other procedures have failed or because the response (e.g., sexual deviance) is strongly reinforced. In such instances, aversive stimuli, including punishment and/or negative reinforcement, constitute a last resort.

SUMMARY AND CONCLUSION

The effectiveness of positive reinforcement in increasing behavior depends on the delay of reinforcement, the magnitude or amount of reinforcement, the quality or type of reinforcer, and the schedule of reinforcement. To maximize performance, reinforcement should be delivered immediately after a response. Moreover, a highly preferred reinforcer should be used. During acquisition of a response, continuous reinforcement should be used until the response has been well established. Subsequently, intermittent reinforcement can be substituted to maintain behavior.

In applied settings, effective use has been made of different types of reinforcers, such as food and other consumables, praise and attention, high-probability behaviors, feedback, and tokens. Each of these types has its advantages and limitations, such as dependence on deprivation and satiation states, ease of administration, and relative effectiveness. Token economies usually incorporate a variety of back-up reinforcers and thus overcome the limitations associated with the use of any single reinforcer.

Contingency contracting refers to a way of structuring a reinforcement program. Each participant in the program negotiates and then formally agrees to the terms of the contract. The reinforcers for performing the target behaviors and penalties for failing to perform those behaviors are made explicit and are agreed upon in writing in advance of the program. The primary advantage of a contract arrangement is that it gives clients an opportunity to develop their own behavior change program and to ensure that the terms are not coercive.

Positive reinforcement represents the major basis for behavioral techniques in applied settings. Positive reinforcement programs are appropriate, not only to increase desirable behaviors but also to decrease or eliminate undesirable behaviors. To accomplish this latter goal, differential reinforcement of other behaviors, alternative behaviors, incompatible behaviors, and low rates of behavior have been very effective.

Negative reinforcement is an alternative procedure for increasing behavior. In most applied settings, it has not been widely used as a behavior change technique. This is largely due to the undesirability of using aversive events if alternative procedures based on positive reinforcement exist. Nevertheless, negative reinforcement has been used successfully, particularly in instances in which positive reinforcement has not been effective or has been difficult to administer.

NOTES

1. A diet high in potassium was encouraged because the patient's medication probably included diuretics (medications that increase the flow of urine). With such medication, potassium is often lost from the body and has to be consumed in extra quantities to maintain bodily functioning.

FOR FURTHER READING

Ayllon, T., & McKittrick, S. M. (1982). *How to set up a token economy*. Austin, TX: Pro-Ed.

Hall, R. V., & Hall, M. C. (1980). *How to select reinforcers*. Austin, TX: Pro-Ed.

Hall, R. V., & Hall, M. C. (1980). *How to use systematic attention and approval*. Austin, TX: Pro-Ed.

Hall, R. V., & Hall, M. C. (1982). *How to negotiate a behavioral contract*. Austin, TX: Pro-Ed.

Iwata, B. A. (1987). Negative reinforcement in applied behavior analysis: An emerging technology. *Journal of Applied Behavior Analysis, 20,* 361–378.

Kazdin, A. E. (1977). *The token economy: A review and evaluation*. New York: Plenum.

Chapter Six

Punishment

TYPES OF PUNISHMENT
    Presentation of Aversive Events
        Verbal Statements
        Electric Shock
        Other Aversive Consequences
    Withdrawal of Positive Consequences
        Time Out from Reinforcement
        Response Cost
    Punishing Consequences Based on Effort
        Overcorrection
        Other Effort-Based Consequences
SELECTING PROCEDURES TO SUPPRESS BEHAVIORS
FACTORS THAT INFLUENCE THE EFFECTIVENESS OF PUNISHMENT
    Delay of Punishment
    Schedule of Punishment
    Source of Reinforcement
    Timing of Punishment in the Response Sequence
    Variation of Punishment
    Reinforcement of Alternative Responses
    General Comments
SIDE EFFECTS OF PUNISHMENT
    Types of Effects
        Emotional Reactions
        Escape and Avoidance
        Aggression
        Modeled Punishment
        Perpetuation of Punishment
    Illustrations from Applied Settings
        Negative Side Effects
        Positive Side Effects
        General Comments

CHARACTERISTICS OF THE PUNISHMENT PROCESS
   Immediacy of Effects
   Specificity of Effects
   Recovery after Punishment Withdrawal
WHEN AND HOW TO USE PUNISHMENT
SUMMARY AND CONCLUSION

Aversive events play a major role in everyday life. Indeed, aversive techniques are deeply enmeshed in many social institutions, including government and law (e.g., fines and imprisonment), education (e.g., failing grades and expulsion), religion (e.g., damnation), international relations (e.g., military coercion), and normal social intercourse (e.g., discrimination, disapproval, and social stigma). Routine interactions of most individuals with both physical and social environments result in aversive events ranging from a burn from a hot stove to verbal abuse from an acquaintance.

In behavior modification, the types of aversive events used and how they are applied differ greatly from punishment practices in everyday life. Before applications are discussed, a few prefatory comments are in order. To begin with, proponents of behavior modification generally avoid the use of punishment whenever possible. One reason, noted in the previous chapter, is that alternative procedures based on positive reinforcement are usually available. Consequently, there may be no need to use aversive consequences. There are many other reasons as well. Punishment is often associated with undesirable side effects, such as emotional reactions (crying), escape from and avoidance of situations (e.g., staying away from a punitive parent), and aggression (e.g., hitting others).

In addition, punishment can foster undesirable associations with regard to various agents (parents, teachers), situations (home, school), and behaviors (doing homework). An important objective in childrearing, education, and socialization in general is to develop positive attitudes and responses toward these agents, situations, and behaviors; their frequent association with punishment may be counterproductive. For example, screaming at a child to practice a musical instrument is not likely to develop a love of music. The constant pairing of aversive events (threats, reprimands, loss of privileges) and the ensuing reactions (child crying) are undesirable and unnecessary for developing the target behavior. As will become clear in this chapter, however, punishment can be beneficial when it is used infrequently and carefully and as part of a more comprehensive program that emphasizes positive reinforcement.

Proponents of behavioral techniques are extremely concerned with abuse and misuse of punishment. Such abuse and misuse have been shown to foster serious problems in children and adolescents. For example, families of deviant children tend to use harsher and more frequent punishment than is used by families of children who function well in everyday life (Kazdin, 1987a). More frequent punishment is not associated with improved behavior. Indeed, both physical and verbal punishment (reprimands) can increase the very behaviors (noncompliance, aggression) that parents, teachers, and others wish to suppress. Unfortunately, the old adage "Spare the rod and spoil the child" still has many adherents. This is unfortunate because a strong case might be made for an opposite contention, "Use the rod and spoil the child."

To be sure, there are many occasions when mild punishment can be useful as part of a behavior change program. And in some cases, people—for example, parents who engage in child abuse to control their children—may need to be trained to administer punishment (and reinforcement) judiciously (Patterson, 1982; Wolfe, 1987). However, the types of punishment procedures, how they are used, and their combination with reinforcement programs make therapeutic applications of punishment very different from its applications in everyday life. The present chapter discusses the various types of punishment techniques, their effects and side effects, and their place in a behavior change program.

TYPES OF PUNISHMENT

Punishment in the technical sense refers solely to the empirical operation (presentation or removal of events) that reduces the frequency of a response. Punishment does not necessarily involve physical pain. Indeed, painful events (e.g., spankings) may not decrease the responses they are designed to punish and thus may not qualify as punishing events. Alternatively, a variety of procedures that serve as punishment do not entail physical discomfort and are not odious to the client.

In behavior modification, several forms of punishment have been developed based on whether aversive events are presented, positive events are withdrawn, or the client's work or effort is required after performance of a particular behavior. Some of the techniques are familiar because they are commonly used in everyday life (e.g., reprimands). However, other techniques, such as withdrawing reinforcing events for very brief periods or requiring clients to practice appropriate behavior, are probably less familiar. Whether the techniques are familiar or not, it is important to examine the effectiveness of different techniques and the manner in which those techniques are most effectively administered.

Presentation of Aversive Events

After a response has been performed, an aversive event such as spanking or reprimand may be applied. There are two types of aversive events, primary aversive stimuli and secondary, or conditioned, aversive stimuli. *Primary aversive stimuli* are inherently aversive events. Such stimuli as electric shock, intense physical assault, bright lights, and loud noises are primary aversive stimuli. Their aversive properties are unlearned. *Secondary, or conditioned, aversive stimuli* acquire their aversive properties by being paired with events that are already aversive. For example, the word *no* serves as a conditioned aversive stimulus for many individuals. The word acquires its aversive value by being paired with such events as physical pain and loss of privileges. Conditioned aversive stimuli that typically control behavior include gestures, nods, frowns, and traffic tickets.

Stimuli may become aversive even if they are not paired with specific aversive stimuli. A stimulus consistently associated with the absence of reinforcement may become aversive. An event signaling that reinforcement will *not* be forthcoming, referred to earlier as an S^Δ, may serve as an aversive event (Azrin & Holz, 1966). The S^Δ serves as a signal that a period of nonreinforcement is in effect. For example, when a child breaks a valuable object, a parent may make a particular facial expression, become silent, and not respond to the child for a while. The parent's nonresponsiveness denotes that the child will not receive reinforcement. During parental silence, virtually no behavior receives approval. The signal or cue (e.g., a facial expression) associated with the parent's nonreinforcement (silence) becomes aversive in its own right.

Verbal Statements.   Verbal statements in the form of reprimands, warnings, disapproval, saying no, and threats are often used in everyday interactions between teacher and student, parent and child, siblings, spouses, friends, and enemies. Verbal statements have been used to suppress behavior in applied research. For example, reprimands and disapproving statements have occasionally been applied in classroom settings to reduce playing during lessons, being out of one's seat, talking without permission, and other disruptive behaviors. Reprimands and disapproval in general have had inconsistent effects. In some cases, for example, disruptive student behavior has been suppressed relatively quickly by saying no after instances of disruptive behavior (Hall et al., 1971). In other cases, reprimands have served as a positive reinforcer, rather than as a punisher. In one classroom, the teacher reprimanded the children by saying "Sit down" when students were out of their seats (Madsen, Becker, Thomas, Koser, & Plager, 1970). Interestingly, the reprimands *increased* the frequency of standing, serving as a positive reinforcer for the behavior they were designed to suppress.

The manner in which verbal statements are delivered may influence their effectiveness. For example, in classroom applications, reprimands are more effective in suppressing child behavior when they are accompanied by looking directly at and grasping the child (Van Houten, Nau, MacKenzie-Keating, Sameoto, & Colavecchia, 1982). Nonverbal components such as glaring or staring at the child, pointing at him or her, or holding the child's arm have been used in several studies in which reprimands have been applied (e.g., Doleys, Wells, Hobbs, Roberts, & Cartelli, 1976; Forehand, Roberts, Doleys, Hobbs, & Resick, 1976). Reprimands are also more effective when they are delivered in close proximity to the child rather than from the other end of the room (Van Houten et al., 1982). In general, reprimands can be effective, especially when accompanied by gestures and other features that may add to their salience or intensity.

Verbal punishment is likely to lose its effectiveness over time. For example, threats have occasionally been used to suppress behavior. When threats signal that some other aversive consequence will follow, they become conditioned aversive events whether the behavior is or is not performed. However, some threats are "idle"—not backed by the threatened consequence. Such threats tend to lose their effects quickly (e.g., Kazdin, 1971; Phillips, Phillips, Fixsen, & Wolf, 1971). Verbal statements are generally likely to produce temporary effects if they are not followed by other consequences, or to require increases in intensity to sustain their effects if they are used by themselves.

Considerations in Using Verbal Statements.   Reprimands and threats are easily administered and, hence, from a practical standpoint are readily available for use as a punishment technique. Also, verbal forms of punishment cause no physical discomfort to the client. Receiving a reprimand may be unpleasant, but such unpleasantness is very different from the kind resulting from more extreme procedures such as corporal punishment. Yet, as mentioned previously, reprimands have been more effective when a child is grasped while reprimanded. The risk of using this procedure is that, in practice, grasping a child is likely to become more intense and may unnecessarily hurt the child. Physical contact with reprimands would need to be supervised closely to avoid misuse. Reprimands alone are commonly used in everyday life and are less objectionable than many other forms of punishment. However, their overuse probably makes them relatively ineffective in ordinary applications.

The major limitation of verbal statements as punishing events is their inconsistent effects; often they produce little or no behavior change. For most of the behaviors brought to treatment, the weak or inconsistent effects of verbal reprimands are not sufficient to achieve therapeutic change. Another consideration is that such people as parents and teachers use reprimands relatively frequently. For example, observations of teachers throughout elementary and high school grades have shown relatively high rates of disapproval and low rates of approval in the ordinary classroom (Thomas, Presland, Grant, & Glynn, 1978; White, 1975). To improve teacher effectiveness, one might not want to increase the use of reprimands, because they are already relatively frequent. Alternative behavior change techniques such as positive reinforcement might be more appropriately implemented.

An important consideration is that reprimands and verbal admonitions in one form or another compose a large part of naturally occurring events in everyday life. Hence, in treatment settings, it may be desirable to train clients to respond to disapproval, if they do not already respond to it. Verbal statements can be made to function as aversive events by pairing them with other events such as physical restraint or removal of positive events. Here the purpose of the program is to develop responsiveness to naturally occurring events.

Electric Shock.   Shock is another aversive event that can be presented after behavior. Although shock has been used relatively infrequently, its unique characteristics and effects warrant mention. Most of its applications have focused on persons who engage in behaviors dangerous to themselves or to others and who have not responded to other procedures. When shock is used in these extraordinary situations, it usually consists of a brief shock to the finger or arm. Because shock is a primary aversive event, even its brief application usually produces rapid and marked suppression of behavior.

Shock may be an alternative when rapid suppression of a serious behavior is needed and when other efforts have failed. For example, Linscheid and Cunningham (1977) used electric shock to eliminate chronic ruminative vomiting in a nine-month-old infant. Constant vomiting after meals had resulted in severe weight loss, malnutrition, and potentially fatal medical complications. The shock was intense enough to evoke a startle reaction but not intense enough to elicit crying. When shock was applied (to the leg) at the onset of vomiting, vomiting dropped from an average of over 100 instances per day to 1 instance per day after only three days of treatment. Follow-up evaluation, nine months after the infant was released from the hospital, revealed that ruminative vomiting no longer occurred and weight gain increased.

The use of shock as a last resort is illustrated by a report published more than 20 years ago (Kushner, 1968). In this application, electric shock was used to suppress uncontrollable sneezing in a female high school student. The girl began to sneeze uncontrollably while hospitalized for treatment of a kidney infection. Before her discharge, the hospital corridors outside her room were freshly painted. The onset of sneezing occurred at this time but continued long after her discharge. Despite a variety of treatments, including psychotherapy, hypnosis, trips to parts of the country with cleaner air, hospitalization, and medication, her uncontrollable sneezing continued. After six months, shock was applied when she came for outpatient treatment sessions. With shock (delivered to her fingertips), her sneezing was rapidly eliminated in only a few treatment sessions. A follow-up evaluation 16 months after treatment showed that uncontrollable sneezing no longer occurred.

In other applications, shock has occasionally been used to suppress such potentially harmful behaviors as self-injury, playing with dangerous equipment, and climbing dangerous places. The rapid and often durable effects of shock have led to its occasional use. Currently, shock is rarely used, partly because its use raises ethical and legal issues but also because many less objectionable but effective alternatives are available. With adults, usually in outpatient treatment, shock has been occasionally used to reduce or eliminate such behaviors as cigarette smoking, overeating, alcohol consumption, and various sexual behaviors, such as fetishes (see Hallam & Rachman, 1976). Shock has not been particularly effective in these instances, and less objectionable procedures with equal or greater effectiveness are readily available.

Considerations in Using Electric Shock.   Shock has been especially useful in cases in which dangerous behavior needs to be suppressed rapidly and alternative procedures have not been effective. Because the procedure is painful, it is usually not resorted to unless alternative procedures have been unsuccessful. Indeed, in the examples provided above, shock was used only after several other procedures had failed to change behavior (e.g., chronic vomiting and uncontrollable sneezing). Given the range of effective alternative techniques, based on both punishment and reinforcement, serious ethical and legal objections might be raised if shock were the first treatment to be considered and applied.

Other limitations militate against the widespread use of shock in applied settings. To begin with, the administration of shock requires special equipment. Hence, shock has generally been restricted to laboratory or treatment settings where clients are seen individually and are closely supervised. In settings where clients are treated in groups, it is not readily feasible to employ shock. In addition, the person using shock must be well trained so that its intensity is not severe and so that accidents due to misuse of equipment do not occur. Even if shock could be applied, professionals and clients are likely to view it as unacceptable for treatment purposes (Kazdin, 1980c). Hence, independently of its effectiveness, its use is restricted to special cases in which extreme procedures appear to be warranted.

Other Aversive Consequences.   A variety of other aversive conse-quences, somewhat less well studied than reprimands and less controversial than shock, have also been used. For example, squirting lemon juice into the client's mouth has been used in a few treatment cases. In one application, lemon juice was used to suppress life-threatening vomiting in a six-month-old infant (Sajwaj, Libert, & Agras, 1974). When the tongue movements that preceded vomiting occurred, lemon juice was squirted (using a syringe) into her mouth. The procedure markedly suppressed episodes of vomiting. At follow-up several months after treatment, it was found that the infant had continued to gain weight and that vomiting had not recurred. Similarly, in another report, squirting lemon juice from a plastic squirt bottle into the mouth of a severely retarded boy effectively eliminated public masturbation (Cook, Altman, Shaw, & Blaylock, 1978).

Another punishment technique that has been used is introducing the smell of aromatic ammonia (smelling salts) contingent upon undesirable behavior. For example, in one report, ammonia was used to suppress self-injurious behavior in two children (Altman, Haavik, & Cook, 1978). Severe hair pulling of a four-year-old girl (who had made herself partially bald) and hand biting of a three-year-old boy (who had damaged the tissues of his fingers) were sup-pressed by breaking a capsule of aromatic ammonia and placing it under the child's nose for a few seconds contingent upon the performance of self-injurious behaviors.

Other punishment procedures are occasionally used. Two of these procedures are spraying a mist of water in the client's face (water mist) and briefly covering the client's face with a piece of cloth or something else that blocks vision (facial screening). For example, water mist and facial screening have reduced self-injurious behavior (face punching, jaw hitting, self-biting) in mentally retarded adolescents (Singh, Watson, & Winton, 1986). The spray of water (at room temperature) or the brief facial screening (five seconds) was contingent upon instances of self-injurious behavior.

The rationale behind many techniques of this kind has been to develop procedures that provide minimal discomfort but can effectively suppress behavior. The use of lemon juice as an aversive event illustrates this rationale. Although the taste of lemon juice is obviously unattractive to most people, its use as an aversive event is probably more socially acceptable than such other procedures as electric shock. Indeed, in one example above, lemon juice was used to suppress severely dangerous behaviors where shock might have been considered as an alternative.

Withdrawal of Positive Consequences

Punishment often takes the form of withdrawing positive events, rather than presenting aversive events after behavior. Familiar examples include the loss of privileges, money, or one's driver's license after behavior. Events that are positively valued and that may even have served as positive reinforcers are taken away as a form of penalty. The two major techniques, each with several variations, are time out from reinforcement and response cost.

Time Out from Reinforcement. Punishment often takes the form of removing a positive event. One procedure for removing a positive event is *time out from reinforcement* (or simply time-out), *which refers to the removal of all positive reinforcers for a certain period of time*. During the time-out interval, the client does not have access to the positive reinforcers that are normally available in the setting. For example, a child may be isolated from others in class for 10 minutes. During that time, he or she will not have access to peer interaction, activities, privileges, and other reinforcers that are usually available.

The crucial ingredient of time-out is delineating a brief period during which reinforcement is unavailable. Ideally, during this period, *all* sources of reinforcement are withdrawn. However, this ideal is not always attained. For example, if a child is sent to his or her room as punishment, removal from the existing sources of reinforcement qualifies as time-out. However, all reinforcement may not be withheld, because the child may engage in any number of reinforcing activities such as playing, listening to music, sleeping, or talking to oneself. Despite these possibilities, time-out usually consists of making reinforcing events unavailable to the client for a brief period.

A variety of time-out procedures have been used effectively in treatment. In many variations, the client is physically isolated or excluded in some way from the situation. The client may be sent to a time-out room or booth, a special place that is partitioned off from others. For example, noncompliance with requests among mentally retarded residents was suppressed by requiring a child to sit in the corner of the room for 40 seconds for an instance of noncompliance (Doleys et al., 1976). Similarly, alcohol consumption among hospitalized chronic alcoholics was suppressed with time-out (Bigelow, Liebson, & Griffiths, 1974). The patients were allowed free access to alcoholic beverages on the ward. During time-out, they were placed in an isolation booth for 10–15 minutes contingent upon drinking.

Although many programs using time-out have employed isolation (removal from the situation) as the time-out procedure, alternative procedures are available that still meet the definition of time-out. One time-out procedure that does not involve removing the individual from the situation was used to suppress disruptive behavior among children (ranging in age from one to three years) who attended a day-care center (Porterfield, Herbert-Jackson, & Risley, 1976). Disruptive behaviors such as hitting or pushing peers, crying and fussing, engaging in tantrums, and breaking toys were punished with time-out procedures while the children engaged in free-play activities. When disruptive behavior occurred, the child was told that the behavior was inappropriate and removed to the periphery of the other children's activity. While away from the center of activity in the room the child was still allowed to observe the activity and the other children. However, the child was not allowed to play with toys. After a brief period, usually less than one minute, the child was allowed to return to his or her activities in the center of the room. Partial removal of children from their activities markedly decreased their disruptive behavior.

Variations of time-out have been used in which the client is not even partially removed from the situation. For example, in one program, time-out was used as part of a reinforcement program for boys in a special education class for mentally retarded children in a state institution (Foxx & Shapiro, 1978). As part of the reinforcement system, the children received praise and smiles (social reinforcement) for performing their work. Each child in the class was given a ribbon to wear around his neck. The ribbon signified to the child and the teacher that the child could receive social and, occasionally, food reinforcers that were administered while the children worked. When any disruptive behavior was performed, a time-out procedure was used. Time-out consisted of removing the child's ribbon for three minutes. Without the ribbon, the child could not receive any of the reinforcers normally administered. This time-out procedure effectively reduced disruptive classroom behavior.

Positive reinforcers have been made unavailable in other ways to accomplish time out from reinforcement. For example, Mansdorf (1977) applied time-out to a mentally retarded adult who refused to comply with staff requests to take a shower. When this resident did not comply, she would simply sit in the dayroom and watch television, listen to music, or go back to bed. Time-out was used for noncompliance by removing her opportunities for reinforcement for a brief period. If she did not comply, television or music was turned off, peers were asked to leave the dayroom, and the pillow and bedding were removed. Essentially, the reinforcers she usually utilized were made temporarily unavailable. If she did comply, these reinforcing events were restored. The procedure was very effective in reducing the number of incidents of noncompliance, as shown in Figure 6–1. The effects were maintained six months after the program had been terminated.

Considerations in Using Time-Out. Time out from reinforcement has been very effective in altering a number of behaviors including psychotic speech, toileting accidents, thumb-sucking, and self-stimulatory and self-injurious behavior (see Hobbs & Forehand, 1977). Usually short time-out durations, such as several seconds or a few minutes, are effective in suppress-

FIGURE 6–1

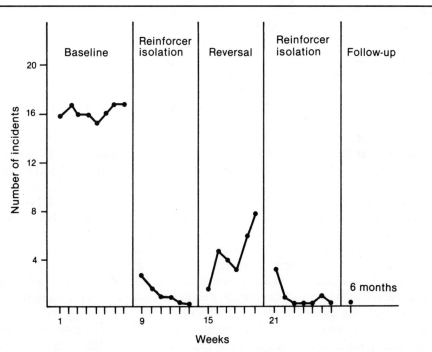

Number of noncompliant incidents per five-day workweek for each experimental condition.

SOURCE: Reprinted with permission from *Journal of Behavior Therapy and Experimental Psychiatry, 8,* 391–393. Mansdorf, I. J. Reinforcer isolation: An alternative to subject isolation in time out from positive reinforcement. Copyright 1977, Pergamon Press Inc.

ing behavior. Longer time-out periods do not necessarily increase the effectiveness of the procedure.

Obvious advantages of time-out are that it can be relatively brief and that it does not involve pain. Additional advantages and disadvantages of time-out depend on the specific form it takes. Removing individuals from the situation in which deviant behavior occurs (such as sending individuals to a time-out room), particularly for extended periods, has potential disadvantages. Removing individuals from the situation in which their performance is a problem reduces opportunities for positive reinforcement in that situation. Hence, the client cannot learn the desired behaviors and the conditions under which those behaviors are appropriate. Also, in some cases, it may be undesirable to leave the client isolated from others because of the opportunity that isolation provides for engaging in maladaptive behaviors. For example, in one report, an autistic child engaged in self-stimulatory behaviors when isolated from others (Solnick, Rincover, & Peterson, 1977).

Isolation from others may also be undesirable for clients who are socially withdrawn. Removal from the social situation may further isolate clients who already have only minimal interaction with others. A main goal of treatment should be to develop prosocial behaviors in the presence of other individuals and not to foster any more isolation, whether physical or social, than may already result from the client's interpersonal deficits.

Many of the objections to time-out are resolved with variations that do not remove the client from the situation. Leaving the client in the situation (such as a classroom) but setting aside brief periods in which reinforcers are not available has many advantages. A client who is allowed to remain in the situation can continue to participate in activities and can perhaps even observe others receive desirable consequences for appropriate behavior. Of course, an individual's behavior may be so disruptive that he or she has to be removed from the situation so as not to disturb or interfere with the activities of others. To handle this possible problem, some programs have allowed individuals to remain in the situation during time-out unless their behavior becomes very disruptive (LeBlanc, Busby, & Thomson, 1974; Porterfield et al., 1976). Using social isolation to back up a less severe form of time-out is an excellent strategy because when this strategy is used, the client is removed from the situation only if necessary.

The extent to which time-out will be effective is likely to depend on the situation from which the client is removed. That ongoing situation, sometimes referred to as "time in," denotes the situation and reinforcing consequences from which the client is withdrawn. If the environment is highly reinforcing (e.g., frequent praise, earning of points, peer interaction), a brief period of time-out is likely to be more effective than it would be if the environment was devoid of reinforcing consequences (Solnick et al., 1977). In practice, time-out does not require that an ongoing reinforcement program or richly rewarding environment be in effect during the time-in period. During any punishment program, some reinforcement should be provided to develop positive and prosocial behavior. Consequently, reinforcement plus time-out is likely to be more effective than time-out alone.

In general, time-out provides an excellent alternative to many of the forms of punishment used in everyday life, such as reprimands and corporal punishment. Very brief time-out, for several seconds or a few minutes, has been effective. Time-out has been especially effective when many reinforcers are available in the setting, so that time out from these reinforcing events is especially aversive (Solnick et al., 1977, Exp. 2). Occasionally, time-out has been ineffective for some individuals and has even served as a positive reinforcer (Foxx & Azrin, 1972; Plummer, Baer, & LeBlanc, 1977; Solnick et al., 1977, Exp. 1). However, these findings are exceptions. The many currently available variations of time-out provide alternatives that are adaptable to most clients and settings.

Response Cost. *Response cost refers to a loss of a positive reinforcer.* With response cost, there is no period during which positive events are unavailable, as is the case with time out from reinforcement (Kazdin, 1972). Response cost requires a penalty of some sort, usually in the form of a fine. Examples of response cost in everyday experience include fines for traffic violations, fees for late filing of income tax or for registering for classes beyond the due date, charges for checks that "bounce," and charges for letters with too little postage.

In applied settings, response cost usually takes the form of a fine. For example, response cost was used as part of a contingency contract for an adult male alcoholic and his wife (Miller, 1972). The husband's excessive drinking was a major source of marital conflict. The contract specified that he could have only one to three drinks a day (instead of the average of seven to eight that he consumed during baseline) and that these could be consumed only before dinner. Any other drinking would require him to pay his wife $20 that she would spend as frivolously as possible, something that was very aversive to him. The wife agreed to refrain from negative verbal responses for her husband's drinking. She was required to pay him a $20 fine if she failed to do this. The husband's drinking decreased quickly and stabilized at a rate within the contract agreement. The effects were maintained up to six months when last observed.

Response cost was used to alter the classroom behavior of two second-grade hyperactive boys (Rapport, Murphy, & Bailey, 1982). The boys had poor attentiveness, high rates of disruptive behavior, and did not complete their academic seatwork. They were informed that they would receive 20 minutes of free time for working on their tasks without disruption but that they would lose 1 minute for each instance of inattentiveness. For example, for one of the boys, numbers from 20 to 1 were listed on cards near the teacher, with each number standing for the number of minutes of free time that remained. For each instance of inattentiveness, the teacher flipped the cards to the next lower value (from 20 to 19, etc.). The number remaining at the end of the lesson constituted the minutes of free time. Contingently withdrawing minutes of free time markedly improved the boys' attentiveness and academic performance. Medication (Ritalin) commonly used for hyperactive children also improved behavior but was less effective than response cost.

Response cost has often been used as part of token economies in which tokens are delivered for some behaviors and taken away for others. For example, in one program with psychiatric patients, fines were levied whenever patients violated a rule of the ward (Upper, 1973). Infractions included such behaviors as getting up late in the morning, undressing or exposing oneself, and shouting. Violations dropped below baseline rates when a fine was subtracted from token earnings. Whether implemented alone or in conjunction with token economies, response cost has altered a wide variety of behaviors such as overeating, disruptive classroom behavior, speech disfluencies, psychotic speech, thumb-sucking, and toileting accidents (see Kazdin, 1977a).

Considerations in Using Response Cost. Response cost, particularly in the form of withdrawing points or tokens after behavior, is relatively easy to implement. One problem that may arise is that clients who lose many points may soon have no further points to lose. However, more points or tokens can be given to such clients at the beginning of a new session or day or can be earned by them for other behaviors to ensure that points can be withdrawn contingent upon the undesired behavior.

One clear benefit of the use of response cost in the form of fines is that the procedure provides the opportunity to deliver positive reinforcers for behavior. If tokens or points are to be withdrawn, they have to be delivered to the client. Behavior change is likely to be more rapid if the tokens are delivered for behaviors incompatible with the responses that are to be suppressed. Hence, when points or tokens are used, reinforcement and punishment in the form of response cost can easily be implemented as part of a single program. Moreover, token reinforcement and response cost combined are more effective than either procedure alone (Phillips et al., 1971; Walker, Hops, & Feigenbaum, 1976).

Punishing Consequences Based on Effort

As a consequence for undesirable behavior, a client can be required to engage in responses that entail work or effort. This is different from presenting the client with an aversive stimulus (e.g., reprimand) or withdrawing a positive event from the client (e.g., response cost). Here the client is required to engage in aversive behavior.

Overcorrection. With overcorrection, the penalty for engaging in an undesirable behavior is performing some other behaviors in the situation. Two components of overcorrection can be distinguished. The first component, referred to as *restitution,* consists of correcting the environmental effects of the inappropriate behavior. Thus, if a child throws food at the dinner table, he or she would be required to clean it up completely. The second component, referred to as *positive practice,* consists of repeatedly practicing the appropriate behavior. For example, the child would be required to place food on his or her plate appropriately several times in a row and perhaps to serve others food as well. These responses are some of the "correct" ways of serving and managing food at the table. Restitution and positive practice are sometimes combined and sometimes used alone, depending on the behaviors that are to be suppressed.

As an illustration, Foxx and Azrin (1972) used restitution and positive practice with a profoundly retarded 50-year-old female who had been hospitalized for 46 years. For several years, this client had engaged in severely disruptive and aggressive behavior, especially throwing things. When she performed a disruptive behavior (e.g., overturning a bed), she was required to correct the physical effects of her behavior on the environment (i.e., turn the bed to its correct position and straighten the spread and pillows). In addition, she was required to rehearse the correct behavior by straightening all of the other beds on the ward. Thus, she had to correct the immediate consequence of whatever inappropriate behavior she performed (restitution) and then to practice repeatedly the correct behavior throughout the ward (positive practice). After 11 weeks of training, she no longer threw objects.

An interesting application of overcorrection was used to eliminate stealing among hospitalized mentally retarded adults (Azrin & Wesolowski, 1974). The residents had a high rate of stealing from one another, especially food during meal and snack times when they purchased items at a commissary (store) in the hospital. A staff member simply required the resident to return the food or the remaining portion if it had been partially consumed. Return of the food did not completely restore the original situation if the food had been partially consumed. With this procedure (called simple correction), stealing remained at a high rate. An overcorrection procedure was implemented that required the resident not only to to return the food but also to purchase more of that food and give it to the victim. The results, illustrated in Figure 6–2, show that theft was eliminated among the 34 residents within a matter of a few days.

It is not possible to have individuals "correct" the environmental consequences of many behaviors that are to be suppressed. The behaviors may not have altered the environment. For example, if a child whines, hits himself, rocks back and forth, or stutters, there are no clear environmental consequences that can be corrected. For such behaviors, positive practice is often used alone. After the undesired behavior has been performed, the client is required to positively practice an appropriate or incompatible behavior. For example, positive practice was used to alter the classroom behavior of six disruptive boys enrolled in a special summer class (Azrin & Powers, 1975). Talking out and being out of one's seat were decreased by having the children who engaged in these behaviors remain in at recess. During this recess period, a child would practice appropriate classroom behavior by sitting in his seat, raising his hand, being recognized by the teacher, and asking permission to get up. This entire sequence was repeated for approximately five minutes, a

FIGURE 6–2

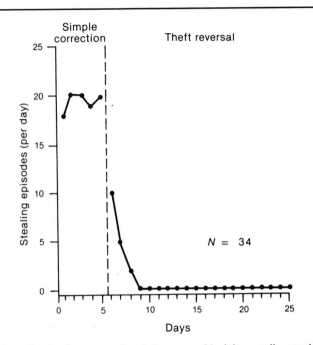

Number of stealing episodes that occurred each day among 34 adult mentally retarded residents in an institution. During the five days of simple correction, the thief was required to return the stolen item. During the theft-reversal (overcorrection) procedure (subsequent to the vertical dashed line), the thief was required to return the stolen item and to give the victim an additional item identical to the one stolen. The stealing episodes consisted of stealing food items from other mentally retarded residents during commissary periods.

SOURCE: Azrin, N. H., & Wesolowski, M. D. (1974). Theft reversal: An overcorrection procedure for eliminating stealing by retarded persons. *Journal of Applied Behavior Analysis, 7,* 577–581. Copyright 1974 by the Society for the Experimental Analysis of Behavior, Inc.

procedure that markedly improved classroom performance. Loss of recess without engaging in positive practice did not achieve the marked changes associated with positive practice.

    Considerations in Using Overcorrection. Overcorrection alone or in combination with other procedures has altered a variety of behaviors such as toileting accidents, aggressive acts, self-stimulatory behaviors, tantrums, nail-biting, and table manners (Foxx & Bechtel, 1983; Ollendick & Matson, 1978). Overcorrection procedures vary widely, depending on the specific behavior that is suppressed and the desired behavior that is developed in its place. The procedures are developed from the general principle of having individuals correct environmental consequences of their actions, where such consequences exist, and practicing the desired behavior repeatedly after each instance of the undesired behavior. The results of a few minutes of corrective training after the undesired behavior has often led to rapid and long-lasting therapeutic effects.

Certainly, the distinguishing feature of overcorrection, in relation to other punishment techniques, is that it focuses on the appropriate behavior that is incompatible with the undesired response. Most forms of punishment do not convey to the client the behaviors that are appropriate. The positive practice component of overcorrection trains desirable behaviors and thus serves an educative function not included in other aversive techniques. Indeed, research has shown that, unlike other punishment procedures, overcorrection not only suppresses inappropriate behavior but also develops positive appropriate behaviors (Carey & Bucher, 1981). There is a related benefit of the procedure. In the usual punishment procedure, parents, teachers, or staff focus their attention on undesirable behaviors that need to be suppressed. Overcorrection shifts attention to desirable behaviors that need to be developed, the priority of any behavior change program.

For use of overcorrection, one must identify both the behavior that will correct the environment and the appropriate behavior that should be performed. When the undesired behavior is performed, the client is immediately required to engage in the sequence of behaviors that restore and overcorrect the action. If simple instructions to complete the requisite behaviors prove insufficient, the client may need to be physically guided (assisted) by the parent or teacher to go through these behaviors. Guiding the client through requisite behaviors can be problematic if the client resists or becomes aggressive (Foxx, 1982). If physical force is necessary, alternative procedures may need to be used.

Another consideration in using overcorrection is that it often requires more supervision than do alternative techniques. The person in charge of the program must ensure that the client goes through the overcorrection sequence for the allotted time and must provide physical prompts if necessary. In some situations, it may not be feasible to provide one-to-one client supervision to conduct overcorrection. For example, in a classroom situation, overcorrection has on occasion been discontinued in part because of the difficulties in supervising overcorrection while managing the rest of the class (Kelly & Drabman, 1977). On the other hand, applications have shown that in a classroom situation overcorrection can be delayed and conducted at recess time or during free periods, when direct supervision of the client need not detract from others in the room (Azrin & Powers, 1975; Barton & Osborne, 1978).

Overall, the rapid and dramatic effects of overcorrection have made this a viable treatment technique for a variety of problems. In many studies, overcorrection has achieved changes in behaviors where other techniques (such as time-out, reprimands, reinforcement of other behavior, and physical restraint) have not proven effective. Although definitive statements about the relative effectiveness of alternative punishment techniques cannot be made at this time, overcorrection appears to be very effective in its own right. In addition, evidence suggests that parents, teachers, and children view overcorrection as a punishment procedure that is more acceptable than such alternatives as isolation (Kazdin, French, & Sherick, 1981).

Other Effort-Based Consequences.   The unique feature of overcorrection is that the behaviors that the client must perform as part of restitution and positive practice are directly related to the behavior that is to be suppressed. However, behaviors involving effort that bear no logical connection to the target behavior have also been effective. The effectiveness of such applications can be expected, based on a variation of the Premack principle. The principle was discussed previously in the context of positive reinforcement in which high-probability (or highly preferred) behaviors (e.g., playing) serve as reinforcers for low-probability (or less preferred) behaviors (e.g., working). The principle also suggests an arrangement of the contingency that can suppress behavior and be used as punishment. Low-probability behaviors can be used as consequences for an undesirable response.

For example, in one program, verbal and physical aggression were suppressed in two emotionally disturbed children in a special education classroom (Luce, Delquadri, & Hall, 1980). One of the children, a seven-year-old boy named Ben, engaged in aggression, severe tantrums, and self-stimulatory behavior. Ben's hitting of other children at school was the target behavior that was to be suppressed. Engaging in exercise was used as the aversive consequence. When Ben hit someone, he was required to stand up and sit down on the floor 10 times (which required less than 30 seconds). Initially, he was physically prompted by the teacher, who helped him up and down. Then, verbal prompts alone were sufficient to ensure that he completed the exercise. The effects of the program, illustrated in Figure 6–3, show that low rates of aggressive behavior were obtained when the exercise contingency was in effect. At a follow-up assessment $1\frac{1}{2}$ years after the program was terminated, Ben's hitting had been completely eliminated.

In a somewhat different procedure, individuals can be required to engage in various aversive chores. For example, Fischer and Nehs (1978) altered the excessive swearing of an 11-year-old-boy. The boy was told that each time he swore, he would be required to wash windows in the residential facility for 10 minutes. The procedure effectively suppressed his swearing. It remained at a low frequency two weeks after the program had been terminated.

Considerations in Using Effort.   The use of effort-based activities as aversive consequences has advantages. The activities (exercises, chores) are quite familiar to parents, teachers, staff, and clients. Consequently, less training is needed in using effort than in using other procedures such as overcorrection, where novel behaviors of the behavior change agent (e.g., special prompting) and the client (e.g., special routine to practice new behavior) may need to be trained and closely supervised.

An important consideration with exercise of other effort-based procedures is whether performing the aversive behavior may interrupt ongoing behavior or be disruptive in the situation. For example, in one study, contingent exercise was used to reduce a boy's inappropriate and bizarre verbalizations in a classroom (Luce & Hall, 1981). Instances of these behaviors were followed by a brief run (20 seconds) around the playground. Although such a procedure suppresses behavior, it may also interrupt sitting at one's desk, remaining in

FIGURE 6–3

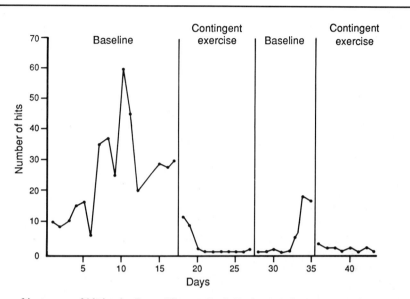

Number of instances of hitting by Ben while at school. During baseline, the aggressive behavior was ignored and no special program was provided to alter it. During the contingent-exercise phase, Ben was required to stand up and sit down on the floor for instances of hitting.

SOURCE: Luce, S. C., Delquadri, J., & Hall, R. V. (1980). Contingent exercise: A mild but powerful procedure for suppressing inappropriate verbal and aggressive behavior. *Journal of Applied Behavior Analysis, 13*, 583–594. Copyright 1980 by the Society for the Experimental Analysis of Behavior, Inc.

the situation, and possibly receiving reinforcement for remaining at a task. Another potential problem, not yet reported, is that engaging in exercise or leaving the situation (going to the playground) may actually serve as a reinforcer (e.g., escape from an aversive task or situation) for some children.

Effort-based procedures such as exercise or chores focus on suppressing undesirable behaviors. With such procedures, unlike overcorrection, no attempt is made to teach an appropriate behavior to replace the target response. For example, one does not want a child to exercise in the classroom or to run around the playground in the middle of a lesson. Overcorrection focuses on developing positive alternative behaviors in addition to suppressing the target response. If feasible in the situation, it may be the most preferable of the effort-based procedures.

SELECTING PROCEDURES TO SUPPRESS BEHAVIORS

The precise punishment procedure selected in any instance may be determined by several considerations, including the severity of the behavior, the danger of the behavior to the client or others, the ease of implementing the procedure in a particular setting, and the training required of the person(s) administering the behavior modification program. For example, response cost might be relatively easily administered and effective with many behaviors and require less time and supervision than would overcorrection. Overcorrection, if more difficult to implement, might be reserved for cases in which less complex procedures proved ineffective. The punishment procedures selected should be the least restrictive or intrusive among those available. Although shock might be effective in suppressing behavior, the severity of the procedure makes it ethically unacceptable unless less severe procedures have failed. Similarly, physically restraining or isolating someone is defensible only if less restrictive procedures (e.g., time-out, response cost) have failed.

When aversive consequences are used to suppress behavior, special consideration might be given to the specific events used and to the possible long-range consequences of using them. Procedures commonly used in everyday life (but usually not in behavior modification programs) often require individuals to engage in tasks that should probably not be used as aversive events. For example, requiring children to stay in from recess or to remain after school, to write "I shall not swear" 500 times on the blackboard, to complete extra homework, or to see the principal when they are disruptive may defeat many of the inherent goals of school. Presumably, we do not want children to learn that these events are aversive. The fact that behavioral programs have occasionally used escape from the classroom as a reinforcer and completion of academic tasks as a punisher (e.g., Harris & Sherman, 1973; MacPherson, Candee, & Hohman, 1974) suggests that important characteristics associated with school are already imbued with aversive properties. Nevertheless, an important goal is to develop positive attitudes and approach responses to these and similar events. To treat various activities or staff as aversive consequences may make school aversive, especially for students who are not obtaining other rewards (e.g., good grades, achievement, peer status, and popularity.)

At present, the long-term consequences of using particular aversive events are not known. Hence, considerations about selection of the events need to be based on information about the individual case and about possible consequences that might result. In short, common sense as well as scientific evidence should enter into the selection of specific punishing consequences.

Behavior modification research has developed and evaluated a large number of aversive techniques. This may seem ironic, given the evidence that, if at all possible, punishment should not be used, and then only as a supplement to a reinforcement program. Yet research on punishment in applied settings has several obligations. Not only should such research develop effective procedures, but the procedures should be humane, socially acceptable to clients, relatively easy to implement, and not readily subject to abuse. The development of alternative punishment procedures has often been based on these considerations.

FACTORS THAT INFLUENCE THE EFECTIVENESS OF PUNISHMENT

The effectiveness of punishment, like that of reinforcement, depends on several conditions. However, the conditions that contribute to the effectiveness of punishment have been somewhat less investigated than the conditions that contribute to the effectiveness of reinforcement. Although punishment has been evaluated extensively in the laboratory (Azrin & Holz, 1966; Hutchinson, 1977), most of the laboratory research dealt with the presentation of aversive events. The removal of positive events has been less well studied. Nevertheless, general statements regarding the conditions that should maximize the effectiveness of punishment can be extrapolated from laboratory and applied research.

Delay of Punishment

Punishment is more effective as positive reinforcement when it is delivered immediately after the target response than when it is delayed. If punishment of the undesirable response is delayed, it immediately follows some other behavior that may be desirable. For example, if a parent punishes a child for some behavior performed earlier that day ("Wait until your father [or mother] comes home"), the delayed punishment would have a weak effect on the undesirable behavior. Moreover, a desirable behavior (e.g., helping with chores) may have been performed in close contiguity with that punishment and may thus be inadvertently suppressed by the punishment. Independently of the specific response that occurs during the delay, if punishment is delayed, it is not likely to be associated with the response that is to be suppressed.

In some cases, punishment is delayed because the undesirable response, such as theft or lying, cannot be detected immediately. The fact that the consequences would be so delayed may raise questions about their likely effects. However, there are ways to bring the consequences in closer proximity to the undesired behaviors. One method is to reenact portions of the previously performed behaviors that occurred and to apply aversive consequences immediately to the reenactment. Such procedures appear to bring the consequences closer to the behavior and lead to response suppression (Van Houten & Rolider, 1988).

Schedule of Punishment

Punishment is more effective when the punishing consequence occurs every time (continuous punishment), rather than once in a while (intermittent punishment). The greater the proportion of punished responses, the greater is the response reduction. However, when punishment is discontinued, recovery of the response is greater with continuous punishment than with intermittent punishment. For example, if time-out is to be used in the home, it should be delivered every time the behavior occurs (continuous schedule). Administering time-out intermittently, rather than after each occurrence of the response, usually leads to less response suppression (Hobbs & Forehand, 1977). However, after a response has been effectively suppressed, punishment can be delivered only intermittently to maintain low rates of the behavior (Calhoun & Lima, 1977; Clark, Rowbury, Baer, & Baer, 1973). In some circumstances and in the use of electric shock, the relationship between punishment schedule and response suppression does *not* hold. There may be no recovery even if punishment was previously delivered on a continuous schedule.

Source of Reinforcement

If a punished response is also positively reinforced, punishment is less effective than if that response is not reinforced. That a punished behavior is performed at all suggests that some reinforcer is maintaining it; otherwise, the behavior would have extinguished. The effect of punishment can be enhanced by removing the source of reinforcement for the punished response. For example, delinquents frequently provide peer social reinforcement for the commission of deviant acts. Punishment of deviant acts is likely to be less effective when there is such reinforcement.

When punishment is used, potential sources of reinforcement for the punished response should be identified and eliminated if possible. In practice, it is sometimes difficult to identify the source of the reinforcement that is maintaining a deviant behavior. However, in many instances, it is evident that teachers and parents socially reinforce behaviors that they wish to suppress. In situations such as the classroom, peers probably reinforce inappropriate behaviors (e.g., clowning, teasing). Punishing disruptive behavior would be expected to have less effect if peers provide reinforcement for those behaviors.

Timing of Punishment in the Response Sequence

The earlier in the response sequence punishment is delivered, the more effective it tends to be. An undesirable response is not a single behavior but a chain or sequence of behaviors that culminates in an act considered undesirable. For example, a child's "theft" of a cookie prior to dinner may consist of a series (chain) of behaviors that includes walking into the kitchen, climbing onto a chair, reaching for the cookie jar, opening the jar, taking a cookie, and eating it. Punishment for going into the kitchen or climbing onto a chair will reduce cookie theft to a greater extent than will punishment after the cookie has been taken and eaten.

The importance of the timing of punishment can be readily explained. If the response chain is completed, the terminal behavior (e.g., cookie consumption) is positively reinforced. Punishment imposed at that time is being used to suppress a response that has just been reinforced. This is not likely to be effective. Moreover, if the chain is completed, the reinforcement of the undesirable response is more immediate than the punishment. As mentioned previously, punishment is more effective when the response to be suppressed is not reinforced than when it is reinforced. Hence, if a response is punished before it is reinforced, punishment should be more effective. Responses early in the chain of behavior may still be reinforced, since behaviors in a chain reinforce prior behaviors in that chain. But the further from the terminal reinforcer a behavior is, the less potent is the reinforcment. Behaviors early in a sequence are further removed from the terminal reinforcer, so their conditioned reinforcing properties are weaker and they are more readily suppressed when punishment is applied. Thus, a punishing consequence (e.g., reprimand) that might be ineffective at the end of the response sequence, might well lead to suppression if administered earlier in the sequence.

A potential problem in applying punishment to initial behaviors in a response chain is that the behaviors at this point in the chain may be part of other response chains that constitute appropriate behavior. To continue our example, punishment of cookie theft might be very effective if it is delivered when the child enters the kitchen. However, entering the kitchen may be a part of appropriate chains, such as washing dishes, feeding a pet, washing one's hands, or hugging one's parents.

Variation of Punishment

Application of aversive events usually consists of a contingency in which a particular consequence (e.g., reprimand or time-out) is applied after the behavior. Recent research suggests that the effects of punishment can be enhanced by varying the punishers that follow behavior (Charlop, Burgio, Iwata, & Ivancic, 1988). For example, rather than using overcorrection, brief time-out, or a reprimand after behavior, the specific consequence can be varied. Thus, on some occasions one of the consequences (time-out) might be used, while on other occasions another consequence (reprimand) would be used. Variation of the aversive consequence leads to greater suppression of the responses than use of any of the individual consequences applied to the behavior. Apparently, there is an adaptation to repeated use of the same consequence that is obviated by variation of the consequence.

The importance of varying the consequences after behavior raises an important point. The effectiveness of mild punishers (e.g., reprimands, time-out) can be enhanced by varying the consequences that are presented. Thus, less severe punishers can be used to suppress behavior if they are varied. An important caution is in order. *Variation* of consequences is to be distinguished from the *combination* of consequences. The findings suggest that application of a consequence after behavior is more effective when that consequence changes; this does not mean in any way that several consequences should be given at the same time after an instance of behavior. The combination of many aversive procedures as a penalty for performance is a misplaced focus and is objectionable for ethical as well as practical reasons.

Reinforcement of Alternative Responses

Punishment is most effective when it is accompanied by reinforcement for performing desirable or prosocial behaviors. *Aversive events of relatively weak intensity can effectively suppress behavior if reinforcement is also provided for an alternative positive response.* Thus, intense punishment is not required to suppress behavior. Mildy aversive events (e.g., grimaces, statements of disapproval, or saying no) may only temporarily suppress undesired behavior. However, their suppressive effect will be enhanced if reinforcement is delivered for positive behaviors.

Even aversive consequences that are not effective by themselves can be effective when they are combined with reinforcement for alternative forms of behavior (Azrin & Holz, 1966). As an example, in one program, an attempt was made to train a profoundly retarded child to walk rather than crawl. Whenever the child crawled, he was restrained (held at the waist for five seconds) (O'Brien, Azrin, & Bugle, 1972). This procedure did not decrease crawling or increase walking. Then the investigators added a positive aspect to the restraint procedure. Whenever the child crawled, he was restrained as before, but he was also aided in walking for a few seconds. Reinforcing an alternative response (continued movement in an upright position), resulted in a dramatic decrease in crawling and an increase in walking. Restraint alone was effective once walking had been established.

Most applications of punishment in behavior modification include reinforcement for desirable behavior. For example, in one program, toddlers were required to sit during the activities in a day-care center as a time-out procedure for disruptive behavior (Porterfield et al., 1976). In addition, approval was provided when a child was playing appropriately. In this and other studies, punishment alone might have been used to suppress behavior. However, suppressing an undesirable behavior does not guarantee that a desirable behavior will take its place. *Punishment usually trains a person in what not to do rather than in what to do.* For example, suppression of fighting in a delinquent does not guarantee the appearance of desirable social behavior.

Overcorrection, as a punishment technique, includes the practice of appropriate behavior to help make punishment more educative than is ordinarily the case. However, the behaviors that are positively practiced in overcorrection are not always desirable prosocial responses. Rather, they are often behaviors that appear to be incompatible with the response that is to be suppressed. For example, one study reported the use of overcorrection to eliminate self-injurious behavior in a psychotic and severely retarded adult (Azrin, Gottlieb, Hughart, Wesolowski, & Rahn, 1975). The positive practice component of the procedure included engaging in fixed bodily postures (e.g., practice in holding the hands away from the body in a sequence of exercises) that were incompatible with hitting oneself. Since these behaviors were not socially desirable in their own right, separate reinforcement contingencies were included to develop appropriate social behaviors and participation in activities on the ward.

For at least three reasons, it is advisable to use positive reinforcement whenever punishment is employed. First, reinforcement for alternative responses increases the efficacy of punishment (Azrin & Holz, 1966). Second, reinforcement can develop appropriate behaviors to displace the inappropriate behaviors that are to be eliminated. Third, positive reinforcement combined with punishment may eliminate undesirable side effects that might result from the use of punishment alone (see below). As a general rule, whether the goal is to increase or decrease a particular behavior, reinforcement techniques should constitute the primary basis of the behavior change program. Any of the various punishment techniques may be a valuable adjunct to reinforcement techniques but perhaps should not be used alone.

General Comments

In the discussion of the factors that influence the effectiveness of punishment, one of the more familiar dimensions considered in everyday life, namely intensity of punishment, was omitted. In everyday applications, such as child rearing, it is often assumed that the greater the intensity of punishment, the greater is the suppression of behavior. Thus, advocates of "spare the rod and spoil the child" often believe that a "really good" spanking is needed to teach a lesson. In general, however, laboratory and applied evidence does *not* support the view that increased intensity of punishment results in increased suppression of a response. There is an exception in laboratory research: the presentation of electric shock at higher intensities has suppressed behavior more quickly than its presentation at lower intensities (Azrin & Holz, 1966). However, this relation does not hold for other aversive events in the laboratory (e.g., noise) or for the many events that are studied in applied settings. For example, louder reprimands, shouts, or threats do not show more suppressive effects than milder forms of these events.

In the withdrawal of positive reinforcers, the more intense punishments are not needed. Even when a reinforcer is withdrawn for a short period (time-out), which does not seem to be an "intense" aversive consequence, response suppression may be dramatic. Occasionally, an increase in the duration of time-out, up to several minutes, has led to greater suppression of behavior (e.g., Hobbs, Forehand, & Murray, 1978). Similarly, for response cost (loss of tokens), larger fines have occasionally suppressed behavior more effectively than smaller fines (Kazdin, 1971). However, these findings do *not* justify long periods of time-out or large fines, because far milder consequences are quite effective. For example, with time-out, extremely brief periods, including periods ranging from 15 to 90 *seconds,* have been very effective in several studies. This is quite different from sending children to their rooms for 30 to 60 minutes, as parents often do, or for eight or nine hours, as abusive parents occasionally do. Such harsh punishments are not only unnecessary but are likely to be ineffective for the child and frustrating for the parents. Much milder punishments, included as part of a program that reinforces prosocial or positive behaviors, can accomplish the goals much more effectively.

SIDE EFFECTS OF PUNISHMENT

Types of Effects

An argument against the use of punishment is that it often results in undesirable side effects. Even though punishment may eliminate the target behavior, it may have other consequences that are worse than the original behavior or at least problematic in their own right. Laboratory research, usually with infrahuman subjects, provides evidence for a variety of undesirable side effects of punishment (Azrin & Holz, 1966; Hutchinson, 1977). These side effects also arise in applied situations where punishment is used.

Emotional Reactions.   Undesirable emotional reactions may result from punishment. These reactions may be temporarily disruptive to the individual. For example, when a child receives a spanking, crying, anger, and similar emotional reactions will probably occur. These reactions are not essential ingredients of punishment, but undesirable concomitant effects. They are undesirable, in part, because they may interfere with new learning. The child may be unresponsive to his social environment until he is no longer upset or angry. An additional consideration is that undesirable emotional reactions are frequently paired with cues in the punishment situation. Eventually, the cues themselves (e.g., a given individual such as a parent or teacher or a given situation such as the home) may produce similar reactions in the absence of punishment.

Escape and Avoidance.   Another side effect of punishment is that it can lead to escape from or avoidance of the punishment situation. If a situation is aversive, an individual can terminate the aversive condition by escaping. Successful escape from the situation is negatively reinforced, because it terminates an aversive condition. Even if the punishing event is only mildly aversive and too weak to suppress behavior, it may still lead to escape behavior (Azrin & Holz, 1966). Hence, the use of aversive stimuli fosters escape and reinforcement of escape behaviors. For example, reliance on punishment in the home may result in attempts to avoid or escape from the home.

Stimuli associated with an aversive situation may also lead to escape. Recall that any event consistently associated with an aversive event becomes aversive in its own right. If one individual is constantly punishing another individual, the punishing agent will take on properties of a conditioned aversive stimulus. The individual whose behavior is punished will attempt to escape from or avoid the punishing agent because of these properties. This side effect is undesirable because if individuals (e.g., children) escape or avoid punishing agents (e.g., parents and teachers), the punishing agents will be unable to provide reinforcement to train desirable responses.

Aggression.   In laboratory work with a variety of species, punishment sometimes results in attacks by one animal on another animal or on the source of punishment (Hutchinson, 1977). In applied programs using punishment, there is the possibility that the punished individual will aggress toward the punishing agent. Attacking the agent may remove the source of punishment, at least temporarily. Hence, the individual's aggression toward the punishing agent is *negatively reinforced* by terminating an aversive event. For example, if an adolescent fights back when being severely beaten by a parent, this may terminate the parental assault. Fighting back, if effective, terminates the aversive consequence by the parent and is negatively reinforced. (Unfortunately, if fighting back is effective, the adolescent's aggressive behavior is reinforced for severe aggressive behavior.)

Modeled Punishment.   The punishing agent *models* (or provides an example of) certain behaviors, namely the use of aversive control techniques that the punished individual may learn. If a parent uses physical punishment with a child, especially harsh punishment, this increases the likelihood that the child will engage in physically aggressive behaviors (Timberlake, 1981). Adults provide models for how to interact with others, Indeed, in interactions with their peers, children appear to use behavioral control techniques similar to the techniques that their parents use to control them (Hoffman, 1960). Thus, it is no surprise that children who are referred clinically for severely aggressive behaviors often come from homes where child and spouse abuse have been evident (see Kazdin, 1987a). Unfortunately, abuse in the home provides effective models that may help train children to become aggressive, apart from other influences operating in the environment. Certainly, caution is required in using aversive techniques—particularly physical punishment—because of the modeling influences of their use.

Perpetuation of Punishment.   Another undesirable side effect of punishment is that its use is reinforced in the person who administers it. Punishment usually results in rapid (though temporary) reduction of the target response. If a parent shouts at a child, the child's behavior is usually altered immediately. Thus, the parent's behavior (shout) is *negatively reinforced* (termination of some undesirable child behavior). Because reinforcement is a powerful technique, particularly if it is immediate, the frequency with which the parent delivers punishment is likely to increase. Even though the punishment is not likely to alter the child's behavior for very long, the failure of the punishment is delayed, whereas the short-term effect is immediate. Hence, the parent is likely to rely increasingly on punishment and runs the risk of encountering the side effects discussed above.

Illustrations from Applied Settings

Negative Side Effects.   Side effects of punishment have been reported in many applications and across a wide range of aversive techniques. For example, in one program, mentally retarded children received verbal reprimands for noncompliance with requests (Doleys et al., 1976). Some of the children showed brief periods of crying, soiling, and wetting their pants. Similarly, reports of programs using overcorrection, response cost, time-out, and shock have occasionally noted that the crying, tantrums, and emotional outbursts of the clients increased and that the clients were generally upset (e.g., Azrin & Wesolowski, 1975; Carey & Bucher, 1981; Matson & Ollendick, 1977). These reports clearly suggest that *emotional side effects* may be associated with punishment.

Studies have also demonstrated that *avoidance* may be associated with punishment. For example, in two studies, children were exposed to adults who administered different consequences during play activities (Morris & Redd, 1975; Redd, Morris, & Martin, 1975). Subsequently, the children were asked to choose the adults with whom they wished to interact. The adults who had been associated with the delivery of punishment (reprimands) were generally not selected for further interaction, whereas those who had been associated with positive reinforcement (praise) were the most frequently selected for further interaction. This research suggests a clear preference for agents who administer reinforcing consequences rather than punishing consequences. Agents who primarily administer punishment are not sought out when clients are given the opportunity for additional interaction. If these findings extend to education and child rearing, children's avoidance of their teacher or parents may be fostered in part by the types of consequences that teachers or parents administer.

Aggression has also been found to be a side effect of punishment. Applications of overcorrection, reprimands, and brief slaps to the hand have effectively suppressed behavior (e.g., Foxx & Azrin, 1972; Mayhew & Harris, 1978). However, increases in attacks on the trainer (e.g., hitting, pinching, throwing things) have been reported early in training. Occasionally, the aggression associated with punishment has been self-inflicted. For example, applications of overcorrection have been associated with increases in self-injurious behavior in some clients (Azrin et al., 1975; Rollings, Baumeister, & Baumeister, 1977).

The negative side effects obtained in using punishment programs appear to be exceptions rather than the rule. And when undesirable side effects appear, they are usually temporary and they usually subside over the course of treatment.

Positive Side Effects.   Occasionally, suppression of behavior leads to positive side effects. For example, in one report, time-out was used to punish the disruptive behavior of a 10-year-old child in a classroom (Jackson & Calhoun, 1977). There was an increase in the child's appropriate social behaviors, such as initiating conversations with peers and joining in activities, even though these were not specifically focused on. Similarly, in another study, reductions in vomiting achieved by using lemon juice were associated with a decrease in episodes of crying and with increases in verbal behaviors (Becker, Turner, & Sajwaj, 1978). Social behaviors, including smiling, communication, and laughing with another resident or a staff member, increased as self-injurious behavior was decreased by the contingent application of water mist or facial screening (Singh et al., 1986). Several studies have found that use of punishment techniques such as overcorrection and time-out are associated with decreases in such behaviors as aggressiveness, whining, and fussing and with increases in participation in activities, attentiveness to others, and smiling.

The positive side effects of punishment have been less well investigated than the negative side effects, both in laboratory and applied research. In general, negative side effects appear to be much more likely than positive side effects. The reason has to do with the effects of aversive events on behavior. Negative side effects such as escape and emotional reactions emerge from mild aversive consequences, even when these consequences are ineffective in suppressing behavior.

General Comments. Undesirable side effects do not necessarily emerge from the use of punishment. Perhaps a major reason that undesirable side effects have been less apparent in applied settings than in laboratory studies is that reinforcement for alternative responses is generally used in conjunction with punishment. For example, if some behavior is reinforced even though other behaviors are punished, the situation and the punishing agent are likely to be less aversive than would be the case if punishment alone were administered. Hence, less escape and avoidance on the part of the client would be evident. In fact, side effects such as avoidance, emotional reactions, and aggression are found less often when punishment is combined with reinforcement for positive behaviors than when punishment is used alone (e.g., Carey & Bucher, 1986). Another reason that undesirable side effects have not been widely found is that mild and brief forms of punishment are generally used in applied settings. Mild forms of punishment are effective in suppressing undesired behavior when reinforcement is delivered for other behaviors. Of course, when mild intensities of punishment are used, it is likely that fewer undesirable side effects will result. Emotional disruption and aggressive behavior are less likely to result from mild forms of punishment than from intense forms resulting from painful stimuli.

CHARACTERISTICS OF THE PUNISHMENT PROCESS

Immediacy of Effects

A reduction in response rate usually occurs immediately following punishment. Using punishment for prolonged periods may result in further suppression. However, if there is no immediate effect, it is probably not advantageous to continue the aversive contingency. It is difficult to specify precisely how immediate the effect of punishment should be to justify being continued. Laboratory work has shown that some response suppression occurs as soon as the punishing stimulus is delivered a few times (Azrin & Holz, 1966).

In applied settings, the rapidity of punishment effects has been especially evident with shock. In a matter of only a few sessions or even one application of shock, behaviors are reduced and sometimes completely eliminated. The rapid and dramatic effects of shock were illustrated in a 14-year-old boy who had a chronic cough (Creer, Chai, & Hoffman, 1977). The cough did not respond to medical treatment or to attempts to remove attention for coughing and to provide praise for periods of not coughing. The cough was so disruptive and distracting to others that the child was expelled from school until his cough could be controlled. After further medical tests proved negative, a punishment procedure was used. Baseline observations revealed that the boy coughed 22 times in a one-hour period. Treatment began by applying a mild electric shock (to the forearm) for coughing. Application of one shock after the first cough eliminated the behavior. The boy immediately returned to school, and he did not suffer episodes of coughing for up to $2\frac{1}{2}$ years after treatment. Since shock is rarely used as an aversive event in applied settings, its effects are not a helpful guide in characterizing the effects of punishment. Nevertheless, the general rule about immediacy of effect holds and is applicable to less intense forms of punishment.

Applications of time-out, verbal reprimands, overcorrection, lemon juice, and other procedures have shown that reductions in behavior occur after one or a few days of punishment (e.g., Marholin & Townsend, 1978; Singh et al., 1986; Wilson, Robertson, Herlong, & Haynes, 1979). Although exceptions to these results can be found, the general pattern is a reduction in behavior relatively soon after treatment is applied. This does not mean that the behavior will be eliminated or suppressed to the desired level in only a few days, but it does mean that beneficial effects of punishment, when they occur, should be evident in client behavior within a relatively brief period (e.g., a few days). If signs of progress are not soon evident, perhaps alternative procedures should be attempted. One would not want to continue punishment without clear signs of progress. Consequently, assessment of behavior is essential as part of a punishment program.

Specificity of Effects

Punishment often leads to effects that are specific to the situation in which the response is punished. Punishing a response in one setting or during one period may not carry over to other settings or other periods. For example, punishment effects achieved in special training sessions in a small room off a ward in an institution may not be evident in the same room after the sessions are over (Marholin & Townsend, 1978) or on the ward after the client leaves the sessions (Rollings et al., 1977). Behaviors suppressed in the treatment setting may continue unless punishment is implemented in the new setting.

The specificity of punishment effects has been evident in other ways. The effect of punishment may be restricted to the presence of the person who previously administered it. For example, verbal warnings and reprimands are sometimes effective only when they are administered by persons previously associated with more severe punishment (Birnbrauer, 1968). Also, the punished behavior may be suppressed only when the person who carried out the punishment contingency is in close proximity to the client (Marholin & Townsend, 1978). In general, response suppression may be limited to the specific conditions associated with punishment. However, the specificity of punishment effects can be overcome by extending the contingency to other conditions.

Recovery after Punishment Withdrawal

The effects of punishment are often quite rapid, so that the frequency of a behavior is reduced in a short time. However, the effect of punishment may not last; when the punishment contingency is withdrawn, the punished behavior may recover or return to its baseline rate. Recovery is likely to occur when punishment has not completely suppressed the response while the contingency was in effect and when reinforcement has not been used to develop an alternative response. As mentioned earlier, whether punishment is highly effective in suppressing behavior depends on a variety of factors. For example, a few electric shocks can completely eliminate self-destructive behavior. Moreover, the suppression is complete and the response does not recover even though the contingency is withdrawn.

Ordinarily, mild forms of punishment will result in recovery after the punishment contingency is withdrawn. Indeed, even when punishment is in effect, the individual may adapt to mild punishment, so that it loses its suppressive effects. For example, the more frequently threats are used, the more they lose their suppressive effects (Phillips et al., 1971). To maximize response suppression with punishment and to minimize recovery, positive reinforcement can be provided for behaviors incompatible with the punished response. When the punishment contingency is removed, the reinforced response will be of a higher relative frequency than the punished response. It will have replaced the previously punished response, and it can be maintained with continued reinforcement.

WHEN AND HOW TO USE PUNISHMENT

In light of the above discussion, it can be seen that punishment should be used cautiously because of its possible undesirable effects and because of ethical considerations that arise in using aversive procedures. As a general rule, other procedures should be employed in advance of punishment. An initial question that should be asked is whether punishment is needed at all. *The fact that a goal may be to suppress behavior does not necessarily mean that the program should be based on punishment.* Response suppression can be achieved with variations of positive reinforcement techniques. As noted in Chapter 5, many reinforcement programs have been designed with the goal of eliminating or reducing undesirable responses. To achieve this goal, differential reinforcement of other behavior (DRO), incompatible behavior (DRI), or alternative behavior (DRA) or differential reinforcement of low rates (DRL) can be used.

Although reinforcement techniques present viable alternatives to punishment, several situations are likely to arise in which punishment will be useful, required, and even essential. First, punishment is essential when the inappropriate behavior may be physically dangerous to oneself or others. Some immediate intervention is required to suppress responses more quickly than is possible through reinforcement and extinction.

Second, punishment is useful when reinforcement of a behavior incompatible with the disruptive behavior cannot be easily administered. For example, if a hyperactive student is literally out of his seat all of the time, it will be impossible to reinforce in-seat behavior. Punishment (along with shaping) may be helpful in initially obtaining the desired response. Eventually, of course, punishment can be faded with increased reliance on shaping with positive reinforcement.

Third, punishment is useful in temporarily suppressing a behavior while another behavior is reinforced. This may be the most common application of punishment in applied settings. However, it should be remembered that mild forms of punishment (e.g., mild reprimands, brief time-outs, and small penalties or costs) are usually sufficient to suppress behavior as long as reinforcement for alternative responses is provided. Indeed, mild punishment can sometimes enhance the effectiveness of reinforcement. In several programs, for example, attempts have been made to decrease disruptive child behavior (e.g., noncompliance, aggressiveness) at home or at school by having parents and teachers provide approval, attention, and praise for appropriate behavior (e.g., following instructions, playing cooperatively). Appropriate child behavior may show little or no improvement. However, when mild punishment is added in the form of a brief time-out or a small response cost, behavior change is often dramatic (Roberts, Hatzenbuehler, & Bean, 1981; Wahler & Fox, 1980; Walker et al., 1981). In general, studies have shown that a combination of mild punishment and positive reinforcement is more effective than either procedure used alone (e.g., Carey & Bucher, 1986; Pfiffner & O'Leary, 1987; Walker et al., 1976).

It is important to address several considerations if aversive techniques are an *ancillary* technique to accompany positive reinforcement. Usually, punishment will suppress undesirable responses but will not train desirable behaviors. Reinforcement is essential to develop appropriate behaviors that replace the suppressed behaviors.

It is important to address several considerations if aversive techniques are to be used. First and perhaps foremost, before aversive techniques are used, it is critical to consider whether alternative interventions are available. Behavior change may be attainable with positive reinforcement alone or combined with mild punishment (e.g., response cost). Reliance on aversive techniques can be justified only if positive reinforcement procedures have proven unsuccessful. Second, and related, if aversive techniques are to be used, they should be the least severe or restrictive interventions possible to achieve the therapeutic ends. More severe or restrictive interventions (e.g., shock, physical restraint) can be justified only if aversive events of lesser intensity or severity have been unsuccessful. Third, the duration of the program should be considered. A program that includes aversive events should have well-specified time limits and well-specified conditions governing its termination or continuation. A final consideration is whether there are clear benefits to the clients that result from treatment. If behavior does not change or show a trend in the desired direction of change, continuation of aversive events is not justified. The above points are minimal guidelines regarding the use of aversive events; they do not exhaust the issues that need to be addressed. Also important are legal guidelines and means of protecting client rights, which are essential to all treatments; these are highlighted in Chapter 13.

SUMMARY AND CONCLUSION

Punishment consists of reducing behavior by presenting aversive events (such as verbal reprimands and disapproval), removing positive events (as in time-out or response cost), and requiring effort and alternative behaviors (as in overcorrection or contingent exercise). Punishment needs to be used carefully to ensure that the procedure will be maximally effective. The most important element in the use of punishment is providing positive reinforcement for behaviors incompatible with the punished response. If an alternative response is reinforced, even mild forms of punishment can change behavior dramatically.

The use of punishment can result in negative side effects, such as emotional reactions, escape from the situation or from the person who administers punishment, aggression, the use of punishment by the punished individual, and overreliance on aversive control procedures. In some instances, positive side effects result from the suppression of deviant behavior. Nevertheless, at present, the possibility of negative side effects makes extensive reliance on aversive procedures somewhat hazardous. Moreover, the success of punishment in achieving its intended effects may be very specific, both in the responses that are altered and in the situations in which behavior change occurs. In general, there is a place for punishment in behavior modification programs, namely as a supplement to reinforcement programs designed to develop prosocial and other appropriate behaviors.

FOR FURTHER READING

Axelrod, S., & Apsche, J. (Eds.) (1983). *The effects of punishment on human behavior.* New York: Academic Press.

Azrin, N. H., & Besalel, V. A. (1980). *How to use overcorrection.* Austin, TX: Pro-Ed.

Azrin, N. H., & Besalel, V. A. (1981). *How to use positive practice.* Austin, TX: Pro-Ed.

Hall, R. V., & Hall, M. C. (1980). *How to use time out.* Austin, TX: Pro-Ed.

Van Houten, R. (1980). *How to use reprimands.* Austin, TX: Pro-Ed.

Chapter Seven

Extinction

FACTORS THAT INFLUENCE THE EFFECTIVENESS OF
EXTINCTION
    Schedule of Reinforcement
    Other Variables Affecting Extinction
    Identifying the Reinforcer Maintaining Behavior
    Controlling the Source of Reinforcement
CHARACTERISTICS OF THE EXTINCTION PROCESS
    Gradual Reduction in Behavior
    Extinction Burst
    Spontaneous Recovery
    Possible Side Effects
APPLICATIONS OF EXTINCTION
WHEN AND HOW TO USE EXTINCTION
OTHER APPLICATIONS OF EXTINCTION
SUMMARY AND CONCLUSION

In the previous chapter, punishment was discussed as a technique for reducing or eliminating a response. Applying specific punishing consequences can reduce the frequency of behavior, particularly when those consequences are accompanied by a reinforcement program designed to develop positive behaviors. The frequency of behavior can be reduced without presenting punishing consequences. Many behaviors are maintained by positive consequences. For example, interruption of others and tantrums, whether in children or adults, are often reinforced by the attention they receive. When there is interest in reducing behavior, extinction can be used to eliminate the connection between the behavior and the positive consequences that follow it.

Extinction refers to withholding reinforcement from a previously reinforced response. A response undergoing extinction eventually decreases in frequency until it returns to its prereinforcement level or is eliminated. Numerous examples of extinction are evident in everyday life. For example, trying to start a defective automobile ceases (extinguishes) after several unsuccessful attempts; warmly greeting an acquaintance each day decreases if he or she repeatedly ignores these efforts; and raising one's hand in class will cease if it is never followed by teacher attention. In each case, the behavior decreases because the reinforcing consequence no longer occurs.

Extinction, like the other principles of behavior modification, refers to a specific relation between behavior and the events after the behavior. In this case, the principle relates the occurrence of a behavior that has been reinforced in the past and the cessation of reinforcing consequences. Although application of the principle can be used to change behavior, extinction often operates in everyday life to foster problem behaviors. For example, in elementary school classrooms extinction often operates with reinforcement to sustain inappropriate behavior. As an illustration, raising one's hand to ask a question is often not attended to by the teacher. The absence of reinforcement is likely to result in extinction of hand raising. Extinction of this behavior that many teachers like is augmented if the teacher reinforces (provides attention to) children who shout out questions or answers. In fact, it is very easy to reinforce disruptive behavior in a class because it receives teacher and peer attention (social reinforcement). On the other hand, quiet and prosocial behaviors such as hand raising or working quietly are often ignored. Although quite simple, this example conveys how appropriate or desirable behavior in a setting may be inadvertently extinguished while undesirable behavior may be systematically, albeit unwittingly, reinforced. The present chapter discusses how to utilize extinction as a way of changing behavior in applied settings.

FACTORS THAT INFLUENCE THE EFFECTIVENESS OF EXTINCTION

Extinction of positively reinforced behaviors is almost always used in a behavior modification program. For example, in a reinforcement program, when a target response is reinforced, nontarget responses that are no longer reinforced are implicitly undergoing extinction. Although extinction is an ingredient in most programs, it may be used as the major technique to decrease undesirable behavior. When extinction is relied on as the major technique, various factors determine whether it will be effective.

Schedule of Reinforcement

The efficacy of extinction and the speed with which the reduction of a response is achieved depend on the schedule of reinforcement that previously maintained the response. A response that has been reinforced every time (continuous reinforcement) rapidly extinguishes when the reinforcer is no longer provided. In contrast, a response that has been reinforced once in a while (intermittent reinforcement) extinguishes less rapidly when the reinforcer is withheld. The more intermittent the schedule (or the less frequent the previous reinforcement), the greater is the resistance of the response to extinction.

The relationship between reinforcement schedules and extinction creates a major problem for behavior change programs that rely exclusively on extinction, because many behaviors are maintained by intermittent reinforcement. For example, incoherent verbalizations of psychiatric patients are often attended to by peers and staff but are sometimes ignored. Decreasing the frequency of these behaviors may be difficult because of the intermittent schedule on which they have been maintained. If all the sources of reinforcement were removed from a behavior previously maintained by intermittent reinforcement, the behavior would eventually decrease and perhaps be eliminated. Intermittent reinforcement *delays* the extinction process, and the delay may be unfortunate. While the long extinction process is under way, it is possible that the response will be *accidentally reinforced*. The possibility of accidental reinforcement during extinction is always a problem—and that problem is exacerbated by a long extinction period.

An example of accidental reinforcement was reported in one of the earliest documented behavioral applications of extinction, a program designed to eliminate a child's bedtime tantrums (Williams, 1959). When the child's parents followed instructions to no longer provide attention for this behavior, extinction proceeded uneventfully and the tantrums were nearly eliminated within a few days. However, one night the child fussed when put to bed by his aunt. She provided a great deal of attention to the tantrum by staying with him until he went to sleep. As a result, the tantrums had to be extinguished a second time, and then they did not occur during the following two years. In this illustration, the accidental reinforcement of the behavior by the aunt merely slowed the extinction process. In more complex situations with many more opportunities for accidental reinforcement (e.g., classrooms where peers may reinforce an inappropriate behavior), extinction may be difficult to apply effectively.

Other Variables Affecting Extinction

The effects of reinforcement schedules on extinction have been more thoroughly studied than the effects of other variables. Yet general statements can be extrapolated from laboratory research on variables that contribute to resistance to extinction. First, the amount or magnitude of the reinforcement used to develop the response affects extinction. The greater the amount of a particular reinforcer given for a response, the greater is the resistance of the response to extinction. Similarly, the longer the response has been reinforced, the greater is the resistance to extinction. Finally, the greater the number of times that extinction has been used in the past to reduce the behavior, the more rapid extinction will be. The individual learns to discriminate periods of reinforcement and extinction more rapidly. If a strong or powerful reinforcer maintained a response and if that response was sustained over a long period, it is likely to be more resistant to extinction than it would be if weak reinforcers had been used and those reinforcers had been delivered over a short period.

Identifying the Reinforcer Maintaining Behavior

Extinction requires that the reinforcer or reinforcers maintaining behavior be identified and that they be withheld when the behavior is performed. While this appears simple enough, in practice it may be difficult to isolate those reinforcers. For example, an emotionally disturbed child's aggressive behavior with peers may be maintained by various reinforcers, such as the control that aggressive behavior exerts over peers, the submissive response of the victims, admiration from friends, or special attention from a teacher or parent. In such a situation, it is difficult to identify which potential reinforcer or combination of reinforcers is maintaining the aggressive behavior. Removing teacher and parent attention may fail to decrease that behavior because other reinforcers are operative. For example, in a classroom program, an attempt to extinguish disruptive behavior by withdrawing teacher attention may have inadvertently served as a reinforcer for that behavior (Madsen, Becker, & Thomas, 1968). The disruptive behavior increased, apparently because it was maintained by reinforcement resulting from peer attention or from the disruptive behavior itself. Empirical observation is the only method for determining which reinforcer is maintaining a behavior. If the consequence is withheld and the behavior declines, this suggests that the consequence served as a positive reinforcer and maintained the behavior. That possibility can be evaluated systematically by using a reversal or other experimental designs, as outlined earlier. The difficulty in carrying out this approach is that the reinforcer is not easily identified if it follows the behavior infrequently (intermittently).

For example, in a psychiatric hospital, disruptive patient behavior may be maintained by attention from a psychiatrist or psychologist. The psychiatrist or psychologist may have little interaction with the patient, yet that interaction may follow particularly bizarre patient behavior. The interaction may be so infrequent that it is assumed not to be responsible for maintaining the bizarre behavior. Consequently, identification of the reinforcer maintaining the behavior is likely to be delayed. If the reinforcer is not quickly identified, there can be considerable delay in beginning the extinction process. For this reason, it is desirable to supplement extinction with other procedures (e.g., reinforcement for appropriate behavior), as will be elaborated later.

Controlling the Source of Reinforcement

Once the reinforcer maintaining an undesirable behavior has been identified, a major problem may be withholding the reinforcer after the behavior. Extinction requires very careful control over reinforcers. Any accidental reinforcement may rapidly reinstate the inappropriate behavior and prolong the extinction process.

For example, in a program conducted several years ago, extinction was used to decrease the delusional talk of a hospitalized psychotic patient (Ayllon & Michael, 1959). The patient consistently talked about her illegitimate child and about the men she claimed were always pursuing her. Her delusional talk had persisted for at least three years. Typically, nurses responded to it by listening to understand and get at the "root" of the problem. When extinction was implemented, the nurses did not attend to the delusional talk and provided attention for sensible talk. At three different times during the extinction phase, however, the delusional talk was accidentally reinforced. Once, a social worker attended to it. On two other occasions, when another employee and volunteers visited the ward, the extinction procedure was again sacrificed. Extinction decreased the delusional talk, and accidental reinforcement appeared to account for temporary increases.

Reinforcement is particularly difficult to control when it is delivered by peers. Parents, teachers, or staff members are often unaware that peers are providing reinforcing consequences for each other's behavior. Clowning in a classroom or stealing among delinquents in the community are examples of such peer reinforcement. Constant surveillance would be required to ensure that no such reinforcement occurred. From a practical standpoint, constant surveillance is usually not possible in either applied settings or the community at large.

One alternative is to enlist peers so that they ignore (extinguish) the deviant behavior of a particular individual. Peers can receive reinforcing consequences for systematically ignoring certain behaviors. If strong peer incentive for extinguishing a response is provided, it is likely that there will be little or no accidental reinforcement. For example, students in one elementary classroom received candy if they ignored a peer who had severe tantrums that consisted of profane screaming and throwing objects (Carlson, Arnold, Becker, & Madsen, 1968). By reinforcing peer behavior, these authors decreased the likelihood of uncontrolled reinforcement.

It is virtually impossible to control reinforcement for some behaviors. For example, autistic children frequently engage in self-stimulatory behaviors such as repetitively playing with objects or their fingers and rocking back and forth. Research has suggested that these behaviors are maintained in part by the sensory stimuli they generate (e.g., auditory, visual, and tactile stimulation) (Rincover, 1978). The behaviors can be extinguished by reducing the stimuli they produce (e.g., by blindfolding the children so that they cannot see what they are doing). However, reducing such stimuli is not feasible or desirable in most settings, so the behavior is likely to be reinforced automatically. Similarly, criminal, aggressive, and bizarre behaviors that one might like to reduce often yield immediate and intermittent reinforcement (e.g., the material goods resulting from theft, the submission of a victim, attention from others). When the source of reinforcement is not easily controlled or eliminated, extinction is neither feasible nor likely to be effective.

CHARACTERISTICS OF THE EXTINCTION PROCESS

Gradual Reduction in Behavior

Although extinction effectively decreases and often eliminates behavior, the *process of extinction is usually gradual*. Unlike punishment, extinction typically does not result in an immediate response reduction. Rather, several unreinforced responses are performed before an effect is demonstrated.

When the undesirable behaviors are dangerous or severely disruptive, the delayed effects of extinction can be deleterious either to the individual himself or to others. For example, the self-destructive behavior of mentally retarded and autistic children is often severe enough to render serious self-inflicted physical damage. Although ignoring the behavior may reduce its frequency, significant physical damage may occur. One child's self-inflicted headbanging resulted in multiple scars over his head and face (Lovaas & Simmons, 1969). During extinction, the child was taken out of physical restraints and placed alone in a small room so that no adults could reinforce (attend to) his destructive behavior. The child's behavior, observed through a one-way mirror, eventually extinguished in 10 sessions over a total of 15 hours. However, from the beginning of extinction until the response finally decreased to zero, the child had hit himself almost 9,000 times. Thus, a great deal of self-inflicted injury occurred during the course of extinction. Although extinction can reduce behavior, dangerous behavior requires an intervention with more rapid results than extinction usually provides.

Extinction Burst

At the beginning of extinction, the frequency of a response may become greater than it was while the response was reinforced. The increase in responding at the beginning of extinction is referred to as a "burst" of responses. Numerous examples of such a burst at the beginning of extinction pervade everyday experience. For example, turning on a radio is usually followed by some sound (e.g., music or news). If the radio no longer works—so that no reinforcement (sound) occurs—attempts to turn on the radio will eventually extinguish. However, before this occurs, the response may temporarily increase in frequency (several on-off turns) and in intensity or vigor.

A burst of responses at the beginning of extinction has occasionally been reported in behavior modification programs. For example, Neisworth and Moore (1972) used extinction to reduce the frequent asthmatic attacks of a seven-year-old boy. The boy's prolonged wheezing, coughing, gasping, and similar responses were usually associated with excessive verbal and physical attention at bedtime. During extinction, his asthmatic attacks when he was put to bed were ignored. When those attacks were shorter than they had been on the previous night, he was rewarded in the morning with lunch money so that he could purchase his lunch at school rather than take his lunch. The results of the program are plotted in Figure 7–1. Of special note is the first phase of extinction (treatment contingencies). At the beginning of extinction, the asthmatic attacks lasted longer than they did during baseline. A similar burst of responses was evident the second time extinction was begun. Eventually, the asthmatic attacks were eliminated, but not before temporarily becoming worse.

A burst of responses is especially serious with behaviors that threaten the client's physical well-being. For example, Wright, Brown, and Andrews (1978) treated a nine-month-old girl who constantly engaged in ruminative vomiting (regurgitating food after eating and between meals). The girl weighed only 8 pounds (her normal weight would have been about 20 pounds) because she received little nourishment from her meals. Because of the excessive staff attention that the girl received from vomiting, an extinction contingency was

FIGURE 7–1

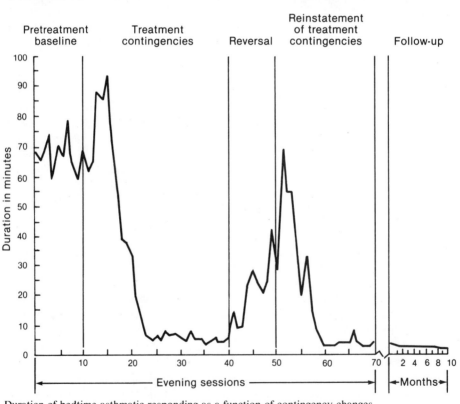

Duration of bedtime asthmatic responding as a function of contingency changes.

SOURCE: Neisworth, J. T., & Moore, F. (1972). Operant treatment of asthmatic responding with the parent as therapist. *Behavior Therapy, 3,* 95–99.

implemented. Staff were instructed to leave the girl's presence immediately when she began to vomit. When she was not vomiting, staff engaged in normal interaction with her, such as holding and looking at her. At the beginning of extinction, there was a burst of vomiting responses. This was especially unfortunate because it meant even greater food deprivation than the girl experienced during baseline. Fortunately, the burst lasted only two days and was followed by a decrease in vomiting and an increase in weight. The benefits of treatment were evident over a year later, when follow-up data were obtained.

A burst of responses may be undesirable even with behaviors that are not physically dangerous. It may be exceedingly difficult for someone to tolerate the undesirable behavior as it intensifies at the beginning of extinction. Thus, during a burst of responses, there is a greater likelihood that these other persons will provide reinforcement for the behavior. For example, if a child's tantrum becomes worse when parents systematically ignore the behavior, the parents may give in to the child and provide attention and comfort. Such parental reinforcement will increase the probability of intense tantrums because it is provided when the behavior is worse than usual. To the parents, of course, extinction may appear to be failing because the behavior has become worse. In reality, however, the effects of extinction are merely beginning.

It is likely that reinforcement during a burst of responses is a basis for undesirable behaviors often seen in children, such as protracted whining and excessive demands for attention. Parents, teachers, or other persons who may be involved in the extinction program need to be prepared for the possibility of a burst of responses so that they do not overreact to a temporary increase in behavior. An initial burst of responses does not always occur. However, when it does occur, the possibility of reinforcement adds to the risk in relying on extinction in the absence of other procedures.

Spontaneous Recovery

After extinction has progressed, a response may temporarily reappear, even though it has not been reinforced. *The temporary recurrence of a nonreinforced response during extinction is referred to as spontaneous recovery.* When a response recovers during extinction, its strength is ordinarily less than it was prior to extinction. For example, if a child's tantrums are ignored, the frequency of tantrums will probably decrease over time, possibly after an initial burst of responses. However, a tantrum may occur after extinction has progressed for some time. Such a tantrum is likely to be of a lower intensity or magnitude than that of the tantrums during baseline.

As with extinction burst, a major concern with spontaneous recovery is that the response will be accidentally reinforced. Spontaneous recovery occurs after several responses have not been reinforced. If reinforcement is provided, it follows a long series of nonreinforced responses. This is tantamount to a highly intermittent reinforcement schedule, which may further increased resistance to extinction. If extinction continues and no accidental reinforcement occurs, the frequency and intensity of the spontaneously recovered response decrease. It is important to realize that the spontaneous recurrence of a response during extinction does not necessarily reflect the ineffectiveness of the procedure. Such recurrences often characterize the extinction process.

Possible Side Effects

Another characteristic of extinction is that the cessation of reinforcement may result in "emotional responses" such as agitation, frustration, feelings of failure, rage, and aggression (Rilling, 1977). Apparently, the transition from positive reinforcement to extinction is aversive and leads to side effects similar to those evident with punishment. Instances of emotional reactions in response to extinction abound in everyday experience. For example, after individuals place money into a malfunctioning vending machine (e.g., reinforcement is no longer delivered), statements of anger, swearing, and aggressive attacks on the machine are common. Individuals who have experienced repeated reinforcement of certain responses may view the cessation of such reinforcement as a failure. When an athlete performs poorly, for example, he or she may swear, express feelings of failure, and throw something to the ground in disgust. The notion of a "poor loser" signifies a person who engages in emotional behavior when his or her responses are not reinforced in a contest—that is, when he or she loses.

Adverse side effects of extinction have occasionally been reported in behavioral programs. For example, to eliminate the effeminate behavior of a boy with a gender identity problem, Rekers and Lovaas (1974) instructed the boy's mother to ignore him whenever he engaged in "feminine" play (with girls' toys). When the mother failed to provide attention for his play behavior, he cried excessively and engaged in aggressive behavior toward her. In fact, a session had to be stopped to reassure the mother that she was doing what she was supposed to and that extinction should be continued.

In general, adverse side effects of extinction have not been well studied in applied settings. Laboratory evidence and reports from some applications suggest that when side effects occur, they are likely to be temporary and to diminish as the target response extinguishes. It is important to be aware that any situation in which reinforcement is no longer provided may become aversive. An aversive situation may result in escape and avoidance and thus reduce the opportunity for providing the client with positive reinforcement for desirable behavior. To avoid this, reinforcement should be delivered for a response other than the one to be eliminated. Thus, there is no net loss in reinforcement for the client. Rather, reinforcement is provided for a new or alternative behavior.

APPLICATIONS OF EXTINCTION

Extinction has been successfully applied to diverse problems. In one of the first demonstrations of this technique, it was used to reduce the frequency with which a psychiatric patient visited the nurses' office (Ayllon & Michael, 1959). The visits had been going on for two years and interfered with the nurses' work. The nurses usually paid attention to the patient when she visited and frequently pushed her back into the ward. After baseline observations, the nurses were instructed not to provide attention to the patient when she visited. Extinction decreased her visits from 16 times a day during baseline to 2 times a day at the end of seven weeks.

Extinction is generally used in conjunction with other procedures, especially positive reinforcement. For example, in a preschool classroom, extinction and reinforcement were used to alter the aggressive behavior of a $3\frac{1}{2}$-year-old boy named Cain who would choke, push, bite, hit, kick, and poke his peers (Pinkston, Reese, LeBlanc, & Baer, 1973). The teacher usually reprimanded the boy, which seemed to have little effect. An extinction program was initiated whereby the teacher ignored his aggressive behavior. Of course, a problem with doing this was that he might seriously injure the victims of his aggression. To avoid that possibility, the teacher immediately interrupted Cain's aggressive activity by attending to the victim and helping the victim begin another activity away from him. While doing this, she ignored Cain. Thus, he did not receive attention from the teacher or submission and adverse reactions from the victim, which also might have helped reinforce his aggressive behavior.

Along with the extinction program, the teacher provided attention (social reinforcement) to Cain whenever he initiated appropriate (nonaggressive) interaction with his peers. The effects of the extinction and reinforcement program appear in Figure 7–2. Extinction reduced Cain's aggressive behavior, as shown in the ABAB design (upper portion of the figure). His aggressive behavior remained low one month after the program (last data point), even though no special procedures remained in effect. The effects of extinction of aggressive behavior were probably enhanced by the reinforcement program (lower portion of the figure), which increased appropriate peer interaction.

Extinction was combined with reinforcement to reduce the delusional speech of four psychiatric patients (Liberman, Teigen, Patterson, & Baker, 1973). The delusional speech included comments about being persecuted, being poisoned by the staff, being injected with monkey blood, being James Bond or an agent of the FBI, and so on. In daily individual interviews with the staff, extinction was used by having the staff simply leave the room (no longer pay attention) when delusional speech began. Each patient could also earn reinforcement that involved an evening chat with a therapist. During the chat, the patient and the therapist were in a comfortable room in which snacks were served. The amount of time earned toward the evening chat depended on how

FIGURE 7–2

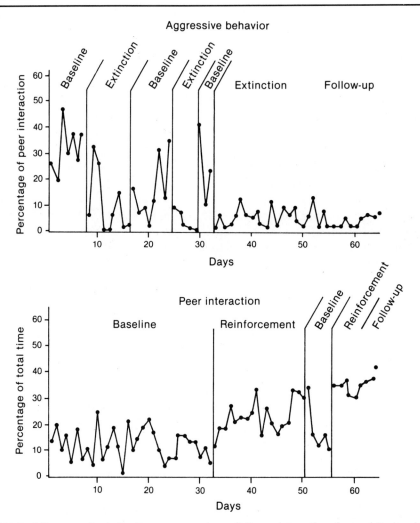

Subject's daily aggressive behaviors as a percentage of all peer interaction observed (top) and his daily peer interaction as a percentage of time observed (bottom).

SOURCE: Pinkston, E. M., Reese, N. M., LeBlanc, J. M., & Baer, D. M. (1973). Independent control of a preschool child's aggression and peer interaction by contingent teacher attention. *Journal of Applied Behavior Analysis, 6,* 115–124. Copyright 1973 by the Society for the Experimental Analysis of Behavior, Inc.

much rational (nondelusional) conversation the patient engaged in during interviews earlier that day. The effects of extinguishing irrational speech and rewarding rational speech can be seen in Figure 7–3. In a multiple-baseline design across four different patients, the effects of treatment appear clear. Rational speech increased when the program was introduced.

FIGURE 7-3

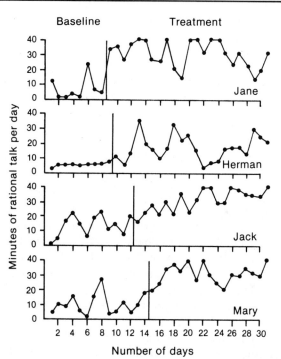

Duration of rational speech before onset of delusions in daily interviews during baseline and treatment (extinction and reinforcement) conditions.

SOURCE: Liberman, R. P., Teigen, J., Patterson, R., & Baker, V. (1973). Reducing delusional speech in chronic, paranoid schizophrenics. *Journal of Applied Behavior Analysis, 6,* 57–64. Copyright 1973 by the Society for the Experimental Analysis of Behavior, Inc.

Many other reports have shown the successful application of extinction alone or in conjunction with other procedures (particularly reinforcement). Hypochondriacal complaints, vomiting, obsessive comments, compulsive rituals, and excessive conversation in the classroom are among the diverse problems that have been treated with extinction and reinforcement. Such applications are particularly noteworthy because they reveal that a number of maladaptive behaviors may be maintained by their social consequences.

WHEN AND HOW TO USE EXTINCTION

Extinction is useful in situations in which the reinforcer that maintains behavior can be readily identified and controlled. In some situations, it is likely that only one or a few reinforcers maintain behavior. For example, parents may attend to a child's tantrum before the child goes to bed. The reinforcers for tantrums may be attention and food, if a snack is given to placate the child. In this example, the reinforcers maintaining behavior are probably limited to attention and food. Each can readily be withdrawn to test this notion. Of course, if there are other relatives in the house (e.g., siblings and grandparents) who can inadvertently provide reinforcement, identifying and controlling the available reinforcers are more difficult. Another consideration in using extinction is whether the burst that may occur will be harmful to the client himself or to others or intolerable to the agents responsible for the client. If the above conditions for extinction can be satisfied, extinction may eliminate the target behavior, so that it is unnecessary to employ other procedures (e.g., punishment).

Extinction is enhanced tremendously when it is combined with positive reinforcement for behavior incompatible with the response to be extinguished. There are many reasons to combine reinforcement with extinction. First, the problems of effectively executing extinction are mitigated. Identifying and controlling reinforcement that maintains the undesirable response are less essential if other reinforcers are provided to develop desirable behavior. Second, the potential undesirable side effects of extinction and the problematic characteristics of the course of extinction are less likely to occur if reinforcement is provided for alternative responses. Providing reinforcement should prevent the side effects that result from reinforcer loss. In addition, a burst of responses and spontaneous recovery may not occur if the reinforced response replaces the extinguished response. Third, extinction may effectively decrease behavior, but it does not ensure that a desirable behavior will replace the eliminated behavior. However, reinforcement can effectively strengthen behavior. If certain undesirable behaviors are extinguished and desirable behaviors are not simultaneously reinforced, extinction may not be very effective. When extinction is terminated, the undesirable behavior is likely to return because no alternative responses have been developed and no alternative means of obtaining reinforcement have been provided. *When extinction or punishment is used, reinforcement should be delivered to develop a behavior that will replace the response to be eliminated.*

OTHER APPLICATIONS OF EXTINCTION

Extinction in applied settings is generally used for behaviors that have been maintained by *positive* reinforcement. In such cases, eliminating the connection between a behavior (e.g., tantrums) and positive reinforcement (e.g., parent attention) can help reduce or eliminate the behavior. Extinction is also used for behaviors that are developed or maintained by *negative* reinforcement. Such applications refer to behaviors that are performed to *avoid* anticipated aversive consequences. For example, individuals who have intense fear related to heights (acrophobia) avoid high places in their everyday lives. There is a connection between heights and aversive consequences (perceived danger). Although there may be little or no real danger in many of the situations that these individuals fear, certainly the anxiety or panic they experience when they approach heights or are actually in situations involving heights is a deeply felt and a genuinely aversive consequence.

It is possible to extinguish responses developed or maintained through negative reinforcement. In such cases, the extinction procedures are generally used in the context of individual therapy for persons who seek treatment, rather than in applied settings such as the home, the school, institutions, and the community. Nevertheless, because such procedures are widely practiced in the context of behavior therapy, it is useful to mention techniques in which the extinction of avoidance behavior is considered to be operative.

Everyday experience teaches us that avoidance behaviors such as fears and phobias are difficult to overcome. The resistance of avoidance behaviors to extinction has been demonstrated in laboratory animal research. In classic experiments, dogs were trained to avoid brief electric shocks by responding to a buzzer that preceded a shock (Solomon, Kamin, & Wynne, 1953). A dog could avoid the shock by jumping over a barrier in the middle of the compartment when the buzzer sounded. The avoidance training procedure was repeated in each side of the compartment. At the beginning of training, the dog was shocked and escaped over the barrier. In a short time, it repeatedly jumped back and forth over the barrier in response to the buzzer. Although the shock was eventually withdrawn from the situation, the avoidance response did not extinguish. The dog never remained in the situation long enough to find out that extinction (removal of shock) began.

Anxiety is presumed to play a role in the development and maintenance of avoidance responses. A previously neutral stimulus elicits anxiety and escape through classical conditioning, described earlier. Cues associated with the unconditioned aversive event can elicit the anxiety and escape response. In the case of avoidance in animals, anxiety or fear increases when the buzzer sounds, because the buzzer preceded shock. Escape from the buzzer reduces fear. Thus, anxiety reduction, by termination of the unconditioned aversive event, negatively reinforces escape. Although the unconditioned aversive event (shock) no longer occurs, successful escape from the anxiety-arousing conditioned aversive event maintains avoidance behavior.

Fear and anxiety in human behavior have often been conceptualized on the basis of avoidance conditioning studied in laboratory research. With humans, it is not clear how most fears develop, as it is in animal research that induces specific fear reactions. However, like laboratory-induced fear, human avoidance behavior is highly resistant to extinction. Fearful persons rarely place themselves in the fear-provoking situation. If they did, escape and avoidance behaviors might extinguish, as described below. Anxiety can be reduced by remaining in the provoking situation to allow the conditioned anxiety to extinguish. Most people do not gain the benefit of extinction because they either do not enter into the situation they fear or only remain in it for a brief period. Thus, avoidance of or escape from the situation is reinforced by anxiety reduction.

Several techniques have been effective in extinguishing avoidance responses. One of the more widely practiced techniques is *systematic desensiti-*

zation, which was derived from a classical conditioning framework (Wolpe, 1958). As mentioned earlier, desensitization alters the valence of the conditioned stimuli so that they no longer elicit anxiety. Anxiety-eliciting conditioned stimuli are paired with nonanxiety states of the client. To achieve a nonanxiety state, the client is usually trained to relax very deeply. Relaxation is eventually paired with actually being in the anxiety-provoking situation or imagining that one is in that situation. For example, in the more commonly used variation of desensitization, the client imagines approaching only mildly provoking situations while he or she is deeply relaxed. As treatment progresses and the client has successfully associated relaxation with these situations, he or she imagines increasingly arousing situations. Eventually, the client can imagine these situations without anxiety. Stimuli that previously elicited anxiety no longer do so. Moreover, the changes in the client's anxiety responses are not restricted to images or thoughts about the situation but eventually extend to the actual situation.

Another technique often used to extinguish avoidance reactions is *flooding*. Flooding nicely illustrates the rationale for extinguishing anxiety responses because it involves exposing the client to anxiety-eliciting stimuli for prolonged periods. Like desensitization, flooding can be conducted in imagination or in the actual situations themselves. The procedure consists of exposing the client to the fear-provoking stimuli directly. For example, a client who is afraid of heights might imagine being in very high places. When the client first imagines such a situation, intense anxiety is produced. However, as he or she continues to imagine the situation for a prolonged period (several minutes or even an hour or more), anxiety decreases. Repeated presentation of the same situation is likely to evoke much less anxiety. As the situation is repeated and others are presented, anxiety is completely eliminated. The conditioned stimuli have lost their capacity to evoke anxiety.

Systematic desensitization, flooding, and related techniques have been successfully used in many programs to overcome anxiety. Each of these techniques exposes the individual to a situation that is usually avoided and prevents or minimizes the need for an avoidance response. Avoidance behavior extinguishes because no untoward consequences actually occur in the situation, and contact with the feared stimuli is actually encouraged. Extinction of avoidance responses may occur inadvertently in the context of counseling or psychotherapy. In therapy, clients frequently express feelings and thoughts that elicit anxiety and guilt in themselves. These feelings and thoughts may be avoided at the beginning of therapy precisely because they evoke anxiety. Therapists typically respond in a permissive and nonpunitive fashion so that maladaptive emotional responses extinguish. As therapy progresses, self-reported and physiological arousal associated with anxiety-provoking topics, such as sex, may decrease over time (e.g., Dittes, 1957).

Behavior therapy techniques have been effective in treating a variety of avoidance and anxiety reactions. Phobias in which specific events or situations are avoided (e.g., heights, flying, open spaces), obsessions (repetitive thoughts), and compulsions (repetitive and ritualistic acts) have been successfully treated with behavioral techniques based on imaginal or real-life (in vivo) exposure. The techniques merely place persons in the situations that arouse anxiety. The situation is presented in special ways, often in conjunction with the use of other techniques for overcoming anxiety (e.g., relaxation training). Many of the behavioral techniques, such as desensitization and flooding, have been quite effective.

SUMMARY AND CONCLUSION

Extinction is often an effective procedure for eliminating behavior. The effectiveness of withholding reinforcement for a response depends primarily on the schedule of reinforcement on which the response has been maintained. Behavior maintained with highly intermittent reinforcement is particularly resistant to extinction. In practice, extinction can be difficult to implement because the source of the reinforcement maintaining behavior cannot always be readily identified and controlled. Several features of extinction warrant consideration.

First, for behaviors that are dangerous (e.g., self-destructive) or highly disruptive (e.g., shouting and screaming), extinction is not recommended. Because the decrease in the undesirable behavior is usually *gradual* during extinction, a large number of responses may be performed before it has been eliminated. If an immediate intervention is required, extinction may be too slow to produce change. Second, the undesirable behavior may increase at the beginning of extinction. If that behavior is inadvertently reinforced when it becomes worse, increasingly deviant behavior may result. Third, extinguished behaviors sometimes recover spontaneously even though they are not reinforced. A potential problem is that inadvertent reinforcement will reinstate these behaviors when spontaneous recovery occurs. Fourth, extinction may be accompanied by undesirable emotional side effects, such as anger or frustration. These side effects are not necessarily inherent in response reduction, but they are likely to occur when alternative means of obtaining reinforcement are not provided.

Although extinction can decrease or eliminate behaviors, it cannot develop new prosocial behaviors to replace the behaviors that have been extinguished. Extinction is most effective when it is used in combination with positive reinforcement for behaviors that are incompatible with or that will replace the undesirable behavior. Such use of extinction is included in most behavior modification programs.

FOR FURTHER READING

Cooper, J. O., Heron, T. E., & Howard, W. I. (1987). *Applied behavior analysis* (chap. 17, Extinction). Columbus, OH: Merrill.

Hall, R. V., & Hall, M. C. (1980). *How to use planned ignoring (extinction)*. Austin, TX: Pro-Ed.

Millenson, J. R., & Leslie, J. C. (1979). *Principles of behavioral analysis* (2nd ed.). New York: Macmillan.

Chapter Eight

Special Technique Variations to Enhance Client Performance

In previous chapters, reinforcement, punishment, and extinction procedures were discussed. By and large, the applications illustrated individual techniques such as the use of token reinforcement or time-out. The illustrations showed that relatively simple and straightforward applications of the procedures are often effective in altering behavior. Actually, the procedures can be applied in a very large number of ways alone and in combination.

For several reasons, it is important to examine variations in the ways behavioral programs can be implemented. To begin with, behavioral programs are not invariably effective when they are applied or not as effective as one would like them to be. For example, the behavior of a hyperactive child may improve with a token reinforcement program, but the improvement may not be great enough to make an important difference to his teachers. Similarly, in a group therapy situation, reinforcement may have increased the extent to which many of the patients participate, yet some of the patients may not have even begun to participate. Or a program may have been designed to change several behaviors but may not have succeeded in changing all of them. In such instances, it is important to be alert to variations in programs that can be implemented.

A major strength of behavioral procedures is that they lend themselves well to evaluation. The effects of a program can be readily evaluated so that one can determine when procedures are not working well. This permits altering the procedures or implementing new procedures to see whether they can produce the desired changes. In many applications, behavioral programs have not worked well initially. However, varying the programs, perhaps by altering the magnitude or type of reinforcement or by adding procedures (e.g., response cost), has led to significant increments in client performance (Kazdin, 1983). There are a host of options that can improve client performance.

Another reason for considering program variations is to convey the range of options available. Different settings have different demands, often practical in nature, that need to be considered when a program is being developed. For example, at home, it may seem reasonable to instruct and train parents to provide reinforcers (e.g., tokens exchangeable for special privileges) for a child who is having special problems. This program needs to be implemented in such a way as not to have an adverse impact on their other children. For larger-scale programs, however, such as programs conducted in day camps, at industrial sites, or in entire cities, it may not be feasible to provide reinforcers based on the performance of each individual because of difficulties in monitoring individual performance or because not enough persons can be deployed to administer such reinforcers. In such circumstances, equally effective variations can be used.

The present chapter considers a number of technique variations that go beyond the variations discussed previously. These variations can be used to enhance client performance when a behavior modification program is not working well or is not working well enough to meet the goals. The present chapter also considers a number of techniques for adapting programs to special characteristics or limitations of various settings.

ENHANCING CLIENT PERFORMANCE

Although behavior modification programs have been effective, occasionally some individuals do not respond to the contingencies or respond only minimally. When a program does not appear to be working or working well, there are a number of components of the program that should be checked. In most instances, the problem stems from how the program is implemented. Features that maximize the effectiveness of a program such as delivery of reinforcers contingently on behavior, immediately after behavior, and on as continuous a schedule as possible are not always easy to implement or to implement consistently. Consequently, ensuring that these features are in place may be all that is needed to improve a program. Similarly, punishment programs based on time-out or reprimands may not work very well initially but can usually be improved by ensuring that the reinforcement program for desirable behavior is also in effect. Even if a program has been implemented reasonably well, there may still be a need for further techniques to enhance performance. Several techniques of this kind can be incorporated into a program.

Prompting

In some cases, the client does not perform the behavior so it cannot be reinforced. Prompting and shaping have already been discussed. However, they warrant consideration here because of their complexities and because of their importance in developing behavior.

Prompting consists of efforts to initiate behavior through some antecedent event. Such efforts are quite common in everyday life. Familiar examples include the nagging of roommates or children. Prompts of this kind are usually likely to be ineffective because they are not associated with consequences (reinforcing) when they are followed by the desired behavior. Moreover, the aversiveness of repeated prompts (constant reminders) probably leads to undesired behaviors (side effects of aversive procedures), such as escape or avoidance as reflected in not listening, "tuning out," leaving the situation, or staying away from the person who provides the prompts. Nevertheless, prompts can be effective in initiating and sustaining behavior.

The types of prompts that have been most frequently studied and are most relevant to programs in applied settings are oral or written instructions. These types of prompts have been fairly well studied in community settings to change such behaviors as littering and failing to recycle waste materials, use seat belts, or conserve energy and water (see Geller, Winett, & Everett, 1982). Many variations of verbal prompts have been studied. Such prompts appear to produce reliable changes on some occasions and little or no change on other occasions. Verbal prompts appear to be more effective when (1) they are delivered immediately before the opportunity to engage in the desired behaviors, (2) they specify the precise behaviors that are to be performed, (3) they are provided in a nondemanding and polite fashion, and (4) the prompted behaviors are followed by immediate reinforcement.

In light of the above, general prompts (e.g., "Please do not litter" or "Please clean up your room this week") are not likely to be very effective. Indeed, the applied research is replete with examples in which general prompts and instructions produce very little or no behavior change. Specific prompts (e.g., "Please dispose of this item in the orange trash bin near the exit" or "Please pick up the laundry from the floor and place your shoes in the closet before leaving for school this morning") are much more likely to be effective.

The effective use of prompts is illustrated by a community-based study to promote seat belt use (Geller, Bruff, & Nimmer, 1985). The prompts were administered by a car passenger (referred to as a "flasher"). A prompt was delivered when the flasher's car and an adjacent car pulled up at an intersection at which both cars were stopped. If the driver of the adjacent car did not have a seat belt on (as evident by an unused shoulder belt in the car), the flasher held up (flashed) a sign (11 × 14 inches) that stated "Please buckle up—I care" and depicted an almost buckled seat belt. Conditions designed to maximize the effect of prompts were present in this situation. The prompt was closely associated with the opportunity to engage in the desired behavior (while in one's car), identified and illustrated the desired behavior (with words and a picture), and was delivered in a nondemanding fashion. If the driver buckled up after the prompt, the prompting card was turned over—the other side stated "Thank you"—to provide social reinforcement. Thus, the prompted behavior was immediately reinforced. Data on buckling were gathered by observers in the back seat of the car from which the prompts were delivered. About 21.5 percent of the prompted drivers buckled their seat belts before leaving the intersection and almost 80 percent did not. Of course those who were influenced by the prompt did not necessarily maintain the behavior. However, the point is only to note that prompts delivered in special ways can help initiate behavior.

If behavior is not changing or is not being performed consistently in a behavior modification program, one of the first lines of attack is to examine the use of prompts. It is important to ensure that these are provided and that they meet the conditions noted above. Prompts can usually be improved to help initiate behavior. At the same time, it is critical to bear their limitations in mind. Prompts are designed to initiate performance. Whether performance is sustained and behavior improves depends on the consequences that follow.

Shaping

Often, "too much behavior" or too stringent demands for behavior change are placed on the person at the beginning of a program. For example, your college roommate may not exercise at all, but, learning of your newly acquired knowledge of behavioral principles and techniques, he or she begs you to develop a behavioral program. Your roommate *can* exercise—he or she used to play tennis or jog five or six days a week. You reason that this is merely a matter of providing some incentive, because your roommate already has the necessary behaviors in his or her repertoire.

You begin the program by telling your roommate that in exchange for exercising four days a week, you will take him or her out for dinner or happy hour on Saturday. You know that it is critical to define "exercise" so that it can be recorded and so that the reinforcer can be delivered contingently for the behavior when it is performed. You and your roommate agree to define exercise to be *at least* 20 minutes of jogging, playing tennis, or engaging in some similar activity to which you both agree. As for the incentives, perhaps you wish to include several reinforcers, so you use a token or point economy. If your roommate exercises for four days, he or she earns 20 points. Any day of exercise over that earns 10 additional points. At the end of the week, your roommate can exchange these points for dinner (20 points) or happy hour (30 points) or save them toward some event that requires more points than can be accumulated in a week, such as $10 (70 points) or a ticket to a live concert (150 points). Because the cause is very worthy, you of course agree to pay for these back-up events as they are earned.

There are a few potential problems with this program. The first is the amount of response (exercise) that is being required. If your roommate has not exercised at all during the previous weeks, the first task is to develop some exercise. An attempt to develop a lot of exercise is likely to fail. Perhaps points should be given for 10 rather than 20 minutes of exercise. As a general rule, a shorter response is more likely to occur than a longer one. Also, a 10-minute response is closer to the baseline level (0 minutes per day) and thus is more likely to be performed. Also, the program requires at least four days of exercise to earn any reinforcers. This means that exercise for one, two, or three days in a given week will not earn points. At the beginning of a program, when the behavior is developing, reinforcers should be provided for any day of exercise.

Also, the points earned in this program are exchanged for back-up events at the end of the week. Although this may be convenient from your standpoint (e.g., you do not have to go out to dinner in the middle of the week), the consequences are too delayed. Behaviors performed early in the week (e.g., on Monday or Tuesday) are not associated with the back-up reinforcers. It would be better to include some back-up events that can be provided on a daily basis (e.g., doing the dishes or running errands for your roommate) in addition to the other reinforcers.

If your program did not increase exercise or had short-lived effects, this would be understandable. The program may need to be revised further so that any short period of exercise is rewarded with points and so that some of the back-up rewards can be bought on any given day. The revised program shapes behavior better by making the demands smaller. It increases the likelihood that the behavior will occur and that the behavior can be reinforced. After a few days of consistent exercise, longer periods of exercise or more days of exercise could be associated with special bonuses. For example, any exercise period of at least 20 minutes could receive an extra token or any week of four or more exercise days could be followed with a 20-point bonus. In this way, one can move toward the original goals. However, one begins a program by reinforcing behavior close to what the person already does. Program failures often result from not shaping behavior gradually and from not moving to more stringent demands only after behavior has become consistent at less stringent levels.

Response Priming

In many instances, the client readily performs the response and has often done so on recent occasions. In such instances, extensive shaping may not be required. The response merely has to be primed in some way. *Response priming refers to any procedure that initiates early steps in a sequence or chain of responses.* Prompts, such as instructions, serve a response-priming function because they initiate performance. However, response priming encompasses more than prompts. As noted earlier, any act can be broken down into a sequence or chain of responses. A difficulty with initiating a sequence of responses is that the final reinforcement (at the end of the chain) is remote. For example, a frequent difficulty with completing a term paper, writing a book, or doing a chore is merely beginning the task. Once the task is begun, the prospect of reinforcement is less remote and the sequence of the requisite behaviors is more likely to be performed.[1] Response priming consists of requiring the client to engage in the initial components of the sequence. Engaging in responses that are early in a sequence increases the probability of performing the final behaviors in the sequence.

Response priming has been used to initiate responses that otherwise have an exceedingly low frequency. For example, a priming procedure was used to increase the frequency with which residents of a nursing home engaged in various activities (McClannahan & Risley, 1975). Several of the residents were physically disabled and confined to wheelchairs or beds, some were mentally retarded, and most had medical disorders. Typically, residents remained in their rooms, did not engage in many activities, sat around the facility, and avoided social interaction. Activities were increased by making equipment and recreational materials (e.g., puzzles and games) available in the lounge. As a resident entered the lounge, he or she was given some materials, even if the materials were not requested. An activity leader demonstrated how to use the materials and provided assistance until the resident began working on them. The priming procedure led to very marked increases in the percentage of residents participating in activities. This procedure illustrates the use of response priming, because residents were encouraged to engage in the initial steps of the response, namely to take the materials and to begin work with them. Once the behavior was begun, it continued.

Priming procedures achieve their effects by making the initial responses easier or more likely. In programs in which the target responses are performed infrequently even though they are in the repertoire of the clients, a priming procedure can be used. Even if the responses are not in the clients' repertoire of responses, the priming procedure can initiate early response components and facilitate shaping.

Reinforcer Sampling

Reinforcer sampling refers to procedures that provide a brief or small sample of the reinforcing event in order to promote greater utilization of that event. Reinforcer sampling is a special case of response priming, but it warrants discussion in its own right. The responses primed are those involving the utilization of a potentially reinforcing event. In reinforcement programs, it is very important that the clients utilize the available reinforcers. The more frequently the reinforcers are used, the more the clients will engage in the target behaviors required to obtain them. The utilization of a reinforcer can be viewed as a sequence of responses. If the initial responses in the sequence can be primed, the likelihood of completing the sequence is increased. To initiate the sequence, a client can engage in the initial part of, or briefly sample, the reinforcing event.

Reinforcer sampling has been used relatively infrequently despite the apparently consistent evidence attesting to its effects. In one of the first reports of the procedure, Ayllon and Azrin (1968a) used reinforcer sampling to increase the frequency with which psychiatric patients engaged in various ward activities. The activities were included in a large list of back-up reinforcers that could be purchased with tokens. The patients were told twice daily that they could go for a walk on the hospital grounds. Payment of tokens was required to engage in the walk. After a few days of baseline, the reinforcer sampling procedure was implemented. Not only were walks announced, but all of the patients were required to assemble outside the ward for a few minutes before deciding whether they would purchase the walk. Essentially, by being required to go outside, the patients *sampled* many of the cues and reinforcers associated with the activity (e.g., outdoor sights, sounds, fresh air). While outside, the patients were asked whether they wished to go for a walk. Those who decided not to go for a walk returned to the ward. The reinforcer sampling procedure increased the utilization of walks. More walks were purchased by patients who had or had not engaged in walks during baseline. During a reversal phase, when the sampling procedure was discontinued, the frequency of walks decreased. However, some patients still continued to engage in more walks than they had engaged in during baseline. In other applications, reinforcer sampling was used to increase the use of recreational and social events (Ayllon & Azrin, 1968b). In each instance, a small sample of the event was provided by entering persons in the activity for a brief period before asking them whether they wished to engage in the full activity.

In general, reinforcer sampling appears to initiate performance among individuals who previously did not engage in the event. For these individuals, reinforcer sampling provides familiarity with the reinforcer, which subsequently augments its use. However, reinforcer sampling does more than provide. It also affects individuals who are already quite familiar with the reinforcer and have utilized it on previous occasions. After reinforcer sampling is terminated, clients may continue to utilize the reinforcer to a greater extent than they did during baseline. Thus, the effects of the sample procedure are maintained.

In any situation in which it is possible to provide a small sample of a reinforcer, the sampling procedure should enhance performance. In utilizing reinforcer sampling, it is usually important to provide only a small sample of the event so as to avoid satiation. If an individual samples a large portion of the event, such as food or an activity, this may amount to noncontingent reinforcement and thus will not increase the behaviors that are required to earn the reinforcer. In applied settings, the effect of a reinforcement program may be relatively weak, in part because the "reinforcers" provide little incentive to engage in the target behaviors. If the activity that is designed to serve as a reinforcer can be made more "valuable" to the client, the likelihood of the client's engaging in the target behaviors to earn that activity is increased.

Vicarious Processes

Performance of a client can be altered by having the client observe the consequences that follow the behavior of other individuals. Individuals are more likely to engage in certain behaviors after observing others (models) receive reinforcing consequences for engaging in those behaviors. In contrast, individuals who observe models receive punishing consequences for engaging in certain behaviors are less likely to engage in those behaviors. These two processes are referred to as *vicarious reinforcement* and *vicarious punishment*, respectively.

Reinforcement.   Vicarious reinforcement, which is widely used to influence behavior, is readily familiar in everyday life. For example, as has been mentioned, slot machines utilize intermittent reinforcement to maintain high rates of behavior (depositing coins) with little payoff (reinforcement). Actually, the behavior is also cleverly maintained by the use of vicarious reinforcement. When playing the slot machines, one invariably sees and hears other players win. Indeed, when someone wins, the slot machine makes loud noises and flashes lights so that the consequences will be conspicuous to others. Similarly, when contests are advertised, reports of happy previous winners are provided to help convey vicarious reinforcement and its effects.

In behavior modification, vicarious reinforcement has been studied in classrooms, the home, and various rehabilitation settings (see Kazdin, 1979a). Investigations have shown that the behavior of one person can be altered by providing reinforcing consequences to others. For example, in a class for behaviorally handicapped children, administering praise to three children for social interaction led to increases in social interaction among children who did not receive praise (Strain, Shores, & Kerr, 1976). Similarly, in another program, praising compliance with parental instructions and imposing time out for noncompliance not only altered the behavior of an uncooperative boy in his home but also improved some behaviors of the boy's brother, although these were not directly praised or punished (Resick, Forehand, & McWhorter, 1976).

Although vicarious reinforcement has been demonstrated in several studies, its effects have occasionally been weak or inconsistent. For example, many persons do not respond when they see others receive reinforcing consequences; for those who do respond, the effects of vicarious reinforcement may be quite temporary (Budd & Stokes, 1977; Christy, 1975; Fantuzzo & Clement, 1981). How reinforcement is administered to the client may influence whether others show vicarious effects. For example, vicarious reinforcement effects are enhanced by delivering reinforcement in a conspicuous fashion and by providing individuals with many opportunities to see others receive reinforcing consequences (Kazdin, Silverman, & Sittler, 1975; Strain et al., 1976).

It is not entirely clear why vicarious reinforcement achieves beneficial effects. The most obvious explanation is that of modeling, in which others see a person receive reinforcing consequences for a particular behavior and then engage in that same behavior to obtain reinforcing consequences. However, copying a model may not account for all of the findings, because the person who is responding vicariously is not always looking at or imitating the person who receives direct consequences (see Kazdin, 1973b, 1977e). For example, in a classroom, it may be that seeing or hearing the delivery of reinforcement (e.g., praise) is a cue to others that the teacher is looking and might also administer reinforcement to them. Praise of one child may serve as a signal (S^D) that other children will be praised if they are behaving appropriately. Hence, children hearing praise may improve their behavior to increase the likelihood that they too will receive praise. Vicarious reinforcement may also draw attention to the specific behaviors that are desired. Delivery of the reinforcing consequences, especially when noting the target behaviors in a conspicuous fashion (e.g., "Look what he did, that's great!"), may help prompt the behavior in persons who do not receive the consequences (Lancioni, 1982).

The cueing function of vicarious consequences is suggested by everyday experience. For example, when one is driving on a highway, seeing a police car and another passenger car next to the road serves as a cue to slow down. The cue suggests that one's driving is being monitored and that a similar consequence (presumably a traffic ticket) might be forthcoming.

Punishment. Vicarious punishment has been less well studied than reinforcement. Nevertheless, research suggests that when the target behavior of one person is punished, the target behavior may decrease both in that person and in other persons (Van Houten, Nau, MacKenzie-Keating, Sameoto, & Colavecchia, 1982). For example, Wilson, Robertson, Herlong, and Haynes (1979) evaluated the vicarious effects of time out from reinforcement in a kindergarten class. One boy with a high rate of aggressive behaviors (e.g., tripping, kicking, and throwing things at others) was placed in time-out for instances of these behaviors. His time-out consisted of sitting for five minutes in a booth in class from which he could not see his peers. When time-out was used, both the boy and his classmates showed a decrease in aggressive acts even though his classmates never experienced time-out for their aggressive behaviors.

In general, the performance of a client may be improved by providing reinforcing and/or punishing consequences to others who are engaging in the target behavior. Of course, vicarious reinforcement and punishment are not substitutes for providing direct consequences to the client. However, they can serve to prompt behaviors by signaling that these behaviors may be reinforced.

Once the client has performed the behaviors, they can be reinforced directly to ensure that they are developed and sustained at high levels (Egel, Richman, & Koegel, 1981; Lancioni, 1982).

GROUP-BASED PROGRAMS

In most of the programs discussed in previous chapters, reinforcing and punishing consequences were applied to individual clients. Even when programs are conducted with groups of individuals, such as a class of students or a ward of patients, consequences are typically provided to individual clients based on their own performance. Although most programs are individualized in this sense, it is possible and often desirable to administer programs in such a way that the peer group is involved in the contingencies. Programs utilizing the peer group can be implemented in several ways (see Greenwood & Hops, 1981; Kazdin, 1977a). Three major methods of using the group are group consequences, team competition, and consequence sharing.

Group Contingencies

Group contingencies refer to programs in which the criterion for reinforcement is based on the performance of the group as a whole. The group must perform in a particular way for the reinforcing consequences to be delivered. For example, a group contingency was used to reduce stealing in three second-grade classes (Switzer, Deal, & Bailey, 1977). Students in these classes frequently stole things (e.g., money, pens, toys) from each other and from the teacher. The investigators assessed the frequency of theft by placing such items as money, magic markers, and gum around the room each day and monitoring their loss. Before initiating the group contingency, the teacher lectured the students by telling them the virtues of honesty and told them they should be "good boys and girls." Later, when the group contingency was implemented, the teacher told the students that if nothing was missing from the classroom the class as a whole could have 10 extra minutes of free time. This was a group contingency because the consequences were based on how the class as a group responded. The group contingency was introduced in a multiple-baseline design. As shown in Figure 8–1, the number of items stolen was not affected by the lecture (weak prompts) emphasizing honesty. On the other hand, whenever the group contingency was introduced into one of the classes, marked reductions in theft were obtained.

A group contingency was used to reduce the shortage of cash in the register of a family-style restaurant (Marholin & Gray, 1976). Cash register receipts were carefully monitored. At the end of each day, the cash in the register was lower than the amount automatically recorded on an internal record of the register. After a baseline period of recording the shortages, a group response cost contingency was devised. If a cash shortage was equal to

FIGURE 8–1

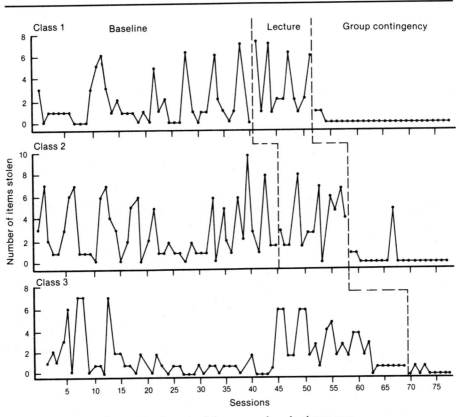

Number of items stolen per day in each of three second-grade classrooms.

SOURCE: Switzer, E. B., Deal, T. E., & Bailey, J. S. (1977). The reduction of stealing in second graders using a group contingency. *Journal of Applied Behavior Analysis, 10,* 267–272. Copyright 1977 by the Society for the Experimental Analysis of Behavior, Inc.

or greater than 1 percent of a day's cash receipts, the shortage was subtracted from the salaries of all the employees who worked at the register that day. The total shortage was simply divided by the number of individuals who worked at the register. Cash shortages were greatly reduced by this procedure, which monitored the performance of all the cashiers as a group and assessed a fine on the basis of the group's performance.

Group contingencies are obviously well suited to situations in which there is a peer group and in which there is interest in fostering similar responses in its members. The previous examples illustrate two areas in which a group contingency was useful—classroom performance and the behavior of employees in a small business. In large-scale community and work applications, group contingencies may play an especially important role. For example, in some business organizations, special incentives are provided if a group (e.g., 90 percent of all employees) engage in a behavior of interest (e.g., donate to a charity, attend an exercise period designed to improve health). In these situations, the interest in developing a particular behavior across many people lends itself well to group contingencies. The effectiveness of such contingencies is evaluated by charting the behavior of the group, rather than the performance of one or a few individuals.

Team-Based Contingencies

Team-based contingencies represent a special type of group contingency but are worthy of separate treatment because of their effectiveness. *In a team-based contingency, a group is divided into two or more subgroups (or teams). Each subgroup functions on a separate group contingency.* As with group contingencies, an individual client can earn or lose for the group and the collective behavior of the group determines what consequences the individual receives. However, the subgroups compete against each other. The consequences are delivered to the subgroup or team with better performance.

For example, Maloney and Hopkins (1973) evaluated the effect of a team contingency on the writing skills of elementary school students attending a remedial summer school session. The students were on one of two teams. They received points for writing behaviors that would improve their compositions, such as increasing the use of different adjectives, action verbs, and novel sentence beginnings. The team that earned the higher number of points (by adding the points for each of its individual members) was allowed to go to recess five minutes early and received a small piece of candy. To ensure that excellent performance was reinforced, both teams could win on a given day if their performance met a prespecified high criterion. The team contingency markedly increased the specific writing skills focused on.

Another program using a team-based contingency focused on the dental hygiene of children in a first-grade class and a second-grade class (Swain, Allard, & Holborn, 1982). The purpose of the program was to increase the cleanliness of their teeth, which was assessed by standard dental procedures measuring the amount of debris or plaque on the teeth. Before baseline, the children were taught how to brush and were provided with a dental kit (toothbrush, toothpaste, and "redcote" tablets that allowed them to detect debris). Daily observations were made on random samples of children in each of the two classes. After baseline, a team contingency was introduced by dividing each class into two teams. Each day, the team that had cleaner teeth received praise, posting of its members' names, and stickers. As shown in Figure 8–2, when the team-based contingency was introduced, the average amount of debris and plaque decreased. Moreover, nine months after the program had been terminated, an unannounced check of the children revealed that the gains had been maintained.

The above programs may have been effective independently of the division

FIGURE 8–2

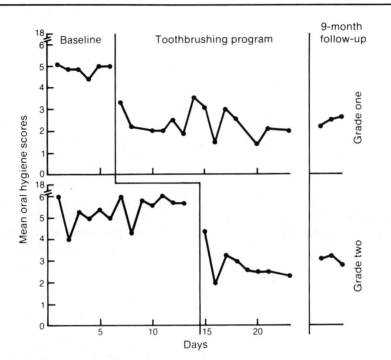

The effects of a team-based contingency on oral hygiene in which lower scores reflect less dental debris and plaque (i.e., cleaner teeth).

SOURCE: Swain, J. J., Allard, G. B., & Holborn, S. W. (1982). The good toothbrushing game: A school-based dental hygiene program for increasing the toothbrushing effectiveness of children. *Journal of Applied Behavior Analysis, 15,* 171–176. Copyright 1977 by the Society for the Experimental Analysis of Behavior, Inc.

into teams, because group contingencies are generally very effective. However, evidence indicates that dividing groups into teams leads to greater changes than does focusing on the group as a whole (Harris & Sherman, 1973). Thus, team competition appears to enhance the effectiveness of group contingencies.

Consequence Sharing

Another type of contingency that involves the group is consequence sharing. *With consequence sharing, the client's peers are involved because they share in the reinforcing consequences earned by the client.* The group members earn the reinforcers, not for their behavior, but when the target client performs certain behaviors.

Consequence sharing is particularly useful in situations in which there is a need to focus on the behavior of only one or a few persons. A reinforcement system can be developed for one person, but the consequences earned by that person can be provided to both him and his peers. When peers share in the consequences, they become involved with the program indirectly and can support and contribute to the client's improvement.

For example, the effect of consequence sharing on the behavior of two mentally retarded elementary school children in a special education class was examined (Kazdin & Geesey, 1977). Tokens were provided for working on academic tasks and paying attention to the lesson. When a predetermined number of tokens had been earned, each of the two children earned a reinforcer selected from a list of reinforcers (e.g., extra recess) that had been developed in advance of the program. As might be expected, contingent token reinforcement improved appropriate classroom performance. However, the token program proved markedly more effective when the reinforcers earned by the two children were given to everyone in the class (consequence sharing) and not just to them.

In another example, consequence sharing was used to improve the behavior of a 50-year-old female psychiatric patient diagnosed as schizophrenic and brain damaged (Feingold & Migler, 1972). The patient participated in a token economy that did not have much impact on her behavior. She engaged in little social interaction, completed her work infrequently, did not keep well groomed, and showed inappropriate verbal behavior. To increase her responsiveness to the program, a consequence-sharing contingency was developed in which two other patients on the ward received the same number of tokens as she earned. In an ABAB design, the target patient's responsiveness to the contingencies was evaluated when she was in the program in which she earned tokens only for herself and when she was in the program in which she earned tokens for both herself and her peers. As shown in Figure 8–3, the number of tokens she earned, and hence the extent of her appropriate job and self-care behaviors, greatly increased during the consequence-sharing contingency.

Consequence sharing is a convenient way to include persons in a program who might otherwise not be included (e.g., classmates, siblings, other family members). The precise reasons why consequence sharing achieves its effects are not known. It may be that the procedure operates by increasing the value of the reinforcing events. Earning for others may be seen as more valuable than earning for oneself. Alternatively, missing opportunities to earn reinforcers may be more aversive when one's peers are involved.

Lotteries

Another type of group program involves a lottery. Lotteries are a familiar technique used in everyday life to raise money. In the usual lottery, several tickets are sold, after which there is a drawing of one or more tickets. The persons whose tickets are drawn earn money or a prize (e.g., a vacation, a car). In everyday life, "buying a lottery ticket" is the behavior that makes one eligible for the prize. In behavioral programs, engaging in some specific target

FIGURE 8–3

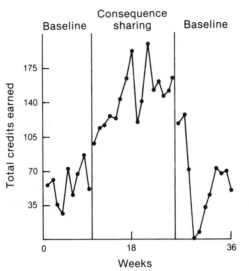

Token earnings during baseline, consequence-sharing, and return-to-baseline phases. During baseline, the patient earned tokens only for herself. During the consequence-sharing phase, she earned tokens for her peers as well as for herself.

SOURCE: Feingold, L., & Migler, B. (1972). The use of experimental dependency relationships as a motivating procedure on a token-economy ward. In R. D. Rubin, H. Fensterheim, J. D. Henderson, & L. P. Ullmann (Eds.), *Advances in behavior therapy* (pp. 121–127). New York: Academic Press.

behavior earns a lottery ticket. *A lottery is a way of arranging reinforcement contingencies to develop specific behaviors in a group of persons.* It is a token economy in which behaviors earn tokens (tickets) that are exchangeable for back-up reinforcers (the prize). In a lottery, there is usually only one back-up reinforcer and not everyone earns it. Thus, a lottery is often used to maximize the amount of behavior generated by a small number of rewards. A lottery is usually group based in the sense that it is applied to large groups of persons. However, in a lottery, unlike the group arrangements discussed previously, each person's behavior is usually unrelated to that of others in the group.

In one application in industry, a lottery was used to reduce absenteeism (Pedalino & Gamboa, 1974). The program was conducted in a manufacturing distribution center. The intervention consisted of a lottery in which an employee who came to work on time received an opportunity to choose a card from a deck of playing cards. At the end of each week, the employee would, ideally, have five cards, which were used as a poker hand. Several of the employees with the highest poker hands received $20. The lottery reduced absenteeism whether it was administered every week or every other week.

Lotteries have been used extensively in community applications of behavioral techniques. Programs concerned with energy conservation, littering, waste recycling, and other community-relevant behaviors have used lottery-based programs. For example, several studies, in an effort to reduce the consumption of gasoline, have provided lottery tickets to persons who decreased the use of their cars. Reductions in mileage, as measured by odometer readings, are rewarded with tickets that are drawn at the end of the week or month to provide small prizes, money, or, in one study, a free keg of beer (see Geller, Winett, & Everett, 1982).

Lotteries are convenient ways to administer reinforcers in group settings. One advantage of lotteries is their ability to dispense relatively large rewards because few rewards are actually provided. The impact of large rewards is especially evident in state lotteries, in which millions of dollars may be provided in a single lottery drawing. That incentive leads to a great deal of behavior (ticket buying). Similarly, but perhaps less dramatically, lotteries can promote a large amount of behavior in a group with relatively few rewards. A potential problem is that such lotteries may not affect the individuals whose behavior is in the need of greatest change, because they will not enter the lottery, not earn tickets for the drawing, or not receive the rewarding consequences when they do. This is not a disadvantage of lotteries per se. If the goal is to alter the behavior of specific individuals, this has to be specified in the contingency. The use of lotteries has been most frequent in cases where the primary interest is in overall group behavior. In such cases, lotteries can be adapted to individuals by combining them with other procedures. For example, individuals could be allowed to earn lottery tickets for themselves and their peers on the basis of their own behavior.

Considerations in Using Group-Based Programs

Group-based contingencies have several advantages. To begin with, they provide an extremely convenient way to implement behavior modification programs. It is easier to administer reinforcing and punishing consequences when the clients are considered as a group than when each client is focused on individually. Indeed, in many of the settings in which behavior modification programs are implemented, few persons are available to conduct individual programs. Hence, group contingencies can often be implemented more readily than individual programs. If individualized contingencies are needed to handle special behaviors of a few clients, those contingencies can be added to the overall group program. The ease of administering group contingencies may explain why people who implement contingencies often prefer group over individualized programs (Drabman, Spitalnik, & Spitalnik, 1974; Rosenbaum, O'Leary, & Jacob, 1975).

Another advantage of group-based contingencies is that they help bring to bear peer sources of reinforcement for behavior. Peers often actively support appropriate behavior so that the group or team can earn the reinforcers. Similarly, with consequence sharing, peers may encourage appropriate behavior so that they can earn the reinforcers. Occasionally, it has been reported that peers brought pressure to bear on other group members or clients whose performance determined their own reinforcers. For example, peers may make threatening verbalizations or gestures or may reprimand target subjects for not earning the reinforcers. More often, group contingencies have been associated with positive side effects, such as increased prompting among peers and reinforcement of one another for appropriate behavior, verbal and nonverbal gestures of friendship (e.g., back-patting), and helping behavior (see Greenwood & Hops, 1981).

The interactions resulting from group-based contingencies may depend on how the program is implemented. Aversive peer interactions may be more likely to result if available reinforcers in the setting are lost when the group does not meet the criterion for performance. Reinforcers normally available in the setting should not depend on group performance, because if they do, individuals may lose events that they would normally receive when their performance is up to standard. Group consequences should include special events or extra privileges over and above what individuals would normally receive, so that reinforcers are not lost because someone else in the group or the target subject did not perform adequately.

Contingencies for the group as well as for individual members are often combined to ensure that individual performance is reinforced and to obtain the added advantages of group incentives. For example, in a program for aggressive elementary school children, selected children received praise and earned points for appropriate social behavior and lost points (response cost) for aggressive acts as part of individual contingencies (Walker, Hops, & Greenwood, 1981). The points that each of these children had left at the end of the day could be exchanged for back-up rewards that the parents agreed to provide at home. A group contingency was also in effect at school, where a special activity was earned by classmates if a child met a specific level of appropriate performance. The group contingency in this program may be especially useful in encouraging and developing appropriate social interaction among aggressive children and their peers.

In another program with group and individual contingencies, seventh-grade students received points for participating in a classroom discussion and were given bonus points for especially well-reasoned discussion statements (Smith, Schumaker, Schaeffer, & Sherman, 1982). In addition to this individual contingency, extra tokens could be earned if all of the students in a given row of seats participated in the discussion. The individual contingency increased participation, and this effect was enhanced by the addition of the group contingency.

PEER-ADMINISTERED CONTINGENCIES

The use of group-based contingencies illustrates an indirect way in which peers are involved in the behavior modification program. The contingencies structure the situation so as to increase peer investment in appropriate behavior. A more direct way to involve peers in the program is to have them administer reinforcing and punishing consequences (McGee, Kauffman, & Nussen, 1977). With peer-administered contingencies, the peers serve as the behavior change agents and provide direct consequences to the target subjects.

Illustrations

Peers have been used in a variety of programs, with considerable success. For example, in one program, peers were utilized to alter disruptive behavior (e.g., noncompliance with teacher instructions, not putting away materials, running, shouting, fighting) in a kindergarten class for children with behavior problems (Smith & Fowler, 1984). Peers provided tokens to a teammate, a child with whom they were paired. Tokens were exchanged for opportunities to participate in special outdoor activities (e.g., kite flying, softball). The peers' tasks were to watch their teammates, to remind them of the appropriate behaviors, and to award tokens. The peers in charge of these responsibilities changed daily. Each day, the children who had earned the maximum number of tokens were entered into a lottery from which the names of peer monitors were drawn the next day. The results indicated that disruptive behaviors decreased with the peer-monitored token reinforcement system.

Peers have been used in the Achievement Place program for predelinquents (Phillips, Phillips, Wolf, & Fixsen, 1973). One of the boys served as a manager of his peers and delivered or fined tokens to develop room-cleaning behavior among them. The manager was responsible for ensuring that the room-cleaning behaviors were completed. He assigned the jobs and provided tokens or fines for the performance of the tasks. When the room was checked by the teaching parents in the facility, he earned or lost tokens based on how well the task had been completed. The peer-manager system of administering consequences was even more effective in obtaining high rates of room cleaning than the system of having contingencies administered by the teaching parents.

In addition to peers, siblings have been used to alter behavior. For example, Doleys and Slapion (1975) used a punishment procedure to alter the verbal behavior of a mildly retarded 15-year-old boy. The boy frequently repeated short verbal utterances. The focus of the program was to suppress such utterances. The boy's program was conducted by his 19-year-old sister. The boy was given 10 points a day at dinnertime if he had not engaged in these utterances. Each time he repeated himself, he would lose a point. When the point earnings accumulated to a large number, he could purchase a game of his choice. As shown in Figure 8–4, when the token reinforcement and response cost program was introduced, repetitions were low and virtually absent. Two weeks after the program was terminated, they remained relatively low.

Siblings have been effectively utilized in other programs. For example, in one program, children (ages six to eight) were trained to increase the social interactions of their physically handicapped and mentally retarded siblings (James & Egel, 1986). The nonhandicapped siblings were trained, using prompting and modeling, to initiate and reinforce social interactions. The training consisted of brief sessions that totaled about 1 to $1\frac{1}{2}$ hours for each

FIGURE 8–4

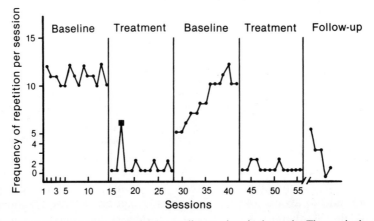

Frequency of repetitions during each of the recording sessions in the study. The particular phase of the study in effect when each of the data points was collected is indicated along the top of the graph. The data point enclosed in a square indicates the frequency of the repetitions recorded on the date that the subject had an epileptic seizure.

SOURCE: Reprinted with permission from *Journal of Behavior Therapy and Experimental Psychiatry, 6,* 61–63. Doleys, D. M., & Slapion, M. J. The reduction of verbal repetitions by response cost controlled by a sibling. Copyright 1975, Pergamon Press, Inc.

nonhandicapped child. The results indicated that social interaction between siblings increased markedly. Moreover, assessment six months later revealed that the effects were maintained.

In the above examples, peers or siblings were used to provide reinforcing consequences. Peers can also be utilized as models for appropriate behaviors and can help prompt such behaviors in others. For example, in a preschool program for "normal" and mentally retarded children, "normal" children were utilized by the teacher as models to help prompt appropriate use of classroom materials among mentally retarded children (Peck, Apolloni, Cooke, & Raver, 1978). During free play, the teacher drew attention to the appropriate behavior of the peer by saying to the mentally retarded child, "Look! See what he is doing? You do it." When the mentally retarded child performed the behavior, his behavior was directly reinforced with praise. Interestingly, peers can be used as models without being trained for this purpose. The teacher or other staff member can merely draw attention to the appropriate peer behavior when it occurs, conveying that such behavior will be directly reinforced if a target child models it.

Considerations in Using Peer-Administered Contingencies

Several advantages have been reported to result from peer administration of the contingencies (Strain, 1981). To begin with, having *the opportunity to work with one's peers* is often a positive reinforcer. For example, Robertson,

DeReus, and Drabman (1976) found that second-grade students decreased their disruptive behavior to earn the opportunity to work with a peer tutor (from the fifth grade) on reading tasks. When opportunities to work with a peer tutor were contingent upon classroom performance, marked changes in student behavior were obtained.

A second and related advantage of peer-administered contingencies is that *the opportunity to serve as a peer behavior change agent* can itself be a reinforcer. Peers often work and pay (in tokens) for the opportunity to participate in the training of another client. For example, in one token economy with predelinquents, youths would bid for the privilege of serving as a manager in the program (Phillips et al., 1973). The privilege was periodically auctioned to the highest bidder—the person who offered the highest number of tokens to purchase it.

A third advantage of peer-administered contingencies is their ancillary side effects. Occasionally, peer-administered contingencies have *improved the social interaction among clients*. For example, peers who administer reinforcing consequences or participate in peer tutoring may show an increase in their social contacts or an improvement in their social status (Abrams et al., 1974; Pigott, Fantuzzo, & Clement, 1986). In addition, peers are evaluated more favorably by clients if they are associated with reinforcing consequences (Sanders & Glynn, 1977). Thus, utilizing peers as behavior change agents can improve aspects of the relationships among peers and target clients. It has also been found that elementary school children who tutor their peers also show gains in the academic areas in which they tutor (Dineen, Clark, & Risley, 1977) and that peers who monitor appropriate playground behavior improve in their own interactions on the playground (Fowler, Dougherty, Kirby, & Kohler, 1986).

A fourth advantage is that peer-administered contingencies occasionally facilitate maintenance and transfer of the behavior. Behaviors developed by peers may be maintained even when the peer-administered contingencies are no longer in effect and may transfer to new settings after the program has been terminated (e.g., Johnston & Johnston, 1972; Stokes & Baer, 1976). When peers administer the contingencies, they may continue to exert stimulus control over the client. The client maintains the behavior in their presence.

Finally, the use of peers as behavior change agents has obvious practical advantages. Utilizing peers enables clients to receive more individualized attention and training than can be provided by the staff. Peers provide an important resource for administering programs that might not otherwise be conducted because of the paucity of staff members in classrooms, institutions, and other settings.

Potential disadvantages are associated with the use of peer-administered contingencies. Peers may not monitor others as well as external agents (teachers, parents). For example, in one program, children who delivered tokens to their peers did not withhold tokens as often as they should have when performance did not meet the criteria (Smith & Fowler, 1984). This occurred only on occasion. Nevertheless, it constituted reinforcing relatively poor performance or noncontingent reinforcement. In the long run, such contingencies might not produce consistent changes in behavior. However, this problem has been reported infrequently, perhaps because feedback and monitoring of peers by an external agent are usually included in the program to ensure that the contingencies are administered as intended. In general, the advantages of peer-based contingencies appear to far outweigh the possible disadvantages. Such contingencies have a variety of side effects that are favorable both to the peers who administer the program and to the recipients of their ministrations.

SUMMARY AND CONCLUSION

Numerous technique variations can be derived from the principles of reinforcement, punishment, and extinction. In the present chapter, some of these variations were illustrated. The different variations have special uses, such as aiding the program when the initial efforts to change behavior have not been effective or taking advantage of special limitations (e.g., difficulties in monitoring behavior for all members in a group) or influences (e.g., the availability of peers as possible aides) to change behavior.

In many behavior modification programs, a small number of persons may not respond to the contingencies or may respond minimally. Several techniques can be implemented to enhance performance. The first step that should be taken is to examine the basic features of the contingencies. The use of prompts represents an initial line of attack. Prompts are likely to initiate the responses of interest if they clearly specify the desired behavior and are provided in close proximity to opportunities to perform that behavior.

In addition to prompts, it is important to evaluate whether the demands placed on performance are too stringent as a point of departure. It is critical to consider shaping in developing behavior even if the client has shown on occasion that he or she can perform the terminal behavior. Building small early segments of the behavior and developing these segments so that they are performed consistently is an initial tactic to enhance performance.

Also discussed were response priming (to help initiate early steps in a response sequence) and reinforcer sampling (providing a sample of the reinforcing event to increase its utilization). Administering positive or negative consequences to others, referred to, respectively, as vicarious reinforcement and punishment, can enhance the performance of persons who do not receive the consequences directly.

Special contingency arrangements that can enhance performance and provide many practical advantages rely on the client's peer group. Group contingencies (in which criteria met by the group serve as the basis of positive reinforcement), team-based contingencies (in which groups may compete against each other), and consequence sharing (in which clients earn consequences for themselves that are shared with others) are primary examples of group-based programs.

Peers provide a potentially valuable resource for the administration of contingencies. Peers can directly administer reinforcing consequences to alter behavior. A variety of benefits accrue from incorporating peers into the administration of reinforcement. Peers who administer reinforcing consequences often improve their own behavior from doing so.

NOTES

1. The effectiveness of response priming is based on chaining, as discussed in Chapter 2. In a chain of responses, each behavior further along in the chain is closer to the final reinforcing consequence. Each response in the chain serves to reinforce the previous response and provides an S^D for subsequent responses. Thus, once the chain of responses begins, it is more likely to be completed. Response priming attempts to begin the early responses in the chain so as to start the sequence.

FOR FURTHER READING

Cooper, J. O., Heron, T. E., & Heward, W. L. (1987). *Applied behavior analysis* (chap. 25, Group-Oriented Contingencies). Columbus, OH: Merrill.

Kazdin, A. E. (1983). Failure of persons to respond to the token economy. In E. B. Foa & P. M. G. Emmelkamp (Eds.), *Failures in behavior therapy* (pp. 335–354). New York: Wiley.

Strain, P. S. (Ed.). (1981). *The utilization of classroom peers as behavior change agents*. New York: Plenum.

Chapter Nine

Self-Control Techniques

The principles of behavior modification describe lawful relations among various environmental conditions and behaviors. The techniques discussed previously represent instances in which one individual (the behavior change agent) manages the contingencies to alter the behavior of another individual (the client). Those techniques can also be applied by the client to control his or her own behavior. When techniques are applied to alter one's own behavior, they are referred to as *self-control* or *self-management techniques*. The present chapter discusses self-control techniques and how they are applied.

INTEREST IN SELF-CONTROL

There are several reasons for interest in self-control techniques within behavior modification. To begin with, self-control techniques can increase the range of applications beyond those available with externally managed procedures. Some of the problems for which people seek therapy—for example, overeating, deviant sexual behavior, obsessive thoughts, and phobic responses—are not readily accessible to the therapist. In such cases, it may be important to have the client help monitor behavior and apply techniques to control behavior in the natural environment. Many of the problems for which individuals seek therapy entail covert or private events (including thoughts, images, fantasies, hallucinations, and dreams) that are not "observable" by anyone other than the individual to whom they occur. As noted earlier, it has been suggested that covert events can be viewed as covert operant responses (referred to as *coverants*) (Homme, 1965). Perhaps covert responses, like overt behavior, can be altered by varying the consequences that follow them. Because the client is the only one who can identify the occurrence of coverants, he or she is in the best position to provide contingent consequences for them. Self-control techniques extend behavior modification procedures to events that are not observable (e.g., thoughts) or are not always readily observed (e.g., eating in everyday situations).

Self-control techniques are also of interest because they help overcome some of the potential limitations and disadvantages of externally administered contingencies. In virtually every behavior modification program, external agents administer the reinforcing or punishing consequences. There are potential disadvantages in relying entirely on externally administered contingencies. First, teachers, parents, and other agents usually miss a great deal of behavior when applying reinforcement. Monitoring several clients in a group situation or one client whose actions extend across many situations makes it virtually impossible to notice, not to mention reinforce, all instances of a target response. Second, the agents who administer contingencies may become a cue for performance of the target behavior because of their association with reinforcement and punishment. That behavior may be performed only in the presence of those who administer reinforcers. Third, and related to the above, the client may perform behaviors less readily in situations in which external agents are not administering reinforcement, because the client can easily discriminate different contingencies across situations. Fourth, individuals sometimes perform better when, instead of having the contingencies imposed on them, they are allowed to contribute to the planning of the program or to choose the behaviors they are to perform (as in contingency contracting).

Yet another reason for interest in self-control is that the goal of behavior modification is to train individuals to control their own behavior and to achieve self-selected goals. Continuous control over a client by an external agent is not an end in itself. Whenever possible, external control is a means for achieving self-control. Self-control and external control can be viewed as opposite ends of a continuum, rather than as discrete procedures. Behavior modification programs vary in the degree to which clients exert control over the contingencies and over the administration of reinforcing or punishing consequences. Self-control techniques attempt to maximize the control that individuals have over the behavior change program. Of course, external control in some form is essential to initiate the program. Therapists train clients to exert self-control by providing recommendations, strong advice, systematic praise, and feedback, all of which are external influences on client behavior. Hopefully, after training has been completed, the clients can apply techniques to themselves to alter new behaviors across different situations. When this final stage is reached, self-control has been achieved.

Self-Control in Everyday Life

People exert control over their own everyday behaviors, such as selecting courses of action, abstaining from particular excesses, adhering to various rituals intended to sustain or recover health, and acting in ways that appear to violate self-interest. In controlling their own behaviors, people use many of the techniques used to control the behaviors of others—that is, they alter the antecedent and consequence conditions.

Individuals have a variety of techniques to control their own behavior in everyday life (Skinner, 1953). First, use is made of *physical restraint,* such as clasping one's mouth to stifle a laugh, covering one's eyes to avoid seeing something, and clasping one's hands to avoid nail-biting. With this technique, individuals place physical restrictions on themselves to achieve a particular end. Second, *changing the stimulus conditions* (or cues) that occasion the response is used to control behavior. For example, one lists appointments or important dates on a calendar so that these stimuli will increase the probability of engaging in certain behaviors at a later date. Third, *depriving or satiating* oneself can be used as a self-control technique. An individual may deprive himself or herself of lunch in anticipation of a special dinner or prior to participation in an athletic event. Fourth, *emotional reactions* can be altered. An individual can prevent an emotional reaction (such as laughing) by eliciting an incompatible response (such as biting one's tongue). Pleasant or unpleasant feelings can be reinstated by conjuring up emotive memories and images. Fifth, individuals use *aversive events* in the environment to control behavior. For example, setting an alarm clock ensures that an aversive event (noise) will be presented. Individuals may also make threatening statements to themselves, such as, "If I don't do this, I'll be late." Sixth, *drugs, alcohol, and stimulants* may be ingested for self-control purposes. Alcohol may be consumed to alter one's mood or alleviate one's anxiety. Coffee may be consumed to increase one's alertness during studying or driving. Seventh, *self-reinforcing and self-punishing* operations are employed to control behaviors. An individual may derogate himself after failing to achieve a goal or praise himself after accomplishing a feat. Finally, *doing something else* is a technique commonly used to control one's own behavior. An individual can engage in behaviors other than the one that leads to aversive consequences. For example, one can alter topics in the middle of a conversation to avoid an argument or whistle a happy tune whenever one feels afraid.

The above techniques used in everyday life allow individuals to control their own behavior. Most of the techniques operate by having individuals perform one behavior (a *controlling* response) to alter the probability of another behavior (a *controlled* response). Thus, a person may chew gum (controlling response) to reduce the likelihood of smoking cigarettes (controlled response). Similarly, a person may wear a blindfold (controlling response) in a well-lighted room to increase the likelihood of sleeping (controlled response). In self-control training, the client is taught how to control a response or to apply a particular technique. The client can then extend the procedure as needed to new situations and behaviors.

Definition of Self-Control

As a general definition, self-control usually refers to those behaviors that a person deliberately undertakes to achieve self-selected outcomes. The person must choose the goals and implement the procedures to achieve them. Debates have frequently emerged in defining self-control (see Brigham, 1982). It has been argued that a person can never "really" control his or her own behavior. When a person appears to be the source of control over a particular behavior, it is possible to explain that behavior on the basis of events in the person's past that have perhaps determined his or her current decision. Hence, a discussion of self-control can easily lead to the perennial debate about free will versus determinism. Yet it is unlikely that behavior is entirely dictated by forces outside the individual's control (e.g., heredity, early home environment) or that the individual acts or chooses a particular course of action entirely free from all external influences (Karoly, 1982).

In behavior modification, self-control is considered to be a matter of degree rather than an all-or-none phenomenon. Behavior change procedures can readily be distinguished by the extent to which the client is in charge and bears responsibility for carrying out the program. The person can be a complete *object* of a treatment procedure that others administer (external control), or the person can completely design and implement treatment for himself or herself (self-control). Also, the person or external agents of change may be involved in varying degrees, so that self-control and external control both operate. *Self-control procedures in behavior modification refer primarily to techniques in which the client plays an active part and occasionally the sole part in administering treatment.*

The notion of self-control usually refers to regulating behaviors that have conflicting consequences, that is, both positive reinforcement and punishment. The reinforcing consequences that follow the behaviors may be immediate, while the punishing consequences may be delayed. Behaviors in this category include excessive consumption of food, cigarettes, alcohol, and drugs. For example, excessive eating results in immediate positive reinforcement derived from the food. However, the aversive consequences that follow overeating, such as physical discomfort, obesity, and the social ostracism attendant upon being overweight, are delayed. Alternatively, the aversive or potentially aversive consequences that follow behaviors may be immediate, and the reinforcing consequences (if present at all) may be delayed. Behaviors in this category include heroic, altruistic, and charitable acts.

Acts of self-control often appear to forgo immediate rewards for future rewards. Thus, a student may forgo the opportunity to attend a party on a Friday night, an apparent act of self-control. The student may sacrifice immediate rewards (entertainment, time with friends) for the prospect of future rewards (doing well in courses that will increase the chances of getting into graduate school). Similarly, people often undergo moderate discomfort in the present to avoid potentially greater discomfort in the future. For example, going to the dentist for cleanings, checkups, and occasional fillings may be uncomfortable in the present. But doing this reduces the chances of much greater discomfort in the distant future, when serious dental problems might otherwise warrant attention.

In the context of treatment, self-control procedures have been applied primarily to behaviors that appear to have immediate positive consequences and delayed aversive consequences. A person performs a response that counteracts or appears to counteract the effects that would be expected from external reinforcers. Thus, refusing a rich dessert after a meal appears to run counter to the expected contingencies. Of course, self-control is often invoked when simplistic accounts of behavior are proposed. Behaviors may normally be controlled by a variety of positive and aversive consequences in the present, past, and future (anticipated consequences). Simply refusing dessert may result from all sorts of influences that are not immediately apparent (pain from eating too much, previous experiences of nausea when overeating, allergic reactions to ingredients in the dessert, anticipation of not being able to get into one's clothes). In applications of self-control, the issue is not whether the individual or other events account for certain sorts of responses. Rather, the focus is on helping the individual bring to bear influences to achieve ends that he or she would like to attain.

Development of Self-Control

Self-control is assumed to reflect a set of behaviors that are learned in much the same way as other behaviors. In early development, a child's behavior is controlled by external agents such as parents and teachers, who set standards and provide consequences for performance. The standards vary for different behaviors. Some parents set high standards for musical or academic achievement but not for mechanical or social skills or household chores. Indeed, standards may vary for different-sex siblings within the same home. Positive reinforcement is provided when the child achieves the standard, whereas punishment (or lack of reward) is provided for performance below the standard. As training continues, achieving a particular standard may take on reinforcing consequences because achievement in the past was paired with external reinforcement. Conversely, the failure to achieve a standard may become aversive by being paired with punishment or lack of reward. Thus, attainment or lack of attainment of an externally or self-imposed standard may contain its own reward or punishment. Through early training, the process of setting standards and providing consequences of achievement eventually becomes independent of external consequences.

The above interpretation of how self-reinforcement and self-punishment patterns of behavior develop has received some support (see Bandura, 1977). Laboratory research has shown that patterns of standard setting and self-reinforcement can be transmitted in ways consistent with that interpretation. For example, individuals can learn to evaluate their own performance based on how others evaluate that performance. Individuals who are rewarded generously by others are more generous in rewarding themselves. Thus, one administers reinforcers to oneself consistent with the way in which others have provided reinforcement.

Modeling is also extremely important in transmitting self-control patterns. For example, children adopt standards of reinforcement that they observe in someone else (a model). If a child is exposed to a model who sets high or low standards for self-reinforcement, the child adopts similar standards for himself (see Bandura, 1977; Karoly, 1977). Individuals exposed to models with low achievement standards tend to reward themselves for relatively mediocre performance. The self-rewarding and self-critical statements made by a model are transmitted to and made by observers.

Self-held standards and self-administered consequences for achievement are also regulated by others in everyday interaction. For example, self-reinforcement for achieving consensually low standards of performance is not looked upon favorably. Students rarely flaunt a D gradepoint average, in part because the standard is consensually low. Thus, standards of performance in self-reinforcing patterns are conveyed through direct reinforcement, modeling, and social control.

TECHNIQUES OF SELF-CONTROL

Self-control patterns can be developed through behavior modification techniques to achieve specific therapeutic ends. Several of the major techniques for training people to control their own behavior can be identified. These techniques are stimulus control, self-monitoring, self-reinforcement and self-punishment, alternative response training, biofeedback, and self-help manuals.[1]

Stimulus Control

Specific behaviors are performed in the presence of specific stimuli. Eventually, the stimuli regularly associated with a behavior serve as cues and increase the probability that the behavior will be performed. Three related types of behavioral problems result from maladaptive stimulus control. First, some behaviors are under the control of stimuli that the client wishes to change. For example, cigarette smoking may be under the control of many stimuli, such as getting up in the morning, drinking coffee, talking with friends, studying, and being alone. It is cued by a variety of situations because it has been repeatedly associated with these situations. Because of these associations, the individual is likely to smoke a cigarette as situations are presented. The therapeutic goal is to eliminate the control that these stimuli exert over smoking.

Second, some behaviors are not controlled by particular stimuli, when such control would be desirable. For example, students who have difficulty in studying often have no particular setting, time, or cues associated with studying. Their studying is not consistently performed in the presence of any particular stimuli. The problem is experienced as difficulty in studying at one's desk or as being easily distracted wherever one studies. The therapeutic goal is to develop stimulus control over study behavior.

Third, some behaviors are under the control of inappropriate stimuli. Sexual deviance such as exhibitionism and fetishism is included in this category. With these behaviors, sexual responses are controlled by stimuli that deviate from appropriate stimuli as determined by social standards. The goal of treatment is to alter the control that some stimuli exert over behavior.

A person who is aware of how certain stimuli control behavior can structure his or her environment to maximize the likelihood that the desired behavior will occur. For example, avoiding a bakery is one example of using stimulus control as a self-control technique. When going by a bakery window, a person unable to "control himself" may enter the bakery and purchase pastries. However, not walking by the bakery or crossing the street just before approaching the bakery can remove the sight of the tempting stimuli (pastries) in the window, so that they cannot exert their influence. Self-control can be attained in the actual tempting situation by gradually approximating the original controlling stimulus in mild doses. The individual tempted by the bakery window can pass the window when the bakery is closed, walk by the window quickly when the bakery is crowded, walk by the window while looking away, and stop by the window after eating a large meal. If the person does not enter the bakery in the presence of increasingly tempting cues, the bakery may no longer exert its influence over his or her behavior.

The use of stimulus control ordinarily requires that a therapist initially consult with the client to explain how stimulus control operates and to help the client identify events that control or fail to control his or her behavior. Actual treatment may consist of helping the client begin to perform behavior under a narrow or new set of stimuli to develop stimulus control or of helping the client to perform new behaviors under familiar stimuli to eliminate existing sources of control. For example, in early applications of stimulus control in behavioral research, clients who failed to study or who ate excessively were instructed to perform the behavior only under certain stimulus conditions (e.g., studying in a special place and at a certain time of the day or eating only at the table and with a full place setting) (Fox, 1962; Goldiamond, 1965). Such procedures were designed to bring behavior under the control of specific stimuli to help increase studying when the clients were in certain situations or to decrease eating when the clients were not in specific situations ordinarily associated with eating.

Insomnia has been treated using stimulus control procedures. For whatever reason insomnia develops, it follows a familiar pattern. A person may be tired before retiring, but as soon as the person goes to bed, he or she may begin to worry about the day's activities. Thus, the stimuli usually associated with sleeping (bed, darkness, and a specific time and place) become associated with behaviors incompatible with sleeping. One adult insomniac went to bed about midnight but was unable to fall asleep until approximately 3 or 4 A.M. (Bootzin, 1972). Before sleeping, he would worry about several mundane problems and finally turn on the television. He would fall asleep while the television was still on. Treatment attempted to bring sleep under control of the stimuli associated with going to bed. The client was told to go to bed when he felt sleepy but not to read or watch television. If unable to sleep, he was to go into another room and stay up as long as he liked. When he again felt sleepy, he was to go back to bed. If he still could not sleep, he was to repeat the procedure. For the first few days of treatment, the client got up four or five times each night before going to sleep. Yet after two weeks, he no longer got up at all. When he went to bed, he stayed there and fell asleep. The client reported sleeping much better and getting much more sleep each night. During a follow-up period conducted up to two months after treatment began, the client got up during the night less than once a week. Thus, the treatment appeared to work very well.

Although stimulus control requires the therapist to explain the principles, techniques, and recommended applications, the clients themselves apply the procedures in their daily lives. Ideally, the clients can extend the use of stimulus control techniques beyond the area that served as the impetus for seeking treatment.

Self-Monitoring

Self-monitoring, or self-observation, consists of systematically observing one's own behavior. Most people are not entirely aware of the extent to which they engage in various behaviors. Habitual behaviors are automatic. People rarely observe their own behavior in a systematic fashion. However, when people are provided with the opportunity to observe their own behavior carefully, dramatic changes often occur.

The reasons that self-monitoring alters behavior are not completely understood. The information obtained through careful observation may provide important feedback about the person's level of behavior. The information conveys whether the behavior departs from a culturally or self-imposed standard of performance. If behavior departs from an acceptable level, corrective action may be initiated until the level has been met (Kanfer, 1977). For example, weighing oneself may provide information that one is overweight and initiate other actions (avoiding snacks, exercising) until the desired weight has been achieved. Thus, although self-monitoring does not itself alter weight, it initiates other behaviors that do.

Self-monitoring may be effective because the act of observation itself may take on reinforcing or punishing properties. For example, for the individual who records hours of study behavior or miles of jogging, each hour or mile tallied may provide reinforcement. Here the act of self-monitoring may operate by providing reinforcement for the behavior.

Although it is not entirely clear why self-monitoring is effective, it has been widely applied as a therapy technique (Kazdin, 1974; Nelson & Hayes, 1981). The use of self-monitoring was illustrated in a program with a 25-year-old woman who complained of obsessive thoughts about cancer of the breast and stomach (Frederiksen, 1975). She was very upset about these frequent thoughts, which appeared to become worse over a six-year period prior to treatment. She was instructed to monitor the frequency of the obsessive thoughts while at home. Keeping a daily tally of the thoughts was associated with a rapid reduction in their frequency from a high of 13 per day to about 2 per day. The woman was then instructed to monitor her thoughts in a more detailed fashion by recording the time of the thought, what she was doing at that time, the specific content of each thought, and so on. When this more detailed assessment procedure was used, her obsessive thoughts decreased further. They did not recur up to four months after treatment.

Self-monitoring has been effectively used with young children in class-room settings. For example, in one study, four learning-disabled children (9–10 years of age) who were behind in academic areas participated in a program in which they self-monitored their classroom behavior (Harris, 1986). In one condition, they monitored whether they were paying attention (by marking yes or no on a sheet) whenever a sound was randomly emitted from a tape recorder. In another condition, they recorded and graphed the number of words they had written at the end of the work period. In general, when one of the behaviors was monitored (i.e., paying attention or words written), on-task behavior and work performance improved.

Investigations have shown that self-recording behavior can influence smoking, overeating, tics, studying, nail-biting, and several other behaviors. However, the effectiveness of self-observation has been inconsistent. A number of studies have shown that self-monitoring does not alter behavior; others have shown that when self-monitoring does alter behavior, the effects are transient. Consequently, self-monitoring is used infrequently as a technique in its own right. It is usually combined with such techniques as self-reinforcement and self-punishment.

Self-Reinforcement and Self-Punishment

Reinforcing and punishing consequences administered to oneself have been used rather extensively as self-control techniques (Gross & Drabman, 1982; Jones, Nelson, & Kazdin, 1977). Clients are trained to administer consequences to themselves contingent upon behavior, rather than receiving consequences from an external agent. Self-reinforcement has received more attention than self-punishment.

The major requirement of self-reinforcement is that the individual be free to reward himself or herself at *any time,* whether or not a particular response is performed (Skinner, 1953). The person who self-administers reinforcers must not be constrained by external pressures to perform a response or to deliver or withhold consequences. An additional requirement to qualify as reinforcement is that the behavior followed by a self-administered consequence must increase in frequency.

In most applications of self-reinforcement, two procedures can be delineated. First, the client can determine the response requirements needed for a given amount of reinforcement. The client controls when to deliver reinforcement and the amount of reinforcement to be delivered. When the client determines the criteria for reinforcement, this is referred to as *self-determined reinforcement* (Glynn, 1970). Second, the client can dispense reinforcement for achieving a particular criterion, which may or may not be self-determined. When the client administers reinforcers to himself or herself, this is referred to as *self-administered reinforcement.* Who administers the reinforcers (oneself or someone else) may not be crucial. The crucial elements are determining *when* to deliver reinforcement and for *what* behaviors. However, if a person is not permitted to self-administer reinforcers, there may be external agents who influence the self-reinforcement process. Thus, self-reinforcement is probably best achieved when the client self-determines and self-administers the reinforcers. Self-reinforcement usually requires the client to observe and record his or her behavior so as to determine whether it has met a criterion. Thus, self-monitoring is an ingredient of the procedure.

Self-reinforcement has been used in several behavior programs conducted in classroom settings. For example, self-reinforcement was used to improve the story writing of elementary school children (Ballard & Glynn, 1975). The children self-recorded the number of sentences, the number of different descriptive words, and the number of different action words on a special sheet. Self-recording did not alter these behaviors. Self-reinforcement was added in which the children were told to administer one point to themselves for increases in the number of sentences they had written. The points were exchangeable for such activities as free time; access to games, art materials, and books; and public display of one's story. The number of sentences increased markedly with self-reinforcement. An extension of the self-reinforcement contingency to the other writing behaviors also showed increases. Interestingly, the quality and interest value of the stories were rated as better during the self-reinforcement phases than during baseline by two university faculty in English who were unaware of the program.

Self-punishment has been used relatively infrequently in behavior modification programs. The reasons are similar to those outlined in the previous discussion of punishment, namely that reinforcement techniques are usually viable alternatives and are less likely to evoke undesirable side effects.

Nevertheless, the utility of self-punishment has been suggested in several instances. For example, self-monitoring and self-punishment were employed with an 11-year-old boy named David, who showed an uncontrollable tic (eye-twitching), a behavior evident since the age of 6 (Ollendick, 1981). Over the years, the tic worsened and came to include uncontrollable movements of his mouth and cheek. David was trained by the therapist to self-monitor his tic at school, using a wrist counter to keep a tally. He was also trained to tense his facial muscles repeatedly when a tic occurred and to do this until the tic stopped. The procedure bears some resemblance to overcorrection (positive practice) and effort-based punishment procedures. In this case, the exercise was self-imposed, first at school and eventually at home as well. The effects of the procedure can be seen in Figure 9–1. Self-monitoring led to a slight reduction in the tic. When the overcorrection procedure was implemented, the

FIGURE 9–1

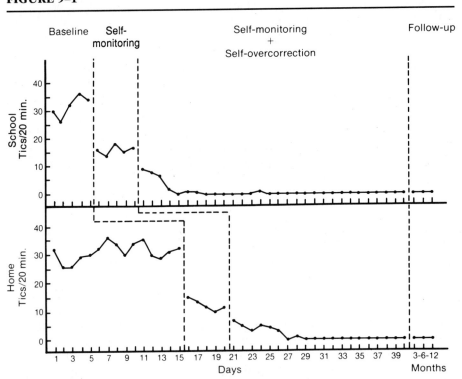

Effects of self-monitoring and self-administered overcorrection across school and home, as evaluated in a multiple-baseline design.

SOURCE: Ollendick, T. H. (1981). Self-monitoring and self-administered overcorrection: The modification of nervous tics in children. *Behavior Modification, 5,* 75–84. Copyright 1981 by T. H. Ollendick. Reprinted by permission of Sage Publications, Inc.

tic was eliminated in each of the settings. Follow-up assessment one year after the end of the program indicated that the tic did not reappear.

One case was reported of a 65-year-old male named Joe, who lived 200 miles away from the clinic (Belles & Bradlyn, 1987). Through arrangements made by phone, a program was devised to alter the number of cigarettes that he smoked. This was corroborated by counts that his wife made unobtrusively. After baseline, Joe rewarded himself for smoking a reduced number of cigarettes. Specifically, for each day on which he met or fell below the criterion number of cigarettes smoked, he provided $3 to a fund for items that he wished to buy. For each day on which he exceeded the criterion, he agreed to send a personal check for $25 to a charity he disliked. To verify this procedure, the check was to be mailed to the investigator, who would then forward the contribution to the charity.

The program was implemented and evaluated in a changing-criterion design so that in many separate phases the criterion for the number of cigarettes was set progressively lower. As shown in Figure 9–2, the criterion (horizontal line) was closely approximated in each phase (B through U). When Joe reached the criterion of five cigarettes per day, he indicated that he wished to remain at that level. The level was maintained and the program was terminated. Follow-up conducted up to 18 months later indicated that smoking remained at this level, obviously well below and much safer than the rate of 80–100 cigarettes each day before the study and baseline (A) phase began.

Self-reinforcement and self-punishment techniques have been applied to a wide range of problems—a craving for drugs, deviant sexual behavior, cigarette smoking, inadequate dating skills, and so on. In many applications, clients do not administer an overt consequence such as money or points. Rather, clients may *imagine* various events or consequences. Imagery-based procedures are addressed later (Chapter 10) because they encompass a variety of techniques in addition to self-reinforcement and self-punishment.

Alternate Response Training

Another self-control technique is training a person to engage in responses that interfere with or replace an undesired response. Essentially, the person is trained to replace one behavior with another. Of course, to accomplish this, the person must have an alternate response in which to engage. For example, people can think pleasant thoughts to control worrying or they can relax to control tension.

The most common focus of alternate response training is the control of anxiety. Relaxation has been widely used as a response that is incompatible with, and therefore an alternative to, anxiety. Typically, a client is trained by a therapist to relax deeply. Many methods for achieving relaxation are available. In behavior therapy, a client is usually trained to tense and relax individual muscle groups. Alternatively tensing and relaxing helps the person discriminate different levels of muscle relaxation. Another relaxation procedure that has

FIGURE 9–2

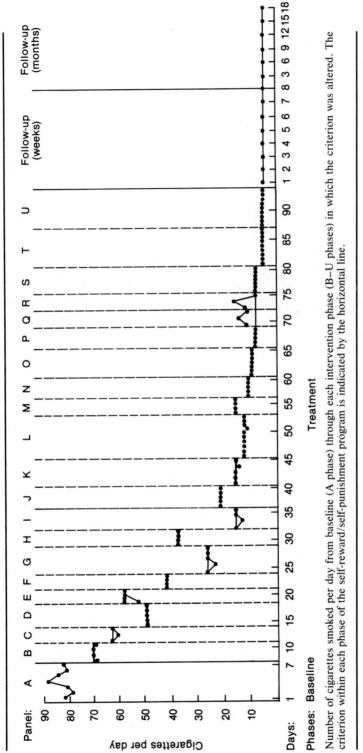

Number of cigarettes smoked per day from baseline (A phase) through each intervention phase (B–U phases) in which the criterion was altered. The criterion within each phase of the self-reward/self-punishment program is indicated by the horizontal line.

SOURCE: Reprinted with permission from *Journal of Behavior Therapy and Experimental Psychiatry, 18,* 77–82. Belles, D., & Bradlyn, A. S. The use of the changing criterion design in achieving controlled smoking in a heavy smoker: A controlled case study. Copyright 1987, Pergamon Press, Inc.

been used is to have the client make suggestions to himself or herself (i.e., self-instructions) of feeling warmth and heaviness in the muscles. Various forms of meditation can also be used to develop relaxation skills. Once relaxation has been learned, it can be used as a self-control technique. The person can use it to overcome anxiety in a variety of situations. Individuals have applied relaxation to themselves effectively in dealing with anxiety regarding interactions with the opposite sex, natural childbirth, public speaking, interviews, and many other problems (see Lichstein, 1988).

Relaxation training has also been used effectively to reduce hypertension (elevated blood pressure). Chronic hypertension is associated with a number of other problems, including heart disease and stroke. Drugs are generally used to deal with hypertension, though there are difficulties that interfere with their long-term use, such as lack of compliance among patients in taking their prescribed medication and side effects of the drugs. Because stress, anxiety, and arousal in general are likely to raise blood pressure, relaxation is a viable procedure to control hypertension. In one report, two adult males with hypertension were trained to relax deeply (Beiman, Graham, & Ciminero, 1978). They were instructed to practice relaxation at home and to apply relaxation when they felt tense or anxious or felt pressures of time or anger with others. Blood pressure readings were taken in the course of their everyday life and during their sessions with the therapist. Relaxation reduced both systolic and diastolic blood pressure. Follow-up assessment, up to six months after treatment, indicated that the effects were maintained and that the blood pressure readings of both clients fell within the normal range.

Varni (1981) used relaxation to treat three hemophilic patients who suffered from severe arthritic pain. The pain resulted from recurrent internal bleeding that affected the joints and caused cartilage and bone damage.[2] Because of possible drug dependency, medication is of limited value in controlling chronic pain. To help control pain, a self-control strategy was developed in which the patients were trained to relax deeply, to engage in deep breathing while saying the word *relax* to themselves, and to imagine themselves in situations previously associated with relief of pain. The patients' reports of pain, illustrated in Figure 9–3, decreased when the self-control training was introduced. The effects were maintained from 7 to 14 months after treatment. Moreover, after treatment, the patients decreased their use of medication to control pain.

Relaxation training is significant as an intervention for several reasons. To begin with, various procedures to induce relaxation (e.g., progressive relaxation, exercises, meditation, biofeedback) have been studied in relation to a number of clinical problems and have been shown to produce change. In addition, relaxation training has been effective in altering a wide range of problems, as already noted. Perhaps relaxation is of special interest because of accumulating evidence regarding the role of stress in placing individuals at risk for physical disease and psychological dysfunction (e.g., depression). For

FIGURE 9-3

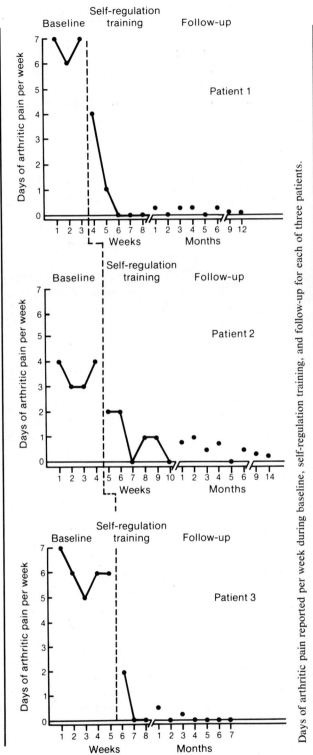

SOURCE: Varni, J. W. (1981). Self-regulation techniques in the management of chronic arthritic pain in hemophilia. *Behavior Therapy, 12,* 185–194. Copyright 1981 by the Association for Advancement of Behavior Therapy. Reprinted by permission of the publisher and the author.

Days of arthritic pain reported per week during baseline, self-regulation training, and follow-up for each of three patients.

example, recent research has suggested that relaxation training enhances the strength of the immune system and reduces the biological impact of stressors (e.g., Kielcolt-Glaser et al., 1985, 1986). Such research raises the possibility that relaxation training may affect functioning in a way that is directly related to bodily defenses against disease.

Biofeedback

Biofeedback consists of providing information to individuals about their ongoing physiological processes (e.g., heart rate, brain wave activity). The information is displayed so that the client can monitor moment-to-moment changes in these processes. Several biofeedback procedures can be distinguished, depending on which physiological processes are monitored and how feedback is administered (see Yates, 1980).

Many physiological processes are directly involved in problems brought for treatment, including hypertension, headaches, epileptic seizures, muscle spasms, cardiac arrhythmias (irregular heartbeat), and anxiety. Generally, biofeedback provides direct ongoing and immediate information to clients about various physiological processes. The goal is to produce a change in the specific response influence or to control the physiological process.

Biofeedback is included here as a self-control procedure because the goal of many biofeedback procedures is to teach clients specific techniques for regulating their own responses in the natural environment. For example, biofeedback may be used to control blood pressure. In treatment sessions, the client may be connected to a device that monitors blood pressure and provides visual feedback (on a TV screen or a digital counter) or auditory feedback (tone) when the blood pressure is above or below a specified criterion. The client can be instructed to decrease the blood pressure and will receive immediate feedback on the extent to which this has been successfully accomplished. Ideally, the client will learn to engage in responses (e.g., pleasant thoughts, relaxation) that are effective in decreasing blood pressure. These responses, hopefully, will be extended to everyday situations long after biofeedback training has been completed.

Biofeedback was used to control the tension headaches of a 39-year-old male who had a 16-year history of severe headaches (Epstein, Hersen, & Hemphill, 1974). A neurological examination failed to reveal organic causes of the headaches. Since research had shown that tension headaches are often associated with contraction of the frontalis (forehead) muscle, muscle relaxation of the frontalis was focused on in this case. To provide feedback, electrodes placed above the client's eyebrows were attached to an electromyograph, which measured muscle tension. The biofeedback consisted of playing music to the client (recordings of his favorite music) whenever the muscle tension was lower than a specified criterion level. He was told that the music was played whenever low levels of muscle tension occurred and that he was to try to keep the music on as much as possible. In an ABAB design, baseline sessions (no feedback) were alternated with biofeedback sessions. As shown in Figure 9–4, biofeedback reduced the client's overall muscle tension. In addition, the client reported a decrease in headaches. To ensure that the client would maintain relaxation when he returned to his normal routine, he was trained to engage in relaxation exercises that he could perform on his own after treatment. Up to a seven-month follow-up, the client reported a low incidence of headaches. Other studies have shown that electromyographic feedback of the frontalis muscles can produce general relaxation that affects responses other than headaches, such as improved respiratory flow among asthmatics, reduced blood pressure among hypertensive patients, reduced sleep latency among clients with insomnia, and reduced tension among individuals suffering from phobias or chronic anxiety (Surwit & Keefe, 1978).

Clinical applications of biofeedback have focused on a variety of responses, including cardiac arrhythmias, tachycardia (accelerated heart rate), hypertension, muscle paralysis and inactivity, seizure activity, sexual arousal, and anxiety (White & Tursky, 1982; Yates, 1980). Biofeedback has been provided in ways that convey not only muscle tension and blood pressure, already illustrated, but also skin temperature, heart rate, brain waves, blood volume, and galvanic skin responses. Although biofeedback has been successful in many reports, researchers have suggested that treatment effects can be more easily obtained with relaxation training, a technique that is easier to implement (because no equipment is required) and more readily extended to the natural environment (Lichstein, 1988). Also, relaxation training can be more readily applied to a wider range of problems because the technology for

FIGURE 9–4

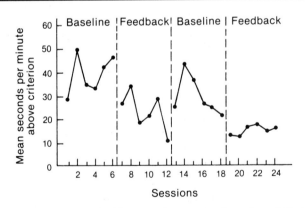

Mean seconds per minute that contained integrated responses above the criterion microvolt level during baseline and feedback phases.

SOURCE: Reprinted with permission from *Journal of Behavior Therapy and Experimental Psychiatry, 5,* 59–63. Epstein, L. H., Hersen, M., & Hemphill, D. P. Music feedback in the treatment of tension headache: An experimental case study. Copyright 1974, Pergamon Press, Inc.

assessing various physiological processes cannot be applied to measure selected clinical problems (e.g., obsessive thoughts).

Another issue has been whether the effects of feedback are sustained after training is completed. Several reports have shown that feedback does not invariably provide a technique that clients implement on their own. Nevertheless, biofeedback has often been shown to result in sustained treatment effects. However, like other self-control methods, biofeedback techniques designed to change behavior have developed to a greater extent than have the methods of ensuring that subjects apply the skills they learn in treatment to their everyday lives.

Self-Help Manuals

Many of the self-control techniques discussed to this point develop skills in clients during treatment sessions. After the skills have been developed, the clients can extend these to the environment to control their own behaviors in a variety of situations. Recently, several self-help techniques have been developed that clients implement for themselves with minimal or no therapist assistance. The techniques have occasionally been referred to as *bibliotherapy* because the procedures are conveyed to potential clients in written form, usually self-help books or manuals that can be purchased in stores or are made available at clinics. Bibliotherapy, or the use of self-help manuals, has been applied to an extraordinary range of problems, including fear reduction, overeating, depression, cigarette smoking, social skills, toileting accidents, sexual dysfunction, and excessive alcohol consumption (Glasgow & Rosen, 1984). The techniques included in these manuals encompass a variety of procedures, alone and in combination. The manuals describe in a step-by-step fashion how the client should proceed to alter his or her problem.

Self-help manuals have been used in adult treatment for a variety of problems. One of the more well investigated applications is the self-administration of systematic desensitization, a treatment designed to reduce anxiety. Rosen, Glasgow, and Barrera (1976, 1977) evaluated the extent to which clients who feared snakes could self-administer desensitization without therapist contact. Desensitization as usually practiced is administered by a therapist. The client is trained to relax deeply and to imagine situations related to the fear while relaxed. By imagining a series of situations related to the fear (such as snakes) while deeply relaxed, the client is eventually no longer anxious in the presence of the actual situations. Rosen and his colleagues provided clients with a written manual that explained how to conduct systematic desensitization. A record was included that trained clients in relaxation. Also provided were instructions to develop scenes that could be imagined and paired with relaxation. The results indicated that completely self-administered desensitization was as effective as therapist-administered desensitization on self-report, overt behavior, and physiological measures of anxiety. Self- and therapist-administered groups were superior to subjects who received either no treatment or a manual that simply contained information about snakes. These results were maintained up to two years of follow-up.

Self-help manuals have been effectively applied to help parents alter the behavior of their children. For example, McMahon and Forehand (1978) examined the effectiveness of a self-help brochure for parents in training appropriate mealtime behaviors in their children. Three normal preschool children from different families participated on the basis of their parents' interest in changing such inappropriate behaviors as playing with food, throwing or stealing food, and leaving the table prior to the end of the meal. An initial consultation in the parents' home explained the procedures. At this point, the parents received a brief brochure (2½ pages) describing how to provide attention and praise for appropriate mealtime behavior and how to use time out from reinforcement (isolating the child in another room) for inappropriate behaviors that the child did not cease to engage in when asked. With only this brief description of reinforcement and time-out, the parents implemented training. The results of training were evaluated by observations of actual eating behaviors in the home. The program was very effective, as shown in the multiple-baseline design across different children, plotted in Figure 9–5. The effects of the program were maintained at follow-up assessment approximately six weeks after treatment. These results are impressive because of the ability of the parents to administer treatment completely on their own.

One of the most widely circulated self-help manuals was developed several years ago for parents who wish to toilet train their children quickly (Azrin & Foxx, 1974). The manual includes a series of procedures based on many of the techniques that have been reviewed: prompting, positive practice, reinforcement, and so on. Instructions, edible rewards, praise, feedback, guidance, and occasional punishment (positive practice) are intertwined to develop the child's self-initiation of toileting skills. The specific procedures on which the manual is based have been carefully researched in experimental studies in which those procedures have produced rapid results. Indeed, the manual suggests that toilet training can be conducted in "less than a day" (average time about four hours). Investigations of how parents actually perform with the manual in training their children have been generally positive. However, evidence suggests that implementing the procedures from reading the book alone is not very effective in developing toileting skills, unless someone is available to provide parents with supervision on how to use the procedures (Matson & Ollendick, 1977).

Self-help manuals have proliferated in recent years (Glasgow & Rosen, 1984). Many of the manuals include techniques that have been shown to alter behavior. However, the manuals themselves often promise more than has been achieved in research. The popularity of the self-help manuals stems from the kinds of promises they often make, such as large and permanent amounts of weight loss, cessation of smoking, and elimination of sexual dysfunction (see

FIGURE 9–5

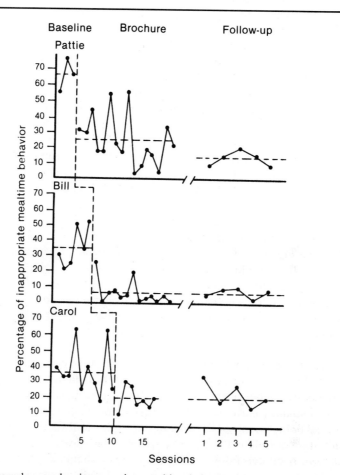

Percentage of intervals scored as inappropriate mealtime behavior. The broken horizontal line in each phase indicates the mean percentage of intervals scored as inappropriate mealtime behavior across sessions for that phase.

SOURCE: McMahon, R. J., & Forehand, R. (1978). Nonprescription behavior therapy: Effectiveness of a brochure in teaching mothers to correct their children's inappropriate mealtime behaviors. *Behavior Therapy, 9,* 814–820. Copyright 1978 by the Association for Advancement of Behavior Therapy. Reprinted by permission of the publisher and the author.

Glasgow & Rosen, 1984). The appeal of these manuals is augmented by their claims of rapid, inexpensive, and marvelously effective cures. Some of the self-help manuals have been shown to enhance functioning. As a general rule, however, the self-help manuals remain untested and are unlikely to produce the sorts of changes suggested by their strong claims.

IMPORTANT CONSIDERATIONS OF SELF-CONTROL TECHNIQUES

Who Is in Control?

To what extent do clients really control their own behavior when self-control techniques are used? These techniques vary considerably in the role they accord clients in implementing treatment. Self-help manuals provide the greatest client autonomy, because when these are used, the therapist exerts little or no direct influence and the clients are left on their own to carry out the procedures. Other self-control techniques, such as self-reinforcement and self-punishment, imply much greater client autonomy than often exists. Even though the clients may play a role in deciding when or how to administer consequences to themselves, many external constraints may strongly influence how the consequences are administered and for what behaviors (Gross & Wojnilower, 1984; Jones et al., 1977). For example, clients are often told *when* to administer consequences and *what* the standards for performance should be. The client may be told that he or she can deliver a reinforcer for *interacting socially,* for performing *correctly* on a task, or for *losing* weight. Self-reinforcement and self-punishment usually require that the client be allowed to administer or not administer the consequences at any time and for any behaviors that he or she sees fit. For reasons that are made clear below, behavior modification programs have usually placed strong constraints on clients so that they have less than complete control over the contingencies.

As has been noted, in terms of the role that clients are given in changing their behavior, self-controlled and externally controlled procedures can be viewed as opposite ends of a continuum. In most techniques, clients exert some control by being involved in selecting the problem focused on in treatment. Beyond this, clients may have some role in implementing the techniques themselves. The degree of involvement that clients can have in their own treatment is an important consideration in deciding which technique to use. Obviously, the amount of control that therapy can delegate to clients is related to such variables as client age, the type of problem focused on, and the setting in which treatment is conducted. Young children would not be expected to control their own hyperactivity with a self-help manual, and prisoners who are repeated sex offenders would not be expected to alter their behaviors by self-monitoring instances of their undesirable behaviors for a few weeks. Problems discussed below, which occasionally arise with various self-control procedures, determine in part whether the self-control technique should be applied or should be expected to accomplish the desired goal.

As a general rule, involving the client in treatment probably is advisable whenever possible. Evidence suggests that clients often prefer techniques that they help design or implement (Kazdin, 1980b). Also, in the case of self-reinforcement, clients occasionally perform better when they dictate the criteria for reinforcement or administer the rewards than when others administer the contingencies (Brigham & Stoerzinger, 1976; Dickerson & Creedon, 1981). The importance of involving clients was evident in a report on the exercise programs of burn victims (Hegel, Ayllon, VanderPlate, & Spiro-Hawkins, 1986). Exercise is critical among burn patients because it prevents skin from contracting over the joints during healing and thus severely limiting the mobility of muscles and joints. The necessary exercise is often stressful and painful. In this successful project, patients engaged in a self-exercise regimen as an alternative to engaging in a program administered by the hospital staff.

Other advantages of involving clients in their behavior modification program are that this may help ensure that the gains achieved are maintained over time and extended to a variety of situations in the client's life. The effects of treatment might be enhanced by training clients to analyze the environmental influences that will arise and to implement specific procedures that will sustain performance. Hence, self-control may be useful in maintaining behaviors once change has been achieved (see Chapter 11).

Adherence to Treatment

An issue that arises in any treatment technique is the extent to which clients will adhere to or carry out the procedures. Self-reinforcement and self-punishment techniques have led to problems in adherence. If an individual is completely free to deliver rewarding or punishing consequences for behavior, will those consequences be administered contingently? The natural contingencies (i.e., the contingencies normally fostered by the environment) may discourage adherence to self-reinforcement and self-punishment contingencies. For example, if a client does not meet a self-imposed performance criterion for self-reward (e.g., studying for two hours), he or she can still self-administer the reward (e.g., going out with friends). If the standards for self-reinforcement are lowered, no immediate penalty will result from an external agent. Essentially, the client might be rewarded for ignoring the performance standard and the entire self-reinforcement contingency. Thus, noncontingent reinforcement and suspension of the contingencies are probably much more likely in self-control programs than in externally managed programs.

In many self-reinforcement studies, the contingencies have not been consistently adhered to over time. For example, in one study, self-reinforcement was used to develop the study skills of college students with low grades (McReynolds & Church, 1973). The students devised "self-contracts" in which they specified small response requirements (e.g., study for a few minutes each day) to acquire reinforcers (e.g., cigarettes or attending a sports event). A new contract was drawn up at the end of a few days as behavior met the previously specified criteria. Despite the fact that the students devised the response criteria themselves—or perhaps because of it—many of them rewarded themselves even though they had not met the requirements for the behavioral contract. These students did not adhere to the contingencies; hence, behavior change should not have been expected.

Self-reinforcement has been most extensively used in classroom settings, where students are permitted to provide reinforcing consequences to themselves for studying and paying attention to the lesson. When students are allowed to determine the number of reinforcers or to decide when they have earned a given number of reinforcers, their standards often diminish. It has been shown that children become increasingly lenient over time and eventually provide reinforcing consequences to themselves for relatively disruptive behavior (see Gross & Drabman, 1982).

In self-reinforcement and self-punishment programs, several procedures have been used to decrease noncontingent or lenient administration of consequences. Such programs usually begin with external reinforcement (by a teacher or parent) to identify the behaviors that should be self-rewarded. This initial phase of externally managed contingencies increases the likelihood that the person will self-administer reinforcement contingently later (O'Brien, Riner, & Budd, 1983). During the self-reinforcement phase, other procedures have been employed to maintain contingent administration of consequences. For example, in classroom programs, external reinforcers are provided by explicitly instructing the children to give themselves rewards only when they have met stringent criteria or by checking the children to see whether they self-reward correctly and threatening punishment if they do not (e.g., Hundert & Bastone, 1978; Robertson, Simon, Pachman, & Drabman, 1979). Although student behavior is effectively controlled by providing externally controlled reinforcing or punishing events or by setting the standards for self-reward, the use of such procedures challenges the notion of *self*-control.

Delivering aversive events to oneself also introduces the problem of leniency. As mentioned earlier, an aversive event administered by an external agent may result in escape or avoidance. There is no reason to believe that this will not happen if aversive events are self-administered. Individuals may avoid applying an aversive event to themselves in one of two ways: by not performing the undesirable behavior or by simply performing the behavior but not applying the aversive event afterward. Programs using self-administered punishment have reported that clients do not administer the consequences to themselves as they should (James, 1981; Wilson, Leaf, & Nathan, 1975). Hence, it is not likely that clients will widely adhere to self-punishment alone.

With both self-reinforcement and self-punishment, clients may discontinue the contingency at any time, because it is under their control. If a client suspends the contingency, even temporarily, that behavior will be reinforced (obtain the positive reinforcer or avoid the aversive event). Hence, a concern with self-control procedures is what will maintain adherence to the contingency. Hopefully, the delayed reinforcing consequences or intended goal of the program (e.g., losing weight) will sustain self-control. However, everyday experience suggests that delayed consequences are not sufficient to maintain adherence to self-imposed contingencies. More often than not, individuals appear to go off diets, resume cigarette smoking, or give up some other contingency that they originally designed. It may be essential to provide individuals with some external reinforcement (perhaps delivered by friend, relative, or spouse) for adherence to the "self-control" contingency. Gradually, external reinforcement might be delivered intermittently and then eliminated altogether. External influences may be critical to the effects of self-reinforcement in other ways. Setting goals publicly (so that others know about them) has been shown to be important in obtaining behavior change in self-reinforcement programs (Hayes et al., 1985). When the contingencies are known to others, social consequences may implicitly serve as an external influence by ensuring that the self-reinforcement program is conducted as intended.

Adherence to treatment has been somewhat of a problem when clients are given self-help manuals and left to their own devices to implement treatment. First, persons left entirely on their own to conduct treatment have relatively high rates of attrition (dropping out of treatment), a finding shown in self-help training for such problems as anxiety associated with public speaking, fears, and sexual dysfunction (Marshall, Presse, & Andrews, 1976; Rosen et al., 1976; Zeiss, 1978). Second, clients who stay in treatment often do not carry out the required procedures when they are left on their own with a self-help manual. For example, investigators have reported that 50 percent or more of the clients who used a self-help manual for the treatment of anxiety failed to complete the procedures that they were instructed to perform (Marshall et al., 1976; Rosen et al., 1976). In a study on the treatment of problem drinkers, approximately one third of the clients said that they had not even read the self-help manual that was used to help maintain treatment gains (Miller, 1977, Exp. 2). For many problems and clients, self-control may provide an adjunct to treatment; however, therapist contact or supervision may be necessary to ensure that the program is carried out. Indeed, research has suggested that reading the materials in a self-help manual and carrying out the prescribed activities are enhanced by contact with a therapist (Glasgow & Rosen, 1984; Holroyd, 1986). At this point, research has not determined which problems or clients are most likely to benefit from self-control strategies and what level of involvement of therapists or other external agents is required to maximize behavior change.

USE OF SELF-CONTROL PROCEDURES

Self-control procedures have been applied to diverse populations, including children and adolescents in classroom settings; inpatient and outpatient clients treated for anxiety, overeating, and alcohol consumption; and parents interested in altering a variety of their children's behaviors at home. Several advantages accrue from the development of self-control procedures. First, such procedures permit various techniques to be more widely extended to the public than would ordinarily be the case with techniques completely carried out by trained professional therapists. In self-control techniques such as stimulus control, self-monitoring, and alternate response training, clients have initial contact with a therapist but carry out the procedures on their own. The initial contact means that little professional time and client expense are involved in beginning and carrying out treatment. With self-help manuals, the potential for widespread dissemination of treatment is even greater than with other self-control techniques. If readers carry out behavior modification techniques presented in manuals, a large number of people might be reached who ordinarily would not even seek treatment.

Another advantage of self-control procedures is that they may be preferred by clients over a therapist-administered treatment. People may prefer implementing a treatment on their own because self-administered treatment may be less expensive and more efficient and because it enables them to play a more direct role in their own treatment. Many clients might be more apt to undergo treatment if they could self-administer the procedures. For example, a Gallup opinion survey indicated that only about 34 percent of cigarette smokers would come for treatment at a clinic and that most cigarette smokers preferred self-help methods (Glasgow & Rosen, 1984). The preference for self-help procedures may extend to a variety of problems.

The application of self-control techniques raises important questions that remain to be resolved. To begin with, the range of clients for whom self-control procedures can be applied has not been elaborated. Perhaps self-control techniques are readily applied to clients who already have enough control to initiate them. Many of the self-control procedures have been carried out on an adult outpatient basis. Inpatient populations, such as mentally retarded persons, psychiatric patients, delinquents, and prisoners, warrant further study in relation to self-control. For many of these groups, treatment is not self-initiated but imposed by the agency or setting. This may reduce the incentives to carry out self-control procedures.

The range of problems for which self-control procedures are effective needs to be evaluated. Currently, applications of self-control procedures encompass a variety of problems, including anxiety, depression, sexual dysfunction, overeating, cigarette smoking, alcohol abuse, and the management of diseases (Holroyd & Creer, 1986; Karoly & Kanfer, 1982). The extent to which various problem areas are amenable to self-control training remains to be researched.

Self-control techniques vary in the extent to which the therapist or some other external agent plays a role in treatment. Contact with the therapist may be important to ensure that treatment is conducted properly, to provide encouragement when problems arise or when the client begins to discontinue the procedures, and to help decide when other procedures should be tried. The role of therapist contact in various self-control procedures needs to be evaluated further.

Although many questions about self-control remain to be resolved, its accomplishments have already been impressive. The available techniques provide clients with a number of alternative means so that they can implement treatment for themselves. Although techniques for controlling one's own behavior have been advocated throughout the history of psychotherapy, only recently have such techniques been evaluated experimentally to establish their effectiveness. The results have demonstrated that for many applications various procedures can help people gain control over their own behavior.

SUMMARY AND CONCLUSION

Self-control refers to the behaviors that an individual deliberately under-takes to achieve self-selected outcomes. Behavioral techniques are applied by the individual rather than by an external agent. Several self-control techniques are discussed. *Stimulus control* allows individuals to control their own behav-ior by altering environmental and situational events that serve as cues for behavior. *Self-monitoring* requires that individuals keep a careful record of the target response. Merely observing one's own behavior often leads to a systematic change. *Self-reinforcement* and *self-punishment* require that indi-viduals apply certain events to themselves following behavior. The crucial aspect of self-reinforcement or self-punishment is the freedom to partake of the reinforcer or not to apply the punishing event.

Alternate response training requires that a client engage in a response that interferes with or replaces the response that the client wishes to control. *Biofeedback* procedures provide information to clients about their physiologi-cal processes. Ideally, clients can learn to control the bodily processes related to the problem for which they sought change. *Self-help manuals* comprise a variety of techniques that have in common the manner in which they are presented to the client. Clients receive written material in brochure or book form that conveys how they are to conduct treatment for themselves. They can use this material to conduct treatment on their own with minimal or no contact with a therapist or consultant.

In many of the self-control techniques, some preliminary training may be needed to convey both the principle behind the technique and the requirements for effective application. However, once the basic principle is understood and the initial training has been completed, the client can implement the treatment intervention and determine the range of behaviors or situations to which it will be applied.

Three major issues pertaining to self-control techniques were discussed. First, in some applications, questions can be raised about the extent to which the client is permitted to self-control. Some of the self-control techniques are embedded in strong external contingencies from a therapist or other agent. Other self-control techniques, such as self-help manuals, often give the client complete autonomy. Second, adherence to treatment has been an issue in various self-control techniques. Clients often do not carry out the procedures on their own, and the contingencies may deteriorate over time. Also, many clients drop out of some self-control programs, and the result may be a lower success rate than might be achieved with therapist-administered treatment. Finally, several advantages are associated with self-control techniques. The techniques allow for the widespread extension of treatment to the public in ways that cannot be readily accomplished with traditional therapist-administered treatment. The costs of treatment are minimal (as in the case of self-help manuals). Contact with a therapist, if any, is very brief. Hence, self-control techniques provide an opportunity for changing behavior on a larger scale than would be achievable with other techniques.

NOTES

1. There are other self-control techniques that cannot be treated here. Additional sources, noted below, detail the full range of self-control techniques.
2. Hemophilia is an inherited disorder of blood coagulation in which there is frequent and difficult-to-control bleeding. The pain for which the patients in this study were treated is caused by repeated internal hemorrhaging, which produces permanent damage to cartilage and bone.

FOR FURTHER READING

Blankstein, K. R., & Polivy, J. (Eds.). (1982). *Self-control and self-modification of emotional behavior: Advances in the study of communication and affect* (Vol. 7). New York: Plenum.

Esveldt-Dawson, K., & Kazdin, A. E. (1982). *How to use self-control.* Austin, TX: Pro-Ed.

Holroyd, K. A., & Creer, T. L. (Eds.). (1986). *Self-management of chronic disease: Handbook of clinical interventions and research.* New York: Academic Press.

Karoly, P., & Kanfer, F. H. (Eds.). (1982). *Self management and behavior change: From theory to practice.* Elmsford, NY: Pergamon Press.

Lichstein, K. L. (1988). *Clinical relaxation strategies.* New York: Wiley.

Watson, D. L., & Tharp, R. G. (1981). *Self-directed behavior: Self-modification for personal adjustment* (3rd ed.). Monterey, CA: Brooks/Cole.

Chapter Ten

Cognitively Based Treatment

Cognitively based techniques refer to a family of procedures that adhere to the general notion that behavior change can be achieved by altering cognitive processes. The cognitive processes that serve as the focus of treatment include perceptions, self-statements, attributions, expectations, beliefs, and images. The assumptions underlying cognitively based techniques are that maladaptive cognitive processes lead to maladaptive behaviors and that changing these processes can lead to behavior change.

Previous chapters have emphasized the importance of environmental changes and how individuals respond to these changes. For example, positive reinforcement and punishment refer largely to external events that are applied to individuals to influence their behavior. Consideration of cognitive processes is a significant addition to treatment approaches because these processes emphasize how the individual perceives the environment. How the environment is perceived can greatly influence the impact of environmental events.

Everyday experience conveys the obvious impact of perceptions. For example, two persons riding a roller coaster may react quite differently, in part because of the different ways in which they perceive the experience. For both persons, the physical characteristics of the ride itself—the "environmental factors"—are essentially the same. Yet one of them may believe that the ride is dangerous and life threatening and feel extremely anxious, whereas the other may believe that the ride is safe and feel excited and exhilarated. During the ride itself, the former may say to himself or herself that something horrible might happen any minute, whereas the latter may say to himself or herself that the ride is wonderful and exciting. The ride can have a different impact on the two persons because of the differences in their perceptions, beliefs, and self-statements.

Differences in perceptions are not to be regarded lightly. The arousal, stress, anxiety, dread, and other biological and psychological signs of these two persons may be dramatically different. Moreover, the events are not just different "in their minds." Their perceptions can have a direct impact on the safety of the experience. The person who views the experience as entirely free from risk might become careless and not take advisable safety precautions. This might increase the risk of injury. The person who views the experience as dangerous might consume alcohol or tranquilizers and thus be unresponsive if an untoward eventuality occurred. Perceptions are not only significant in their own right but also through their influence on behavior.

The interrelationships among cognitive processes, environmental events, and behavior are perhaps more clearly conveyed in the context of social behavior. For example, a person who believes that other people are very friendly may initiate social responses (greetings, conversations) with acquaintances and strangers. The belief (cognitive process) leads to greeting and chatting with others (behavior), which in turn generate environmental consequences (e.g., attention, praise, and other sources of reinforcement from others). These consequences are likely to affect the person's perceptions and behaviors in the future. This small-scale example conveys how cognitive processes and environmental events mutually influence each other.

INTEREST IN COGNITIVE PROCESSES

Interest in cognitive processes as behavior change procedures can be traced to many influences in both basic and clinical research. Basic research in developmental psychology has been especially significant—in particular, research on how cognitive processes and language emerge in childhood and on how language affects behavior. It has been shown that early in childhood children often talk out loud to describe what they are doing and to regulate or influence their own actions (Zivin, 1979). This can be observed in situations in which children seem to be narrating what they are doing as they play with toys or dolls and engage them in various activities. Over the course of development, speech becomes internalized and private, so that adults have private thoughts before or during their actions. Private speech can be observed by having children and adults say out loud what they are thinking or by having them answer questions about what they are thinking as they engage in various activities. Theory and research in child development have elaborated the emergence and importance of cognitive processes over the course of childhood (e.g., Kohlberg, Yaeger, & Hjerthuim, 1968; Piaget, 1928).

Within clinical work, cognitive processes have been shown to relate to a number of clinical problems, including depression, anxiety, social withdrawal, and eating disorders (Guidano & Liotti, 1983). As an example, consider depression, a disorder characterized by sadness, lack of interest in activities, and often such other symptoms as disturbances of sleep and eating. Typically, depressed persons view themselves as failures, see their world as filled with loss, and feel pessimistic and hopeless about the future (Beck, 1976). These beliefs are related to the various symptoms of depression as well as reduced interactions with others and a lack of interest in activities. Suicidal thoughts or attempts, which are often associated with depression, have been identified with even more specific beliefs. Research suggests that in both children and adults the belief that things are hopeless, more than other characteristics of depression such as sadness and more than the severity of depression, is related to suicide ideation, attempt, and completion (Beck, Kovacs, & Weissman, 1975; Kazdin et al., 1983). A number of forms of psychotherapy and medication are available for depressed persons. One effective treatment, referred to as *cognitive therapy,* focuses directly on altering the belief system of depressed persons (Beck, Rush, Shaw, & Emery, 1979).

Many other clinical problems appear to have important cognitive features that may lead to maladaptive behavior. For example, aggressive children appear to have a predisposition to perceive their interpersonal environment in ways that help promote their aggressive reactions. Such children often perceive as hostile ambiguous social situations in which the intent of others is not clear (Dodge, 1985). Thus, if an aggressive child is accidentally bumped in the hall while walking to class, he is more likely than a nonaggressive child to see this as an act of aggression. Understandably, when such situations are perceived as hostile, the child is more likely to respond aggressively (Deluty, 1981). A number of other cognitive processes have been shown to relate to aggressive behavior (Kazdin, 1985b), and some of these will be illustrated in the discussion of specific techniques later in the chapter.

Most cognitively based techniques are applied in the context of psychotherapy sessions in which children, adolescents, or adults are seen individually or in a group by professional therapists. Treatment focuses on specific processes that are designed to alter behavior. This context is different from that of applied settings where contingencies in the environment are managed by parents, teachers, hospital staff, peers, or others directly in the situations in which problem behaviors have emerged. However, it is not easy to clearly delineate how and by whom cognitively based techniques are administered. These techniques are often used as self-control procedures in which individuals learn a particular technique that they can apply as needed to situations in everyday life. Also, in many applications, parents and teachers have been trained to help children at home and at school (Spivack & Shure, 1982; Weissberg et al., 1981). Thus, cognitively based techniques are sometimes used in applied settings, as are techniques based on reinforcement and punishment practices. Finally, cognitively based techniques are often used in combination with reinforcement and punishment techniques in applied settings. Selected applications of cognitively based techniques are also illustrated in the present chapter.

ILLUSTRATIVE TECHNIQUES

Self-Instructions and Self-Statements

What people say to themselves has been considered important in controlling their own behavior (Zivin, 1979). It has been suggested that the influence of one's own speech on behavior results from childhood learning. The speech of external agents (e.g., parents) controls and directs behavior in early childhood. The child eventually develops a self-directed and verbal repertoire that derives from the speech of these external agents. For example, children praise and criticize themselves in ways that they observe in adult models. Similarly, children verbally administer self-instructional statements to guide their actions. While the instructions of others continue to influence behavior throughout life, self-instructional statements also exert control. Self-instructional statements, while usually private or covert, are sometimes evident in everyday life when an individual "thinks out loud" and describes a course of action that he believes he should pursue. For example, in preparing to ask an employer for a raise, an individual may tell himself what he would say when the situation arises. Indeed, the individual may use self-verbalization while engaging in the actual conversation.

Self-instruction training has been used as a behavior change technique. Individuals are trained to make suggestions and specific comments that guide their own behavior in a fashion similar to being instructed by someone else. Investigations have shown that children and adults can be trained to make statements to themselves that guide their behavior.

For example, in one application, self-statements were used to treat headaches (Holroyd, Andrasik, & Westbrook, 1977). Adult clients reporting a history of headaches (average of six years) were trained to identify thoughts about events or situations that precipitated stress. They practiced reappraising stressful events with self-statements (e.g., "What am I thinking to induce my distress?") and emitting self-instructions that helped cope with such situations (e.g., "Calm down, concentrate on the present," "Imagine myself for a moment carefree, at the beach"). They were encouraged to implement their coping skills at the first sign of a headache. Treatment resulted in reported reductions in headaches. These self-instruction clients showed greater reductions than did persons who received biofeedback or no treatment. The effects were maintained up to a 15-week follow-up assessment.

Occasionally, self-statements are used to help individuals control undesirable and repetitive thoughts. The client is trained to stop his or her bothersome thoughts with a technique that is appropriately called *thought stopping*. The technique proceeds in a manner similar to self-instruction training. First the therapist models the desired statement, and then the client states the instruction aloud and, eventually, covertly. For example, Hackmann and McLean (1975) used thought stopping to treat obsessive-compulsive clients. When a client had an obsessive thought or imagined a ritualistic behavior, the therapist at first hit the desk with a ruler and shouted "Stop!" in order to interrupt the obsessive thought. After a few trials, the therapist said "Stop" without using the ruler. The client was instructed to shout "Stop!" aloud to interrupt his or her obsessive thoughts. Later, the client was instructed to say "Stop" in a whisper and then subvocally. In this way, clients learned how to effectively interrupt their obsessive thoughts without the aid of the therapist. Treatment effectively reduced obsessive thoughts in only a matter of a few sessions. Other applications of thought stopping have attested to its efficacy, but the technique is less well researched than other self-statement methods.

Self-statements have also been used to control anxiety. For example, the effects of different types of self-instruction were compared in helping young children handle fear of the dark (Kanfer, Karoly, & Newman, 1975). Children trained to make self-statements reflecting competence ("I can take care of myself in the dark") were better able to remain in the dark than children instructed to make statements that reevaluated the situation (e.g., "The dark is a fun place to be") or distract themselves with other types of statements (e.g., "Mary had a little lamb"). Thus, the types of self-statements that individuals make may determine the effectiveness of training.

Problem-Solving Skills Training

Cognitively based treatment has been applied extensively to children and adolescents in programs that develop interpersonal problem-solving skills (Spivack & Shure, 1982). The programs are based on evidence that children and adolescents with adjustment problems have deficits in various cognitive processes that underlie social behavior. Specific problem-solving skills that have been well studied and in which deficits are evident among maladjusted children are listed in Table 10–1. These skills are considered the basis for social behaviors that individuals perform in everyday situations.

For example, children with adjustment problems often have difficulty in identifying alternative solutions to interpersonal problems (e.g., resolving an argument), the consequences of their behaviors (e.g., the reactions of others), and the steps that need to be taken to achieve a goal (e.g., how to make friends). These and related skills can be developed by training the children to use problem-solving steps and self-statements in various games, academic tasks, and real-life situations. Training helps the children to think about the particular task, problem, or situation, the behaviors that need to be performed, and the alternative courses of action that are available, and then to select a particular solution. As in self-instruction training, the children ask specific questions or make specific self-statements to help themselves develop

TABLE 10-1 Problem-Solving Skills that Relate to Adjustment

1. *Alternative solution thinking*—the ability to generate different options (solutions) that can solve problems in interpersonal situations.

2. *Means-end thinking*—awareness of the intermediate steps required to achieve a particular goal.

3. *Consequential thinking*—the ability to identify what might happen as a direct result of acting in a particular way or choosing a particular solution.

4. *Causal thinking*—the ability to relate one event to another over time and to understand why one event led to a particular action of other persons.

5. *Sensitivity to interpersonal problems*—the ability to perceive a problem when it exists and to identify the interpersonal aspects of the confrontation that may emerge.

SOURCE: Adapted from Spivack, G., Platt, J. J., & Shure, M. B. (1976). *The problem-solving approach to adjustment*. San Francisco: Jossey-Bass.

problem-solving skills (e.g., "What am I supposed to do? What is my plan? How do I do it?"). They are trained to answer these questions when confronted with interpersonal situations in which their behavior is problematic and to identify and carry out socially appropriate solutions to problems.

A number of studies have shown that problem-solving skills training can decrease disruptive and impulsive behavior and increase peer popularity among children and adolescents (see Kazdin, 1985b; Kendall & Braswell, 1985; Spivack & Shure, 1982). Many of these studies have focused on children who are mildly disruptive or impulsive at school. With such children, the effects of training are maintained up to two years later (Shure & Spivack, 1982). With more severely disturbed children and adolescents such as those who show aggressive or delinquent behavior, cognitively based treatment that focuses on problem-solving skills training has led to significant changes at home, at school, and in the community, and these gains are evident up to one year later (Arbuthnot & Gordon, 1986; Kazdin, Esveldt-Dawson, French, & Unis, 1987; Lochman, Burch, Curry, & Lampron, 1984). To date, however, most of these studies have shown that the changes do not return the children to normative levels of functioning. The children remain less aggressive than they were before treatment, less aggressive than children who did not receive treatment, but they are still more aggressive than children who are functioning well at home and at school. Because severely disturbed aggressive children often do not respond to various forms of treatment, the gains shown with problem-solving skills training are promising.

Problem-solving skills training has been used in a variety of areas. For example, the approach has been effectively applied with mothers who neglect their children. Parental neglect refers to a chronic failure of parents to meet their children's needs with regard to physical safety, health, nutrition, and emotional development. For legal purposes, neglect is often considered with physical abuse in the sense that they both reflect extreme, harmful, and maladaptive child-rearing practices. Neglectful parents may have deficits in judgment and behavior, because they fail to anticipate the needs of their children and the consequences of their neglect. Problem-solving training was applied to mothers whose neglect had been adjudicated (Dawson, de Armas, McGrath, & Kelly, 1986). This project focused on three mothers (ages 20 to 27) who had been identified by child-protective services as neglectful and referred for treatment. Several vignettes related to the care of children were constructed based on past reports and the mothers' descriptions of situations in which they failed to meet their children's needs. Each of the vignettes was read aloud to the parent, who was asked to engage in the problem-solving approach—to define the problem, to consider possible solutions, to describe the consequences and obstacles of each solution, and to choose the best solution. Here is a sample vignette:

> You and your mother have an argument on the phone. She tells you that you can just forget about bringing your children over tonight for her to baby-sit while you go out with your boyfriend (husband). It's 5 P.M. You don't have any money to hire a baby-sitter. The story ends with you and your boyfriend (husband) going out for the evening (Dawson et al., 1986, p. 213).

During baseline, problem situations were presented to see how each mother managed the care of her children—whether she identified a plan to solve the problem, selected various means or steps toward the goal, and identified obstacles that would interfere with completing appropriate behaviors. The problem-solving skills training approach was then taught individually to each mother, using modeling, shaping, and feedback. The effects of training were evaluated in a multiple-baseline design. As shown in Figure 10–1, each mother's solutions to the problems (vignettes) included more of the problem-solving skills components than did her baseline performance. Effectiveness ratings were also completed by social workers associated with each case to assess the extent to which the mother improved in her child-rearing practices, as reflected in such activities as solving child-related problems in the home, performing responsibilities, and providing food, clothing, and child care. Effectiveness ratings increased after treatment for each of the mothers. At follow-up 15 months later, only one of the mothers was available for reassessment on the vignettes. She continued to show high levels of problem-solving skills. The other two mothers, who had moved, had had full custody of their children restored by the child welfare department, with no further reports of neglect.

Imagery-Based Procedures

Several cognitively based techniques rely on imagery. Clients imagine various events in specific ways that lead to change in their behavior. For many imagery-based procedures, clients imagine alternative ways of behaving or

FIGURE 10-1

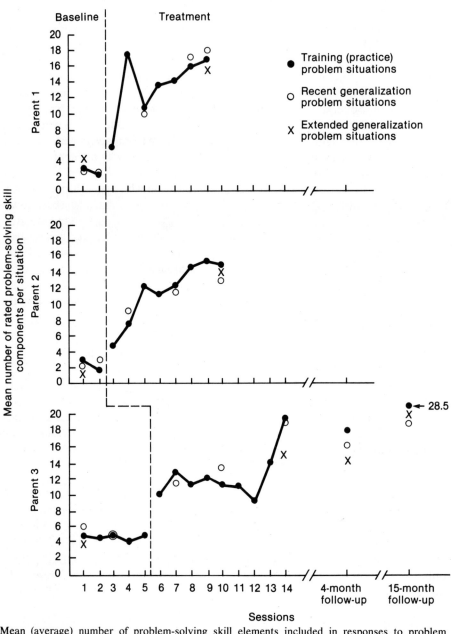

Mean (average) number of problem-solving skill elements included in responses to problem situations for each parent.

source: Dawson, B., de Armas, A., McGrath, M. L., & Kelly, J. A. (1986). Cognitive problem-solving training to improve the child-care judgment of child neglectful parents. *Journal of Family Violence, 1,* 209–221.

specific positive and negative consequences to develop or suppress behaviors. The rehearsal of various behaviors in imagery has been shown to influence actual behavior under a number of circumstances.

One procedure based on imagery is referred to as *covert sensitization* (Cautela, 1967). The procedure consists of having clients imagine themselves engaging in an undesirable behavior (e.g., overeating or excessive alcohol consumption). When this image is vivid, the clients imagine an aversive consequence associated with the behavior (e.g., feeling nauseous). The purpose of treatment is to build up an aversion toward stimuli that previously served as a source of attraction. The procedure is referred to as *covert* because it is conducted in imagination. The clients do not have to engage in behavior but only to imagine it as associated with particular consequences. The effects of treatment, however, carry over to actual behavior.

Covert sensitization was used with an adult male who was in a psychiatric facility because of his multiple sexual deviations (Hayes, Brownell, & Barlow, 1978). His history included attempted rape, multiple fantasies involving sadistic sexual acts (e.g., forced sexual acts with bound women, the use of pins and whips during intercourse), and exhibitionism. He had been arrested for both attempted rape and exhibitionism. Treatment consisted of having him imagine aversive consequences associated with situations in which exhibitionistic and sadistic acts are performed. This was a typical exhibitionistic scene with aversive consequences: (Hayes, Brownell, & Barlow, 1978)

> "I call her over to the car. She doesn't see what I'm doing. I say, 'Can you please help me with this?' She looks down and sees my dick. It's hard and she's really shocked. Her face looks all kinds of distorted. I quick drive away. As I drive away, I see her look back. I think, 'Oh, shit, she's seen my license plate!' I begin to worry that she might call the police. . . . I get home and I'm still worried. My wife keeps saying, 'What's wrong?' . . . As we all sit down to dinner, I hear a knock on the door. I go open it, and there are four pigs. They come charging in and throw me up against the wall and say, 'You're under arrest for indecent exposure!' My wife starts to cry and says, 'This is it! This is the last straw!' "

After several days of treatment, similar scenes were developed to associate imagined aversive consequences with sadistic acts. Over the course of treatment, sexual arousal was directly measured by the degree of the client's erection (penile blood volume) as the client viewed slides of exhibitionistic, sadistic, and heterosexual scenes. For example, heterosexual slides displayed pictures of nude females and sadistic slides displayed nude females tied or chained down in a number of provocative positions. The client also reported his degree of arousal to cards describing various sexual situations.

The effects of covert sensitization were evaluated in a multiple-baseline design, since the procedure was introduced at different points in time for scenes related to exhibitionism and sadism. As shown in Figure 10–2, both physiological arousal and self-reported attraction to deviant sexual stimuli decreased as a function of treatment. On the other hand, arousal to heterosex-

FIGURE 10-2

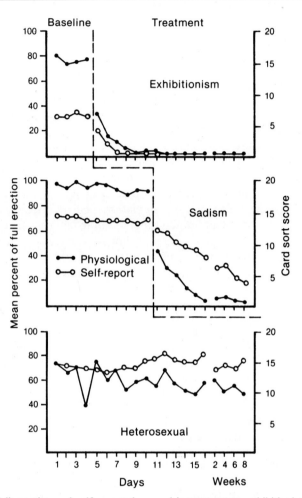

Percentage of full erection and self-reported arousal in response to exhibitionistic, sadistic, and heterosexual stimuli during baseline, treatment, and follow-up phases. Card sort data are daily averages in the baseline and treatment phases and weekly averages in the follow-up phase.

SOURCE: Hayes, S. C., Brownell, K. D., & Barlow, D. H. (1978). The use of self-administered covert sensitization in the treatment of exhibitionism and sadism. *Behavior Therapy, 9,* 283–289. Copyright 1978 by the Association for Advancement of Behavior Therapy. Reprinted by permission of the publisher and the author.

ual stimuli was never focused on and did not change. Moreover, these effects were maintained up to eight weeks after treatment.

Imagery is frequently used as part of procedures to treat anxiety and fear. Mentioned previously were two procedures, systematic desensitization and flooding, in which the individual is exposed to anxiety-provoking situations.

The situations can be presented in imagination or by exposure to the actual situations. Imagery is often a convenient basis for treatment because of the ease with which a wide range of situations can be presented and presentation of the situations can be controlled. For example, an *imagery-based flooding procedure* was used to treat Joseph, a 6½-year-old boy, who suffered from posttraumatic stress disorder (Saigh, 1986). This disorder is a reaction to a highly stressful event or experience. Its symptoms include persistently reexperiencing the trauma (e.g., in thoughts and dreams), avoidance of stimuli associated with the trauma, numbing of responsiveness, outbursts of anger, difficulty in sleeping, and exaggerated startle responses. Joseph was a Lebanese boy who experienced the disorder after exposure to a bomb blast. His symptoms included trauma-related nightmares, recollections of the trauma, depression, and avoidance behavior.

To treat Joseph, five scenes were developed that evoked anxiety (e.g., seeing injured people and debris, approaching specific shopping areas). He rated his discomfort as each scene was described to him. After Joseph was trained to relax, the scenes were presented to him for extended periods (over 20 minutes). During this exposure period, he was asked to imagine the exact details of the scenes. The five scenes were incorporated into treatment in a multiple-baseline design, so that exposure to the scenes occurred in sequence or at different points in time. In each session, Joseph rated his discomfort in response to all of the scenes.

The results are presented in Figure 10–3. As evident, Joseph improved markedly after only 10 sessions (1 session of baseline assessment, 10 sessions of treatment). Assessment immediately after treatment and six months later indicated that the scenes no longer caused discomfort. Perhaps more important are the results from other measures. Before and after treatment, Joseph was assessed in the marketplace where the bomb blast had occurred. After treatment, he showed less avoidance of the area and remained in it longer. Other measures, including assessment of anxiety, depression, and classroom performance at school, also indicated improvement after treatment. Thus, imagery-based treatment appeared to affect several important areas of functioning.

Another imagery-based procedure, referred to as *covert modeling* (Cautela, 1976), consists of imagining a person other than the client engaging in various behaviors that the client would like to develop. Modeling, a behavior therapy technique in its own right, is conducted by having clients observe another person (e.g., the therapist) engaging in behaviors that the clients would like to develop (e.g., approaching a feared situation, engaging in social interaction). In this way, the clients become able to engage in the same behaviors.

In covert modeling, clients *imagine* rather than observe models. Covert modeling has been used in outpatient treatment to train shy adults to act more assertively in a variety of social situations (Kazdin, 1984). In treatment, these clients imagine a person similar to themselves behaving assertively in such

FIGURE 10-3

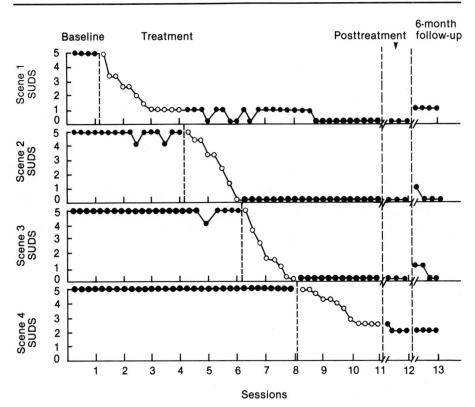

Joseph's ratings of discomfort, referred to as Subject Units of Disturbance (SUDS), in which 5 = maximum discomfort and 0 = no discomfort. Assessment was conducted to measure the discomfort caused by each scene during the treatment sessions. Treatment reflects the period in which imagery-based exposure (flooding) focused on the specific scene.

SOURCE: Reprinted with permission from *Behaviour Research and Therapy, 24*, 685–688. Saigh, P. A. In vitro flooding in the treatment of a 6-yr-old boy's post-traumatic stress disorder. Copyright 1986, Pergamon Press, Inc.

situations as returning merchandise at a store, asking an apartment landlord to make needed repairs, responding to high-pressure salespersons, and asking one's employer for a raise. This enabled the clients to effect changes in their overt behavior.

Imagery-based procedures have been applied to a variety of problems, such as anxiety, sexual deviation, inassertiveness, obsessions, and alcohol consumption (Kazdin & Smith, 1979). However, evidence on the effectiveness of these procedures is limited to a small number of problems. The procedures are usually conducted in treatment sessions in the presence of a therapist. However, they can also be viewed as self-control techniques because clients can imagine various scenes in their everyday life to handle problems that arise long after contact with the therapist has been terminated. By rehearsing in imagination behaviors that may be difficult to perform, or by imagining rewarding or aversive consequences to facilitate or inhibit responses, clients can control their own behavior.

Stress Inoculation Training

Stress inoculation training is designed to help individuals cope with stressful events, such as situations in which anxiety, anger, or pain arise (Meichenbaum & Cameron, 1983). The approach teaches a variety of cognitive and self-control skills to reduce the impact of these events. The medical notion of "inoculation" is used to convey the idea that clients are exposed to small or manageable doses of the stressful event that do not overwhelm their defenses (Novaco, 1979).

Treatment helps clients to identify stressful events and the cognitions that arise when clients are confronted with these events, to evaluate the events differently by applying various coping strategies, including relaxation, imagery, and adaptive self-statements, and to practice the coping skills in both treatment sessions and everyday life. Training helps clients replace maladaptive cognitive appraisals (interpretations) of the events with positive evaluations and self-statements. To accomplish this, self-control and cognitive components are included in treatment.

Because of the relevance of stress in several areas of life and the importance of coping skills, stress inoculation has been applied to a broad range of problems, such as controlling anger among hospitalized patients or delinquents and reducing stress among persons whose jobs expose them to frequent crises (e.g., law enforcement officers, probation counselors). Several applications have utilized stress inoculation training to help individuals cope with stressful medical procedures.

For example, the technique has been used effectively for patients (ages 14–62) who were undergoing elective surgery (Wells, Howard, Nowlin, & Vargas, 1986). The anxiety and pain associated with surgery make the notion of inoculation against stress particularly relevant. In this project, patients were assigned either to the stress inoculation or to a control condition that was the standard hospital preparation for surgery. Stress inoculation patients were instructed about the stress associated with surgery and taught to identify cognitive and physical cues associated with or leading to stress (e.g., increased heart rate, negative self-statements). They were also instructed in the use of relaxation, deep breathing, pleasant imagery, and coping and positive self-statements. Training was completed prior to surgery. Assessment revealed that before and after training, but prior to surgery, the anxiety of the patients in the stress inoculation training group decreased. In contrast, the anxiety of the patients in the control group increased. After surgery, the patients who had received stress inoculation reported less anxiety during their recovery in the hospital and lower pain intensity than did the patients in the control group. Moreover, the patients who had received stress inoculation were rated by nurses as having adjusted better to their hospitalization. Thus, the study demonstrated that stress inoculation reduced both preoperative and postoperative distress.

Stress inoculation training has also been applied to children who were undergoing stressful medical procedures. One program focused on children with leukemia who were being given a special medical test (bone marrow aspiration) to identify whether cancer cells were present (Jay, Elliot, Katz, & Siegel, 1987). The test, which requires the injection of a needle through bone and the suction of bone marrow, is both stressful and painful, despite the use of local anesthetics. Distress, reports of pain, and blood pressure were significantly lower for the children who received stress inoculation training than for the children who received mild tranquilizers.

Special populations have also received stress inoculation training to help them cope with the complications of physical disease. For example, a recent program focused on adults who suffered from multiple sclerosis, a physical disease of the central nervous system (Foley, Bedell, LaRocca, Scheinberg, & Reznikoff, 1987). The physical symptoms of this disease include impairment of sensory, motor, visual, bladder, and other functions. Many patients are restricted to wheelchairs or the use of crutches. Apart from the physical symptoms of multiple sclerosis, its psychological complications may include anxiety, depression, poor body image, and low self-esteem. Stress inoculation training was used to increase coping skills and to reduce psychological symptoms. Patients were randomly assigned to stress inoculation training or to routine care, which included various forms of psychotherapy and medication. The stress inoculation patients were trained in muscle relaxation; self-monitoring of stressors, thoughts, feelings, and behavior; the use of imagery and reinterpretation or cognitive reappraisals of the situation; and role play of these coping strategies. Stress inoculation training led to reductions in anxiety and depression and to improved ability to cope with stressors. These effects were maintained at a six-month follow-up assessment. The patients who had been given routine care did not improve on these measures and hence were eventually given stress inoculation training.

Combined Procedures

As already noted, cognitively based techniques are often used in the context of psychotherapy. In applied settings, select cognitively based techniques are used by themselves or, more often, in combination with various reinforcement and punishment procedures. Cognitive procedures such as the use of self-statements to control behavior may be combined with direct reinforcement of the desired behaviors.

For example, to control violent temper outbursts in an institutionalized mentally retarded adult, several procedures were used (Harvey, Karan, Bhargava, & Morehouse, 1978). Externally imposed contingencies included time out from reinforcement for complaining (which preceded temper tantrums) and token reinforcement for periods without complaining. Self-administered procedures included relaxation training and the use of self-statements to help the person remain calm and to exert control over problematic situations. The combined procedures dramatically reduced temper tantrums. The effects were maintained when behavior was assessed one year after treatment had ended.

Cognitively based treatment and reinforcement contingencies were combined in a program for adolescents who were considered to be in need of controlling their anger (Feindler, Ecton, Kingsley, & Dubey, 1986). These adolescents were hospitalized on an inpatient service for behaviorally and emotionally disturbed youths. The intervention consisted of eight weeks of training in relaxation, self-instruction, use of coping statements, self-monitoring of anger and conflict experiences, and problem-solving skills. Modeling, rehearsal, and practice were used to train the skills. In addition, a reinforcement system was invoked in which points were provided for patient compliance and participation. At the end of treatment, those who were given the training engaged in fewer rule violations in the hospital and received fewer restrictions to their room than did those who were not given the training. Additional measures such as reduced impulsiveness and increased ratings of self-control by staff improved for those who were given the cognitive-behavioral training. Further assessment indicated that the effects of training were maintained two months later.

Programs similar to the above have been reported in which cognitively based interventions were combined with externally imposed contingencies utilizing token or social reinforcement (e.g., Alford, 1986; Snyder & White, 1979) and may have been more effective than the individual procedures used alone. To date, however, evidence has not demonstrated that cognitively based procedures increase the efficacy of alternative reinforcement and punishment programs for problems in the home, classroom, hospitals, or other applied settings. Further tests are needed to evaluate the benefits of adding one type of technique to the other.

EVALUATION AND CURRENT STATUS

Cognitively based interventions have been used in many applied settings, particularly in classrooms where the disruptive behavior of young children has been studied. There are many techniques and procedural variations, and their effects cannot be summarized simply. Extensive evidence has emerged regarding the effectiveness of some of the techniques. For example, several studies have attested to the effectiveness of cognitive therapy as a treatment for depression in adults. This technique is applied to clients seen in individual therapy. In applied settings such as the home and the school, the effectiveness of many cognitively based treatments is not as well established. Some of the ambiguities and effects may be illustrated by highlighting applications of self-instruction and problem-solving skills training.

Outcome Ambiguities in Applied Settings

Self-Instruction Training. Research has shown that self-instruction training can help impulsive children slow down in performing a number of tasks (Kendall & Braswell, 1985). There are several ambiguities regarding the extension of this work to the behavior of children in applied settings. The ambiguities can be illustrated by highlighting two studies with young children.

Several years ago, self-instruction training was used effectively with three Head Start children who were highly disruptive in class (Bornstein & Quevillon, 1976). After baseline data on in-class behavior were obtained, self-instruction training was administered. Training was conducted for two hours outside the classroom, where the children worked on tasks (e.g., copying figures, solving problems). For each task, an experimenter modeled the type of question that the child should ask (e.g., "What does the teacher want me to do?"), directions (e.g., "I'm supposed to copy that picture"), and self-praise (e.g., "I really did that one well"). In general, the instructions were designed to convey how to complete work successfully for a variety of tasks. The children were instructed to administer instructions to themselves—first aloud, then in a whisper, and finally without sound (covertly). As shown in Figure 10–4, self-instruction training was administered in a multiple-baseline design across children and was associated with marked increases in on-task behavior. Classroom performance clearly improved. Moreover, these effects were maintained several weeks after treatment was initiated.

It might be expected that the immediacy, magnitude, and durability of the effects illustrated in the figure would be cause for tremendous encouragement. However, several investigators have tried to repeat this demonstration, a process referred to as *replication,* with little or no success (e.g., Bryant & Budd, 1982; Friedling & O'Leary, 1979). For example, Billings and Wasik (1985) tried to follow closely the procedures implemented in the original study. They provided self-instruction training to Head Start children who were disruptive in class and evaluated the training in a multiple-baseline design across children. Figure 10–5 presents the results for three children (Brian, Elliott, and John) who received training and for a fourth child (Andy) who did not. With an effective intervention, classroom behavior would have been expected to improve after training was introduced, as in the original study of Bornstein and Quevillon (1976). The effects are unclear. In this study, as in a number of others, self-instruction training did not alter performance.

The ambiguities surrounding the effects of self-instruction training are a matter of current research. Investigations have focused on the reasons why self-instructions might change behavior. In one study, first- and second-grade children received self-instruction training to improve their performance on

FIGURE 10-4

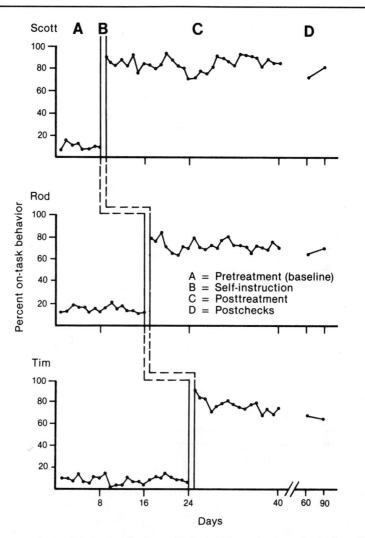

Daily percentage of on-task behaviors for Scott, Rod, and Tim across experimental conditions.

SOURCE: Bornstein, P. H., & Quevillon, R. P. (1976). The effects of a self-instructional package on overactive preschool boys. *Journal of Applied Behavior Analysis, 9,* 179–188. Copyright 1976 by the Society for the Experimental Analysis of Behavior, Inc.

arithmetic tasks (Roberts, Nelson, & Olson, 1987). The training focused on how to approach the task and complete the problems. The children who received self-instruction training improved, but further analyses revealed that the improvement was not associated with using the self-instructions after training. In fact, the children tended not to use self-instructions unless they

FIGURE 10-5

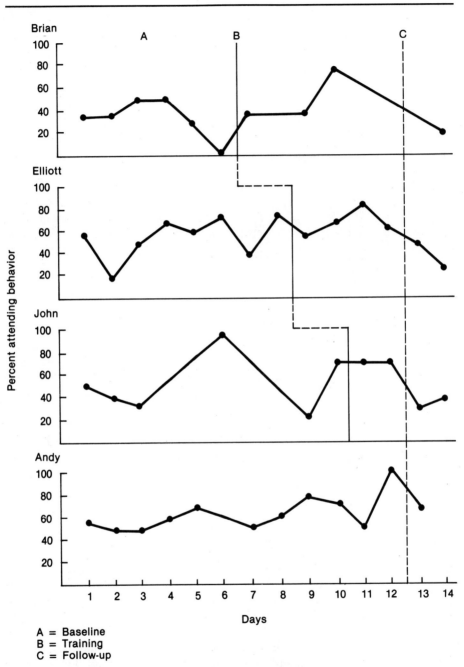

A = Baseline
B = Training
C = Follow-up

Daily percentage of attending behavior in class across conditions.

SOURCE: Billings, D. C., & Wasik, B. H. (1985). Self-instructional training with preschoolers: An attempt to replicate. *Journal of Applied Behavior Analysis, 18*, 61–67. Copyright 1985 by the Society for the Experimental Analysis of Behavior, Inc.

received reinforcers (tokens) for doing so. The investigators suggested that self-instructions may improve performance by providing clear instructions on how to approach a task, rather than by altering cognitive processes that putatively underlie behavior. This suggestion is consistent with other work showing that instructions from an external agent (e.g., parent, teacher) can speed up the acquisition of behavior (e.g., Resick, Forehand, & Peed, 1974). The findings raise questions about how self-instructions work and about whether they provide an intervention that operates differently from instructions provided from an external agent.

Problem-Solving Skills Training.   Problem-solving skills training, as discussed earlier, has enjoyed widespread application and some success. An issue that has emerged in many studies has to do with the effects of such training on performance in applied settings. In many studies, evaluation of the effects of the training on a number of laboratory-based measures has shown that children do utilize the problem-solving skills in which they have been trained. Additional measures have focused on behavior and measures of adjustment at home and at school. On measures of behavior in applied settings, the effectiveness of problem-solving procedures has been less consistent.

For example, problem-solving skills training was incorporated into the curriculum for elementary school children in grades 2–4 (Weissberg & Gesten, 1982). In one variation of the program, children received 34 lessons (20–30 minutes each) and opportunities to review skills and practice in resolving interpersonal conflicts. Major areas of the training were recognizing feelings in oneself and others, identifying interpersonal problems, generating alternative solutions, considering consequences, and integrating problem-solving skills. Use of the skills covered in these lessons was integrated with classroom activities, such as solving minor problems between children. Several evaluations of the program showed that the children who received training in problem-solving skills improved significantly as compared to the children who did not receive such training. However, the impact of problem-solving skills training on teacher ratings of classroom adjustment has been equivocal; some studies have shown gains, but other studies have not (e.g., Gesten et al., 1982; Weissberg et al., 1981).

Two recent studies evaluated the impact of problem-solving skills training on elementary school children (Nelson & Carson, 1988). The results from both studies indicated that improvement in performance on measures reflecting knowledge of and skills in the problem-solving approach was greater for the children who received the training than for the children who did not receive it. However, measures of behavioral adjustment, peer acceptance, and children's views about themselves were not consistently altered. The study raises questions about the extent to which problem-solving skills can effect changes in behavior in the home, at school, and in the community. Mentioned earlier were studies of problem-solving skills for treatment of antisocial behavior in children. Here changes in behavioral adjustment have been achieved; however, the effects have been weak.

General Comments

The ambiguities surrounding self-instruction training and problem-solving skills training result from the presence of positive outcome effects on some occasions but not on other occasions. Occasional exceptions or studies that do not obtain identical results are not rare in scientific research. One reason for seeming inconsistencies is that the effects can depend on a variety of conditions that are not well understood, such as characteristics of the clients, the persons who administer the intervention, and the setting. When there are conflicting findings, one set of findings is not necessarily "true" and the other necessarily "false." One need not decide whom to believe. From the standpoint of developing interventions for classroom or other applied settings, the inconsistent effects reflect an important statement regarding the status of the interventions.

Self-instruction training and problem-solving skills training as interventions for applied settings are not yet sufficiently well understood, and the variables that make these interventions effective are not yet clear. Factors on which their effectiveness may depend include the age, intelligence, race, gender, and developmental level of the clients and many characteristics related to how the interventions are implemented (Bornstein, 1985; Cole & Kazdin, 1980). As these and other variables are evaluated, it is likely that the effects of self-instruction training and problem-solving skills training in applied settings can be more reliably produced.

In contrast, a great deal is known about the application of positive reinforcement and about many of the conditions that contribute to its effectiveness. For example, and as detailed previously (in Chapter 5), it is known that delay, magnitude, type, and schedule of reinforcement can contribute to the extent of behavior change. If favorable conditions are not carefully implemented, as when very delayed or intermittent consequences are used, reinforcement programs are not likely to change behavior. Cognitively based interventions have been less well studied than positive reinforcement in applied settings. Parallel information about the factors to ensure their effectiveness is not yet available. Thus, when a given study shows that a cognitively based intervention has produced some behavior change, this suggests that the intervention holds promise. However, more needs to be understood before the intervention can be used reliably to produce change.

SUMMARY AND CONCLUSION

Cognitively based techniques are a family of procedures. The common feature of these procedures is the view that cognitive processes (perceptions, self-statements, attributions, expectations, beliefs, and images) relate in significant ways to maladaptive behavior and that change in these processes leads to behavior change. Most cognitively based techniques are applied in the context of psychotherapy, in which the client is seen by a therapist in individual or group treatment sessions. Several of these techniques were presented to illustrate cognitive approaches.

Self-instruction training develops patterns of instructing oneself how to perform. These patterns enable individuals to analyze situations and to specify the requirements for their own behavior. The instructions are designed to prompt and guide performance. *Problem-solving skills training* develops cognitive problem-solving processes that underlie interpersonal behavior. The individual uses a specific type of self-statement to identify effective solutions and approaches to interpersonal situations. *Imagery-based techniques* consist of having the client imagine various behaviors and consequences that are designed to alter overt behavior. Imagery used to rehearse appropriate behavior can affect how one performs in the actual situation. *Stress inoculation training* focuses on developing cognitive and self-control skills to reduce the impact of stress. Individuals are trained to monitor events and their evaluations of events; to use coping strategies such as relaxation, imagery, and positive self-statements; and to apply coping skills in everyday life.

Cognitively based techniques are used in applied settings either by themselves or in combination with reinforcement and punishment techniques. The most common application has been self-instruction training or problem-solving skills training in the schools to improve classroom deportment and adjustment. Applications of cognitively based techniques in applied settings have been less extensively evaluated than applications of reinforcement and punishment techniques. The effects of cognitively based techniques have been promising but somewhat inconsistent. It has been suggested that these techniques increase the effectiveness of reinforcement and punishment techniques, but this suggestion warrants further research.

FOR FURTHER READING

Cautela, J. R., & Kearney, A. J. (1986). *The covert conditioning handbook.* New York: Springer.

Kendall, P. C., & Braswell, L. (1985). *Cognitive behavioral therapy for impulsive children.* New York: Guilford.

Meichenbaum, D., & Jeremko, M. E. (1983). *Stress reduction and prevention.* New York: Plenum.

Spivack, G., & Shure, M. B. (1982). The cognition of social adjustment: Interpersonal cognitive problem solving thinking. In B. B. Lahey & A. E. Kazdin (Eds.), *Advances in clinical child psychology* (Vol. 5, pp. 323–372). New York: Plenum.

Chapter Eleven

Response Maintenance and Transfer of Training

Techniques discussed in previous chapters have altered many behaviors among a wide range of clients. Dramatic changes in behavior are obviously impressive, but do those changes last? What happens when behavioral programs are discontinued or when clients leave the special settings in which the programs have been conducted? The issues raised by these questions, often referred to as generalization, constitute the topic of the present chapter.

The term *generalization* has been employed very loosely to signify that behavior changes carry over (or generalize) to conditions other than those included in training. However, generalization can include a variety of phenomena. It can refer to behavior changes that carry over to other situations, periods, or settings than those in which the behavioral program was implemented (Drabman, Hammer, & Rosenbaum, 1979; Stokes & Baer, 1977). The extension of behavior changes over time is usually referred to as *response maintenance* or resistance to extinction. The question addressed by response maintenance is whether behavior change is maintained after the program has been terminated. The extension of behavior changes to new situations and settings is usually referred to as *transfer of training*. The question addressed by transfer of training is whether behavior change extends to situations not included in the program (e.g., to the home when the program is conducted in the classroom). Transfer of training can also mean the extension of behavior changes to the presence of other persons. For example, behaviors trained in the presence of parents may not carry over to other adults (guests, teachers), siblings, or peers.

Response maintenance and transfer of training are not uniquely relevant to behavior modification. They apply to any enterprise or activity in which behavior change is a goal. Thus, they represent critical issues for child rearing, education, religion, psychotherapy, and many other areas besides behavior modification. For example, a major issue in psychotherapy is whether positive changes that take place in the therapist's presence (e.g., reduced guilt or anxiety in talking about a particular topic) are maintained when the client completes therapy and interacts with others in everyday situations. Similarly, in education, a major hope is that after completing their formal education (maintenance), people will continue to read and educate themselves in everyday life outside the classroom (transfer). Governments are interested in having citizens maintain their law-abiding behaviors (e.g., traveling within the speed limit) even when the contingencies (e.g., surveillance by police officers) are not in effect.

Response maintenance and transfer of training have received special attention in behavior modification for three reasons. First, an obvious priority for treatment is developing ways of changing behavior. Only after effective procedures for changing behavior have been developed is it meaningful to raise questions about response maintenance and transfer of behavior. Until recently, few effective procedures were available to alter many of the problem behaviors to which behavioral procedures have been effectively applied. For example, until recently, few effective procedures were available to increase the use of seat belts among automobile drivers and passengers. Evidence emerged noting that special reinforcement contingencies could markedly increase seat belt use (e.g., Roberts & Fanurik, 1986). After it has been shown that initial changes are quite possible, the questions of maintaining behavior and ensuring the transfer of behavior to other situations (e.g., when the person is a driver or a passenger, when the person is in his or her car or in the car of others) take on primary importance. Indeed, other studies have shown that the maintenance and extension of seat belt use is feasible (e.g., Sowers-Hoag, Thyer, & Bailey, 1987). Now that effective change procedures are at hand for many behaviors, maintaining changes and ensuring their transfer to new situations have taken on increased importance.

Second, evaluations of behavioral techniques have often suggested that maintenance and transfer may not occur after treatment. For example, many studies have used an ABAB (or reversal) design, in which treatment is temporarily withdrawn in a return-to-baseline phase. When this is done, behavior usually reverts to or near baseline levels. Such loss of behavior during a reversal phase may provide a preview of coming attractions, namely loss of the acquired behavior once the behavior change program has been terminated. Similarly, in multiple-baseline designs, contingencies are often introduced, one situation at a time, into different situations, such as the home, the classroom, and the playground. Behavior change in one situation usually occurs without behavior changes in other situations until the program (e.g., reinforcement) has been introduced into those situations. This suggests that newly developed behaviors are not likely to transfer to new situations without special contingencies.

Third, behavior modification programs usually require the use of reinforcement and other contingencies that differ from the contingencies available in everyday life. For example, children who have behavioral and academic problems at school or psychiatric patients who engage in bizarre behaviors may be placed in a special classroom or ward where the contingencies are highly conducive to behavior change. This raises the obvious question of what will happen to these persons when they return to ordinary settings, where the contingencies are not programmed to promote desirable behaviors.

In some situations, response maintenance is not an issue because the program is intended to remain in effect. For example, employees are often provided with incentives, such as bonuses for exceeding a sales quota or bonuses for using exercise facilities (because improved fitness reduces employee absenteeism). The reinforcement contingencies may remain in effect permanently. In such situations, special procedures for maintaining behavior may not be required.

In most of the programs in which behavioral techniques are applied, the program is intended to be a temporary tool for developing behavior so that it is performed consistently. In such programs, the assumption is that the person will return to a setting or situation in which the specific contingencies are not present. Maintenance of the behavior in that setting or situation is obviously critical and must be planned before the contingencies are withdrawn.

Response maintenance and transfer of training can readily be distinguished in the abstract, but in practice they often go together. For example, if a psychiatric patient leaves a token reinforcement program in the hospital and returns home, both response maintenance and transfer of training are important. Reinforcement for the specific target behaviors is no longer forthcoming (i.e., extinction), so the responses may not be maintained. At the same time, the setting is different, so the acquired behaviors may not carry over (i.e., transfer). The extent to which the behaviors will transfer and be maintained will determine the success of the patient's return to the community.

Response maintenance and transfer need not always go together. For example, in classroom situations, reinforcement programs are often implemented at one time of day (e.g., morning). Transfer of training can refer to whether behavior also changes during times of day (e.g., afternoon) or in situations (e.g., the playground) in which the reinforcement program has not been implemented. Response maintenance or resistance to extinction is not relevant here, because the target behaviors are still reinforced in the morning. The issue is whether the reinforced behaviors transfer or generalize to other situations while the program is in effect. The present chapter examines the evidence bearing on both response maintenance and transfer of training. It also discusses techniques to increase the likelihood that behaviors will be maintained and will carry over to new situations.

RESPONSE MAINTENANCE

At the outset, it is important to note that behaviors do not always revert to preprogram or baseline levels when the contingencies are withdrawn. Behaviors are often maintained after a program has been terminated. Maintenance of behavior has been evident in a variety of settings and for many populations whose behaviors have been assessed from several months to several years after the termination of programs (e.g., Bushell, 1978; Griffin, Locke, & Landers, 1975; Paul & Lentz, 1977). Thus, loss of behavior is by no means inevitable.

However, when responses are maintained after the reinforcing or other consequences have been withdrawn, the reason is usually unclear. One would expect behaviors to reflect the contingencies that currently operate in the environment. When the contingencies are withdrawn, one can only speculate why the behaviors are maintained. Various explanations have been offered. First, it is possible that behaviors developed through a reinforcement program may come under the control of other reinforcers in the setting. For example, in a classroom, withdrawal of a token economy may not lead to the loss of appropriate behaviors. Because the teacher has been consistently paired with the delivery of token reinforcement, he or she may serve as a stimulus for appropriate behavior and may continue to serve as a powerful source of reinforcement after the token reinforcement has been withdrawn. Second, behaviors may be maintained because of reinforcement resulting directly from the behaviors themselves. Many behaviors result in their own reinforcement. For example, reading, social interaction, or eating skills may be maintained once they have been developed. Each of these behaviors may be reinforced by the consequences that naturally follow their execution.

Finally, behavior may be maintained after the reinforcers have been withdrawn, because the behavior of the persons who administered the program (parents, teachers, peers, hospital staff) has changed in some permanent fashion. For example, if a contingency contract system in the home is withdrawn, a child's desirable behavior may still be maintained at a high level because the parents may then provide reinforcement (allowance and praise) and punishment (loss of privileges) more systematically than they did prior to the contract system. Unfortunately, there is very little evidence that the behavior of those who administer a behavior modification program is permanently altered (see Kazdin & Moyer, 1976). As soon as a program is withdrawn, the agents who administer the program frequently revert to the behaviors they previously used to control client behavior.

Each of the above explanations of response maintenance is usually offered after the fact. After behavior fails to reverse when a program is withdrawn, an investigator may speculate why this occurred. Any of the explanations may be correct in a given instance. However, maintenance of behavior is more clearly understood when it is predicted in advance on the basis of the special procedures used to develop resistance to extinction, rather than when extinction does not occur and has to be explained.

Despite the above examples and explanations of response maintenance, removal of the contingencies usually results in a decline of performance to or near baseline levels. This has led authors to state that if response maintenance is the goal of the behavior modification program, it has to be programmed systematically into the contingencies, rather than merely hoped for as a desirable side effect (Baer, Wolf, & Risley, 1968, 1987; Stokes & Baer, 1977).

TRANSFER OF TRAINING

Transfer of training can refer to different phenomena, depending on whether one is speaking of transfer across situations, settings, or the persons who implement the contingencies. In most programs, changes of behavior in one situation do not result in a transfer of those changes to other situations or settings, either while the program is in effect or after it has been withdrawn. Indeed, the stimulus conditions controlling behavior are often quite narrow, so that behavior changes are restricted to the specific setting in which training has taken place and even to the persons who administered the program. Although transfer of training across situations and settings is the exception rather than the rule, many examples are available.

In one program, physically handicapped and mentally retarded persons learning to function in the community were trained to engage in appropriate pedestrian skills (e.g., approaching and crossing intersections safely) (Page, Iwata, & Neef, 1976). Although training was conducted in a classroom situation, the skills transferred to actual performance in the city streets. Similarly, in a classroom reinforcement program, behaviors altered during one part of the day, such as the morning or the afternoon, sometimes transferred to other parts of the day even though performance during those other parts was not reinforced (Kazdin, 1973a).

Despite these and other encouraging reports, transfer of training to situations or settings in which a program has not been conducted usually does not occur unless the program is continued across situations or settings. Even when some transfer of the behavior occurs, it may be restricted to new situations that bear a very close resemblance to the training sessions. For example, Liberman, Teigen, Patterson, and Baker (1973) found that training psychiatric patients to speak rationally, without reference to delusions, transferred from training sessions to similar sessions in which the contingencies were not in effect. However, the treatment effects did not generalize to the ward in everyday interactions that these patients had with the staff. As is the case with response maintenance, transfer of training usually has to be programmed directly to ensure that changes extend beyond the conditions of training.

PROGRAMMING RESPONSE MAINTENANCE AND TRANSFER

The initial priority for behavior modification in applied settings has been to develop techniques that reliably alter behavior. Consequently, the technology for changing behavior has received much greater attention than the technology for developing maintenance and transfer of behavior. In the last several years, however, tremendous progress has been made in the areas of maintenance and transfer by identifying the different types of generalization that need to be developed, by elaborating the principles that suggest how these types of generalization might be developed, and by describing methods of assessing and evaluating generalization (e.g., Drabman et al., 1979; Horner, Bellamy, & Colvin, 1984; Pigott, Fantuzzo, & Clement, 1986; Rusch & Kazdin, 1981). Several specific techniques have been identified to ensure that behaviors will be maintained and will transfer to new situations (e.g., Albin, Horner, Koegel, & Dunlap, 1987; Stokes & Osnes, 1986). The present section reviews major techniques for achieving these ends. Techniques to achieve maintenance and transfer will be treated together because they are often focused on simultaneously in a given program and also because the techniques that accomplish one often affect the other. Procedures that are more suited to maintenance than to transfer, or vice versa, will be noted as such.

Bringing Behavior Under Control of the Natural Contingencies

Perhaps the most obvious procedure for ensuring that behavior will be maintained and will transfer to new situations is to bring it under the control of the consequences that naturally occur in the environment. Reinforcing and punishing consequences that ordinarily follow behavior in everyday life may be sufficient to maintain behavior once it has been well established. Also, if behavior comes under the control of the natural contingencies, transfer of training will not be a problem, because the consequences in the new situations may sustain the behavior. For example, praise and attention from others as well as the consequences that follow from the behavior itself, as in the case of eating and reading, may sustain performance.

Baer (Baer, Rowbury, & Goetz, 1976; Baer & Wolf, 1970; Stokes & Baer, 1977) has introduced the concept of *behavioral traps* to convey the rationale behind maintenance and transfer that result from the natural contingencies. According to this concept, once a client's behavior has been developed, it should be "trapped" into the system of reinforcers that is available in the environment. The purpose of behavioral interventions should be to bring the client's behavior up to the level sustained by the natural consequences. Initially, his or her behavior may be developed by extraneous reinforcers (e.g., tokens, food and other consumables, or praise) that the environment normally would not provide. However, after that behavior has been developed, other reinforcers (e.g., contact with peers) may sustain its high level.

Baer et al. (1976) provided an example of a program in a preschool classroom in which the target behavior appeared to be maintained by the natural reinforcers. To increase social interaction in a withdrawn boy, the teacher provided social reinforcement (attention, expressions of interest) whenever he socialized with his peers. In several phases of an extended ABAB design, teacher praise was alternately delivered and withdrawn. Two results emerged from the program. First, the teacher's praise was responsible for the boy's increased interaction. Second, over time, his interaction was maintained even when the teacher did not deliver praise. Apparently, the reinforcement resulting from peer interaction tended to maintain his social behavior after it had been well developed. That behavior was, as it were, trapped into the network of peer interactions and thus no longer required the behavior modification program. Other research has shown that training such social behaviors as smiling, sharing, and providing positive physical contact among children changes the social behaviors of their peers (Cooke & Apolloni, 1976). Thus, behaviors may be maintained by mutual social reinforcement among peers and target subjects even when the contingencies administered by the persons who initiated the program have been withdrawn.

There are several problems with the strategy of developing behaviors to a level at which they come into contact with the naturally available reinforcers in order to ensure that behaviors will be maintained and will carry over to a variety of situations. To begin with, behaviors that appear to be of the kind that the natural environment will maintain are very often not maintained at all. For example, even social interaction (the subject of the above example of trapping) is usually not maintained in children or adults after the contingencies have been withdrawn (e.g., Kazdin & Polster, 1973; Strain, Shores, & Kerr, 1976; Strain, Shores, & Timm, 1977). Similarly, behaviors that are followed by immediate reinforcement, such as appropriate eating skills (e.g., O'Brien, Bugle, & Azrin, 1972) or smiling to others (e.g., Reisinger, 1972), are not automatically maintained by the natural environment. At present, it is difficult to identify in advance which behaviors will be maintained by naturally occurring events in the environment or which situations will automatically support newly developed behaviors.

A related difficulty in relying on naturally occurring reinforcers to maintain behavior pertains to how the social environment operates. The natural network of reinforcers does not necessarily promote or maintain appropriate behavior (Stokes & Osnes, 1986). Deviant or disruptive behaviors are likely to receive attention or notice in everyday situations such as the home or the school.

Parents, teachers, hospital staff, and peers often attend to and reinforce inappropriate behavior as a matter of course. For example, disruptive behaviors are often directly reinforced by attention from one's peers (e.g., Sanson-Fisher, Seymour, Montgomery, & Stokes, 1978). Thus, the natural contingencies often seem to operate against the maintenance and transfer of prosocial behavior.

Perhaps the major obstacle to using the natural contingencies as a way to support desirable behavior is the lack of clear guidelines as to how this should be done. The procedures for improving behaviors are well developed. But procedures have not been developed for structuring the situation so that the target behaviors are invariably trapped by the social environment.

For individuals functioning normally in society, many adaptive behaviors are maintained by the natural environment. Yet most individuals have received extensive social training and respond to a variety of subtle external and self-imposed influences. In contrast, individuals in treatment, rehabilitation, and educational settings (for whom most behavior modification programs are conducted) are trained to respond to external consequences in carefully programmed situations. It is no surprise, therefore, that their behaviors are not maintained when the consequences are withdrawn and they are placed in a social situation for which they have not been prepared. What often happens is that when a behavior modification program has been withdrawn, behaviors are maintained for a few persons but not for others. If behaviors continue, perhaps they are being maintained by the naturally occurring reinforcers. If behaviors are not maintained when a program has been withdrawn, specific procedures can be implemented to achieve response maintenance and transfer of training. Because unplanned and unprogrammed maintenance and transfer of behavior are exceptions rather than the rule, it is usually advisable to implement one or more of the procedures discussed next.

Programming Naturally Occurring Reinforcers

In many programs, the consequences used to alter behavior are not ordinarily available in the setting where clients will eventually function. For example, tokens or candy usually do not follow behavior in the classroom or on a hospital ward. However, consequences that are normally available can replace the extraneous events that were used to alter behavior initially. Programming naturally occurring consequences, as does the technique discussed above, utilizes available events in the environment to maintain behavior or to achieve transfer. However, instead of depending on the natural contingencies to support or trap behavior, naturally occurring events can be substituted systematically to sustain performance.

The programming of naturally occurring reinforcers has been used successfully in many programs that were concerned with both response maintenance and transfer of training. For example, Kallman, Hersen, and O'Toole (1975) treated a male patient who complained that he could not walk. Although the patient had no organic problem, he was hospitalized and confined to a wheelchair. Social reinforcement was used to develop his standing and walking in the hospital. Eventually, he walked by himself. He returned home, where the treatment effects were maintained for about a month. Then he said that he could not walk and he returned to the hospital. His walking was developed, and he again returned home. Videotaped interactions of the patient and his family revealed that his family had previously attended to his disability and had ignored his attempts to walk. Hence, to maintain walking, the patient's family was trained to reinforce walking and to ignore (extinguish) complaints of being unable to walk. After the family was trained, follow-up indicated that the behavior was maintained up to 12 weeks after treatment. In this program, social consequences in the natural environment were used to sustain the gains that had been achieved in treatment.

The importance of training relatives to ensure response maintenance and transfer has been emphasized in the treatment of autistic children (Lovaas, Koegel, Simmons, & Long, 1973). Follow-up assessment of the behavior of autistic children one to four years after treatment showed that children whose parents had been trained to carry out the behavioral procedures maintained their gains outside the treatment facility and indeed improved slightly. On the other hand, children who had been institutionalized where the contingencies were not continued lost the gains that they had achieved in treatment.

Teachers in regular classrooms have been trained to continue the contingencies initiated in a special setting to achieve both transfer and maintenance (Walker, Hops, & Johnson, 1975). Highly disruptive children participated in a token economy in a special education classroom to develop appropriate classroom behavior. After improvements had been achieved, the children were returned to their regular classrooms. In some of these classrooms, the teachers conducted a behavioral program to sustain the gains that had been achieved in the special education classroom. The children who returned to a classroom where some of the contingencies were continued maintained their behavior in the new settings to a much greater extent than did the children who returned to a classroom where no program was in effect. When the special contingencies in the regular classrooms had been terminated, the behavioral gains were maintained among the children who had continued the program in their regular classrooms. Thus, the substitution of one program for another helped maintain behavior transfer and helped transfer it to a new setting, even though the program was eventually discontinued.

In general, behaviors may need to be developed with special contingencies to achieve high and consistent levels of performance. However, after behavior has been developed, contingencies utilizing sources of influence available in the natural environment can be substituted. The natural contingencies may not automatically sustain appropriate behavior, as has been noted in the discussion of behavioral traps. However, if naturally occurring consequences are altered to support behavior, they provide a useful transition between highly programmed contingencies and the haphazard and often counterproductive contingencies of the natural environment.

Gradually Removing or Fading the Contingencies

Losses of behavioral gains following a behavior modification program may result from abruptly withdrawing the reinforcing and punishing consequences. Gradually removing or fading the program is likely to be less discriminable to the client than the abrupt withdrawal of consequences. Eventually, the consequences can be eliminated entirely without a return of behavior to its baseline rate.

Fading of the contingencies can be accomplished in many ways. One of the most frequently used ways has been reported in token economies in institutional settings. For example, with psychiatric patients, token economies are often divided into steps or levels. As patients progress, they pass through the various levels of the program. As patients perform the target behaviors consistently, they move to higher levels in the system, at which more reinforcers may be available (to encourage further progress). At the highest level, few or no contingencies may be in effect, so that the patients can learn to function without direct and immediate consequences.

Paul and Lentz (1977) used a leveled token economy to fade the contingencies for chronic psychiatric patients. At the first level, the patients needed to perform only minimal levels of behavior (such as attending activities) to earn tokens. As they moved to higher levels, they could earn more tokens and they had access to a larger range of backup reinforcers. At the highest level, they could buy themselves off the system. They used a credit card instead of tokens, and they had access to all of the available reinforcers as long as they continued to perform adequately.

The purpose of using levels is to develop higher levels of performance over time and to reduce the highly structured contingencies that maintain performance. Ideally, the highest level in the program will resemble the contingencies that one is likely to encounter outside the setting. To ensure that performance is maintained at a high level, clients can be given the privilege of earning themselves off the highly structured contingencies (as in a token economy) only if their performance meets a particular criterion (Kazdin & Mascitelli, 1980). If a client's performance continues at a high level with few or no contingencies, behavior is more likely to be maintained when the client leaves the setting.

The contingencies can be faded in ways other than using levels in a token reinforcement program. An alternative procedure is to check behavior and provide reinforcing consequences less often over time. For example, Rosen and Rosen (1983) reduced stealing in a seven-year-old boy who frequently took things from his classmates. Points (exchangeable for extra recess and other reinforcers) were provided if he did not have other children's possessions; fines were invoked if he did. The boy was checked every 15 minutes and received or lost points accordingly. This procedure effectively reduced his stealing. The program was then faded by checking and providing consequences only once every two hours. As shown in Figure 11–1, when the program was faded, virtually no stealing occurred. During the follow-up phase, checking, points, and fines were discontinued. The effects of the program were maintained over a 31-day follow-up period.

Gradually withdrawing the contingencies may be very useful because it prepares clients for the conditions under which they must normally function. In everyday living, the contingencies are often unsystematic and the consequences for performance, if any, may be delayed. The gradual withdrawal of contingencies provides a transition between a highly programmed environment and one that is less well programmed with regard to given target behaviors. At present, several other studies have shown that fading the consequences leads to maintenance of behavior (e.g., Friman & Hove, 1987; Gross & Ekstrand, 1983; Van Houten, Nau, & Marini, 1980). Thus, fading represents a maintenance strategy that should probably be routinely incorporated into behavioral programs.

FIGURE 11–1

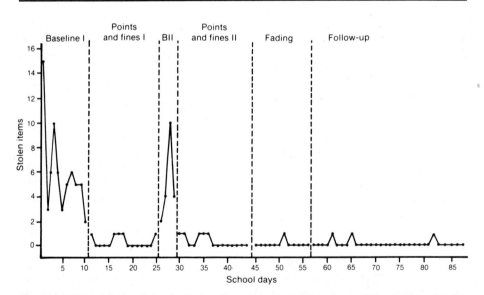

Number of items stolen each day during baseline and intervention (points and fines) phases. During the fading phase, consequences were provided less frequently for behavior. In the follow-up phase, the program was discontinued.

SOURCE: Rosen, H. S., & Rosen, L. A. (1983). Eliminating stealing: Use of stimulus control with an elementary student. *Behavior Modification, 7,* 56–63. Copyright 1983 by H. S. Rosen & L. A. Rosen. Reprinted by permission of Sage Publications, Inc.

Expanding Stimulus Control

One reason that behaviors may not be maintained and may not transfer to new settings is that clients readily form a discrimination between the conditions in which reinforcement (or punishment) is (S^D) and is not delivered (S^Δ). Behavior becomes associated with a narrow range of cues that may include specific behavior change agents (e.g., parents or teachers) who administer the program and the specific setting in which the contingencies are in effect (e.g., the classroom rather than the playground or the home). As soon as the program is withdrawn or the setting changes, clients discriminate that the desirable behavior is no longer associated with certain consequences. Thus, responses are not maintained and do not transfer to new situations.

Maintenance and transfer can be developed by expanding the breadth of the stimuli that exert control over behavior (Horner et al., 1984). The procedures used to expand stimulus control may vary as a function of the type of transfer that is of interest. For example, in some programs, client behavior may be restricted to the presence of the specific persons who conduct training and implement the contingencies. In these cases, the narrow control exerted by the staff may be expanded by introducing more staff into training. For example, Stokes, Baer, and Jackson (1974) trained four severely and profoundly retarded children to engage in greeting responses (hand waving), using one staff member in the institution as the trainer in special experimental sessions. Although the behaviors were developed in this way, observations revealed that the children usually did not greet other staff members who approached them. The behavior was apparently under quite narrow stimulus control. The stimulus control was expanded by having a second staff member also conduct training. The additional training not only increased greeting responses to this staff member but also resulted in greeting responses to several other staff members who had not been associated with the training. Thus, the behavior was no longer under the narrow stimulus control of the trainer.

Usually, it is of interest to ensure that behavior transfers simultaneously across several dimensions, including staff members, activities, situations, and settings. For example, Emshoff, Redd, and Davidson (1976) used praise and points (exchangeable for money) to develop positive interpersonal comments among four delinquent adolescents. To develop behavior that would transfer across a variety of stimulus conditions, two of the clients were trained under conditions that varied across activities (e.g., during games and discussions), trainers, locations in the facility, and the time of day. Unlike the clients who were trained under constant training conditions, the clients who received this highly varied training made positive comments under several tests for generalization when tokens were delivered noncontingently, when a new trainer was introduced, and when the activity, setting, and trainer all varied. Not only was transfer of training improved by varying the training conditions, but the clients who were trained in this way also showed superior maintenance of the behavior three weeks after training had been terminated.

As another example, Koegel and Rincover (1974) developed such behaviors as attending to a task, imitating, speaking, and recognizing words among autistic children. Although these behaviors were increased, performance did not transfer beyond the one-to-one situation with the staff member used in the training sessions. When a child was placed with others in a group situation, the trained behaviors decreased. To develop transfer to the classroom situation, various stimulus conditions of the classroom were gradually introduced into training. Other children, the classroom teacher, and teacher aides were included in the training situation to associate performance of the target behavior with a variety of stimuli. After the stimulus conditions were expanded in training, behavior transferred to the classroom.

The above studies illustrate that transfer of training and response maintenance can be established by introducing various components of the situation in which transfer is desired or by expanding the range of the individuals who administer the contingencies. From these studies, it appears that the stimulus conditions of the transfer setting need to be introduced while training is still in effect. As the stimuli that exert control over behavior broaden, the likelihood that the behavior will be performed in new situations and in the presence of a variety of people is markedly increased. It is important to note that not all of the conditions across which transfer is desired need to be introduced into training. Only a few of the new stimulus conditions need to be introduced, after which transfer extends to new settings and to people who have had no association with the training.

Training Individuals to Respond to the "General Case"

Expanding stimulus control, which consists of introducing a broad range of stimuli into training, has been conducted for many years. Recently, this approach has been developed more systematically in a strategy referred to as *training the general case*. This strategy trains the individual to perform the target behavior across a variety of stimulus conditions so that the behavior does not come under the control of a narrow range of cues.

A number of specific steps are employed to teach the general case (Horner, Eberhard, & Sheehan, 1986). These steps are listed in Table 11–1. Consider the steps with a hypothetical program designed to teach a shy, withdrawn child to socialize with peers at school. The target behavior may consist of speaking with other children. In Step 1, we note the specific situations in which we wish the behavior to occur. In our example, we decide that we would like the child to engage in the behavior during recess, at lunch, and during free time in class. In Step 2, we identify the salient stimulus characteristics that vary among these conditions. Among such characteristics are differences in the number of children present, in daily activities, in settings, and in the amounts of structure provided in the situations. In this step, an indefinite number of characteristics might be identified, but the success of the strategy does not depend on identifying every conceivable characteristic on

TABLE 11–1 Requirements for Training the General Case

Step 1 Specify the set of stimulus situations across which a behavior is to be performed after training has been completed.

Step 2 Define the range of relevant dimensions or characteristics across which they vary.

Step 3 Define the range of response variations or the different behaviors required across the set of stimulus situations.

Step 4 Select and teach examples that sample from the range of the stimulus and response domains (as specified in Steps 2 and 3).

SOURCE: Adapted from Horner, R. H., Eberhard, J. M., & Sheehan, M. R. (1986). Teaching generalized table bussing: The importance of negative teaching examples. *Behavior Modification, 10,* 457–471.

which the situations vary. The task is merely to identify some of the salient characteristics that differentiate the situations.

In Step 3, we specify the variations of the target behaviors that are required in these situations. The behaviors might include initiating conversation, approaching others, responding to initiations of others, joining a group that is already engaged in an activity, and starting an activity with another person. Finally, in Step 4, we select for training exemplary situations that represent the stimulus and response domains of interest. Thus, training might be carried out in different social situations, with different persons present, and with different social cues. Using the overall approach, training systematically programs behaviors for performance in diverse situations.

Several studies have evaluated general-case training as a means of ensuring transfer of behaviors across stimulus conditions. One such study was designed to teach the simple skill of putting on a shirt to mentally retarded persons (8–23 years old) who lived in community group homes (Day & Horner, 1986). Two training methods were used. The first method consisted of single-instance training, in which individuals were trained (prompts, praise) to put on a single type of shirt (T-shirt). The second method consisted of general-case training, in which additional types of shirts were presented in training (T-shirt, tank top, turtleneck). These shirts sampled a broader range of stimulus conditions (e.g., type of collar, sleeve length, fit, fabric), and as a consequence they also required the broader range of responses entailed in "putting on a shirt." At different points in training, individuals were tested (without prompts or reinforcement) to see the extent to which they could put on a wide range of shirt types, including types that had not been part of training. General-case training led to a much broader performance across a range of new stimulus conditions than did single-instance training.

Other studies have utilized the general-case training approach to develop self-care and community-relevant skills among mentally retarded persons, including skills in dressing, using vending machines at school and in the community, shopping, and bussing cafeteria tables (e.g., Horner, Albin, & Ralph, 1986; Horner, Eberhard, & Sheehan, 1986). The results have shown that behavior transfers to a broader range of stimulus conditions with general-case training than with the usual single-case training. Few studies have examined the extent to which long-term maintenance is enhanced by general-case training (Sprague & Horner, 1984). However, research on expanding stimulus control, mentioned previously, has suggested that maintenance is also enhanced by developing behavior under a broad range of stimulus conditions. In general, training the general case appears to be an important strategy to ensure that behaviors are not restricted to features of the training setting.

In some cases, practical obstacles may prevent introducing diverse stimuli conditions into training. For example, many behavioral programs focus on developing community-related skills among various populations. Training is often conducted in the community to help train the general case. However, it may be difficult to make diverse settings available for training purposes. One alternative may be to use videotaped vignettes illustrating the diverse settings in which the behaviors are to be performed, a procedure that also facilitates generalization across settings (Haring, Kennedy, Adams, & Pitts-Conway, 1987).

Schedules of Reinforcement

As mentioned earlier, resistance to extinction can be enhanced by using intermittent reinforcement. After behavior has been well established, reinforcing consequences can be delivered intermittently. The intermittence of the reinforcement can be increased, so that very little reinforcement is provided for behavior. Resistance of behavior to extinction once reinforcement is withdrawn is a function of the intermittence of the reinforcement. The more intermittent (or thinner) the reinforcement schedule, the greater is the resistance to extinction.

Intermittent reinforcement has been used to maintain behavior in several programs. In one demonstration, intermittent reinforcement was used to maintain social behavior among two male mentally retarded adults who attended a sheltered workshop (Kazdin & Polster, 1973). Because these men had engaged in little social interaction, they received tokens for talking with their peers. During three work breaks, they were told that they would receive tokens for interacting with peers socially. Each client received a token for each of the peers with whom he had spoken during each break. Thus, every interaction was reinforced. Figure 11–2 shows that during the first phase in which reinforcement was given, the daily average number of both clients' interactions gradually increased. Then, during a reversal phase in which tokens were withdrawn, their interactions decreased. When reinforcement was reinstated, one of the clients (S_1) received tokens as he had before (i.e., continuous reinforcement). The other client (S_2) was told that he would receive tokens only once in a while (i.e., intermittent reinforcement). At first, the second client received tokens during two of the work breaks. Eventually, all of his token reinforcement was withdrawn. As Figure 11–2 shows, during a second reversal

FIGURE 11–2

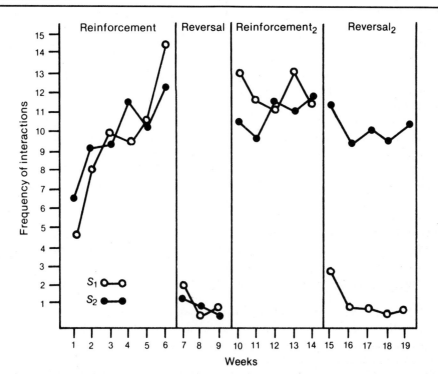

Mean frequency of interactions per day during reinforcement, reversal, reinforcement₂, and reversal₂ for Subject 1 (S₁) and Subject 2 (S₂).

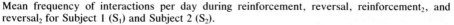

SOURCE: Kazdin, A. E., & Polster, R. (1973). Intermittent token reinforcement and response maintenance in extinction. *Behavior Therapy, 4*, 386–391.

phase, the client whose behavior had been continuously reinforced showed an immediate decline in social interaction. However, the client whose behavior had been intermittently reinforced maintained a high rate of social interaction. Thus, intermittent reinforcement appeared to help maintain behavior.

Intermittent reinforcement was also shown to enhance maintenance in a project designed to increase the selection of nutritious snacks among three children (ages four–five) enrolled in a day-care center (Baer, Blount, Detrick, & Stokes, 1987). Each day, the children were offered a choice of snacks that were considered nutritious (fruit, vegetable) or relatively nonnutritious (cookie, cracker). The children were trained to identify the nutritious snacks, to state that they would choose such snacks, and then to select such a snack afterward. If the children completed this sequence, they were allowed to draw from a grab bag that included cards listing consequences (reinforcers) that they would receive (e.g., hugs, tickles, stickers). After the behavior had been developed, the opportunities to select from the grab bag were made increasingly intermittent. At first, consequences were given every day (100 percent of the days). This was faded over periods of 5–10 days so that the consequences were delivered only 67 percent and then 33 percent of the days. Eventually, no consequences were provided. The results indicated that behavior was maintained up to seven weeks after the reinforcement had been terminated.

Instead of eliminating reinforcement completely, some investigators continue the use of intermittent reinforcement to maintain behavior at a high level. Intermittent reinforcement is quite effective, of course, while the reinforcement is still in effect. For example, Phillips, Phillips, Fixsen, and Wolf (1971) gave or withdrew points on the basis of the degree to which predelinquents cleaned their rooms. After the behavior had been well established, the reinforcing and punishing consequences became increasingly intermittent. The rooms were checked daily, but reinforcement or punishment occurred only once in a while. Although the consequences were delivered on only 8 percent of the days checked, the behavior was maintained at a high level. The consequences were not completely withdrawn, so the effect of intermittent reinforcement on extinction was not evaluated.

Intermittent reinforcement can be readily incorporated into most programs. It is important to make the schedule of reinforcement increasingly intermittent to increase resistance to extinction. It is unclear whether highly intermittent reinforcement forestalls extinction only temporarily or can virtually eliminate extinction even after a long extinction period. Behaviors reinforced intermittently have been maintained up to several months or a year after the intervention has been terminated (Hall, Cooper, Burmaster, & Polk, 1977; Morin, Ladouceur, & Cloutier, 1982).

Delay of Reinforcement

Behavior may also be maintained by gradually increasing the delay between reinforcement and the target behavior. When behavior is initially developed, immediate reinforcement is usually essential to ensure a high rate of responding. As behavior stabilizes and becomes well established, the delay between behavior and the reinforcing consequences can be increased without a loss in performance.

In maintaining behavior, the effectiveness of delaying reinforcement following a response has not been widely studied, although delay of reinforcement has often been used as part of other maintenance strategies such as fading the contingencies and altering reinforcement schedules. An illustration of how delays can be used was provided in three classrooms where reinforcement was contingent upon the appropriate behavior of the group (Greenwood, Hops, Delquadri, & Guild, 1974). After behavior had achieved a relatively high level, a delay was introduced in earning the group consequences. The classes were required to perform high levels of behavior for an increasing number of consecutive sessions before the reinforcer was delivered. A maximum delay of

10 sessions was attained before earning the reinforcer. Follow-up data three weeks after the program ended revealed that appropriate classroom behaviors were maintained.

A major purpose of delaying reinforcement is to maintain behavior after the program has been entirely withdrawn. Yet while the program is in effect, delayed reinforcement may increase generalization of behavior over time or across situations. For example, the effects of immediate and delayed reinforcement in maintaining the behavior of preschool children were compared (Fowler & Baer, 1981). Individual target behaviors (e.g., sharing, cooperative play) were identified, depending on the problem areas of each child. Behavior was observed for two classroom periods each day. Reinforcement (stickers exchangeable for toys) and feedback for performance of the target behavior were provided for performance in the first class period each day. When reinforcement and feedback were provided immediately after that period, behavior improved; but the changes were not evident in the second period. When the consequences were delayed until the end of the day (even though they were provided only for how well the children did in the first period), performance improved in both periods. Thus, delayed reinforcement promoted maintenance of behavior across both periods. It is likely that with delayed reinforcement the children were less able to discriminate the behaviors and periods for which reinforcement was provided, so they sustained their behavior at high levels to maximize their chances of receiving reinforcement.

In general, delayed reinforcement is not a reliably effective method for changing behavior initially. Yet it can be effective in maintaining behavior over time (e.g., Dunlap, Koegel, Johnson, & O'Neill, 1987). The shift from immediate to delayed reinforcement may be important in behavior change programs because most of the reinforcers available in the social environment are delayed. Hence, it is important to wean a client from immediate reinforcement. Behaviors should be well established before long delays are invoked. When delayed reinforcement is introduced, performance should be observed closely to ensure that there is no loss of behavioral gains. Eventually, reinforcement may be withdrawn entirely or delivered only after long delays, without a loss in performance.

Peer Facilitators

Peers may be utilized to help maintain behavior and to develop transfer across a variety of situations. If behavior comes under the stimulus control of the persons who implement the contingencies, it may be important to involve peers in the administration of consequences. Because peers have contact with the client across a variety of situations, their presence may provide the client with cues to continue the target behavior across these situations. After the specific contingencies have been terminated, peers may still influence the client's behavior.

Many programs utilizing peers as behavior change agents have been conducted in classroom settings (see Strain, 1981). For example, Lancioni (1982, Exp. 1) trained normal fourth-grade children as tutors to help socially withdrawn mentally retarded children engage in cooperative play, activities, and self-help skills. The tutors were trained to model the target behaviors and to provide prompts and social reinforcement. For their assistance, the tutors received tokens. They worked with retarded children in activities in special sessions outside the classroom, which increased the social behavior of the retarded children. Moreover, the changes in the behavior of the mentally retarded children transferred to social interaction with other children and to a play situation in which training had not been conducted. After training had been terminated, performance was maintained over a two-week follow-up period. These results suggest that the use of peers may facilitate both transfer of training and response maintenance.

Similarly, in another program, three junior high school students were trained to serve as tutors for children in need of remedial reading instruction (Greer & Polirstok, 1982). The tutors were trained to administer approval for on-task behavior and to ignore disruptive behavior. They received token reinforcement for their delivery of approval. The results indicated that the target children improved in their performance in reading assignments. After the tutors no longer received token reinforcement for helping the target children, they continued to provide approval and the target children maintained their improvements in reading. These results illustrate a potential advantage of peer-based reinforcement. Once peers have been trained, they may continue to provide reinforcement to persons under their charge. Alternatively, they may serve as discriminative stimuli and (through stimulus control) help promote the target behaviors altered in training.

Other investigations have shown that peer-administered contingencies sometimes lead to maintenance and transfer of behavior to situations other than those in which training has been conducted (Peck, Cooke, & Apolloni, 1981). However, the use of peers as facilitators of transfer and maintenance remains to be exploited. In many of the situations in which behavioral programs are conducted, peers, siblings, or other inmates or residents might be involved in monitoring the behavior of a target subject.

Self-Control Procedures

As noted earlier, one reason why changes in behavior are not maintained and do not transfer is that behavior comes under the stimulus control of external agents (e.g., parents, teachers, staff) and the restricted situations (e.g., home, classroom, ward) in which training is conducted. Perhaps, training clients to control their own behavior would prevent behavior changes from being lost when a program is withdrawn. Also, because the client implements the contingencies in self-administered programs, such programs can be executed across situations.

Few programs have carefully tested the effects of self-control strategies on long-term maintenance in applied settings. Promising results have been obtained in selected instances. For example, Wood and Flynn (1978) demonstrated the potential effects of self-reinforcement on maintaining behaviors among six male predelinquents who lived in a family-style residential facility. The boys participated in a token economy in which points for appropriate social, academic, and self-care behaviors could be exchanged for various privileges in the setting. Self-reinforcement was employed to develop room cleaning for each boy's room (e.g., having the bed made, leaving no objects on the bedspread or dresser). Some of the boys first received tokens administered by the staff for keeping their rooms clean. The others were instructed to administer points to themselves for their room-cleaning behaviors. Self-administered points were monitored by the staff to ensure that the boys evaluated their behaviors accurately. Eventually, all of the boys were placed on a self-evaluation and self-reinforcement system.

Interestingly, at the end of the program, all of the contingencies were withdrawn to assess whether room-cleaning behaviors were maintained. The results, which appear in Figure 11–3, show that instructing the boys to clean

FIGURE 11–3

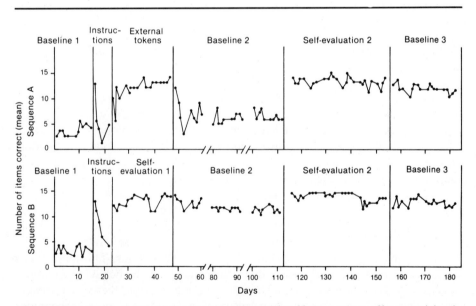

Mean number of room-cleaning behaviors correctly completed by two groups of boys receiving the conditions in a slightly different sequence. During the self-evaluation phases, the boys self-administered the reinforcing consequences based on evaluations of their own behavior.

SOURCE: Wood, R., & Flynn, J. M. (1978). A self-evaluation token system versus an external evaluation token system alone in a residential setting with predelinquent youths. *Journal of Applied Behavior Analysis, 11,* 503–512. Copyright 1978 by the Society for the Experimental Analysis of Behavior, Inc.

their rooms had little effect on their behavior. However, in the third phase, points administered by the staff (top portion of the figure) or by the boys themselves (bottom portion) improved room cleaning. For each set of boys, self-evaluation and self-reinforcement later led to high levels of room cleaning; and this effect was maintained up to 22 days after the contingencies had been terminated. Thus, the self-evaluation procedure appeared to maintain high rates of the target behavior.

In another demonstration, self-control techniques were used with parents of preschool children who had been referred for treatment (Sanders & Glynn, 1981). The children were noncompliant, demanding, and difficult to manage at home. The parents were trained to provide prompts and praise for appropriate behavior, to deliver feedback, and to use reprimands and withdrawal of reinforcers for inappropriate behavior. Initially, training was conducted by a therapist who visited the home. After the parents' skills had been developed, a self-management training procedure was provided to help the parents maintain their skills. They were trained to monitor their own behavior, to structure the situation to foster appropriate child behavior, to identify target behaviors, and to monitor their children's progress. The initial training increased the parents' skills (e.g., use of social reinforcement), which decreased disruptive child behavior in the home. With the self-management training, the parents' skills were maintained in the home and generalized to community settings (shopping trips, visits to relatives), where disruptive child behavior also decreased. Moreover, a three-month follow-up assessment indicated that the parents' skills and low rates of disruptive child behavior were maintained.

Self-reinforcement may have its limitations as a technique for achieving maintenance. To begin with, persons allowed to self-reward often become increasingly lenient over time, so that reinforcers are delivered even though the desired behaviors are not performed. Second, behaviors are often not maintained after self-reinforcement contingencies have been withdrawn. Indeed, small or no differences in response maintenance have been found, depending on whether an external agent or the clients themselves previously administered the reinforcers (see Jones, Nelson, & Kazdin, 1977).

In classroom applications, self-control contingencies have sustained performance as long as the contingencies were in effect and were monitored by others, such as a teacher. Special incentives for accurate self-reward, including points or praise and reprimands, may be necessary to ensure that the contingencies are executed to promote appropriate behavior. This amounts to continuation of a program, rather than maintenance of the behavior without a specific reinforcement program. Thus, for applied settings, there is at present only sparse evidence showing that self-reinforcement can maintain behavior without careful monitoring of the contingencies by an external agent, such as a teacher.

From the standpoint of maintenance, self-control procedures provide a useful adjunct that may help effect the transition from externally managed contingencies to the contingencies in the natural environment. Self-reinforcement, self-monitoring, and self-evaluation, alone or in combination, involve the client more directly in the program and provide less reliance on external agents, such as parents or teachers. In this sense, self-control procedures may be considered part of a more general strategy of fading the contingencies (cf. Gardner, Cole, Berry, & Nowinski, 1983; Mank & Horner, 1987).

Cognitively Based Procedures

Cognitively based techniques such as self-instruction training and problem-solving skills training constitute special self-control procedures that may also be useful in maintaining behavior and promoting transfer. These procedures focus on developing skills that individuals can apply to a variety of situations and settings.

Burgio, Whitman, and Johnson (1980) used self-instruction training with mentally retarded children (IQs ranging from 45 to 71) who were highly distractible in class. The children were trained to carry out self-instruction steps while completing academic tasks (arithmetic and printing). Training markedly improved their performance in the special training sessions conducted outside class. The gains transferred to classroom performance on academic tasks. Moreover, attentive behavior and teacher ratings of the children's distractibility in class also improved.

Apart from transfer of training, response maintenance occasionally results from self-instruction training. For example, in a classroom setting, Bornstein and Quevillon (1976) trained disruptive children to administer self-instructions to develop appropriate classroom behavior. Attentive behavior markedly increased, and these effects were maintained several weeks after training. However, as discussed previously (Chapter 10), the effects of self-instruction in altering classroom behavior have been inconsistent.

Cognitively based interventions have frequently improved various problem-solving skills (e.g., thinking of solutions to problems). However, the gains do not always transfer to actual behavior outside the training sessions. For example, Robin, Kent, O'Leary, Foster, and Prinz (1977) worked with mother and daughter dyads among children (11–14 years old) who had "excessive disagreements" with their parents. Training helped parents and children define problems and identify and implement solutions. Performance on various measures of problem-solving skills improved, but the gains did not extend to communication in the home. In some studies, self-instruction training and problem-solving skills training have altered behavior in applied settings such as the home and school (e.g., Arbuthnot & Gordon, 1986; Kazdin, Esveldt-Dawson, French, & Unis, 1987; Lochman, Burch, Curry, & Lampron, 1984). Yet many other studies do not show transfer of training (see Kazdin, 1982d; Urbain & Kendall, 1980). Additional work is needed to identify the factors in self-instruction training that can be used to facilitate transfer of training and response maintenance.

Duration of Intervention Programs

Many behavioral programs have been implemented in settings such as the classroom, home, or community for relatively brief periods (e.g., several days or a few weeks). Marked changes in behavior can be achieved even in such brief periods. However, maintenance and transfer may be especially unlikely in programs implemented for relatively brief treatment periods. If one wishes to develop durable behaviors that are performed in many different situations, an extended period of training may be necessary.

The duration of the program appears to be related to response maintenance and transfer of training, though the effects of duration on maintenance and transfer have not been carefully tested. Yet, a few behavior modification programs have been carried out for protracted periods (from several months to a few years). In such instances, the results have suggested that the responses are maintained and transfer to new situations. For example, in the Paul and Lentz (1977) program, psychiatric patients who participated in a token economy over several months continued to show gains 1½ to 5 years after the program, and these gains were reflected in community adjustment. Thus, both maintenance and transfer appeared to be achieved. As another example, a behavior modification program was implemented in elementary school grades over a period of several years and grade levels (Bushell, 1978). The program led to changes in behavior that were still evident two years after the program had been terminated and the children had entered classrooms where reinforcement programs were not in effect.

Programs in place for extended periods often provide intensive treatment effort. For example, in a program for autistic children (under four years of age), behavioral intervention was provided in the child's home, school, and community (Lovaas, 1987). Treatment focused on eliminating maladaptive behavior (e.g., self-stimulation, aggression) and developing a variety of prosocial (e.g., play) and cognitive-academic skills (e.g., language, reading, writing). The program involved parents, teachers, and trained undergraduates so that almost all of the child's waking hours were devoted to developing adaptive behaviors. Treatment was provided for 40 hours a week, 365 days a year, for two to six years. The results indicated that 47 percent of the children were eventually placed in normal first-grade classes and improved markedly on standardized intelligence tests. These gains were not evident in control children who were not involved in the training program. Here the gains of the program appeared to transfer to regular public school functioning.

The above programs do not show unequivocably that the longer a program is in effect, the more likely it is that behaviors will be maintained and will transfer to new settings. To obtain this information, research would need to compare the effects of a program applied to different children for different durations. Yet some evidence has suggested that programs in effect for brief periods show little maintenance and that maintenance increases as treatment is continued. For example, in one program, peer interaction was developed among withdrawn elementary school children (Paine et al., 1982). The children received token reinforcement at recess and in-class training for social behavior. Behaviors improved, but the gains were lost in return-to-baseline phases. Treatment was introduced and withdrawn repeatedly in separate phases over time. With each successive treatment phase, less of the desired social behavior was lost when baseline conditions were reintroduced. By the end of the program, behaviors were maintained and the children remained within the normal range of social interaction without continuing treatment.

The reasons why behaviors were maintained are unclear. It is possible that as a behavior is performed for an extended period, reinforcers that naturally occur in the environment or are provided by the behavior itself begin to control the behavior. Indeed, such effects seem evident in everyday life. Engaging in exercise or eating special foods may initially require some special incentive program. However, once the behaviors have been performed for an extended period, they often seem to be maintained "on their own." Similarly, in behavioral programs, repeated opportunities to perform a behavior appear to influence maintenance (Greenwood, Delquadri, & Hall, 1984; Horner, Williams, & Knobbe, 1985). Thus, evidence points to the importance of such factors as repeated performance of the behavior over time. However, the process of developing behavior so that it becomes fixed in one's repertoire (i.e., relatively impervious to moment-to-moment contingencies) is not well understood. Additional research is needed in the context of behavioral programs to examine whether, in fact, programs in effect for longer periods of time are related to maintenance of behavior change once the program has been terminated.

Procedures Used in Combination

The previously discussed procedures for promoting response maintenance and transfer of training are not mutually exclusive. In fact, many of the procedures can be viewed as variations of a more general strategy. For example, many of the procedures are designed to make the training situation increasingly similar to the nontraining situations so that stimulus control over the desired behavior is relatively broad. Thus, altering the delivery of reinforcement so that it is increasingly intermittent and delayed, fading the contingencies altogether, fading the presence of the trainer, and using peers who are present in the natural settings might all be viewed as efforts to develop behavior so that it is not connected to, or performed exclusively in the presence of, a narrow range of conditions.

Another reason for not viewing the procedures for promoting maintenance and transfer as mutually exclusive is the way they are employed. Investigators frequently use several procedures simultaneously to maximize the likelihood that responses will be maintained and will transfer to new situations. For example, Ayllon and Kelly (1974) restored the speech of an 11-year-old mentally retarded girl who had not spoken in class for over eight months.

Candy and social reinforcement were provided to shape components of speech (e.g., opening her mouth, blowing air out of her lips, making a sound, and eventually verbally responding to questions). To ensure that behaviors would be maintained and would transfer from the sessions in the counselor's office to the classroom, several techniques were used simultaneously.

First, over the course of training, the schedule of reinforcement was made increasingly intermittent. Second, praise was substituted for primary reinforcement (candy) so that the behavior would come under the control of naturally occurring reinforcers in the environment. Third, stimuli associated with the classroom were introduced into the counselor's office so that the training situation would increasingly resemble the classroom. Thus, other children, a blackboard, and desks were added to the training situation. Fourth, to foster the girl's speaking in the presence of her peers, a group contingency was introduced. Candy was provided to the group if each child in the training session, including the target child, answered questions asked by the trainer. Fifth, training was extended to the classroom, in which the trainer and later the teacher administered reinforcement. Overall, the training consisted of eight sessions outside the classroom followed by seven more sessions in the classroom. The girl's verbal responses increased markedly over the course of treatment. A follow-up assessment one year after training had ended indicated that the responses were maintained at the level achieved during training and transferred across three new teachers and settings within the school.

Similarly, Haney and Jones (1982) used several procedures to maintain behavior in a program designed to teach mentally retarded children how to escape from fires in their home. The training consisted of instructions, modeling, rehearsal, and social and tangible (candy) reinforcement. Several complex sequences of behaviors were taught, so that the children could assess how dangerous the situation was and how to behave accordingly. After the behaviors had been well established, the training program was faded, using several procedures. First, prompts were gradually decreased to reduce reliance on the trainer. Second, reinforcement was provided for increasingly large sequences of correct behavior. Finally, external reinforcement from the trainer was replaced by self-reinforcement, under which the children took their rewards for correct completion of the appropriate escape behaviors. Assessment six months after the program had been terminated indicated that the behaviors were maintained.

Many other behavior modification programs have combined various techniques to promote response maintenance and transfer, such as substituting naturally occurring reinforcers for more contrived reinforcers and expanding stimulus control so that the training situation resembles natural stimulus conditions (Koegel, O'Dell, & Koegel, 1987); fading the contingencies and using self-reinforcement and delayed reinforcement (Turkewitz, O'Leary, & Ironsmith, 1975); substituting one program for another and expanding stimulus control (Walker et al., 1975); using delayed and intermittent reinforcement and fading the presence of the trainer (Dunlap et al., 1987); and using peers, shifting from edible to social and from continuous to intermittent reinforcement, and increasing the delay of reinforcement (Lancioni, 1982).

In general, each of the procedures designed to promote maintenance and transfer emphasizes a different aspect of the contingencies that control behavior. The focus on any single factor, such as the stimuli that exert control over the response, the scheduling of consequences, and fading of the contingencies, may be limited when applied individually. In many of the situations in which maintenance and transfer are required, it is likely that several procedures would have to be programmed systematically. Current research represents an important beginning by looking at several specific techniques for achieving maintenance and transfer.

SUMMARY AND CONCLUSION

Two major issues in evaluating behavior modification programs are maintenance of behavior once the program has been withdrawn and transfer of the behavior to other situations and settings than those in which training has taken place. These issues are referred to as response maintenance and transfer of training. Maintenance and transfer are not automatic by-products of a behavior modification program. Rather, they usually have to be programmed directly by including specific procedures in the program.

Recently, advances have been made in developing techniques that help maintain behavior and help ensure its transfer. Major techniques of this kind are (1) bringing behavior under the control of the natural contingencies, (2) programming naturally occurring reinforcers, (3) gradually removing or fading the contingencies, (4) expanding stimulus control over behavior, (5) training individuals to respond to the general case, (6) altering the schedules of reinforcement, (7) increasing the delay of reinforcement, (8) using peer facilitators, (9) using self-control procedures, and (10) using cognitively based procedures. These techniques vary in the extent to which they have been evaluated and in the extent to which they achieve maintenance, transfer, or both. The techniques are often combined in many programs to maximize the likelihood that durable and broad changes in performance will be attained. Hence, the effectiveness of individual techniques is often difficult to determine. Nevertheless, present work suggests that several of the techniques can be implemented to maintain high levels of performance and to extend these levels to the new situations in which the client will function.

FOR FURTHER READING

Albin, R. W., Horner, R. H., Koegel, R. L., & Dunlap, G. (Eds.). (1987). *Extending competent performance: Applied research on generalization and maintenance.* Eugene: University of Oregon.

Baer, D. M. (1981). *How to plan for generalization.* Austin, TX: Pro-Ed.

Kazdin, A. E., & Esveldt-Dawson, K. (1981). *How to maintain behavior*. Austin, TX: Pro-Ed.

Stokes, T. F., & Osnes, P. G. (1986). Programming the generalization of children's social behavior. In P. S. Strain, M. J. Guralnick, & H. M. Walker (Eds.), *Children's social behavior: Development, assessment, and modification* (pp. 407–443). New York: Academic Press.

Chapter Twelve

Current Applications of Behavioral Techniques

MEDICAL APPLICATIONS
  Prevention
  Eating Disorders
  Pain
  Adherence and Compliance
PERSONAL SAFETY
  Seat Belt Use
  Special Situations for Children
  Business and Industry
CONTEMPORARY CONCERNS IN EVERYDAY LIFE
  Traffic Control
  Energy Conservation
  Littering
  Waste Recycling
  Employment and Job-Related Skills
ADDITIONAL APPLICATIONS
LARGE-SCALE APPLICATIONS
  Education
  Delinquent Youths
  Work-Site Applications
LONG-TERM FOLLOW-UP
SUMMARY AND CONCLUSION

Previous chapters have presented alternative techniques derived from operant conditioning principles and methods of assessing and evaluating the impact of these techniques on behavior. The techniques were illustrated by drawing on examples of behavioral problems with various populations, settings, and behaviors. As the illustrations may reflect, most behavior modification programs have been conducted in school classrooms, the home, institutional settings for mentally retarded persons or psychiatric patients, and facilities for delinquents. The initial applications focused on clients and behaviors that were traditionally regarded as central to education, treatment, and rehabilitation. Understandably, these areas have been emphasized because of the long-recognized need for techniques to alter behavior.

Behavioral techniques have been extended to many other areas. The extensions were prompted by successes of the techniques in altering a variety of behaviors within traditional domains of treatment and education. In addition, if operant conditioning principles describe relations between environmental events and behavior with any degree of generality, the techniques should be relevant to a wide range of behaviors in diverse settings. The previous chapters have hinted at the breadth of applications with occasional examples illustrating a relatively novel problem or focus. The present chapter conveys more clearly the range of applications by sampling some of the areas of current work.

MEDICAL APPLICATIONS

Behavior modification techniques are being applied increasingly to problems that relate to physical health and illness. Applications of behavioral science to the prevention, diagnosis, and treatment of problems of physical health have recently emerged as an area referred to as *behavioral medicine* or, more generally, *health psychology*. The domain of behavioral medicine encompasses a wide range of problems, including adherence to medical regimens such as exercising, following a special diet, or taking medicine; the treatment of a variety of disorders, including cardiac arrhythmias, hypertension, seizures, headaches, pain, and muscle spasms; and behaviors that can impair or promote physical health (see Doleys, Meredith, & Ciminero, 1982). Although examples throughout previous chapters have illustrated applications of behavioral medicine, it is important to highlight the area here.

Prevention

In many cases, serious illness and disease can be averted by engaging in preventive behaviors. A number of studies have focused on developing behaviors to reduce the risk of disease or to detect the early onset of disease so that treatments can be effectively applied. Only a few of the many areas in which this has been accomplished can be sampled here.

Behavioral interventions have also been applied to the prevention of life-threatening disease. The direct treatment of such clinical problems as alcohol and drug abuse and cigarette smoking reduces the risk of many other diseases. However, such studies are treatment studies in that they focus on problematic target behaviors. Other studies have focused on prevention even when no immediate target behavior is in need of direct intervention. As an example, cancer is of obvious concern because of the multiple forms it may take and the often poor prognosis. Early detection is extremely important because the survival rates for many cancers are much greater if the cancer is treated before it has spread (metastasized). Behavioral techniques have been applied to increase early detection through self-examination. Instructions, feedback, and reinforcement have been used to train women and men, respectively, to self-examine for early symptoms of breast or testicular cancer (e.g., Friman, Finney, Glasscock, Weigel, & Christophersen, 1986; Hall et al., 1980). The relatively few studies in this area have shown that the requisite behaviors can be developed and maintained after training has been terminated.

Behavioral interventions have focused on a number of areas that are critical even if not life threatening. For example, considerable work has been conducted on dental care to prevent tooth decay, gum disease, and loss of teeth. Although environmental interventions (fluoridation of community water supplies) have helped, individual care of one's teeth remains critical. Interventions for different facets of dental care have been studied. Evaluating interventions have been facilitated by the availability of measures to assess various degrees of dental plaque. Such measurement permits evaluation of the extent to which persons are brushing and flossing effectively.

In one project, children were trained to floss their teeth to reduce plaque. Instructions, prompts (reminder cards at home), self-monitoring, and intermittent reinforcement were quite effective in reducing plaque (Dahlquist & Gil, 1986). The intervention was maintained in the home by shifting the assessment and reinforcement procedures from an experimenter to the parents. Other studies have shown that behavioral techniques can increase the frequency and quality of toothbrushing and tooth flossing in children and adults (Claerhout & Lutzker, 1981; Iwata & Becksfort, 1981).

Eating Disorders

Behavioral techniques have been applied to a variety of eating disorders that can lead to or reflect physical disease, including obesity, ruminative vomiting, anorexia nervosa, and bulimia. For example, anorexia nervosa, a disorder invariably found in young women, involves reduced food consumption that results in extreme loss of weight. Women with anorexia nervosa lose at least 20 percent of their normal body weight, have a marked fear of becoming obese, and resist gaining weight. The physical consequences of significant weight loss include an emaciated appearance, cessation of menstruation, and, in severe cases, death.

In one program, several anorexia nervosa patients were treated using a contingency contract system (Pertschuk, Edwards, & Pomerleau, 1978). Hospitalized patients were told that a daily weight gain of one-half pound was required in order to earn certain privileges on the ward. Individualized contracts were drawn up in writing and signed by the therapist and the patient. The patients were told that they were responsible for gaining weight and that they could request nutritional counseling if they wished assistance. During baseline, the patients had generally continued to lose weight. However, during the contract period (about two weeks), they showed an average weight gain of about 4.2 kilograms (9.3 pounds). Follow-up assessment ranging from 3 to 28 months indicated that the patients had continued to gain weight after discharge from the hospital. Other reports have suggested successful treatment of anorexia nervosa with reinforcement and feedback techniques, contingency contracting, desensitization, and other behavioral procedures alone or in combination (e.g., Hauserman & Lavin, 1977; Monti, McCrady, & Barlow, 1977).

Pain

Behavioral techniques have been applied to treat pain associated with a variety of disorders. The techniques are usually applied to alter many of the behaviors associated with pain—for example, to increase the amount of time hospitalized patients remain out of bed; to reduce signs of pain such as grimacing, moaning, complaining, and walking in a guarded or protective manner; and to decrease reliance on medication.

Pioneering work applying behavioral techniques to chronic pain was reported several years ago by Fordyce and his colleagues (Fordyce et al., 1974). In one of the studies, patients with back pain (due to a variety of physical disorders) participated in a treatment program for approximately seven weeks within the hospital. During treatment, the patients received social reinforcement from their families and from staff for engaging in increased activity (e.g., going on walks) in the hospital. Complaints, moaning, inactivity, and grimacing were ignored. After treatment, the patients reported less intense pain, reduced their intake of medication, and increased the amount of time they spent out of bed. Other studies have shown that reinforcement from staff can increase activities (e.g., walking, riding a stationary bicycle) and reduce pain among hospitalized patients diagnosed with chronic back pain (Cairns & Pasino, 1977).

Many applications of behavioral techniques to pain are conducted at home, rather than in hospital settings. For example, Miller and Kratochwill (1979) used time out from reinforcement to reduce the frequency of stomachache complaints in a 10-year-old girl named Karen. There was no evidence of organic impairment, and medication had not eliminated the complaints. Analysis of the home environment suggested that reinforcement (staying home from school, watching television, playing with toys, being waited on with food, drink, and social attention) might be maintaining the complaints. Karen's mother was instructed to use a time-out whenever Karen complained. When Karen complained about her stomach, she was told to rest in her room. Although some reinforcers (books) were available, television, toys, and games were not available. The curtains were drawn and the door was almost closed so that Karen could rest quietly. The main feature of the time-out appeared to be a reduction of attention from the mother for complaining. The effects of the program are illustrated in Figure 12–1. In the third phase, there was an accidental return to baseline when Karen vomited and received extra attention for a four-day period. The program was implemented again, and

FIGURE 12–1

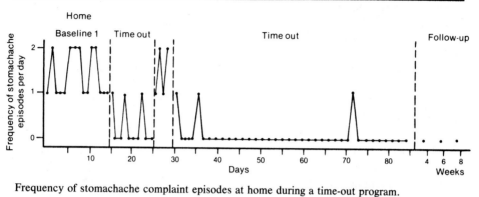

Frequency of stomachache complaint episodes at home during a time-out program.

SOURCE: Miller, A. J., & Kratochwill, T. R. (1979). Reduction of frequent stomachache complaints by time out. *Behavior Therapy, 10,* 211–218. Copyright 1979 by the Association for Advancement of Behavior Therapy. Reprinted by permission of the publisher and the author.

Karen's complaints declined. Follow-up several weeks and one year after treatment indicated no further complaints of pain.

Other reports have suggested that behavioral techniques, including biofeedback, relaxation training, incentive systems, and cognitive-behavioral strategies such as the use of self-statements, can be used to treat pain associated with chronic disease, menstruation, and intercourse (see Doleys et al., 1982; Turk, Meichenbaum, & Genest, 1983). Specific disorders such as headaches and back pain represent areas in which several techniques have been studied.

Adherence and Compliance

Adherence to medical regimens is an important area of concern because many forms of medical and psychological treatment depend on client compliance with treatment recommendations. Yet estimates have suggested that up to 50 percent of medical patients do not comply with their prescribed regimens (Gillum & Barsky, 1974).

Behavior modification has been used to increase adherence to a variety of treatment procedures. For example, Lowe and Lutzker (1979) treated a juvenile diabetic named Amy, who had been hospitalized repeatedly as a result of not adhering to her prescribed medical regimen. To ensure a blood sugar balance, she had been prescribed a special diet, insulin injections, and exercise. She had been instructed to conduct urine tests several times daily to measure the effect of balancing diet, insulin, and exercise. She had also been told to maintain personal hygiene, especially with regard to foot care because of poor circulation to her feet, loss of sensation in her feet, and possible injuries that might become infected if not detected. Unfortunately, Amy did not follow the approriate diet, conduct urine tests, or engage in foot care (wash and inspect for cuts and bruises).

   To increase compliance with this medical regimen at home, the investigators gave Amy a "memo" (written instructions) that told her how to complete the desired behaviors and at what times this should be done each day. Later, a token economy was devised in which Amy earned points (exchangeable for rewards daily or at the end of the week) for engaging in the tasks required to manage her diabetes. The effects of the program are presented in Figure 12–2, which graphs Amy's daily percentage of completion of the desired tasks. Introducing the memo increased Amy's adherence to the diet (bottom portion

FIGURE 12–2

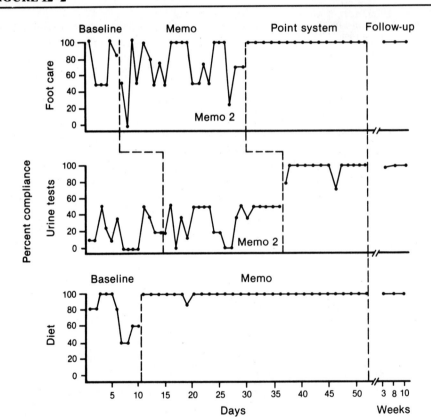

Percentage of compliance to medical regimen for foot care, urine tests, and diet.

SOURCE: Lowe, K., & Lutzker, J. R. (1979). Increasing compliance to a medical regimen with a juvenile diabetic. *Behavior Therapy, 10,* 57–64. Copyright 1979 by the Association for Advancement of Behavior Therapy. Reprinted by permission of the publisher and the author.

of the figure) but did not affect her other behaviors. The token system, however, markedly improved her adherence to the requirements regarding foot care and urine tests. During the follow-up period, the experimenter was no longer formally involved in the program. Amy's parents continued the program, and her behaviors were maintained at a high rate.

Another program focused on improving the ability of 19 children (ages 8 to 12) to control their diabetes (Epstein et al., 1981a). The children and their parents received training in procedures to assess urine glucose levels, to adjust insulin doses as needed, to follow a special diet, and to exercise. When the children received points for accurately assessing their urine glucose levels and for following diet and exercise regimens, their control of their glucose levels increased substantially. The gains were maintained up to 10 weeks after treatment had ended.

Reinforcement techniques have also been used to increase compliance with special diet, exercise, and medication regimens among patients with a variety of disorders, including renal dysfunction, hypertension, asthma, and coronary disease, to mention a few (see Russo & Varni, 1982; Stuart, 1982). These applications are especially significant because of the life-threatening consequences associated with failure to follow prescribed treatments.

PERSONAL SAFETY

Behavioral techniques have been increasingly applied to areas of safety to prevent injury and death in a variety of situations. The significance of safety-related behaviors can be attested to in many ways. For example, among adults, accidents are the fourth leading cause of death (after heart disease, cancer, and stroke). Accidents involving motor vehicles and work accidents are the two categories of accidents that result in the highest death rates (Sulzer-Azaroff, 1982). Interventions that can decrease the likelihood of injury and death from accidents are obviously important. The range of safety-related behaviors and situations to which behavioral techniques have been applied is extensive and can only be sampled here.

Seat Belt Use

The use of seat belts in automobiles is a major safety issue, given evidence that use of seat belts can prevent approximately half of all the deaths and injuries that would occur in their absence among motor vehicle passengers. As one illustration of work in this area, seat belt use was increased among children who attended an after-school day-care program (Sowers-Hoag, Thyer, & Bailey, 1987). Seat belt use was assessed at the end of each day as the parents picked up the children. Each parent drove to a loading zone, at which time a staff member went to get the child and bring the child to the car. Seat belt use was measured by noting whether the child had belted himself or herself before the car left the loading zone. The intervention to develop seat belt use included educational information for the children about the use of seat belts, assertiveness training through role play to help children ask as needed where to find or how to fasten the seat belt, and practice in using different kinds of seat belts. Also, a reward system was used in which the children who used seat belts were eligible for a lottery on the next day in which they could earn a small prize (valued at between $0.24 and $0.59). A child's chances of earning a prize on the next day was relatively high (50 percent). After the program was in effect, the performance criterion for eligibility for the lottery was increased to two consecutive days of seat belt use.

Although the program was applied to all of the 158 children at the facility, the intervention was evaluated with only 16 of the children. The intervention was introduced in a multiple-baseline design across two groups of children. As is evident in Figure 12–3, child seat belt use was increased when the intervention was introduced. When the frequency of the lottery was reduced and two days of seat belt use was required, seat belt use remained high. A follow-up assessment was conducted three months after the program had been terminated. The results indicated a high level of seat belt use (75–86 percent).

Special Situations for Children

There are a host of situations in which children are at risk because of their age, lack of knowledge, inexperience, and stage of development. Several foci illustrate efforts to apply behavioral techniques to improve child safety at home and in the community. Child abduction is obviously a major social and parental concern. In one investigation, preschool children (three to five years old) were trained to protect themselves against abduction by strangers (Poche, Brouwer, & Swearingen, 1981). Children were initially selected for participation if they were susceptible to abduction, which was assessed by having a stranger (actually someone working in the study) approach a child and ask whether he or she would leave the preschool with him. Unfortunately, approximately 90 percent of the children agreed to go with the stranger after being given simple verbal inducements, though no child was actually taken from the setting.

Training was conducted at various places around the school. Adults were trained to lure children by using verbal ploys to encourage children to leave with them. Physical force, of course, was not used to encourage the children to leave. (Such force is rarely used by persons who actually abduct children.) Such statements as these were made to the children: "Would you like to go with me for a walk?" and "I've got a nice surprise in my car." The target behaviors, derived from interviews with parents, consisted of making a brief verbal comment to the stranger and then getting away as quickly as possible. The training consisted of modeling the desired behaviors, having the child rehearse the desired behaviors, and providing the child with social and tangible reinforcement (e.g., praise, stickers) for correct responding. Practice continued across different situations and across different types of approaches by the adults. The results indicated that the children learned the requisite behaviors

FIGURE 12–3

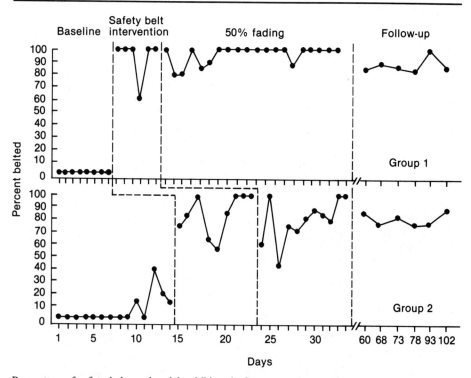

Percentage of safety belt use by eight children in Group 1 and eight children in Group 2.

SOURCE: Sowers-Hoag, K. M., Thyer, B. A., & Bailey, J. S. (1987). Promoting automobile safety belt use by young children. *Journal of Applied Behavior Analysis, 20,* 133–138. Copyright 1987 by the Society for the Experimental Analysis of Behavior, Inc.

and were not amenable to being lured by the adults. The effects generalized to assessment in a naturalistic situation out in the community and were maintained up to 12 weeks after training had been completed. Subsequent research has shown that children can be trained in skills to avoid abduction with a specially made videotape that presents the training sequence (Poche, Yoder, & Miltenberger, 1988). The program could be widely disseminated because of its videotape form, accompanied by instruction in its use.

In another program, mentioned earlier, elementary school children were trained to engage in behaviors that would enable them to escape from emergency fire situations in their home (Jones, Kazdin, & Haney, 1981a). The children were trained in simulated bedrooms at school. The desired escape behaviors were selected from fire safety manuals and after consulting with firefighters, who identified problem situations and lifesaving behaviors. The target behaviors were extremely complex sequences of responses to avoid being overcome by smoke (e.g., rolling out of bed, crawling to a door or window), to make decisions based on the extent and location of the hypothetical fire, and to select among alternative escape routes. Training included instructions, feedback, modeling, and both external reinforcement and self-reinforcement. The results indicated that the children did not have the requisite responses prior to training but developed them at a high level when the program was executed. Moreover, the responses were maintained at a two-week follow-up assessment. Subsequent research indicated that the behaviors developed in these children tended to decrease several months after training (Jones, Kazdin, & Haney, 1981b). However, the behaviors can be maintained if the training program is faded gradually (Haney & Jones, 1982).

Child safety has been the focus of several other applications of behavioral techniques, such as interventions to reduce the number of child safety hazards (e.g., fire, electricity, poisons) at home (Tertinger, Greene, & Lutzker, 1984) and to manage the situations of "latchkey children"—children who return to an unsupervised home after school (Peterson, 1984). In these studies, efforts have been made to increase the safety of the home or to help the children manage in situations in which an adult is not available.

Business and Industry

Many applications of behavior modification have been conducted in industry to promote safe practices on the part of employees (e.g., wearing protective devices, using potentially dangerous equipment properly) and management (e.g., removing work hazards). An excellent illustration can be seen in a study of safety in open-pit mining (Fox, Hopkins, & Anger, 1987). The study was conducted at two open-pit mines, one in Wyoming and the other in Arizona. Uranium was extracted and processed at one of the mines; coal was extracted and processed at the other. The two mines used similar equipment (e.g., trucks, bulldozers) and procedures (e.g., strip mining, crushing, storing materials). The goals of the program were to decrease job-related injuries, days lost from work due to such injuries, and costs (e.g., due to medical care, insurance, and equipment damage) among employees in each mine.

An incentive in the form of tokens (trading stamps) was provided at the end of each month to workers who had not been injured or had not required medical care because of an accident. Trading stamps were also given to all members of a group that worked under a particular supervisor if no one in the group had been injured. Bonus stamps were available to workers whose suggestions for improving safety in the facility were adopted. Trading stamps could also be lost (response cost) for missing work due to injury or for causing an accident. The trading stamps could be exchanged at a nearby redemption center that carried hundreds of items (e.g., small appliances, barbecue grills, spice racks, clocks). The program was introduced to each mine in a multiple-baseline design and integrated with the mine's routine practices for several years. Figure 12–4 shows a marked reduction in the number of accidents

FIGURE 12–4

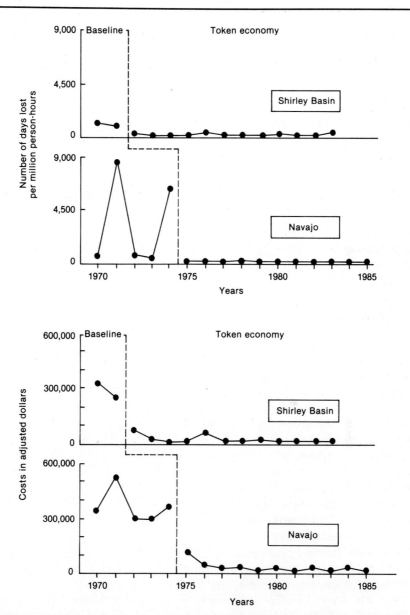

Yearly number of days lost from work, per million person-hours worked, because of work-related injuries (upper figure) and yearly cost, adjusted for hours worked and inflation, resulting from accidents and injuries (lower figure).

SOURCE: Fox, D. K., Hopkins, B. L., & Anger, W. K. (1987). The long-term effects of a token economy on safety performance in open-pit mining. *Journal of Applied Behavior Analysis, 20,* 215–224. Copyright 1987 by the Society for the Experimental Analysis of Behavior, Inc.

among workers (upper panel) as well as a reduction in monetary costs to the company (lower panel). Also of interest is the long-term use of the program and the continuation of the improved safety.

Several other applications in industry have shown that behavioral techniques can enhance worker safety. The interventions have utilized feedback to workers, prompts and reinforcement for behaviors that promote safety, and modeling of safe work practices. These interventions have promoted safe employee practices to avoid injury and have effectively reduced hazards leading to accidents and exposure to toxic and potentially carcinogenic substances in the air (Alavosius & Sulzer-Azaroff, 1986; Hopkins et al., 1986; Sulzer-Azaroff & de Santamaria, 1980).

CONTEMPORARY CONCERNS IN EVERYDAY LIFE

Behavioral techniques have been extended to several areas that reflect issues, concerns, and experiences in everyday life. Applications have extended to such problems as traffic control, energy, conservation, littering, waste recycling, employment, and job performance (see Geller, Winett, & Everett, 1982).

Traffic Control

The control of automobile traffic has served as the focus of a number of studies designed to reduce accidents and injury. Applications in this area might also be conceived as extensions to safety and prevention. Several studies have focused on speeding because of the direct relation of speeding to automobile accidents and death. Already mentioned (Chapter 5) was the effect of feedback in reducing the number of drivers speeding on the highway (Van Houten, Nau, & Marini, 1980). The feedback consisted of a road sign that indicated the percentage of drivers not speeding on the previous day as well as the best percentage on all previous days. Both speeding and the number of traffic accidents were decreased.

An extension of the program used similar feedback procedures on streets in major cities in Canada and Israel (Van Houten et al., 1985). In one of the studies, other procedures were added to the roadside feedback. Drivers were occasionally stopped and received a warning fine for speeding or praise (a thank-you note) for adhering to the speed limit. The results of the interventions indicated reductions in speeding and traffic accidents.

Also related to traffic accidents is the manner in which drivers approach yellow and red lights. Increased accident risk is associated with approaching an intersection when the traffic light changes to yellow or red. The likelihood of going through a yellow or red light has to do in part with the timing of lights from one intersection to the next. A recent demonstration assessed the percentage of drivers leaving one intersection who went through a yellow or red light at the next intersection (Jason, Neal, & Marinakis, 1985). As a result of the assessment, the timing sequence of the traffic lights at the two intersections was altered so that the change to the yellow light occurred much sooner at the second intersection. Thus, drivers going through a green light at the first intersection were more likely to have a red light at the next intersection, and therefore to stop. Manipulating the timing sequence markedly increased the number of cars that stopped correctly at the second intersection. As a result of the change, accidents were reduced by approximately 33 percent.

Approximately 18 percent of the persons killed in traffic accidents are pedestrians (see Jason & Liotta, 1982). A question of applied significance is whether pedestrian behavior can be changed to reduce the number of accidents. A major source of pedestrian accidents is crossing the street outside the crosswalks (jaywalking) or stepping into traffic without warning. Studies have shown that such interventions as prompting, feedback, and reinforcement can effectively train children and adults to cross streets safely and to provide warnings to drivers (e.g., Van Houten, Malenfant, & Rolider, 1985; Yeaton & Bailey, 1978).

Energy Conservation

Consumption of electricity, gasoline, and home heating oil and gas has been a worldwide concern because of the limited energy resources available from usable fossil fuels and because of the increased demand for energy. Several investigations have examined whether behavioral techniques can be used to curb energy consumption. For example, in a four-month project designed to reduce fuel oil consumption in the home, Seaver and Patterson (1976) studied 180 households randomly drawn from rural communities. These households were assigned randomly to one of three conditions: feedback, feedback plus social commendations, and no treatment. At the time of fuel delivery, the feedback households were told how much fuel they had consumed relative to the same period in the previous year and how much money they had saved or lost. The feedback-plus-commendation households received the above feedback plus social recognition (in the form of a decal saying "We are saving oil") if they had reduced their fuel consumption. The feedback-plus-commendation households used significantly less fuel than did the other households. The feedback-alone households and the no-treatment households did not differ from each other. Several other studies have shown that interventions involving feedback, monetary reinforcement, and self-monitoring effectively reduce home energy consumption (Geller, Winett, & Everett, 1982).

A major source of fuel consumption is the use of automobile gasoline. A number of applications have used behavioral techniques such as token reinforcement, feedback, or small incentives to promote the use of mass transit (buses) instead of personal automobiles or to promote driving less than usual (Foxx & Hake, 1977; Geller, Winett, & Everett, 1982). For example, one study increased the use of car pools by providing token reinforcement and special parking privileges to university students who formed such pools (Jacobs,

Fairbanks, Poche, & Bailey, 1982). Conservation of energy and a decrease in pollution are two benefits that can result from the extension of such programs to reduce one-person use of cars.

Littering

Littering in public places is a matter of social concern, both because it is unsightly and because of the tremendous expense of cleanup. Estimates suggest that millions of dollars are required to clean major highways alone (Keep America Beautiful, 1968). Campaigns and public appeals have not been very effective in reducing littering. Incentive systems have effectively reduced littering or increased the removal of existing litter in such settings as national forests, schools, movie theaters, university campuses, and athletic stadiums (Osborne & Powers, 1980). Instructions and prompts (e.g., posters, small signs, and conspicuously marked trash cans with antilitter messages) have increased the correct disposal of litter (Geller, Winett, & Everett, 1982). However, the use of incentives has generally been more effective in improving the deposit as well as the cleanup of litter.

For example, one program was directed at decreasing the litter on the grounds in a 15-square-block urban housing area that included over 390 low-income families (Chapman & Risley, 1974). Litter was collected in residential yards, public yards, streets, sidewalks, and other areas. Providing small monetary incentives (10 cents for filling up a litter bag or for cleaning yards rather than merely turning in filled litter bags) reduced the amount of litter observed in the neighborhood, as measured by sampling 25 randomly selected yards. Paying children for clean yards was more effective than paying them for full litter bags. Both incentive conditions demonstrated the utility of reinforcement in maintaining low levels of litter in a community setting.

Many applications to reduce the amount of litter have relied on monetary incentives. Yet such interventions need not be expensive. For example, in one program, individuals who picked up litter were given a ticket to win a prize of $20 (Powers, Osborne, & Anderson, 1973). The tickets were drawn from a lottery, so the money was not provided to each of the individuals who participated. A lottery system is a useful way to sustain high levels of a behavior without providing money or a prize to each individual who performs it.

Waste Recycling

A concern related to littering is the accumulation of waste products in the environment. For some waste products, recycling is an alternative approach to litter control. If waste products (e.g., metal cans, paper, returnable bottles) can be recycled, they become a resource. In one program, the recycling of paper was increased on a university campus (Geller, Chaffee, & Ingram, 1975). Several dormitories had collected wastepaper to be sold to a paper mill at $15 per ton and eventually recycled. Different interventions were implemented to increase their collection of wastepaper. One intervention consisted of a "recycling contest" between men's and women's dormitories. The dorm that collected more paper would receive a bonus of $15. Another intervention consisted of a raffle in which each student who brought paper to the collection room received a ticket. Tickets were drawn each week and earned prizes, including monetary certificates redeemable at retail stores for clothing, groceries, furniture, and other items varying in monetary value. Both the contest contingency and the raffle contingency increased the amount of paper that was brought to the collection rooms of the dormitories, but more paper was brought and more individuals brought paper when the raffle contingency was used.

Extrinsic reinforcers are not always necessary to increase recycling. In one project, residents of three apartment complexes were merely informed of the location of recycling containers that were being used to collect newspapers (Reid, Luyben, Rawers, & Bailey, 1976). Near the containers, which were placed in the laundry rooms of the apartment complexes, were instructions explaining their use. In addition, residents were interviewed briefly prior to the program and prompted about the use of the containers. Over a period of several weeks, the amount of newspapers collected increased relative to baseline levels.

Employment and Job-Related Skills

Obtaining and keeping a job entails problems of obvious social significance. Lack of employment, aside from its economic implications, is associated with a number of social ills including crime, "mental illness," alcoholism, medical neglect, and family dysfunction (Warr, 1987). Behavioral programs have improved job interview skills, success in obtaining employment, and on-the-job performance.

A few studies have examined procedures for helping individuals to obtain employment. For example, Azrin, Flores, and Kaplan (1975) developed a job-finding club to train unemployed persons in skills that would enhance their opportunities for obtaining a job. Members were paired into dyads, so that each member would have someone to provide support and encouragement. Also, members were trained to search for jobs through various sources (e.g., former employers, relatives), role-played job interviews, received instructions in dress and grooming, learned to prepare a résumé, and expanded their job interests. Persons who participated in the program found employment within a shorter time period and received higher wages than persons who did not participate. Three months after participation in the program, 92 percent of the clients had obtained employment, compared with 60 percent of the persons who did not participate.

Behavioral techniques have also improved job interview skills. For example, in one program, former hospitalized psychiatric patients were trained in interview skills (Furman, Geller, Simon, & Kelly, 1979). The clients were trained to provide positive information about themselves and their experiences, to make appropriate nonverbal gestures while speaking, to express interest and enthusiasm for the potential position, and to ask appropriate questions. The training used role-playing, practice, videotaped feedback, prompts, and praise for appropriate behavior. The effects of training for one person are illustrated in Figure 12–5. At the end of training, an experienced job interviewer, unfamiliar with the training program, rated interview skills as improved.

FIGURE 12–5

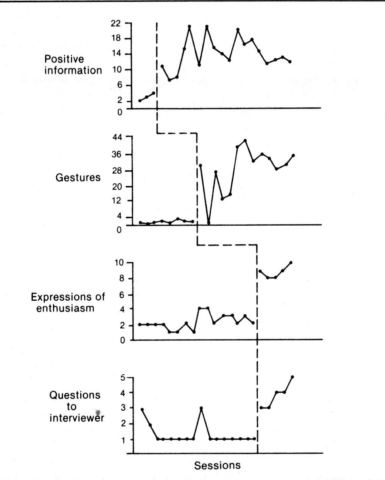

Job interview training for one client as evaluated in multiple-baseline introduction of giving positive information, gesturing, asking questions, and expressing enthusiasm for the position.

SOURCE: Furman, W., Geller, M., Simon, S. J., & Kelly, J. A. (1979). The use of a behavioral rehearsal procedure for teaching job interviewing skills to psychiatric patients. *Behavior Therapy, 10,* 157–167. Copyright 1979 by the Association for Advancement of Behavior Therapy. Reprinted by permission of the publisher and the authors.

On-the-job performance has been improved in several behavior modification programs. Emery Air Freight Corporation is a frequently cited example of the use of reinforcement in industry ("New Tool," 1971). To improve many aspects of company operations, Emery used feedback, praise, and social recognition to reinforce job performance. For example, in one application, the cost of delivering airfreight was reduced by shipping several smaller packages in a large container. Employees who worked on the loading dock received feedback and praise for shipping packages in larger containers, thus saving money. Use of the containers increased 95 percent and remained at a high level for almost two years, saving the company approximately $650,000 per year.

Many other businesses have relied on reinforcement contingencies to improve both employee performance and morale. For example, a small company that produced egg cartons used a token economy to recognize the efforts of employees and to increase productivity (Nelton, 1988). Employees earned 25 points a year for perfect attendance, 20 points a year if no disciplinary action was formally noted, and 15 points for working a year without lost time due to injury. Five points were deducted for each day of absence. Points were also earned for cost-saving or safety suggestions and for community service. Employees who reached 100 points were awarded a jacket with the company logo and the words "The 100 Club." Reports from employees indicated that the program was well liked. Production improved as well, although the role of the token reinforcement program was not specifically evaluated.

The previous examples are only a sampling of a plethora of applications of behavioral techniques to business and industry. Feedback and incentive systems have altered absenteeism, tardiness, production and sales, and employee-customer interactions (see Frederiksen, 1982). Although most of the applications have focused on small businesses (such as a single store, restaurant, or local company), some of the programs have been implemented by large industries with offices throughout the United States (e.g., Mirman, 1982).

ADDITIONAL APPLICATIONS

Extensions of behavior modification to social, environmental, health-related, and safety problems represent only a few of the innovative directions that the field has taken. Consider some of the other areas of application. Behavioral techniques have been applied to the *elderly,* such as nursing-home residents and geriatric patients. Programs based on social or token reinforcement have increased their social interaction, physical activity, and recovery from physical injury. Their self-care skills (e.g., self-bathing), eating habits, and leisure-time activities have been improved as well (see Burgio & Burgio, 1986).

Interventions have been extended to facets of *crime* other than the rehabilitation of delinquents and criminals. For example, prompting and police patrol techniques have effectively reduced shoplifting in department stores and burglary rates in communities (McNees et al., 1976; Schnelle et al., 1978). For years, behavioral applications have focused on delinquent youth and adult criminals in various settings (Burchard & Lane, 1982).

Behavioral techniques have been applied to diverse aspects of family life. Clinically important examples include the focus on special populations, as in training the parents of children with various dysfunctions, including antisocial behavior and autism, or training parents who engaged in abusive child-rearing practices (see Kazdin, 1987a; Schreibman, 1988; Wolfe, 1987). Many other applications have focused on everyday concerns of parents, rather than extreme clinical problems. For example, applications have utilized reinforcement techniques to train fathers to provide better care for their newborn infants (Dachman, Alessi, Vrazo, Fuqua, & Kerr, 1986, Exp. 2), to reduce television viewing, and to increase the reading of school-age children (Wolfe, Mendes, & Factor, 1984), and to increase family socialization and interaction when families go out to eat (Green, Hardison, & Greene, 1984).

Athletic performance has been the focus of several studies. Feedback, modeling, and praise have improved the performance of athletes and increased the effectiveness of coaching. The acquisition of skills related to the sport of interest (e.g., executing football plays or engaging in exercises correctly) and the quality and speed of performance have been enhanced in applications to football, gymnastics, tennis, and track (e.g., Allison & Ayllon, 1980; Shapiro & Shapiro, 1985).

Overall, the above illustrations convey the breadth of behavioral applications. Some of these applications reflect areas of work that have not been within the traditional purview of psychological interventions. Indeed, these extensions have led to the emergence of new disciplines or subdisciplines or new areas of work in which behavioral techniques merge with other fields, as reflected in areas bearing such labels as behavioral medicine, behavioral pediatrics, behavioral ecology, and behavioral geriatrics.

LARGE-SCALE APPLICATIONS

Most applications of behavioral techniques have been on a relatively small scale, as reflected in programs designed for one or a few individuals. The focus on individuals is obviously essential when particular clients require special treatment programs. Similarly, many demonstrations have focused on small groups or intact units of individuals, such as students in a classroom, patients on a psychiatric ward, or youths in a facility for delinquents. This focus is also essential because effective interventions are needed for a wide range of populations in special settings. In the last several years, behavioral techniques have been applied on a much larger scale. The large-scale extensions have followed naturally from the promising evidence of the small-scale demonstrations. Many of the areas to which behavioral techniques have been extended are relevant to large segments of the population, such as the community at large.

Education

Perhaps the largest extensions of behavioral techniques have been in the schools. One program, referred to as Behavior Analysis, was developed for disadvantaged elementary school children (Bushell, 1978).[1] The program included over 7,000 children in approximately 300 classrooms (from kindergarten through third grade) in 15 cities throughout the United States. The program relied heavily on token reinforcement to promote academic performance. It also included several other components, such as instructing children in small groups within the class, using academic curricula that permitted evaluation of student progress, specifying performance criteria for teachers and students, and providing special training and feedback to teachers regarding their performance and the progress of their students. The gains in academic performance of students who participated in the program were markedly greater than the gains of students in traditional classrooms. Moreover, those gains were still evident two years after the program had been terminated and the children in the program had entered classrooms where token reinforcement was not in effect.

In other educational programs, behavioral techniques have been extended to encompass entire schools, entire school districts, or classrooms from several schools (e.g., Boegli & Wasik, 1978; Greenwood et al., 1987; Rollins, McCandless, Thompson, & Braswell, 1974; Thompson, Braswell, Persons, Tucker, & Rollins, 1974). Favorable results from these programs indicate that academic performance and classroom deportment can be altered in large-scale applications of behavioral techniques.

Delinquent Youths

Programs for delinquent youths have also been extended on a relatively large scale. Approximately 20 years ago, a behavioral program for predelinquents was developed in a single home-style setting in Kansas (Achievement Place). The program consists of several components, including a token economy managed by a well-trained couple (teaching parents), programs to train children in several skill areas, and procedures to help reintegrate children into the community (Kirigin, Braukmann, Atwater, & Wolf, 1982). Multiple studies demonstrated the effects of various reinforcement and punishment techniques in altering behaviors in the facility, at school, and in the community. The program has since been extended to over 150 group homes throughout the United States and a few foreign countries (Jones, Weinrott, & Howard, 1981).

Work-Site Applications

Many applications of behavioral techniques have focused on health-related behaviors such as alcohol consumption, cigarette smoking, weight control, and nutrition (see Brownell, 1982). Although most of these programs have been implemented with small numbers of individuals as part of a special treatment project, large-scale extensions have increased. For example, incentive programs have been implemented in industrial settings (e.g., Dow Chemical Company) to alter the cigarette smoking of hundreds of people (Danaher, 1980). The Dow Chemical program was initiated when the company discovered that it lost $500,000 because of missed workdays due to the illness of persons who smoked. Cigarette smokers were given the opportunity to win a large prize (a boat and motor worth $42,400) for each month of not smoking. Smaller incentives ($1 each week and the opportunity to win $50 quarterly) were also provided for nonsmoking. Four hundred employees participated in the program. After one year of the program, abstinence from smoking was reported for 75 percent of these employees. Several programs have been reported in which work sites were used as the basis for recruiting large numbers of clients to control diet, weight, and hypertension and to manage stress (Brownell, 1982).

LONG-TERM FOLLOW-UP

Apart from large-scale applications, the scope of behavioral interventions has changed in yet another way. When behavior modification first emerged as an area of study, the primary question was whether interventions could change behavior and whether behavioral changes were due to the specific procedures used. Small-scale projects were emphasized, and treatments were implemented and withdrawn in brief phases (as part of ABAB designs) to see whether the program was responsible for the changes. The preliminary work was restricted largely to the short-term effects of treatments.

Over the years, the efficacy of behavioral techniques for many problems has become firmly established. For example, to mention only two areas, hundreds of studies have demonstrated the ability to readily alter the adaptive and deviant behaviors of hospitalized psychiatric patients and the academic performance and deportment of children and adolescents in the classroom. The need no longer exists to show that behavioral interventions can produce change in these populations and settings. What is needed is evidence that long-term gains can be sustained.

Several programs have focused on long-term maintenance of changes and on the transfer (generalization) of treatment effects. For example, in a program for hospitalized psychiatric patients, mentioned previously, a token economy was used to develop a variety of adaptive behaviors on the ward, such as attending activities, engaging in self-care behaviors, or engaging in social interaction (Paul & Lentz, 1977). The effects of the program, relative to routine hospital care or milieu treatment (provided to other groups), were marked. Patients who participated in the token economy showed greater changes while in the hospital and greater rates of discharge. Moreover, the gains were evident from 1½ to 5 years after the patients had left the hospital. The impact of treatment on long-term maintenance is an important extension over previous work.

In school settings, the assessment of long-term effects has increased over the last several years with quite promising results. For example, the Behavior

Analysis program, already mentioned, indicated that the academic gains of elementary school students were maintained up to two years after the program had ended (Bushell, 1978). Similarly, in a junior high school program for adolescents with behavioral problems, token reinforcement led to reductions in expulsions, suspensions, and academic failure. At follow-up assessment three to four years later, gains were still evident (Heaton & Safer, 1982; Safer, Heaton, & Parker, 1981). Adolescents who participated in the program showed higher rates of entrance into high school and of school attendance, better classroom conduct, and lower rates of withdrawal from school, compared to adolescents who did not participate in the program.

Long-term follow-up has not always shown the continued benefits of behavioral treatment. For example, the Achievement Place program for delinquent youths has produced mixed results. The youths live in a home-style facility but continue to attend regular school and generally function in the community. Evaluation of the program has shown that while youths are in the facility, they show fewer contacts with police and the courts and higher rates of school attendance than those of delinquent youths who are on probation or who participate in traditionally managed settings (Kirigin, Wolf, Braukmann, Fixsen, & Phillips, 1979; Kirigin et al., 1982). Yet one to two years after treatment, rates of criminal offense and reinstitutionalization are not significantly better among Achievement Place youths than among youths who have received other types of programs.

Long-term effects have been more promising in applications of behavioral techniques with aggressive children who come to the attention of mental health professionals. For example, in one of the more carefully evaluated treatment programs for aggressive children, parents are trained to identify, define, and observe behavior; to administer praise, tokens, and mild forms of punishment; and to negotiate conflicts and contingency contracts (see Patterson, 1982). Several evaluations of the program have shown that it reduces deviant child behavior at home and at school to the level of normally functioning children and that the gains are maintained one year after treatment has been terminated (Fleischman, 1981; Patterson & Fleischman, 1979). These results are quite promising because severe aggressive behavior in children and adolescents has been resistant to most forms of psychological treatment (Kazdin, 1985b).

The above projects are significant because they address important problems in several applied areas. The work is especially noteworthy because it goes beyond demonstrating that behavior changes can be achieved. For the changes to be significant, evidence is needed that they can be maintained and that they enhance the long-term, everyday-life functioning of the persons who have achieved them.

SUMMARY AND CONCLUSION

The principles of operant conditioning describe relations between behavior and environmental events and hence should be generally applicable when there is interest in changing behavior. This does *not* mean that all behavior is the same, that behaviors in everyday life can be altered in a fashion identica! to the alteration of behaviors under laboratory control, or that all people are alike. Rather, the general applicability of the principles means that arranging antecedent and consequent events in a systematic way is likely to change behavior. Extended applications of behavior modification have been possible in large part because of its method of evaluating interventions. The assessment of behavior over time in many settings has permitted evaluation of interventions and their effects. The behavioral approach to problem identification and evaluation has helped translate significant problems into concrete behaviors that can be altered.

As is evident in the present chapter, behavioral techniques and evaluation approaches have been widely extended. The chapter covered a broad number of areas of application, but many of these areas were not covered in depth to convey the full range of applications and other areas (e.g., applications by the military or in college teaching) were omitted entirely. Among the areas illustrated in the present chapter were prevention of disease, eating disorders, pain control, adherence to medical regimens, seat belt use, dangerous situations for children, safety in business and industry, traffic control, energy conservation, littering in public places, waste recycling, and employment and job-related skills. Apart from the extension of behavioral techniques to many areas of everyday life, the characteristics of behavioral applications have changed in many ways. Although most behavioral programs have been small-scale demonstrations of what behavioral techniques can accomplish, an increasing number of them have been conducted on a large scale, especially in education, in facilities for delinquent youths, and at work sites. Another change has been the increased attention to long-term effects. Both large-scale applications and the long-term effects of behavioral programs are in need of much further attention, a point that will be raised in the next and final chapter.

NOTES

1. The program was part of Project Follow Through, a demonstration project that was designed to follow up the gains provided in an early, federally funded program, Head Start. Project Follow Through tested the effects of several types of educational programs, one of which was behavior analysis.

FOR FURTHER READING

Burgio, L. D., & Burgio, K. L. (1986). Behavioral gerontology: Applications of behavioral methods to the problems of older adults. *Journal of Applied Behavior Analysis, 19,* 321–328.

Geller, E. S., Winett, R. A., & Everett, P. B. (1982). *Preserving the environment: New strategies for behavior change.* Elmsford, NY: Pergamon Press.

Holroyd, K. A., & Creer, T. L. (Eds.). (1986). *Self-management of chronic disease: Handbook of clinical interventions and research.* New York: Academic Press.

Williamson, D. A. (1987). Recent advances in behavioral medicine. *Behavior Modification, 11,* 259–263.

Chapter Thirteen

Critical Issues and Future Directions

Previous chapters have presented different principles and techniques of behavior change and illustrated a wide range of applications. It should be evident that behavioral techniques have been effectively applied to many areas of functioning of children, adolescents, and adults. It is fairly safe to say that these techniques have been extended to more areas of human functioning than have any other approaches to therapy, education, or rehabilitation. However, behavioral techniques are not just a matter of applying techniques to behavior. There are a number of considerations related to how the behavioral approach is carried out and to the social, ethical, and legal context in which behavioral programs are conducted. The present chapter considers critical features of the behavioral approach, the social context in which behavioral techniques are administered, and directions for future work.

CRITICAL ELEMENTS OF THE BEHAVIORAL APPROACH

At first blush, the success of behavioral interventions might be considered a result of the generality of operant conditioning principles and of the techniques derived from them. Indeed, it is true that positive reinforcement, for example, has considerable generality and can be used to alter behavior in the laboratory or applied settings and among many infrahuman species and humans. However, there are other features that make pivotal contributions to the effectiveness of behavioral interventions. It is useful to consider critical elements of the behavioral approach at a somewhat higher level of abstraction. At this level, one can go beyond the specific principles and techniques and examine a few critical elements or steps underlying the approach. It is important to make these critical elements explicit because they account for the ability to extend behavioral techniques effectively to many novel areas of application.

Task Analysis

Description and Illustration.   A critical step in developing effective programs consists of identifying the precise behaviors that need to be assessed and that serve as the focus of the intervention. In many of the programs reviewed in previous chapters, one or two relatively simple target behaviors served as the focus. Yet the behavioral approach has been able to address complex sets of behaviors. Altering more complex sets of behaviors is facilitated by a process referred to as *task analysis*. Task analysis is a way of proceeding from the general goal of the program to a number of small, trainable, and highly concrete behaviors. The purpose of task analysis is to identify the specific behaviors that are required and to break down or divide a complex sequence of behaviors into component parts that can be trained.

A task analysis may be deceptively simple because the behaviors that are eventually selected may seem obvious and straightforward. The initial component of task analysis is to identify what the desired behaviors are. This component may follow from an evaluation of appropriate or competent behavior among persons who are performing well (Van Houten, 1979). Thus, if one wishes to develop social skills in a socially withdrawn or rejected child, an initial task is to examine the competent social behavior of children who are functioning well (i.e., are accepted or popular). Competent social behavior helps identify the terminal behaviors that are required. In some cases, the desired behaviors are identified by soliciting the input of persons who are in a special position because of their expertise. Such persons are consulted to identify what behaviors are to be performed or how they are to be performed. For example, developing a program of special practices to prevent disease or to detect a disease early may require soliciting the views of health experts. The behaviors they identify (e.g., methods to check oneself for early signs of disease) are translated into concrete behaviors that form the goals of the program.

However the requisite behaviors are identified, a critical component of task analysis is to specify those behaviors in small, trainable units. This component may be difficult, because there are no firm rules for determining how behaviors are to be divided or what units are trainable. Training may require smaller or larger units of behavior, depending on the initial levels of client skill or ability. Along with identifying the specific trainable components, the order or sequence of the behaviors needs to be specified. Training then proceeds to develop each individual component into the larger sequence until the entire set of behaviors has been trained.

Task analysis is nicely illustrated in a behavioral program for mentally retarded and physically handicapped adults (ages 19–33) who lived in federally subsidized apartments for handicapped persons (Williams & Cuvo, 1986). The adults selected for this project had failed to keep up (i.e., clean and take care of) their apartments and were therefore in danger of losing them. Indeed, these persons had already received fines and eviction had been threatened. In this project, the goal was to train them to keep up their apartments so as to meet the criteria invoked under their contracts.

The training focused on four areas—care of the refrigerator, the air-conditioning and heating unit, the electric range, and other appliances. Each of these areas was divided into a number of concrete behaviors. The behaviors were identified by consulting the appliance manuals, home maintenance texts, and housekeeping personnel of the housing project. Consider one of the areas of focus, care of the refrigerator. The investigators divided the task into 26 behaviors, listed in Table 13–1, that would satisfy the overall goal of properly caring for the refrigerator. Completing these behaviors would constitute appropriate cleaning and defrosting of the refrigerator. The list includes no unusual behaviors, given the demands of the task. Yet the detailed analysis of the task provides a critical condition for effective intervention. With the steps so carefully identified and described, the task of providing instructions (prompts) and reinforcement is greatly facilitated. In passing, it is important to note that the skills were effectively trained and were maintained when assessed 1½ years later. All of the participants passed inspection when governmental agencies checked their apartments almost two years after the training.

In a quite different focus, adult males (ages 25–35) were trained to examine themselves for signs of testicular cancer (Friman, Finney, Glasscock, Weigel, & Christophersen, 1986). Such self-examination is important because testicular cancer is the third leading cause of death of men ages 15–40. To train correct

TABLE 13–1   Task Analysis of Refrigerator Upkeep

1.   Open refrigerator door.

2.   Open freezer door.

3.   Determine whether or not the freezer requires defrosting (½ inch of ice or not). * If less than ½ inch of frost is present, close freezer and refrigerator door. If ½ inch or more frost is present, go on to Step 4.

4.   Turn temperature control dial to "off" position.

5.   Remove food from freezer compartment.

6.   Remove food from freezer tray.

7.   Set freezer to winter position.

8.   Optional: Remove food from refrigerator shelves.

9.   Secure refrigerator door open.

10.   Secure freezer door open (unless Step 13 is performed).

11.   Remove frost from freezer.

12.   Let the frost in the freezer melt into the freezer tray on its own or

13.   Place a pan of hot water in the freezer to speed melting.

14.   After all the frost has melted, wipe down the freezer, drying any water that is present.

15.   Remove freezer tray.

16.   Empty the freezer tray of any water that may have been collected.

17.   Wipe dry the freezer tray.

18.   Set freezer tray to summer position.

19.   Return freezer tray back to correct position.

20.   Replace food into freezer tray.

21.   Replace food into freezer.

22.   Replace food on refrigerator shelves.

23.   Return temperature control dial to the number 3–4 position.

24.   Shut freezer door.

25.   Shut refrigerator door.

26.   Allow to cool back down (one–two hours before reuse).

SOURCE: Williams, G. E., & Cuvo, A. J. (1986). Training apartment upkeep skills to rehabilitation clients: A comparison of task analytic strategies. *Journal of Applied Behavior Analysis, 19,* 39–52. Copyright 1986 by the Society for the Experimental Analysis of Behavior, Inc.

self-examination, it was first critical to identify precisely what behaviors were required. The list of required behaviors was obtained by discussing the task with urologists and by consulting written and film materials about testicular cancer. The specific behaviors that constitute appropriate self-examination are listed in Table 13–2. Again, careful identification of the requisite behaviors

TABLE 13–2   Tasks Required for Testicular Self-Examination

1. Gently pulls scrotum so that it hangs freely.

2. Uses fingers and thumbs of both hands to isolate and examine one testicle.

3. Locates the soft tender mass (the epididymis and spermatic cord) on top of and extending behind the testicle.

4. Rotates the entire surface area of the testicle between fingers and thumbs.

5. Uses fingers and thumbs to isolate and examine the other testicle.

6. Locates the soft tender mass on top of and extending behind the testicle.

7. Rotates the entire surface area of the testicle between fingers and thumbs.

SOURCE: Friman, P. C., Finney, J. W., Glasscock, S. G., Weigel, J. W., & Christophersen, E. R. (1986). Testicular self-examination: Validation of a training strategy for early cancer detection. *Journal of Applied Behavior Analysis, 19,* 87–92. Copyright 1986 by the Society for the Experimental Analysis of Behavior, Inc.

greatly facilitated evaluation of the program and effective training. Individuals were successfully trained in self-examination and reported continuing performance of the behaviors up to several months later.

In many behavioral applications, task analysis has been crucial in breaking down complex behaviors so that they can be assessed and trained. Task analyses have been extremely helpful in training persons in cardiopulmonary resuscitation (CPR) techniques to help revive individuals who have suffered a heart attack (Seaman, Greene, & Watson-Perczel, 1986), in teaching adults with a diagnosis of autism to purchase items in stores (Haring, Kennedy, Adams, & Pitts-Conway, 1987), in training persons with physical handicaps to use their hearing aids (Tucker & Berry, 1980), and in teaching persons to care for the physically handicapped (Neef, Parrish, Egel, & Sloan, 1986).

General Comments.   The persons who design behavioral interventions often do not have the expertise needed to identify the desired behaviors for a task analysis. To identify such behaviors, they may have to consult experts or other persons with special knowledge in specific areas. In the above examples, this was done to determine what behaviors were required for apartment upkeep and for correct self-examination for signs of testicular cancer. The task of the person designing the behavioral program is to translate into concrete steps and small units of behavior the larger goals or practices that have been identified.

A complexity of task analysis has to do with the degree of specificity of the individual behaviors and with the unit or amount of behavior that any one step should include. For some behaviors or clients, many small units of behavior may be grouped into one step in the task analysis; for other behaviors or clients, many more steps may have to be delineated and trained separately. As an example, training dressing skills might require different steps in a task analysis for severely retarded children than for nonretarded children. Division of the behavior into smaller units might facilitate training with the children functioning at a lower level. There are no firm guidelines for delineating the number of steps, but it is likely that the decision will be based on the complexity of the goal, the initial behaviors (baseline level) of the persons who are to be trained, and the speed with which the behaviors are acquired during training.

The effectiveness of behavioral interventions very much depends on identifying specific behaviors so that they can be assessed and trained. Once specific behaviors have been identified, they can often be changed. Many behavioral techniques (e.g., shaping, feedback, positive reinforcement) can readily alter the specific behaviors of interest and ensure performance of the desired sequence of responses. However, the initial task is careful identification and specification of the behaviors to be changed. The significance of this task is easily overlooked because it is much less dramatic than the techniques actually used to alter behavior.

Assessment and Evaluation

The effectiveness of behavioral techniques owes as much to the methods of assessment and evaluation as to the specific techniques that are used. Assessment in behavioral programs consists of direct measurement of the behaviors of interest. For example, if a task analysis reveals 10 different behaviors that constitute appropriate eating for severely retarded persons, appropriate job performance for factory workers, or appropriate study skills for college students with academic difficulties, the specific behaviors are measured directly.

Assessment of these behaviors is continued over time. Continuous assessment before, during, and after training is crucial to the approach (Kazdin, 1981a). Baseline assessment is essential to identify the level of functioning or performance prior to training. If training produces the desired changes, assessment will reveal a departure from baseline levels of performance. By observing performance during baseline and intervention phases, one can see clearly whether the intervention is having the desired effects. A major reason why behavioral techniques are so effective is that it is relatively easy to tell when a program is failing or is not working as well as desired.

As a hypothetical example, a behavioral program might reduce the rate of fighting of an aggressive child from 20 fights per day to 10 fights per day. A change of this magnitude is likely to be quite evident when graphed over time Yet the results would also convey that the program needs to be changed. For the program to be successful, virtual or complete elimination of fighting is required. The assessment provides essential *feedback* to the investigator about whether alternative techniques need to be pursued (Hayes & Nelson, 1986). Indeed, in many behavioral programs, the procedures designed to alter behavior were initially ineffective (see Kazdin, 1983). For example, defiant and aggressive child behavior in the home or at school is often unaffected by simply having parents or teachers praise appropriate child behavior (e.g., Wahler & Fox, 1980; Walker, Hops, & Greenwood, 1981). The undesired behavior may not decrease until mild punishment (time out, response cost) is added to the contingencies. The decision to alter the contingencies in these and many other applications was made possible by the data obtained through direct assessment of behavior. Clear information that an intervention is not working serves as a prompt for the therapist, trainer, or investigator to do something differently. For many other approaches to treatment, information about the impact of the intervention is either obtained after treatment has been completed or is not obtained at all. Consequently, one cannot alter treatment if it is not working.

A major difficulty with many approaches to education, therapy, and rehabilitation is that one cannot tell when programs are succeeding or failing (i.e., obtaining or not obtaining the goals) or falling somewhere in between. If one accepts for a moment the importance of continuous assessment to evaluate change, one can view the behavioral approach in a broader light. The approach does *not* require adherence to specific principles or techniques, such as those derived from operant conditioning. If one believes that a specific intervention can produce change, the method of behavior analysis can be used to test that intervention directly. Indeed, the behavioral approach to assessment and evaluation has been used to test such interventions as the effects of various medications on psychiatric problems, the impact of various foods on behavior, and various nonbehavioral approaches to psychotherapy (Kazdin, 1982c). It is this larger approach that needs to be more widely embraced, because it permits evaluation of the effectiveness of interventions.

Multicomponent Interventions

Behavioral programs are highly varied even when the same term (e.g., reinforcement program) is used in referring to them. For example, when investigators report the use of a token economy, the available variations and range of options can make the interventions in a given program quite different among different settings (Kazdin, 1977a). Nevertheless, in many of the extensions of behavioral techniques to novel areas of application, one can discern a distinct strategy for developing effective interventions.

In a significant proportion of behavioral programs, the intervention includes multiple components. Table 13–3 lists commonly used components and states the purposes toward which they are directed. The components address three facets of the contingency, namely antecedents, behaviors, and consequences. As a package, they focus on facets critical to the development of the target behavior (education, instructions, and modeling), correct execution and improved rendition of the target behavior (rehearsal, practice, and corrective feedback), and increased frequency or consistency of performance (reinforcement). These components in various forms have been used as a package in many studies, including studies designed to develop personal safety

TABLE 13–3   Components Commonly Used as Part of Behavioral Interventions in Applied Settings

Components of the Intervention	*Purpose*
Antecedents	
1. Education	Description of the behaviors and the rationale for their importance.
2. Instructions	Verbal or written prompts designed to describe the behaviors and the conditions and way in which they are performed.
3. Modeling	Visual prompt to illustrate how the behavior is to be performed and to direct attention to difficult or complex portions of the behavior; illustration of the sequence or order of several behaviors that go together.
Behavior	
4. Rehearsal and practice	Opportunities to perform the behavior, so that instructions (prompts), feedback, and reinforcement can be provided.
Consequences	
5. Feedback	Information designed to correct or improve portions of the behavior.
6. Reinforcement	Consequences to increase the frequency of performance of the behavior or to develop consistency of performance.

skills among children (Sowers-Hoag, Thyer, & Bailey, 1987), to train hospital staff to use behavioral techniques (Parsons, Schepis, Reid, McCarn, & Green, 1987), and to enhance conversational skills among nursing home residents (Praderas & MacDonald, 1986).

Using the multiple components together frequently leads to marked changes in behavior. However, after the intervention has shown an effect, it is not clear what aspect of the intervention was responsible for change or whether all of the components were necessary. In general, investigators who apply behavioral approaches are interested in developing strong or highly effective interventions that can be used in a variety of situations. The goal has been to obtain large changes in behavior and to maintain those changes over time. As a result, large multicomponent packages of treatment are often selected. There has been less interest in dissecting interventions by looking at the effects a program exerts with or without a particular component. In fact, several demonstrations are available that utilize only one or two of the components. For example, material reviewed in the chapters on reinforcement, punishment, and extinction illustrates procedures that do not involve multiple components. Thus, there is evidence regarding the impact of such isolated interventions as modeling, feedback, and social and token reinforcement. However, more comprehensive intervention packages combining different components are often used so as to maximize the likelihood of behavior change.

General Comments

Task analysis, assessment, and evaluation are central components of behavior analysis and contribute significantly to the demonstrated effectiveness of the approach. The special significance of these components is that they reflect a strategy that can be applied to evaluate a variety of interventions, whether or not the interventions are conceived as behavioral. This is important because the primary commitment of clinical or applied work is (or at least should be) to ameliorate significant problems (e.g., problem child behavior, academic deficiencies, depression, poor nutrition) and to improve client functioning, rather than to promulgate a specific approach (e.g., family, cognitive, or behavior therapy). Task analysis, assessment, and evaluation techniques provide a way of testing with individual clients and large groups of individuals whether an intervention designed to change behavior or some other facet of human functioning actually does so. Assessment and evaluation in particular can contribute to the selection of effective interventions, whether or not these interventions derive from behavioral principles.

THE SOCIAL CONTEXT OF TREATMENT

The approach toward intervening to change behavior refers to the manner of identifying behaviors and evaluating the impact of the intervention. Much broader considerations need to be taken into account in deciding what behaviors to alter, what techniques to use, and whether the outcomes attained are very important. The goal of clinical and applied research is not only to develop effective procedures but also to ensure that those procedures take into account the concerns of society and the concerns of the consumers of treatment (parents, teachers, clients). Three areas of social concern seem to be especially relevant in light of recent developments in behavior modification, namely the behaviors that serve as the focus of behavioral treatments, the social acceptability of the treatments used, and the utility or importance of the outcomes achieved.

Focus of Treatment

Considerable agreement exists regarding the goals of most therapeutic programs, whether or not they are behavioral programs. Thus, there is reasonable consensus that behavior change techniques should be applied to improve the academic behaviors of children who are doing poorly in school, to decrease the symptoms of depressed psychiatric patients, to eliminate the self-destructive behavior of autistic or mentally retarded children, to decrease antisocial behavior among delinquents, and to develop behaviors that prevent disease. In most instances, the focus of treatment does not raise major questions. However, situations occasionally arise that pose fundamental questions about the focus and social implications of treatment.

Social and moral questions about the focus of treatments can be illustrated in the controversy associated with the application of behavioral techniques to a boy named Kraig who engaged in cross-gender behaviors (Rekers & Lovaas, 1974). As noted previously (Chapter 2), Kraig, who was almost five years old, engaged in several feminine behaviors, including dressing up as a girl, playing with cosmetics, and showing pronounced feminine mannerisms, gestures, and gait. He mimicked subtle feminine behaviors of an adult woman. He also seemed to avoid masculine behaviors, and he constantly played with girls. Kraig's cross-gender behaviors appeared extreme, and they led to social isolation and ridicule. Also, because cross-gender behaviors in childhood are sometimes associated with sexual deviance in adulthood, the need to intervene seemed especially urgent. In any case, Kraig's parents sought treatment.

Rekers and Lovaas developed masculine behaviors such as playing with toys typical of little boys (e.g., soldiers, guns, airplanes), engaging in aggressive behaviors (e.g., playing cowboys and Indians, playing with a dart gun and a rubber knife), and dressing in masculine-typed clothes (e.g., army shirt, football helmet). Such behaviors as dressing in girls' clothes, playing with dolls, taking the role of the girl in games, and showing feminine gestures were decreased. In therapy sessions, Kraig's mother attended to his masculine behaviors and ignored his feminine behaviors; at home, his parents used token reinforcement to develop gender behaviors that were considered more sex appropriate. The program was very effective in altering Kraig's cross-gender behaviors, and 26 months after treatment, his sex-typed behaviors were considered to have become "normalized." Indeed, follow-up revealed not only the absence of pretreatment feminine behaviors but also expanded sex-role activities characteristic of boys (e.g., more rough-and-tumble play, interest in camping out).

Fundamental questions have been raised about the focus of this study (Nordyke, Baer, Etzel, & LeBlanc, 1977; Rekers, 1977; Winkler, 1977). Developing masculine behaviors explicitly adheres to social stereotypes about how little boys and girls and, later, men and women, should behave. Yet traditional sex-role behaviors may be questioned—they are not necessarily psychologically "healthy" or natural. Indeed, females who are high in femininity and males who are high in masculinity often show such characteristics as high anxiety, low self-esteem, and low social acceptance (Bem, 1975). Similarly, it has been found that the intelligence of children who show high sex-typed behaviors is lower than that of those whose behaviors are less sex-typed. The important point here is that fostering sex-typed behavior reflects a value stance and that the adjustment of the individual or the welfare of society may not necessarily be enhanced by stronger sex-typed behaviors.

On the other side of the issue, Rekers and Lovaas (1974; Rekers, 1977) noted that the severity of Kraig's cross-gender behavior, the possibility of his sexual deviance in adulthood, and his parents' concern over his social adjustment suggested the need to intervene. The issue extends beyond any particular case, and it raises questions about areas of treatment that are controversial and value laden. Scientific research cannot resolve the many questions that arise. For example, it is not known that children with cross-gender behaviors in fact later become deviant. If this were known, additional questions might be raised about whether the deviance (e.g., transvestism) would necessarily harm the individual or society. Obtaining informed consent from the persons involved in treatment does not resolve the problem, because neither the therapist nor the client (or his parents) can be truly informed. Insufficient information exists about the consequences of treating or failing to treat the problem, so the long-term risks and benefits of treatment cannot be known.

In other, albeit related areas of clinical interventions, issues have been raised about whether some behaviors should be treated at all. For example, Davison (1976) argued some years ago that treating homosexuality explicitly acknowledges sexual preferences for the same sex as a "problem." Yet the problem may not be sexual preferences per se, but adjusting to a world that has strong biases against homosexuality. Many homosexuals may be driven to treatment because of the tremendous pressures associated with staying in the "closet." Therapists are not apt to treat heterosexuals who wish to be homosexual or to expand their sexuality to include homosexual relations. So, it has been argued, perhaps homosexuals should not be treated for their sexual preferences. Independently of the stand that a particular person may take, this issue clearly illustrates the role that values may play in selecting target behaviors.

Concerns over the social value of target behaviors selected in behavioral and other forms of treatment arise with behaviors that may evoke fewer emotional responses than are evoked by sex-role behaviors and sexual preferences. For example, classroom applications of behavioral techniques frequently focus on making children well behaved, so that they remain in their seats, do not speak without permission, and attend to their lessons (Winett & Winkler, 1972). Most of these applications have not included especially deviant children who engaged in severely disruptive or dangerous behavior (e.g., hyperactivity, aggression). Yet, for many years, the focus on having mildly disruptive or inattentive children pay attention went unchallenged. A large number of investigations have since shown that improving attentiveness among students in the classroom does not improve academic performance. Perhaps proponents of behavior modification have been too apt to embrace goals selected by others—having "well-behaved and quiet children"—while neglecting major goals of education such as improved academic performance. A shift in the research focus in educational settings has shown that improving academic performance has frequently, as a side effect, improved classroom attentiveness and reduced disruptive behavior (Kazdin, 1981b). Thus, concerns that many teachers have about discipline can be remedied by improving academic behaviors. Unless severe behaviors are apparent, the focus on classroom deportment might be appropriately redirected to academic accomplishment.

In general, the focus of treatment needs to be given careful consideration. In fact, that focus may reflect priorities that are not necessarily in the best interests of the client or of society at large. The techniques used to alter behavior may be ethically neutral, in the sense that by themselves they do not necessarily dictate a target focus. Yet those techniques are invariably applied in situations in which a definite value structure is implicit. Recognition of the social context in which behaviors need to be developed is an important step in deciding how the techniques for altering behavior should be applied.

The value questions raised in connection with changing particular target behaviors have, of course, not been resolved. Yet some attention has been given to whether the target behaviors selected are important from the standpoint of the social context in which the individual functions. For example, Minkin et al. (1976) were interested in developing conversational skills in predelinquent girls. Any of a large number of skills might be trained to improve social interaction. What behaviors should be taught? To answer this question, the investigators first asked "normal" junior high school and college girls to converse to see how people without social skills problems interacted. Videotaped recordings of the conversations were made so that observers could examine social interaction. The investigators identified behaviors that seemed important in conversation, including providing positive feedback to another person, indicating that one understands what was said, asking questions for clarification, and talking for a longer time. Other college students and people from the community (e.g., a gas station attendant, homemakers) rated the tapes on the basis of how well they reflected overall conversational skills. The judges' ratings correlated with the specific behaviors identified as important by the investigators. Higher rates of performing those behaviors led to more positive evaluations of overall conversational skills.

The above procedures were completed to select the behaviors that might be relevant to teach the predelinquent girls whose conversational skills were deficient. The girls were trained using instructions, practice, feedback, and token reinforcement. At the end of training, the girls improved on the specific skills and judges' ratings of their conversation indicated that they were up to the average level of university and junior high school students in overall conversational ability.

Identifying behaviors that people in everyday life regard as important is referred to as *social validation* (Wolf, 1978). Social validation can refer to selecting behaviors that the social community regards as important or evaluating whether the changes achieved in treatment are important. In either case, the social context (consisting of evaluations of laypersons or others who may be in contact with the client) helps determine whether the focus or accomplishments of treatment are really important. Behavior modification techniques may be able to change a variety of behaviors, but which behaviors should be changed is usually a function of what people in everyday life identify as important. Increasingly, investigators are utilizing the evaluations of people in everyday life to determine the behaviors that need to be trained. While people in everyday life are not in a position to say what behaviors are "correct" or "healthy," their opinions often reflect behaviors that determine who is considered deviant or abnormal. With many populations, the goal is to return clients to the community. Adequate functioning in the community may mean developing behaviors that enable persons to adapt to their social situations.

Treatment Outcomes

The social context of behavioral treatment also arises in evaluating changes in performance. Although dramatic changes often result from behavioral interventions, it is still appropriate to ask whether the changes are really important and whether they make a difference in the lives of the clients. The social context in which the clients perform is an important consideration in answering these questions.

Normative Levels. As noted previously, social validation considers whether the amount of change achieved in treatment is important. One way to evaluate its importance is to determine whether it brings the client within the normal range of functioning, that is, to the levels of peers who have been identified as not showing problems that warrant treatment. For example, in one program, appropriate eating was developed in mentally retarded residents of a state hospital who seldom used utensils, constantly spilled food on themselves, stole food from others, and ate food previously spilled on the floor (O'Brien & Azrin, 1972). Using prompts, verbal praise, and food reinforcement, training increased the appropriate eating behaviors of these residents. Nevertheless, one can still ask whether the improvements achieved were really very important and whether the eating skills of the residents approached those of people regarded as normal in this regard. To address these questions, the investigators compared the eating habits of the group that received training with the eating habits of "normals." Observers recorded the eating behavior of customers in a local restaurant. The level of inappropriate eating behaviors is illustrated by the dashed line in Figure 13–1. Evidently, the level of inappropriate eating behaviors among the mentally retarded residents was even lower than the normal rate of inappropriate eating behaviors among people eating in a restaurant. Thus, the changes achieved with training brought the residents' eating behaviors to acceptable levels of people functioning in everyday life.

Several reports have evaluated whether the behaviors of deviant, socially disruptive, or withdrawn children, the behaviors of unassertive or shy adults,

FIGURE 13–1

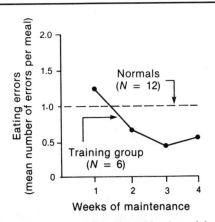

Mean number of improper responses per meal performed by the training group of retardates and the mean number of improper responses performed by normals.

SOURCE: O'Brien, F., & Azrin, N. H. (1972). Developing proper mealtime behaviors of the institutionalized retarded. *Journal of Applied Behavior Analysis, 5,* 389–399. Copyright 1972 by the Society for the Experimental Analysis of Behavior, Inc.

and the speech of psychiatric patients have been raised to the normative behavior levels of individuals functioning adequately in everyday life (Kazdin, 1977d). By comparing behavioral changes with the behavior levels associated with adequate functioning, behavior modification has relied increasingly on the social context to help determine whether treatment effects are beneficial.

Subjective Evaluations.   Another method for evaluating whether the behavior changes achieved are important is to ask people in contact with the client or in a position of expertise whether the changes have made a difference. For example, Jones, Kazdin, and Haney (1981a) trained children in correct responses to several emergency fire situations that can arise in the home. Sequences of emergency escape behaviors were trained by means of instructions, shaping, modeling, feedback, and reinforcement as the children practiced escape under simulated conditions. To measure whether the differences in the children's level of behavior before and after treatment were important, firefighters were asked to evaluate child behavior across various emergency situations. The firefighters rated the likely consequences that the baseline and trained levels of child performance would have in a real fire. They indicated that given trained rather than baseline levels of performance, the children were much less likely to be burned severely or to be burned to death in each of the emergency situations. Thus, performance after training was judged to have important consequences in emergency fire situations.

Most often, the outcomes of intervention programs are not a matter of life and death but a matter of degree. Determining whether these outcomes are important and make a difference requires fine distinctions and judgments of the client and others. As an illustration, a recent program focused on a college student named Steven who wished to eliminate two muscle tics (uncontrolled movements) (Wright & Miltenberger, 1987). The tics involved head movements and excessive eyebrow raising. Individual treatment sessions were conducted in which Steven was trained to monitor and identify when the tics occurred and in general to be more aware of their occurrence. In addition, he self-monitored the tics throughout the day. Assessment sessions were conducted in which he read at the clinic or the college library and observers recorded the tics. The impact of self-monitoring and awareness training procedures was evaluated in a multiple-baseline design in which the two muscle tics were focused on in sequence. As shown in Figure 13–2, both of the tics declined in frequency when treatment was applied.

A central question is whether the reduction was very important or made a difference to either Steven or others. At the end of treatment, Steven's responses to a questionnaire indicated that he was no longer distressed by the

FIGURE 13–2

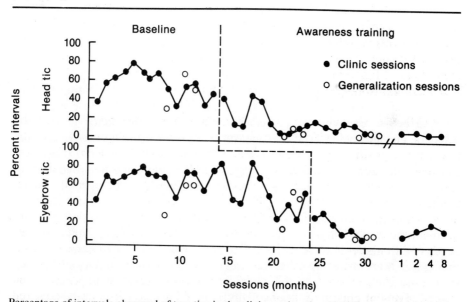

Percentage of intervals observed of two tics in the clinic sessions in which Steven sat and read for 25-minute periods and in generalization sessions (various places in the college library). Observers recorded the tics in these sessions across baseline and treatment phases.

SOURCE: Reprinted with permission from *Journal of Behavior Therapy and Experimental Psychiatry, 18,* 269–274. Wright, K. M., & Miltenberger, R. G. Awareness training in the treatment of head and facial tics. Copyright 1987, Pergamon Press, Inc.

tics and that he felt that they were no longer very noticeable to others. In addition, four observers rated randomly selected pretreatment and posttreatment videotapes. These were videotapes of assessment periods in which direct observations had been made of Steven's tics. The observers rated the tics from the posttreatment tapes as not at all distracting, normal to very normal in appearance, and small to very small in magnitude. In contrast, they rated the tics from the pretreatment tapes as much more severe on these dimensions. The observers were then told which videotapes were the posttreatment tapes and were asked to report how satisfied they would have been if they had achieved the same results. All of the observers reported that they would have been satisfied with the treatment results. The evaluations from Steven and independent observers help attest to the importance of the changes achieved and provide information that cannot readily be discerned from the reductions graphed from direct observations.

Subjective evaluations of treatment effects have been used to assess whether improvements in the writing skills of children are reflected in ratings of the creativity or interest value of their compositions, whether individuals who have been trained in public speaking skills are evaluated more positively by their audiences, and whether people in contact with deviant children see their behaviors differently after treatment (see Kazdin, 1977d). Although the opinions of others in contact with clients do not necessarily reflect actual changes in performance, such opinions are important as a criterion in their own right because they often serve as a basis for seeking treatment in the first place and because they typify the evaluations that the clients will encounter after leaving treatment.

Social Impact Measures.   Measures of social impact are another type of measure that helps to socially validate treatment outcomes. These measures refer to behaviors evident in everyday life and of importance to parents, teachers, and society at large. The measures are often gross indexes of change. For example, social impact measures for programs designed to improve academic functioning, to decrease aggressive behavior, and to prevent coronary illness might be school grades, arrest records, and mortality rates, respectively.

Consider a behavioral program that is designed to train social skills in a shy and withdrawn child. Training may develop such behaviors as maintaining eye contact with the trainer, improving on nonverbal indexes of attentiveness, asking questions of the other person, and manifesting other conversational and interpersonal skills that a task analysis may have revealed as important. The effects of training may be dramatically evident in, say, a multiple-baseline design across behaviors or situations. The importance of the changes achieved can be established by assessment of normative levels of functioning or by subjective evaluation, as discussed previously. Yet another way would be to see whether the changes are reflected on impact measures of significance to parents and teachers. For example, after training, does the child participate in more activities with other children or invite friends home, and is he or she welcomed by others? Such measures are often regarded as the "bottom line" by consumers of treatment (i.e., those who request and pay for treatment). A measure of the social impact of treatment, or measures significant to consumers of treatment, can socially validate intervention effects.

Social impact measures have often been used in behavioral approaches. For example, in studies that improve safety practices in business and industry, the benefits are often reflected in the number of injuries and accidents (Fox, Hopkins, & Anger, 1987). Similarly, efforts to alter the habits of drivers have not only reduced speeding, the target behavior of interest, but are also reflected in reductions in accidents (Van Houten, Malenfant, & Rolider, 1985). In these studies, injuries and accidents are measures of obvious social importance.

Measures of social impact raise special problems. The measures often rely on records of various agencies (e.g., schools, the courts) that are often collected inconsistently (Kazdin, 1979b). Also, the measures may "miss" a great deal of important behavior. For example, any program designed to reduce delinquent behavior might measure the arrest record of a child or adolescent or the extent to which a child or adolescent has contact with the police or the courts. Yet the police often do not count all of their contacts with youths, and even if they do, most delinquent acts are not detected by them (Empey, 1982). Consequently, their records cannot be expected to measure change accurately. Nevertheless, social impact data are a useful means of seeing whether the improvements identified on specific behaviors are reflected directly on measures of primary interest to consumers of treatment and society at large. When such measures show a change, they convey important evidence that the impact of an intervention was socially important.

Treatment Techniques

The selection of target behaviors and the evaluation of treatment outcome are not the only areas in which the social context is relevant. The techniques that can be used to alter behavior must consider people's opinions about what is appropriate and what should be done. It may be of little use to develop effective treatments if the procedures are highly objectionable to the people who need them (e.g., parents, teachers, clients) or to the people for whom they will be used (e.g., children, patients).

Recently, attention has been given to the public reaction to the procedures used in treatments and to whether treatments are viewed as acceptable ways of changing behavior. The notion of *treatment acceptability* refers to judgments by laypersons, clients, and others of whether treatment procedures are appropriate, fair, and reasonable for the problem that is to be treated. There are a number of reasons for the interest in the acceptability of treatment. One reason is that client rights are protected if institutional review committees, laypeople, and clients themselves evaluate whether proposed treatment procedures are acceptable in light of the client's problem. A second reason is that procedures need to be designed that are not only effective but also desirable or preferred among alternative treatments that might produce change.

Moreover, treatment acceptability is likely to relate to adherence to procedures. Clients and therapists are more likely to carry out treatments that they view as highly acceptable. In outpatient treatment, clients are more likely to remain in treatment if the procedures used are palatable or positive. Indeed, aversion techniques often have high dropout rates, presumably because the techniques, even if effective, are not very acceptable.

Research has examined how people evaluate treatment and whether treatment procedures are acceptable. For example, in one project, young psychiatric inpatients, their parents, and hospital staff were asked to evaluate several procedures that were applied to children (hypothetical cases) for highly deviant and disruptive behavior at home and at school (Kazdin, French, & Sherick, 1981). The procedures were described in detail and the subjects rated the extent to which the different treatments were consistent with commonly held notions of what treatment should be, whether the treatments were fair or cruel, whether the treatments were appropriate for clients who could not give consent, and so on. Marked differences among the treatments were shown in a measure that assessed the overall acceptability of treatment. The children, parents, and staff agreed in their ordering of treatments. A reinforcement technique (in which appropriate behavior was reinforced as a way of reducing inappropriate behavior) was evaluated as much more acceptable than the alternative treatments. Time out (involving 10 minutes of isolation) was rated as the least acceptable treatment. Positive practice and medication to control disruptive behavior were intermediate in overall acceptability.

Evaluations of acceptability can be useful in choosing among variations of the same type of treatment. It may be that alternative versions of a treatment that are likely to be similar in their effectiveness vary widely in their acceptability to consumers. For example, several versions of time out from reinforcement are available, including variations that do not remove the person from the situation. Variations of time out that remove the individual from the situation may not be any more effective than those that do not. However, people tend to view time out without isolation as a much more acceptable treatment (Foxx & Shapiro, 1978; Kazdin, 1980c; Porterfield, Herbert-Jackson, & Risley, 1976). Apart from variations of a given technique, specific characteristics of a given treatment have been examined. From such evaluations, we have learned that acceptability of treatment is influenced by a number of factors such as whether the client is involved in planning the program; the adverse side effects of treatment; the age, sex, and race of the child; and whose opinion about treatment is solicited (e.g., parent versus child) (Elliott, 1988; Kazdin, 1980b, 1980c, 1981c).

People's views of treatment acceptability probably depend on many factors such as how it is applied, who applies it, the severity of the problem, and the number of alternative treatments that have been tried. It is important to understand the factors that influence acceptability so that procedures incorporating the factors that potential consumers see as important can be developed and so that effective procedures can be presented to consumers in clinically sensitive ways. Recent studies have suggested that procedures known to be effective in changing behavior can be made more acceptable to consumers by efforts to describe the procedures better or by including positive reinforcement in programs designed to reduce behavior (Mudford, 1987; Singh & Katz, 1985). These studies suggest that views of the acceptability of treatment can be influenced both by variations in procedures and by the manner in which procedures are presented.

Traditionally, treatment techniques have been evaluated by looking at how effective they are on various measures of personality and behavior. Obviously, the effectiveness of a treatment is extremely important. However, treatments, whether behavioral or nonbehavioral in orientation, need to be evaluated along many dimensions (Kazdin & Wilson, 1978; Strupp & Hadley, 1977). Some of these dimensions reflect broader concerns than the extent of therapeutic improvement for a particular client. Client evaluations of procedures, the ease of implementing techniques, the costs of treatment, and similar considerations illustrate the expanded criteria that are being used to evaluate treatment. Within behavior modification, the criteria include concerns about the importance of the changes achieved as well as consumer satisfaction with the treatments themselves and how they are conducted.

THE ETHICAL AND LEGAL CONTEXT

Several ethical and legal issues must also be taken into account in designing and implementing interventions. Most of the ethical and legal issues associated with treatment apply broadly across disciplines (e.g., psychology, psychiatry, social work, counseling) and treatment approaches (e.g., family, humanistic, and other approaches). A few such issues have been raised in relation to behavioral techniques. These issues are highlighted here.

Behavior Control and Individual Freedom

The behavioral approach represents explicit attempts to alter specific behaviors in the context of education, treatment, rehabilitation, or everyday life. The focus on behavior and behavior change may raise special concerns about efforts to "control" people. The very term *behavior modification* may imply efforts to control, manipulate, or otherwise tinker with other people's lives. Indeed, the term, rather than the procedures it describes, is what seems to evoke negative reactions (Kazdin & Cole, 1981; Woolfolk, Woolfolk, & Wilson, 1977).

There are no inherent or unique control issues raised by behavioral techniques that are not also raised by other approaches to treatment. Behavioral techniques do not necessarily embrace particular goals or an agenda for changing society. The issue relevant to behavioral interventions is not "control'' or the dictating of objectives but the bearing of behavioral interventions on the many goals of individuals, families, and society at large. Obvious examples of such goals are the education of young people, the minimization of crime, and the prevention of disease. The issue is whether behavioral or other forms of intervention can contribute something to facilitate the achievement of these goals. For example, in classroom settings, many of the attempts of teachers to control student behavior are based on corporal and verbal punishment. The issue here is not whether child behavior should be controlled to achieve certain goals. The goals of improved academic performance, appropriate classroom behavior, and increased enjoyment of specific activities such as reading are widely agreed upon. The issue is whether behavioral interventions have anything to offer that will improve attainment of these goals. Techniques discussed in previous chapters, especially those based on positive reinforcement, appear to offer means that can greatly improve upon many of the techniques ordinarily used in everyday life (e.g., lectures, pleas, repeated instructions, threats, verbal and physical punishment).

Behavioral principles and techniques do not argue for a particular way of life or particular goals. Indeed, the same principles and techniques have been applied to quite different styles of living. For example, behavioral principles and techniques have been applied to communal living. Twin Oaks is a small community in Virginia that has been developed on the basis of operant conditioning principles and specific practices outlined in *Walden Two* (Skinner, 1948). The community, begun in 1967, is organized on the basis of a token economy in which credits are earned for performing the work and activities that the community requires in order to function. The lifestyle of the community embraces such values as sharing of assets, individual autonomy, and self-government in a way different from that of mainstream community life (Kinkade, 1973). But behavioral principles and techniques can also be used by individuals as part of self-control techniques for advancing personal rather than communal goals. In general, the goals of professionals concerned with the welfare of individuals is to increase effective living, personal choices, and freedom from behaviors that may restrict functioning in everyday life. The goals of behavior modification do not differ from the goals of other approaches to the welfare of individuals.

Misuse of Reinforcement and Aversive Techniques

Reinforcement and aversive techniques can include many practices for altering behavior. It is not difficult to conceive of ways of misusing these techniques under the guise of laudatory purposes.

Contingent Consequences and Environmental Restraint.   A basic feature of behavior modification programs is the contingent delivery of reinforcing events to alter behavior. The potential for abuse in withholding reinforcers (e.g., food, activities) is readily conceivable. There are multiple sources for the protection of clients with whom such abuses might be practiced. Within the "helping" professions (such as psychology, psychiatry, social work, and counseling), various ethical codes are designed to protect the rights of clients. In addition, legal decisions have helped clarify the rights of the clients who are most vulnerable to abusive conditions.

Separate legal decisions have held that involuntarily confined populations such as psychiatric patients, mentally retarded persons, and institutionalized delinquents have the right to a variety of events and activities. For example, they have the right to receive nutritionally balanced meals, to receive visitors, to sleep in a comfortable bed, to be given a place for their clothes, to engage in regular exercise, and to watch television (see Martin, 1975). As a rule, these basic events and activities cannot be used as reinforcers and made contingent upon behavior. However, this has not interfered with the development of effective programs. Reinforcement programs for involuntarily confined individuals can provide back-up events beyond those to which these individuals are entitled by right and which the setting normally provides. In such instances, use is generally made of token economies in which a large number of back-up events are provided, including *extra* privileges and activities and access to a store where tokens can purchase diverse items (e.g., Paul & Lentz, 1977).

Most applications of behavioral techniques are made in cases where issues of constitutional and legal rights are not raised. For example, adults in their own behalf and in their children's behalf often seek treatment and agree to and help design the program that will be used in treatment, and they reserve the right to change their minds. In such cases, the participants provide their consent to engage in treatment. Other protections of the client, noted later, are aimed at ensuring that the program will not misuse contingent events.

Use of Aversive Techniques. Behavior modification relies much more heavily on positive reinforcement than on negative reinforcement and punishment. Yet the punishment techniques of behavior modification have come under judicial review. Actually, the courts had been evaluating punishment long before the development of behavior modification, because physical restraint, corporal punishment, and inhumane conditions were often used under the guise of treatment or rehabilitation. The courts seek to protect individuals from "cruel and unusual" punishment, as specified by the Eighth Amendment of the U.S. Constitution.

Most of the judicial rulings on punishment do not apply to the procedures used in behavior modification, because the more dramatic and intrusive forms of punishment, such as chaining individuals or beating them, have never been part of the behavioral techniques. However, it is important to consider the judicial rulings on punishment procedures that may be a part of behavior modification. Court decisions reached about punishment, of course, depend heavily on the specific procedures that are used. Obviously, the considerations governing a few minutes of isolation (one form of time out) differ from those governing electric shock or very long periods of isolation. Indeed, the courts have ruled that extended periods of isolation are not permissible and that during brief periods of isolation the clients must have adequate access to food, lighting, and sanitation facilities (*Hancock v. Avery*).

Electric shock is rarely used as a punishing event, but the courts have delineated rather clear restrictions governing its use. For example, in one decision (*Wyatt v. Stickney*), shock was restricted to extraordinary circumstances, such as when a client is engaging in self-destructive behavior that is likely to inflict physical damage. Moreover, shock should be applied only when another procedure has been used unsuccessfully, when a committee on human rights within the institution has approved of the treatment, and when the client or a close relative has consented to its use. The fact that the courts permit the use of mild shock under any circumstances probably reflects their recognition that the procedure can permanently eliminate a behavior (e.g., self-injurious acts) after only a few applications.

The courts have not addressed most of the forms of punishment that are currently used in behavior modification, but some court rulings have focused on punishments that bear a resemblance to behavioral techniques. Isolation or seclusion, for example, resembles time out from reinforcement. However, several characteristics of time out make it different from the punishments that the courts consider. In particular, the brevity of time out (one minute to a few minutes), the multiple variations of the time-out procedures (e.g., with and without isolation), the procedures used during the "time in" period (e.g., reinforcement of positive behaviors), and the settings in which time out is usually applied (e.g., classroom, home) make the time out from reinforcement quite different from the isolation and seclusion considered by the courts. Many other behavioral procedures, such as overcorrection, positive practice, and response cost (all of which are in relatively common use), are not considered by the courts. These procedures are for milder forms of punishment than the types of aversive interventions that have come before the courts.

Protection of Client Rights

Many ethical and legal issues arise in any form of treatment, particularly treatment for clients who are involuntarily confined. Consequently, a number of safeguards have emerged to protect client rights, including international codes and national guidelines to cover clinically relevant research (see Kazdin, 1978). In addition, organizations of professionals involved in clinical research have generally provided guidelines. The full range of regulations, codes, and guidelines is too extensive to review here, but a few of the sources of protection warrant mention.

One set of guidelines that has been offered raises a number of questions that therapists (or persons who design and implement the program) should adequately address prior to implementing therapy. The questions, which appear in Table 13–4, are intended to ensure that the procedures are appropriate and that the client (or guardian) is fully aware of the intervention. These

TABLE 13–4   Ethical Issues for Human Services: Selected Questions to Guide Professional Practice

The questions related to each issue have deliberately been cast in a general manner that applies to all types of interventions, and not solely or specifically to the practice of behavior therapy. Issues directed specifically to behavior therapists might imply erroneously that behavior therapy was in some way more in need of ethical concern than non-behaviorally oriented therapies.

In the list of issues the term *client* is used to describe the person whose behavior is to be changed, and *therapist* is used to describe the professional in charge of the intervention; *treatment* and *problem,* although used in the singular, refer to any and all treatments and problems being formulated with this checklist. The issues are formulated so as to be relevant across as many settings and populations as possible. Thus, they need to be qualified when someone other than the person whose behavior is to be changed is paying the therapist, or when that person's competence or the voluntary nature of that person's consent is questioned. For example, if the therapist has found that the client does not understand the goals or methods being considered, the therapist should substitute the client's guardian or other responsible person for "client," when reviewing the issues below.

A. Have the goals of treatment been adequately considered?
B. Has the choice of treatment methods been adequately considered?
C. Is the client's participation voluntary?
D. When another person or an agency is empowered to arrange for therapy, have the interests of the client been sufficiently considered?
E. Has the adequacy of treatment been evaluated?
F. Has the confidentiality of the treatment relationship been protected?
G. Does the therapist refer the clients to other therapists when necessary?
H. Is the therapist qualified to provide treatment?

SOURCE: Association for Advancement of Behavior Therapy. (1977). Ethical issues for human services. *Behavior Therapy, 8,* v–vi. Copyright 1977 by the Association for Advancement of Behavior Therapy. Reprinted by permission of the publisher and the author.

guidelines are not directed specifically toward behavior modification procedures, because behavior change procedures in general, whether behavioral or not, raise similar ethical issues. The questions are intended to guide those who implement any form of psychological treatment.

Apart from legal statutes and professional guidelines, other means aid in the protection of client rights. Clients or individuals acting in their behalf (e.g., parents) must provide *informed consent*. Informed consent refers to agreement to the intervention and to the conditions under which the intervention is provided. For consent to be informed, the individual must be competent to make rational decisions, must understand the intervention and the available options, and must act without duress. The issues of consent have been raised most frequently with involuntarily confined persons (e.g., hospitalized psychiatric patients). The purpose of informed consent is to ensure understanding of and agreement with the procedures. Individuals in treatment can revoke their consent at any time.

In addition to requiring consent, institutions that provide treatment or rehabilitation services have institutional review boards that consider the procedures being proposed for treatment. These boards may include experts in the area of treatment as well as lawyers and laypersons who provide different perspectives regarding controversial applications of treatment. Many, if not most, of the procedures applied are considered standard and need not undergo special review. However, special procedures (e.g., aversive consequences) or applications involving special populations that cannot act on their own behalf (e.g., children) are reviewed routinely to ensure that individual rights are protected.

Another means of protecting individual rights is the use of a contractual arrangement between the therapist and the client. A behavioral contract is used whenever possible to involve all of the parties that are included in the program. The contract can make explicit the goals of treatment, the procedures that will be used, and the likely risks and benefits. A useful feature of a contract is that it enables the client and his or her guardians to negotiate the final goals of treatment. Active client participation in the design of treatment is likely to make treatment fairer than it would be if treatment were unilaterally imposed on the client. Including the client in the development of the contract may have manifold benefits, such as making the treatment more acceptable and fostering communication (negotiation) between the parties involved (e.g., parent and child, spouses) (cf. Barbrack & Maher, 1984; Kazdin, 1980b).

CURRENT ISSUES AND FUTURE DIRECTIONS

Extensions of behavioral techniques to a wide array of populations, efforts to implement behavioral programs on a relatively large scale, and evidence for the long-term effects of treatment suggest that behavioral techniques may be effective in addressing multiple personal and social problems. The evidence attesting to the effectiveness of behavioral techniques in many areas of treatment, rehabilitation, and education is truly impressive. Yet the accomplishments of these techniques need to be viewed in perspective.

Limitations of the Approach

Behavioral techniques do not always achieve the desired outcomes, even in reasonably well circumscribed situations (e.g., the home or classroom) in which many contingencies can be carefully implemented and closely monitored. Behavioral techniques bring to bear important influences, such as various positive reinforcers. When these events are administered in special ways (e.g., immediately after behavior, on a continuous or rich reinforcement schedule, and contingent upon behavior), behavior changes are often dramatic.

Yet limitations should be expected in the effects that are produced. Antecedent events (e.g., prompts) or consequences (e.g., reinforcers) do not exhaust the range of the factors that influence normal and maladaptive behavior. The expansion of behavioral techniques to include cognitive events (self-statements, imagery) enhances the potential of treatment by increasing the range of the influences that can be brought to bear to produce therapeutic change. But even the addition of cognitive and environmental influences does not exhaust the range of the factors that control behavior. Biological predispositions (e.g., temperament), genetic endowment, and environmental factors that usually cannot be controlled in treatment (e.g., family living conditions, maladjustment of parents) may delimit the types of effects that any treatment can achieve. Thus, no single set of interventions can be expected to invariably solve the clinical and other problems to which it is applied.

As an example of the range of influences, consider the problems of antisocial behavior in children. Serious antisocial behaviors in children (aggression, stealing, tantrums, destructiveness, lying and related behaviors) is influenced by harsh child-rearing practices, serious psychological dysfunction (depression, antisocial behavior, alcoholism) in the parent(s), child temperament, genetic endowment, and many other factors (see Kazdin, 1987a). These and other influences do not invariably determine that a child will become antisocial, but they increase the risk that serious antisocial behavior will develop. Training parents in behavioral techniques (parent management training) has been one of the most effective interventions for treating antisocial children (Patterson, 1982). Yet it would be quite understandable if changing parent-child interaction and altering the contingencies of reinforcement in the home did not totally eliminate the problems of such children. Antisocial behavior seems to be influenced by many factors other than the reinforcement contingencies in the home. Indeed, parent management training has been very effective in some applications but has produced mixed effects in others (see Kazdin, 1987b). Although further improvements in treatment are likely to be made, the complexity of the problem of child antisocial behavior and the number of factors that influence such behavior will probably continue to present obstacles to any treatment approach.

In general, the effects of behavioral techniques have been quite effective in altering a number of behaviors in the context of clinical treatment and of extensions to society. The influences of these techniques on behavior extend beyond the current contingencies of reinforcement. This does not mean that altering the contingencies will be ineffective. However, it does mean that limitations in the effects of any approach to intervention may be expected.

Program Failures

In many applications, behavioral problems may initially fail to achieve the desired changes in behavior. The conclusion reached may be that behavior modification "does not work" or that the procedures "do not really apply" to this client. As a general and quite tentative rule, the less experience one has with behavioral techniques, the more likely one is to conclude that a program does not work. This may well reflect a bias against admitting failure among proponents of behavior modification. Yet in several instances in which the issue of program failure arises, an alternative explanation seems quite plausible.

For example, parents who are learning behavioral techniques for managing their children invariably note that these techniques are not new and that they have been using the techniques all along. They often claim that their use of reinforcement (praise or allowance) or time out (sending the child to his or her room) has not worked. Parents are usually correct in this claim. However, careful inquiry or direct observation of their behavior in the home reveals that the procedures they have tried are not even close approximations of the ways in which reinforcing and punishing consequences are applied in behavioral programs. For example, parents often say that they have used reinforcement to alter behavior but that it has not helped. However, positive reinforcers need to be administered immediately after behavior, on a continuous or close to continuous schedule, and contingent upon performance. As important, the target behaviors need to be carefully specified, so that reinforcement can be applied consistently and the results measured to see whether the program is having impact. Once these and related conditions (e.g., use of prompts, shaping) are faithfully observed, one may be in a better position to say that the procedures have not worked.

In many applications of behavioral techniques in which the contingencies *are* implemented correctly, the programs may fail to achieve the desired changes. Here too one is tempted to conclude immediately, but perhaps mistakenly, that behavioral techniques do not work. Interestingly, several studies have shown that slight modifications in the program when clients have failed to respond (using some of the techniques discussed in Chapter 8) often produce the desired behaviors (Kazdin, 1983). Thus, an initial judgment that treatment has failed may be controverted by additional applications of treatment and additional evaluations of progress. For example, defiant and aggressive child behavior in the home or at school is often unaffected by simply having parents praise appropriate child behavior (Herbert et al., 1973; Wahler & Fox, 1980; Walker et al., 1981). The undesired behaviors may not decrease until mild punishment (response cost, time out) is added to the contingencies. Such demonstrations illustrate the importance of carefully evaluating the effects of treatment, so that the therapist or trainer can determine when other procedures are needed to produce the desired outcomes.

A related point that warrants mention pertains to how behavioral techniques are implemented. The principles of reinforcement, punishment, and extinction and the techniques derived from those principles are relatively simple. However, considerable skill is required to implement the techniques so as to attain the desired outcomes. The techniques need to be implemented systematically and consistently and with knowledge of the factors that influence their effects. Many successful programs have devoted considerable attention to ensuring that behavior change agents (parents, teachers, hospital staff) are well trained. Once these change agents have been trained, their behaviors are often monitored carefully to ensure that the contingencies are carried out correctly (e.g., Bushell, 1978; Patterson, 1982; Paul & Lentz, 1977). The importance of training behavior change agents and monitoring their execution of behavioral techniques has been learned from repeated demonstrations that without such training and monitoring, programs often deteriorate or simply fail outright (Bassett & Blanchard, 1977; McLaughlin et al., 1983; Scheirer, 1981). What distinguishes behavior modification techniques from everyday uses of reward and punishment is *how* the techniques are applied and evaluated. The successful applications illustrated throughout this book depend on very careful implementation and evaluation of behavioral techniques.

Extensions of Behavioral Techniques

Extrapolation from present work in behavior modification suggests that the focus of treatments will continue to expand. Over the brief history of behavior modification as a formal movement, the trend toward an expanding focus can be readily identified. In early applications beginnning over 30 years ago, behavioral techniques were directed primarily to special populations such as psychiatric patients, the mentally retarded, autistic children, and delinquents. Applications with these populations have continued by extending the range of the techniques and target behaviors studied and by extending the duration of treatment effects. In the last decade, additional populations and settings have been investigated. Prominent examples include the applications of behavioral techniques to medical problems, geriatric populations, and business and industry.

Current work points toward continued expansion of applications in several directions. First, behavioral techniques are being increasingly applied to behavior in everyday life. At one level, such techniques are being used to deal with social and community problems (e.g., crime, energy conservation) whose solution can affect the quality of life for society as a whole. At another level, they are increasingly available to help people improve the quality of their personal lives.

Second, large-scale applications are likely to continue in the foreseeable future. Applications to deal with social problems at the level of community, city, state, and country may raise concerns about attempts to control behavior and dictate goals to others. Efforts to regulate many behaviors are already being made. Behavioral techniques may be valuable in increasing the effectiveness of efforts to encourage behaviors that have been identified as desirable (e.g., encouraging parents to obtain vaccinations for their children, encouraging children to eat well-balanced meals, and encouraging people not to drive when intoxicated).

Finally, for several years, further attention is likely to be devoted to the dissemination of current findings on behavioral techniques and their application. Identification of effective interventions is an obviously important step, but by itself is not enough. A major task is to disseminate what has been learned, so that treatments can be more widely applied. There have been efforts to disseminate techniques that have been shown to be effective. For example, books and manuals have been prepared for parents and teachers to help them learn behavioral techniques and apply them at home and in school (e.g., Azrin & Foxx, 1974; Blechman, 1985; Clark, 1985; Forehand & McMahon, 1981). Also, behavioral programs for the treatment of psychiatric patients and delinquent youths have been disseminated to facilities other than those in which they were originally developed (see Bacher, Liberman, & Kuehnel, 1986). The obstacles to disseminating behavioral procedures are quite formidable. Among the obstacles are the difficulty of integrating new procedures within institutional structures (e.g., hospitals) that are hard to penetrate and the difficulty of ensuring that the procedures, if adopted, are implemented correctly.

Efforts to disseminate current findings do not mean that all of the questions regarding behavioral techniques have been answered or that the most effective approaches are known. Yet there are large numbers of people with behavioral problems for which effective treatments have already been identified and many everyday behaviors whose alteration could have a significant impact on education, interpersonal relations, health, and other areas. A source of frustration is the failure to disseminate current techniques widely. However, only recently has there been an accumulation of scientific knowledge about effective practices that warrant widespread dissemination.

FOR FURTHER READING

Baer, D. M., Wolf, M. M., & Risley, T. R. (1987). Some still-current dimensions of applied behavior analysis. *Journal of Applied Behavior Analysis, 20,* 313–328.

Franks, C. M. (Ed.). (1984). *New developments in behavior therapy: From research to clinical application.* New York: Haworth Press.

Hopkins, B. L. (1987). Comments on the future of applied behavior analysis. *Journal of Applied Behavior Analysis, 20,* 339–346.

Kunkel, J. H. (1987). The future of JABA: A comment. *Journal of Applied Behavior Analysis, 20,* 329–334.

Glossary

A

ABAB design   See **reversal design.**

alternate response training   A technique used in therapy (such as desensitization) and as a self-control strategy in which the individual is trained to engage in a response (e.g., relaxation) that interferes with or replaces another response that is to be controlled or eliminated.

aversive event   A stimulus that suppresses a behavior that it follows or increases a behavior that results in its termination.

avoidance   Performance of a behavior that postpones or averts the presentation of an aversive event.

B

back-up reinforcer   An object, activity, or event (primary or secondary reinforcer) that can be purchased with tokens. A reinforcer that "backs up" the value of tokens.

baseline   The frequency with which behavior is performed prior to initiating a behavior modification program. The performance rate used to evaluate the effect of a behavior modification program. Operant rate of behavior. The initial phase of reversal, multiple-baseline, changing-criterion, and simultaneous-treatment designs.

behavior   Any observable or measurable response or act. (The terms *behavior* and *response* are used synonymously.) Behavior is occasionally broadly defined to include cognitions, psychophysiological reactions, and feelings, which may not be directly observable but are defined in terms that can be measured by means of various assessment strategies.

behavioral control   Exerting power or influence over others by altering the environmental contingencies to achieve a definite end.

behavioral medicine   The application of behavioral procedures to problems of physical health and illness. Applications of this kind focus on problems related to the prevention, diagnosis, and treatment of physical disorders or on behaviors with consequences related to health and illness.

behavioral trap   Refers to the notion that once a client's behavior has been developed, it may become entrenched in and maintained (i.e., trapped) by the social system of available reinforcers in the client's everyday environment. That is, behaviors initially developed through special contingency arrangements may be maintained by ordinary, naturally occurring contingencies after the program has been withdrawn.

bibliotherapy   A form of self-help treatment that is conveyed to clients through written materials such as manuals and books. This form of treatment involves little or no therapist assistance.

biofeedback   Procedures that provide information to clients about their ongoing physiological processes. Providing this information to the client enables the client to monitor moment-to-moment changes in these processes.

C

chain   A sequence of behaviors that occurs in a fixed order. Each behavior in the sequence serves as a discriminative stimulus (S^D) for the next response. Each behavior in the sequence (except the first behavior) also serves as a conditioned reinforcer that reinforces the previous response.

chaining   Developing a sequence of responses in reverse order, so that the last response in the sequence is developed first, the next to the last response is trained second, and the remaining responses are trained in the reverse order of their performance once the sequence is finally performed. Developing a complex behavior by training individual components of the behavior in a reverse order.

changing-criterion design   An experimental design in which the effect of the program is evaluated by repeatedly altering the criterion for reinforcement or punishment. If the target behavior matches the criterion as the criterion is repeatedly altered, this suggests that the contingency is responsible for the behavior change.

classical (or respondent) conditioning   A type of learning in which a neutral (conditioned) stimulus is paired with an unconditioned stimulus that elicits a reflex response. After the conditioned stimulus is repeatedly followed by the unconditioned stimulus, the association between the two stimuli is learned. The conditioned stimulus alone will then elicit a reflex response. In classical conditioning, new stimuli gain the power to elicit respondent behavior.

client   The person for whom the behavior modification program has been designed and implemented. Used in the present text as a generic term to include the patient, student, subject, child, or other person for whom the intervention has been planned.

cognitively based treatment   An approach that considers cognitive processes such as thoughts, beliefs, and perceptions to play a major role in the conceptualization and treatment of clinical problems.

cognitive processes   Internal events such as thoughts, beliefs, self-statements, perceptions, and images.

conditioned aversive stimulus   An initially neutral event that acquires aversive properties by virtue of being paired with other aversive events or with a signal that no reinforcement will be forthcoming.

conditioned reinforcer   See **secondary reinforcer.**

conditioned response   A reflex response elicited by a conditioned stimulus in the absence of the unconditioned stimulus. This response resembles, but is not identical to, the unconditioned response. See **classical conditioning.**

conditioned stimulus   A previously neutral stimulus that, through repeated associations with an unconditioned stimulus, elicits a reflex response. See **classical conditioning.**

consequence sharing   A contingency arrangement in which the consequences earned by one person are provided to both that person and his or her peers.

contingency   The relationship between a behavior (the response to be changed) and the events (consequences) that follow the behavior. Sometimes events that precede the behavior (antecedents) are also specified by a contingency.

contingency contract   A behavior modification program in which an agreement or contract is made between a person who wishes behavior to change (e.g., a parent) and the person whose behavior is to be changed (e.g., a child). The contract specifies the relationship between behavior and its consequences.

contingent delivery of a reinforcer   The delivery of a reinforcer only when a specified behavior has been performed. Contrast with **noncontingent delivery of a reinforcer.**

contingent upon behavior   An event (e.g., praise, tokens, time out) is contingent upon behavior when the event is delivered only if that behavior is performed.

continuous reinforcement   A schedule of reinforcement in which a response is reinforced each time it is performed.

control group design   An experimental design in which the effect of the program is evaluated by comparing (at least) two groups, a group that receives the program and another group that does not receive the program.

coverant   A private event such as a thought, a fantasy, or an image that is not "observable" to anyone other than the individual who is experiencing it. Private events can be viewed as responses that can be altered by varying the consequences that follow them. The term *coverant* is a contraction of the terms *covert* and *operant.*

covert event   A private event such as a thought, a fantasy, or an image. See **coverant.**

covert sensitization   An imagery-based treatment in which clients imagine themselves engaging in an undesired behavior (e.g., overeating) and then imagine an aversive event or state (e.g., vomiting). The treatment is designed to decrease the undesired behavior.

cue   See **discriminative stimulus (S^D).**

D

delay of reinforcement   The time interval between a response and delivery of the reinforcer.

deprivation   Reducing the availability of, or access to, a reinforcer.

differential reinforcement   Reinforcing a response in the presence of one stimulus (S^D) and extinguishing the response in the presence of other stimuli (S^Δ). Eventually, the response is consistently performed in the presence of the S^D but not in the presence of the S^Δ.

differential reinforcement of alternative behavior (DRA)   Delivery of a reinforcer after any response that decreases the likelihood that an undesired behavior will occur. The reinforced response may be incompatible with the behavior that is to be reduced (DRI) or may be any behavior other than the one that is to be reduced (DRO).

differential reinforcement of incompatible behavior (DRI)   Delivery of a reinforcer after a response that is incompatible or competes with a target response that is to be suppressed. The effect is to increase the frequency of the incompatible response (e.g., cooperative play) and to decrease the frequency of the undesirable target response (e.g., fighting).

differential reinforcement of low rates (DRL)   Delivery of a reinforcer for reductions in performance of the target behavior. Reinforcers may be delivered for reduction in the overall frequency of a response within a particular period or for an increase in the amount of time that elapses between responses. A DRL schedule can reduce the frequency of a target response.

differential reinforcement of other behavior (DRO)   Delivery of a reinforcer after any response except the target response. The effect of reinforcing only behaviors other than the target response is to decrease the target (unreinforced) response.

discrete categorization   A method of assessing behavior in which behaviors are dichotomously scored as having occurred or not occurred. This method is very useful when several behaviors are to be scored.

discrimination   Responding differently in the presence of different cues or antecedent events. Control of behavior by discriminative stimuli. See **stimulus control.**

discriminative stimulus (S^D)   An antecedent event or stimulus that signals that a certain response will be reinforced. A response is reinforced in the presence of an S^D. After an event becomes an S^D by being paired with reinforcement, its presence can increase the probability that the response will occur.

disease model   A general approach in medicine in which symptoms (e.g., fever) are viewed as a result of some underlying disease or pathology (e.g., bacterial infection) and treatment, ideally, is directed at the underlying disease. This approach was transferred to abnormal behavior by positing an underlying "psychological disease." The intrapsychic model in psychology is consistent with the disease approach in medicine.

duration   A method of recording behavior that measures the amount of time in which a behavior is performed.

E

elicit   To automatically bring about a response. Respondent or reflex behaviors are elicited by unconditioned stimuli. Contrast with **emit** and **operant behavior.** See **classical conditioning.**

emit   To perform a response spontaneously. Operant behaviors are emitted. They are controlled primarily by the consequences that follow them. Contrast with **elicit** and **respondent.** See **operant conditioning.**

escape   Performance of a behavior that terminates an aversive event.

experimental design   The program plan that determines how the effect of the experimental contingency will be evaluated. The plan for evaluating whether the behavior modification program, rather than various extraneous factors, was responsible for behavior change.

extinction   A procedure in which the reinforcer is no longer delivered for a previously reinforced response.

extinction burst   An increase in the frequency and intensity of responding at the beginning of extinction.

F

fading   The gradual removal of discriminative stimuli (S^D), including such prompts as instructions or physical guidance. Initially, developing behavior is often facilitated by prompts. However, in most situations, it is important to fade the prompt. Fading can also refer to the gradual removal of reinforcement, as in the progressive thinning of a reinforcement schedule.

fixed-interval schedule   A schedule of administering reinforcement. In an FI schedule, reinforcement is given to the first occurrence of the target response after a fixed time interval elapses.

fixed-ratio schedule   A schedule of administering reinforcement. In an FR schedule, an unvarying number of occurrences of the target response is required for reinforcement.

frequency   The number of times that a response occurs. See **rate of responding.**

functional relationship   A relationship between behavior and the experimental condition or contingency. A functional relationship is demonstrated if behavior systematically changes when the contingency is applied, withdrawn, and reapplied.

G

generalized conditioned reinforcer   A conditioned reinforcer that has acquired reinforcing value by being associated or paired with a variety of other reinforcers. Money is a generalized conditioned reinforcer.

group contingencies   Contingencies in which the group participates. There are two major variations: (1) An individual's behavior can determine the consequences delivered to the group, and (2) the behavior of a group as a whole determines the consequences that each member of the group receives.

H

high-probability behavior   A response that is performed with a relatively high frequency when the individual is given the opportunity to select among alternative behaviors. See **Premack principle.**

I

imagery-based techniques Cognitively based behavior modification procedures that rely on the presentation of events in imagination. See **covert sensitization.**

incompatible behavior A behavior that interferes with, or cannot be performed at the same time as, another behavior.

informed consent Agreeing to participate in a program with full knowledge about the nature of the treatment and about the program's risks, benefits, expected outcomes, and alternatives. Three elements are required for truly informed consent—competence, knowledge, and volition.

intermittent reinforcement A schedule of reinforcement in which only some occurrences of a response are reinforced.

interval recording An assessment strategy in which behavior is observed as having occurred or not occurred. Observations are usually made in a single period (e.g., 30 minutes) that is divided into small intervals (e.g., 15 seconds). Behavior is scored as having occurred or not occurred during each of the small intervals.

interval schedule of reinforcement A schedule in which reinforcement is delivered on the basis of the amount of time that passes before a response can be reinforced. Contrast with **ratio schedule of reinforcement.**

intrapsychic model The view that overt behavior, whether "normal" or "abnormal," is a result of underlying psychological processes and that the underlying processes must be treated before the overt behavior can be changed.

L

latency The time between the presentation or onset of a stimulus and the occurrence of behavior.

M

model The person whose behavior is observed or imitated in observational learning.

modeling See **observational learning.**

multiple-baseline design Experimental designs that demonstrate the effect of a contingency by introducing the contingency across different behaviors, individuals, or situations at different points in time. A causal relationship between the experimental contingency and behavior is demonstrated if each of the behaviors (individual or situation) changes only when the contingency is introduced.

multiple-baseline design across behaviors An experimental design in which baseline data are gathered across two or more behaviors. First, the experimental contingency is applied to one of these behaviors while baseline conditions remain unchanged for the other behaviors. Then, after all of the behaviors have stabilized, the experimental contingency is applied to a second behavior. This process is continued until the experimental contingency has been applied to all of the behaviors.

multiple-baseline design across individuals   An experimental design in which baseline data are gathered across two or more individuals. First, the experimental contingency is applied to one of these individuals while baseline conditions remain unchanged for the other individuals. Then, after behavior has stabilized for all of the individuals, the experimental contingency is applied to a second individual. This process is continued until the experimental contingency has been applied to all of the individuals.

multiple-baseline design across situations   An experimental design in which baseline data are gathered across two or more situations. First, the experimental contingency is applied to behavior in one of these situations while baseline conditions remain unchanged for behavior in the other situations. Then, after behavior has stabilized in all of the situations, the experimental contingency is applied to behavior in a second situation. This process is continued until the experimental contingency has been applied to behavior in all of the situations.

N

naturally occurring reinforcers   Uncontrived reinforcing events that are usually available as part of the environment. Such events include attention, praise, completion of an activity, and mastery of a task.

negative reinforcement   An increase in the frequency of a response that is followed by the termination or removal of a negative reinforcer. See **negative reinforcer.**

negative reinforcer   An aversive event or stimulus whose termination increases the frequency of the preceding response. The increase in frequency of the response that terminates or removes the aversive event is called "negative reinforcement."

noncontingent delivery of a reinforcer   The delivery of a reinforcer independently of behavior. The reinforcer is delivered without reference to how the individual is behaving. Contrast with **contingent delivery of a reinforcer.**

O

observational learning   Learning by observing another individual (a model) engage in a behavior. In such learning the observer need not perform the behavior or receive direct consequences for his or her performance.

observer drift   The gradual departure of observers from the definitions that they are supposed to use when they record behavior. If this happens, recorded changes in the target behavior may reflect changes in how responses are being scored rather than the effects of the program.

occasion   Presenting an S^D and thus increasing the likelihood that a response will be performed. Certain cues in the environment (e.g., music) occasion certain responses (e.g., singing).

operant behavior   Emitted behavior that is controlled by its consequences.

operant conditioning   A type of learning in which behaviors are altered primarily by regulating the consequences that follow them. The frequency of operant behaviors is altered by the consequences that they produce.

operant rate See **baseline.**

overcorrection A punishment procedure that consists of two components. First, the environmental consequences of the undesirable behavior must be corrected (e.g., cleaning up a mess). Second, correct forms of desirable behavior must be thoroughly rehearsed or practiced (e.g., cleaning up messes made by several other people).

overt behavior Behavior that is publicly observable and measurable. Contrast with **covert event.**

P

paraprofessional A person such as a parent, teacher, or peer who works with the mental health professional to implement a treatment program.

positive practice Repeatedly practicing appropriate responses or responses incompatible with an undesirable response that is to be suppressed. This is a component of overcorrection, but it is often used alone as a punishment technique when the response that is to be suppressed (e.g., a self-stimulatory behavior such as rocking) has no clear environmental consequences that can be corrected.

positive reinforcement An increase in the frequency of a response that is followed by a positive reinforcer. See **positive reinforcer.**

positive reinforcer An event whose presentation increases the probability of a response that it follows.

Premack principle Of any pair of responses or activities in which an individual freely engages, the more frequent one will reinforce the less frequent one.

primary reinforcer A reinforcing event that does not depend on learning to achieve its reinforcing properties. Food, water, and sex are primary reinforcers. Contrast with **secondary reinforcer.**

prompt An antecedent event that helps initiate a response. A discriminative stimulus that occasions a response. Instructions, gestures, physical guidance, and modeling cues serve as prompts.

psychodynamic view An explanation of personality that accounts for behavior by positing underlying psychological forces—drives, impulses, or personality dynamics.

punishment Presentation of an aversive event or removal of a positive event contingent upon a response that decreases the probability of the response.

R

rate of responding The frequency of responding is often expressed in relation to the amount of time that a behavior has been observed. The rate of responding equals frequency (number of occurrences of the behavior) divided by time (seconds or minutes).

ratio schedule of reinforcement A schedule in which reinforcement is delivered on the basis of the number of responses that are performed. Contrast with **interval schedule of reinforcement.**

reinforcement   An increase in the frequency of a response when the response is immediately followed by a particular consequence. The consequence can be either the presentation of a positive reinforcer or the removal of a negative reinforcer.

reinforcer sampling   A case of response priming in which the purpose is to develop or increase the utilization of an event as a reinforcer. Providing the client with a sample or small portion of the event increases the likelihood that the entire event can serve as a reinforcer.

reliability of assessment   In behavioral research, this term usually refers to interobserver agreement, or the consistency with which different observers working independently score a target response. The method used to calculate agreement depends on the method used to assess behavior (e.g., frequency, interval, or duration). The calculation usually yields a percentage of agreement between observers.

resistance to extinction   The extent to which a response is maintained once reinforcement is no longer provided.

respondent   Behavior that is elicited or controlled by antecedent stimuli. Reflexes are respondents because their performance automatically follows certain stimuli. The connection between such unconditioned respondents and the antecedent events that control them is unlearned. Through classical conditioning, respondents may come under the control of otherwise neutral stimuli.

response   See **behavior.**

response cost   A punishment procedure in which a positive reinforcer is lost contingent upon behavior. With this procedure, unlike time out from reinforcement, no time limit to the withdrawal of the reinforcer is specified. Fines are a common form of response cost.

response covariation   The tendency of several responses to change together, even when only one of the responses serves as the focus for change. In a person's repertoire, many behaviors may be correlated. If that is the case, changing one of those behaviors often changes behaviors with which it is correlated.

response deprivation hypothesis   The frequency of a target behavior can be increased if a preferred behavior is contingent upon first performing the target behavior. The effectiveness of this contingency is considered to depend on the fact that unless the target behavior is performed, the individual is deprived of performing the preferred behavior (i.e., cannot engage in it freely at the baseline rate). See **Premack principle.**

response generalization   Reinforcement of one response increases the probability of other responses that are similar to and resemble that response. Contrast with **stimulus generalization.**

response priming   Any procedure that initiates early steps in a sequence of responses. By initiating those early steps, response priming increases the likelihood that the terminal response in the sequence will be performed.

restitution   A component of overcorrection that consists of correcting the environmental effects of the undesired or inappropriate behavior. See **overcorrection.**

reversal design   An experimental design in which the target behavior of a subject or a group of subjects is assessed to determine baseline performance. The experimental condition is then introduced, and it is maintained until the target behavior changes. A reversal phase follows in which the experimental condition is withdrawn. Finally, the experimental condition is reintroduced. A functional relationship is demonstrated if the target behavior changes during each of the phases in which the experimental condition is presented and if it reverts to baseline or near baseline levels when the experimental condition is withdrawn. Also called an "ABAB design."

reversal phase   A phase in the reversal design in which the program is withdrawn or altered to determine whether the target behavior reverts to baseline or near baseline levels. During a reversal phase, one of three changes is usually made: (1) the program is withdrawn; (2) the consequences are delivered noncontingently; or (3) the consequences follow a DRO schedule.

S

satiation   Providing an excessive amount of the reinforcer. A loss of effectiveness that occurs after a large amount of the reinforcer has been delivered.

schedule of reinforcement   The rule denoting how many or which responses will be reinforced.

S^D See **discriminative stimulus.**

S^Δ An antecedent event or stimulus that signals that a certain response will not be reinforced.

secondary (or conditioned) reinforcer   An event that becomes reinforcing through learning. An event becomes a secondary reinforcer by being paired with other events (primary or conditioned) that are already reinforcing. Praise and attention are examples of secondary reinforcers. Contrast with **primary reinforcer.**

self-administered reinforcement   Refers to the client's delivery of the reinforcer to himself or herself.

self-control   Refers to those behaviors in which an individual deliberately undertakes to achieve self-selected outcomes by manipulating antecedent and consequent events.

self-determined reinforcement   Refers to the client's specification of the criteria for reinforcement.

self-help manuals   Books, manuals, or brochures that are designed to teach clients how to implement treatments for themselves. Usually little or no therapist contact is required. The client merely applies the specified techniques in a step-by-step fashion.

self-instruction training   A self-control technique in which individuals prompt their own behavior by providing covert self-instructions or statements that direct and guide it.

self-monitoring   Assessing or recording one's own behavior. Sometimes used as a self-control technique.

self-punishment   Providing oneself with punishing consequences contingent upon behavior.

self-reinforcement   Providing oneself with reinforcing consequences contingent upon behavior. For a procedure to qualify as self-reinforcement, the client must be free to partake of the reinforcer at any time, whether or not a particular response has been performed.

self-statements   The statements that people make to themselves either aloud or privately (covertly). Self-statements are utilized in various treatment techniques, such as self-instruction training.

shaping   Developing a new behavior by reinforcing successive approximations toward the terminal response. See **successive approximations.**

simultaneous-treatment design   An experimental design in which two or more interventions are implemented during the same treatment phase. The interventions are balanced (varied) across different conditions, such as the time of day in which treatment is implemented. The simultaneous-treatment design is useful for comparing the relative effectiveness of two or more interventions.

social learning theory   A conceptual framework within behavioral research that integrates the influence of different types of learning (classical, operant, and observational learning) in explaining how behavior develops and is maintained and altered. Social learning theory emphasizes the significance of cognitive processes in mediating the influence of environmental events and in actively influencing performance, the interrelationship of cognitions and the environment, and the influence that cognitions and the environment have on each other.

social reinforcers   Reinforcers that result from interpersonal interaction, such as attention, praise and approval, smiles, and physical contact.

social validation   Refers to the evaluation of the social importance of both the behavior focused on in treatment and the changes achieved in treatment. The applied or clinical significance of behavioral programs is often evaluated after treatment by comparing the behavior of the target subject with that of persons who perform adaptively or by soliciting the opinions of persons in the community with whom the client interacts.

spontaneous recovery   The temporary recurrence of a behavior during extinction. A response that has not been reinforced may reappear temporarily during the course of extinction. The magnitude of such a response is usually lower than its magnitude prior to extinction.

stimulus   A measurable event that may have an effect on a behavior.

stimulus control   The presence of a particular stimulus serves as an occasion for a particular response. The response is performed only when it is in the presence of a particular stimulus. See **discriminative stimulus.**

stimulus generalization   Transfer of a trained response to situations or stimulus conditions other than those in which training has taken place. The behavior generalizes to other situations. Contrast with **response generalization.**

subjective evaluation   A method used to evaluate whether the changes achieved by a behavioral program make an important difference to various consumers of treatment, including the clients themselves, persons in contact with them, and persons who are in a position to evaluate the behaviors of interest. This method solicits the opinions and subjective evaluations of potential consumers to help decide whether these changes are important or make a difference in everyday situations.

successive approximations   Responses that more and more closely resemble the terminal behavior that is being shaped. See **shaping.**

T

target behavior   The behavior to be altered or focused on during a behavior modification program. The behavior that has been assessed and is to be changed.

task analysis   An initial stage in developing a program. The stage consists of identifying the precise behaviors that need to be developed, dividing those behaviors into concrete steps that can be trained, and setting the sequence (or order) in which the training will take place.

team-based contingency   A group contingency in which the members of a group earn reinforcers on the basis of the group's performance. In addition, use is made of subgroups or teams that compete to earn reinforcers between the teams.

terminal response   The final goal of shaping or the behavior that is achieved at the end of shaping. See **shaping.**

time in   The situation from which a person is removed when time out from reinforcement is used and access to available reinforcers is thus withdrawn for a brief period. The effectiveness of time out depends in part on how reinforcing that situation is.

time out from reinforcement   A punishment procedure in which, contingent upon behavior, access to positive reinforcement is withdrawn for a brief period. Isolation from a group exemplifies time out from reinforcement.

token   A tangible object that serves as a generalized conditioned reinforcer. It can be exchanged for back-up reinforcers from which it derives its value. Poker chips, coins, tickets, stars, points, and check marks are commonly used as tokens. See **token economy.**

token economy   A reinforcement system in which tokens are earned for a variety of behaviors and are used to purchase a variety of back-up reinforcers. A token economy is analogous to a national economy, in which money serves as a medium of exchange and can be earned and spent in numerous ways.

training the general case   A strategy designed to ensure that behaviors are performed across a variety of stimulus conditions (e.g., in different situations, in the presence of different persons) in which the behaviors will be required. The strategy requires that variations of different stimulus conditions be included during training.

transfer of training   The extent to which responses trained in one setting transfer to settings other than the one in which training took place. See **stimulus generalization.**

U

unconditioned response   A reflex response elicited by an unconditioned stimulus. See **classical conditioning** and **respondent.**

V

variable-interval schedule   A schedule of administering reinforcement. In a VI schedule, the first occurrence of the target response after a given interval has elapsed is reinforced. However, the time interval changes each time that reinforcement is delivered; the interval is variable. The schedule is denoted by the average time that must elapse before a response can be reinforced.

variable-ratio schedule   A schedule of administering reinforcement. In a VR schedule, a number of occurrences of the target response are required for reinforcement. The number of required responses varies each time that reinforcement is delivered. The schedule is denoted by the average number of times that the response must occur before reinforcement is delivered.

vicarious punishment   Punishment of one individual sometimes decreases performance of the punished behavior in individuals who have not been directly punished. A spread of punishment effects to individuals whose behaviors have not been directly punished.

vicarious reinforcement   Reinforcement of one individual sometimes increases performance of the reinforced behavior in individuals who have not been directly reinforced. A spread of reinforcement effects to individuals whose behaviors have not been directly reinforced.

References

Abrams, L., Hines, D., Pollack, D., Ross, M., Stubbs, D. A., & Polyot, C. J. (1974). Transferable tokens: Increasing social interaction in a token economy. *Psychological Reports, 35,* 447–452.

Alavosius, M. P., & Sulzer-Azaroff, B. (1986). The effects of performance feedback on the safety of client lifting and transfer. *Journal of Applied Behavior Analysis, 19,* 261–268.

Albin, R. W., Horner, R. H., Koegel, R. L., & Dunlap, G. (Eds.). (1987). *Extending competent performance: Applied research on generalization and maintenance.* Eugene: University of Oregon.

Alford, B. A. (1986). Behavioral treatment of schizophrenic delusions: A single-case experimental design. *Behavior Therapy, 17,* 637–644.

Allen, K. D., & Stokes, T. F. (1987). Use of escape and reward in the management of young children during dental treatment. *Journal of Applied Behavior Analysis, 20,* 381–390.

Allen, L. D., & Iwata, B. A. (1980). Reinforcing exercise maintenance: Using existing high-rate activities. *Behavior Modification, 4,* 337–354.

Allison, M. G., & Ayllon, T. (1980). Behavioral coaching in the development of skills in football, gymnastics, and tennis. *Journal of Applied Behavior Analysis, 13,* 297–314.

Altman, K., Haavik, S., & Cook, J. W. (1978). Punishment of self-injurious behavior in natural settings, using contingent aromatic ammonia. *Behaviour Research and Therapy, 16,* 85–96.

Arbuthnot, J., & Gordon, D. A. (1986). Behavioral and cognitive effects of a moral reasoning development intervention for high-risk behavior-disordered adolescents. *Journal of Consulting and Clinical Psychology, 54,* 208–216.

Association for Advancement of Behavior Therapy. (1977). Ethical issues for human services. *Behavior Therapy, 8,* v–vi.

Ayllon, T., & Azrin, N. H. (1968a). Reinforcer sampling: A technique for increasing the behavior of mental patients. *Journal of Applied Behavior Analysis, 1,* 13–20.

Ayllon, T., & Azrin, N. H. (1968b). *The token economy: A motivational system for therapy and rehabilitation.* New York: Appleton-Century-Crofts.

Ayllon, T., & Haughton, E. (1964). Modification of symptomatic verbal behaviour of mental patients. *Behaviour Research and Therapy, 2,* 87–97.

Ayllon, T., & Kelly, K. (1974). Reinstating verbal behavior in a functionally mute retardate. *Professional Psychology, 5,* 385–393.

Ayllon, T., Layman, D., & Kandel, H. J. (1975). A behavioral-educational alternative to drug control of hyperactive children. *Journal of Applied Behavior Analysis, 8,* 137–146.

Ayllon, T., & Michael, J. (1959). The psychiatric nurse as a behavioral engineer. *Journal of the Experimental Analysis of Behavior, 2,* 323–334.

Azrin, N. H., Flores, T., & Kaplan, S. (1975). Job-finding club: A group-assisted program for obtaining employment. *Behaviour Research and Therapy, 13,* 17–27.

Azrin, N. H., & Foxx, R. M. (1971). A rapid method of toilet training the institutionalized retarded. *Journal of Applied Behavior Analysis, 4,* 89–99.

Azrin, N. H., & Foxx, R. M. (1974). *Toilet training in less than a day.* New York: Simon & Schuster.

Azrin, N. H., Gottlieb, L., Hughart, L., Wesolowski, M. D., & Rahn, T. (1975). Eliminating self-injurious behavior by educative procedures. *Behaviour Research and Therapy, 13,* 101–111.

Azrin, N. H, & Holz, W. C. (1966). Punishment. In W. K. Honig (Ed.), *Operant behavior: Areas of research and application* (pp. 380–447). New York: Appleton-Century-Crofts.

Azrin, N. H., & Powers, M. A. (1975). Eliminating classroom disturbances of emotionally disturbed children by positive practice procedures. *Behavior Therapy, 6,* 525–534.

Azrin, N. H., & Wesolowski, M. D. (1974). Theft reversal: An overcorrection procedure for eliminating stealing by retarded persons. *Journal of Applied Behavior Analysis, 7,* 577–581.

Azrin, N. H., & Wesolowski, M. D. (1975). Eliminating habitual vomiting in a retarded adult by positive practice and self-correction. *Journal of Behavior Therapy and Experimental Psychiatry, 6,* 145–148.

Bacher, T. E., Liberman, R. P., & Kuehnel, T. G. (1986). Dissemination and adoption of innovative psychosocial interventions. *Journal of Consulting and Clinical Psychology, 54,* 111–118.

Baer, D. M., Rowbury, T. G., & Goetz, E. M. (1976). Behavioral traps in the preschool: A proposal for research. *Minnesota Symposia on Child Psychology, 10,* 3–27.

Baer, D. M., & Wolf, M. M. (1970). The entry into natural communities of reinforcement. In R. Ulrich, T. Stachnik, & J. Mabry (Eds.), *Control of human behavior* (Vol. 2, pp. 319–324). Glenview, IL: Scott, Foresman.

Baer, D. M., Wolf, M. M., & Risley, T. R. (1968). Some current dimensions of applied behavior analysis. *Journal of Applied Behavior Analysis, 1,* 91–97.

Baer, D. M., Wolf, M. M., & Risley, T. R. (1987). Some still-current dimensions of applied behavior analysis. *Journal of Applied Behavior Analysis, 20,* 313–328.

Baer, R. A., Blount, R. L., Detrick, R., & Stokes, T. F. (1987). Using intermittent reinforcement to program maintenance of verbal/nonverbal correspondence. *Journal of Applied Behavior Analysis, 20,* 179–184.

Ballard, K. D., & Glynn, G. (1975). Behavioral self-management in story writing with elementary school children. *Journal of Applied Behavior Analysis, 8,* 387–398.

Bandura, A. (1965). Influence of models' reinforcement contingencies on the acquisition of imitative responses. *Journal of Personality and Social Psychology, 1*, 589–595.

Bandura, A. (1977). *Social learning theory*. Englewood Cliffs, NJ: Prentice-Hall.

Barbrack, C. R., & Maher, C. A. (1984). Effects of involving conduct problem adolescents in the setting of counseling goals. *Child and Family Behavior Therapy, 6*, 33–43.

Barlow, D. H., & Hayes, S. C. (1979). Alternating treatments design: One strategy for comparing the effects of two treatments in a single subject. *Journal of Applied Behavior Analysis, 12*, 199–210.

Barlow, D. H., & Hersen, M. (1984). *Single-case experimental designs: Strategies for studying behavior change* (2nd ed.). Elmsford, NY: Pergamon Press.

Barton, E. J., & Osborne, J. G. (1978). The development of classroom sharing by a teacher using positive practice. *Behavior Modification, 2*, 231–250.

Bassett, J. E., & Blanchard, E. B. (1977). The effect of the absence of close supervision on the use of response cost in a prison token economy. *Journal of Applied Behavior Analysis, 10*, 375–379.

Beck, A. T. (1976). *Cognitive therapy and emotional disorders*. New York: International Universities Press.

Beck, A. T., Kovacs, M., & Weissman, A. (1975). Hopelessness and suicidal behavior: An overview. *Journal of the American Medical Association, 234*, 1146–1149.

Beck, A. T., Rush, A. J., Shaw, B. F., & Emery, G. (1979). *Cognitive therapy of depression*. New York: Guilford.

Becker, J. V., Turner, S. M., & Sajwaj, T. E. (1978). Multiple behavioral effects of the use of lemon juice with a ruminating toddler-age child. *Behavior Modification, 2*, 267–278.

Beiman, I., Graham, L. E., & Ciminero, A. R. (1978). Self-control progressive relaxation training as an alternative nonpharmacological treatment for essential hypertension: Therapeutic effects in the natural environment. *Behaviour Research and Therapy, 16*, 371–375.

Belles, D., & Bradlyn, A. S. (1987). The use of the changing criterion design in achieving controlled smoking in a heavy smoker: A controlled case study. *Journal of Behavior Therapy and Experimental Psychiatry, 18*, 77–82.

Bem, S. L. (1975). Sex role adaptability: One consequence of psychological androgyny. *Journal of Personality and Social Psychology, 31*, 634–643.

Bigelow, G., Liebson, I., & Griffiths, R. (1974). Alcoholic drinking: Suppression by a brief time-out procedure. *Behaviour Research and Therapy, 12*, 107–115.

Billings, D. C., & Wasik, B. H. (1985). Self-instructional training with preschoolers: An attempt to replicate. *Journal of Applied Behavior Analysis, 18*, 61–67.

Birnbrauer, J. S. (1968). Generalization of punishment effects: A case study. *Journal of Applied Behavior Analysis, 1*, 201–211.

Blankstein, K. R., & Polivy, J. (Eds.). (1982). *Self-control and self-modification of emotional behavior: Advances in the study of communication and affect* (Vol. 7). New York: Plenum.

Blechman, E. A. (1985). *Solving child behavior problems—At home and at school*. Champaign, IL: Research Press.

Boegli, R. G., & Wasik, B. H. (1978). Use of the token-economy system to intervene on a schoolwide level. *Psychology in the Schools, 15,* 72–78.

Bootzin, R. R. (1972). Stimulus control treatment for insomnia. *Proceedings of the 80th Annual Convention of the American Psychological Association, 7,* 395–396.

Bornstein, M. T., Bellack, A. S., & Hersen, M. (1977). Social-skills training for unassertive children: A multiple-baseline analysis. *Journal of Applied Behavior Analysis, 10,* 183–195.

Bornstein, P. H. (1985). Self-instructional training: A commentary and state-of-the-art. *Journal of Applied Behavior Analysis, 18,* 69–72.

Bornstein, P. H., & Quevillon, R. P. (1976). The effects of a self-instructional package on overactive preschool boys. *Journal of Applied Behavior Analysis, 9,* 179–188.

Breyer, N. L., & Allen, G. J. (1975). Effects of implementing a token economy on teacher attending behavior. *Journal of Applied Behavior Analysis, 8,* 373–380.

Brigham, T. A. (1982). Self-management: A radical behavioral perspective. In P. Karoly & F. H. Kanfer (Eds.), *Self-management and behavior change: From theory to practice* (pp. 32–59). Elmsford, NY: Pergamon Press.

Brigham, T. A., & Stoerzinger, A. (1976). An experimental analysis of children's preference for self-selected rewards. In T. A. Brigham, R. Hawkins, J. W. Scott, & T. F. McLaughlin (Eds.), *Behavior analysis in education.* Dubuque, IA: Kendall/Hunt.

Bristol, M. M. (1976). Control of physical aggression through school- and home-based reinforcement. In J. D. Krumboltz & C. E. Thoresen (Eds.), *Counseling methods* (pp. 180–198). New York: Holt, Rinehart & Winston.

Brown, J. (1987). A review of meta-analyses conducted on psychotherapy outcome research. *Clinical Psychology Review, 7,* 1–23.

Brownell, K. D. (1982). Behavioral medicine. In C. M. Franks, G. T. Wilson, P. C. Kendall, & K. D. Brownell (Eds.), *Annual review of behavior therapy: (Vol. 8). Theory and practice* (pp. 156–207). New York: Guilford.

Bryant, L. E., & Budd, K. S. (1982). Self-instructional training to increase independent work performance in preschoolers. *Journal of Applied Behavior Analysis, 15,* 259–271.

Budd, K. S., & Stokes, T. F. (1977, August). *Cue properties of praise in vicarious reinforcement with preschoolers.* Paper presented at the meeting of the American Psychological Association, San Francisco.

Burchard, J. D., & Lane, T. W. (1982). Crime and delinquency. In A. S. Bellack, M. Hersen, & A. E. Kazdin (Eds.), *International handbook of behavior modification and therapy* (pp. 613–652). New York: Plenum.

Burgio, L. D., & Burgio, K. L. (1986). Behavioral gerontology: Application of behavioral methods to the problems of older adults. *Journal of Applied Behavior Analysis, 19,* 321–328.

Burgio, L. D., & Tice, L. (1985). The reduction of seizure-like behaviors through contingency management. *Journal of Behavior Therapy and Experimental Psychiatry, 16,* 71–75.

Burgio, L. D., Whitman, T. L., & Johnson, M. R. (1980). A self-instructional package for increasing attending behavior in educable mentally retarded children. *Journal of Applied Behavior Analysis, 13,* 443–459.

Bushell, D., Jr. (1978). An engineering approach to the elementary classroom: The Behavior Analysis Follow Through project. In A. C. Catania & T. A. Brigham (Eds.), *Handbook of applied behavior analysis: Social and instructional processes* (pp. 525–563). New York: Irvington.

Cairns, D., & Pasino, J. A. (1977). Comparison of verbal reinforcement and feedback in the operant treatment of disability due to chronic low back pain. *Behavior Therapy, 8,* 621–630.

Calhoun, K. S., & Lima, P. P. (1977). Effects of varying schedules of time out on high- and low-rate behaviors. *Journal of Behavior Therapy and Experimental Psychiatry, 8,* 189–194.

Carey, R. G., & Bucher, B. B. (1981). Identifying the educative and suppressive effects of positive practice and restitutional overcorrection. *Journal of Applied Behavior Analysis, 14,* 71–80.

Carey, R. G., & Bucher, B. B. (1986). Positive practice overcorrection: Effects of reinforcing correct performance. *Behavior Modification, 10,* 73–92.

Carlson, C. S., Arnold, C. R., Becker, W. C., & Madsen, C. H. (1968). The elimination of tantrum behavior of a child in an elementary classroom. *Behaviour Research and Therapy, 6,* 117–119.

Catania, A. C. (1984). *Learning* (2nd ed.). Englewood Cliffs, NJ: Prentice-Hall.

Cautela, J. R. (1967). Covert sensitization. *Psychological Reports, 20,* 459–468.

Cautela, J. R. (1976). The present status of covert modeling. *Journal of Behavior Therapy and Experimental Psychiatry, 7,* 323–326.

Chapman, C., & Risley, T. R. (1974). Anti-litter procedures in an urban high-density area. *Journal of Applied Behavior Analysis, 7,* 377–384.

Charlop, M. H., Burgio, L. D., Iwata, B. A., & Ivancic, M. T. (1988). Stimulus variation as a means of enhancing punishment effects. *Journal of Applied Behavior Analysis, 21,* 89–95.

Christophersen, E. R., Arnold, C. M., Hill, D. W., & Quilitch, H. R. (1972). The home point system: Token reinforcement procedures for applications by parents of children with behavior problems. *Journal of Applied Behavior Analysis, 5,* 485–497.

Christy, P. R. (1975). Does use of tangible rewards with individual children affect peer observers? *Journal of Applied Behavior Analysis, 8,* 187–196.

Claerhout, S., & Lutzker, J. D. (1981). Increasing children's self-initiated compliance to dental requirements. *Behavior Therapy, 12,* 165–170.

Clark, H. B., Greene, B. F., Macrae, J. W., McNees, M. P., Davis, J. L., & Risley, T. R. (1977). A parent advice package for family shopping trips: Development and evaluation. *Journal of Applied Behavior Analysis, 10,* 605–624.

Clark, H. B., Rowbury, T., Baer, A. M., & Baer, D. M. (1973). Time out as a punishing stimulus in continuous and intermittent schedules. *Journal of Applied Behavior Analysis, 6,* 443–455.

Clark, L. (1985). *SOS: Help for parents.* Bowling Green, KY: Parents Press.

Cole, P. M., & Kazdin, A. E. (1980). Critical issues in self-instruction training with children. *Child Behavior Therapy, 2,* 1–23.

Cook, J. W., Altman, K., Shaw, J., & Blaylock, M. (1978). Use of contingent lemon juice to eliminate public masturbation by a severely retarded boy. *Behaviour Research and Therapy, 16,* 131–134.

Cook, T. D., & Campbell, D. T. (Eds.). (1979). *Quasi-experimentation: Design and analysis issues for field settings.* Skokie, IL: Rand McNally.

Cooke, T. P. & Apolloni, T. (1976). Developing positive social-emotional behaviors: A study of training and generalization effects. *Journal of Applied Behavior Analysis, 9,* 65–78.

Creer, T. L., Chai, H., & Hoffman, A. (1977). A single application of an aversive stimulus to eliminate chronic cough. *Journal of Behavior Therapy and Experimental Psychiatry, 8,* 107–109.

Dachman, R. S., Alessi, G. J., Vrazo, G. J., Fuqua, R. W., & Kerr, R. H. (1986). Development and evaluation of an infant-care training program with first-time fathers. *Journal of Applied Behavior Analysis, 19,* 221–230.

Dahlquist, L. M., & Gil, K. M. (1986). Using parents to maintain improved dental flossing skills in children. *Journal of Applied Behavior Analysis, 19,* 255–260.

Danaher, B. G. (1980). Smoking-cessation programs in occupational settings. *Public Health Reports, 95,* 149–157.

Dapcich-Miura, E., & Hovell, M. F. (1979). Contingency management of adherence to a complex medical regimen in an elderly heart patient. *Behavior Therapy, 10,* 193–201.

Davison, G. C. (1976). Homosexuality: The ethical challenge. *Journal of Consulting and Clinical Psychology, 44,* 157–162.

Dawson, B., de Armas, A., McGrath, M. L., & Kelly, J. A. (1986). Cognitive problem-solving training to improve the child-care judgment of child neglectful parents. *Journal of Family Violence, 1,* 209–221.

Day, H. M., & Horner, R. H. (1986). Response variation and the generalization of a dressing skill: Comparison of single instance and general case instruction. *Applied Research in Mental Retardation, 7,* 189–202.

Deitz, S. M. (1977). An analysis of programming DRL schedules in educational settings. *Behaviour Research and Therapy, 15,* 103–111.

Deitz, S. M., & Repp, A. C. (1973). Decreasing classroom misbehavior through the use of DRL schedules of reinforcement. *Journal of Applied Behavior Analysis, 6,* 457–463.

Deitz, S. M., Repp, A. C., & Deitz, D. E. D. (1976). Reducing inappropriate classroom behavior of retarded students through three procedures of differential reinforcement. *Journal of Mental Deficiency Research, 20,* 155–170.

Deluty, R. H. (1981). Alternative-thinking ability of aggressive, assertive, and submissive children. *Cognitive Therapy and Research, 5,* 309–312.

DeMaster, B., Reid, J., & Twentyman, C. (1977). The effects of different amounts of feedback on the observer's reliability. *Behavior Therapy, 8,* 317–329.

DeRisi, W. J., & Butz, G. (1975). *Writing behavioral contracts: A case simulation practice manual.* Champaign, IL: Research Press.

Dickerson, E. A., & Creedon, C. F. (1981). Self-selection of standards by children: The relative effectiveness of pupil-selected and teacher-selected standards of performance. *Journal of Applied Behavior Analysis, 14,* 425–433.

Dineen, J. P., Clark, H. B., & Risley, T. R. (1977). Peer tutoring among elementary students: Educational benefits to the tutor. *Journal of Applied Behavior Analysis, 10,* 231–238.

Dittes, J. E. (1957). Extinction during psychotherapy of GSR accompanying "embarrassing" statements. *Journal of Abnormal and Social Psychology, 54,* 187–191.

Dodge, K. A. (1985). Attributional bias in aggressive children. In P. C. Kendall (Ed.), *Advances in cognitive-behavioral research and therapy* (Vol. 4, pp. 73–110). New York: Academic Press.

Doleys, D. M., Meredith, R. L., & Ciminero, A. R. (Eds.). (1982). *Behavioral medicine: Assessment and treatment strategies.* New York: Plenum.

Doleys, D. M., & Slapion, M. J. (1975). The reduction of verbal repetitions by response cost controlled by a sibling. *Journal of Behavior Therapy and Experimental Psychiatry, 6,* 61–63.

Doleys, D. M., Wells, K. C., Hobbs, S. A., Roberts, M. W., & Cartelli, L. M. (1976). The effects of social punishment on noncompliance: A comparison with time out and positive practice. *Journal of Applied Behavior Analysis, 9,* 471–482.

Domjan, M., & Burkhard, B. (1986). *The principles of learning and behavior* (2nd ed.). Monterey, CA: Brooks/Cole.

Dorsey, M. F., Iwata, B. A., Ong, P., & McSween, T. E. (1980). Treatment of self-injurious behavior using a water mist: Initial response suppression and generalization. *Journal of Applied Behavior Analysis, 13,* 343–353.

Drabman, R. S., Hammer, D., & Rosenbaum, M. S. (1979). Assessing generalization in behavior modification with children: The generalization map. *Behavioral Assessment, 1,* 203–219.

Drabman, R. S., Spitalnik, R., & Spitalnik, K. (1974). Sociometric and disruptive behavior as a function of four types of token-reinforcement programs. *Journal of Applied Behavior Analysis, 7,* 93–101.

Dunlap, G., Koegel, R. L., Johnson, J., & O'Neill, R. E. (1987). Maintaining performance of autistic clients in community settings with delayed contingencies. *Journal of Applied Behavior Analysis, 20,* 179–184.

Egel, A. L., Richman, G. S., & Koegel, R. L. (1981). Normal peer models and autistic children's learning. *Journal of Applied Behavior Analysis, 14,* 3–12.

Elliott, S. N. (1988). Acceptability of behavioral treatments: Review of variables that influence treatment selection. *Professional Psychology: Research and Practice, 19,* 68–80.

Empey, L. T. (1982). *American delinquency: Its meaning and construction.* Chicago: Dorsey Press.

Emshoff, J. G., Redd, W. H., & Davidson, W. S. (1976). Generalization training and the transfer of treatment effects with delinquent adolescents. *Journal of Behavior Therapy and Experimental Psychiatry, 7,* 141–144.

Epstein, L. H., Beck, S., Figueroa, J., Farkas, G., Kazdin, A. E., Daneman, D., & Becker, D. (1981a). The effects of targeting improvements in urine glucose on metabolic control in children with insulin-dependent diabetes. *Journal of Applied Behavior Analysis, 14,* 365–375.

Epstein, L. H., Figueroa, J., Farkas, G. M., & Beck, S. (1981b). The short-term effects of feedback on accuracy of urine glucose determinations in insulin-dependent diabetic children. *Behavior Therapy, 12,* 560–564.

Epstein, L. H., Hersen, M., & Hemphill, D. P. (1974). Music feedback in the treatment of tension headache: An experimental case study. *Journal of Behavior Therapy and Experimental Psychiatry, 5,* 59–63.

Eysenck, H. J. (1952). The effects of psychotherapy: An evaluation. *Journal of Consulting Psychology, 16,* 319–324.

Fantuzzo, J. W., & Clement, P. W. (1981). Generalization of the effects of teacher- and self-administered token reinforcers to nontreated students. *Journal of Applied Behavior Analysis, 14,* 435–447.

Favell, J. E., McGimsey, J. F., & Jones, M. L. (1978). The use of physical restraint in the treatment of self-injury and as positive reinforcement. *Journal of Applied Behavior Analysis, 11,* 225–241.

Feindler, E. L., Ecton, R. B., Kingsley, D., & Dubey, D. R. (1986). Group anger-control training for institutionalized psychiatric male adolescents. *Behavior Therapy, 17,* 109–123.

Feingold, L., & Migler, B. (1972). The use of experimental dependency relationships as a motivating procedure on a token-economy ward. In R. D. Rubin, H. Fensterheim, J. D. Henderson, & L. P. Ullmann (Eds.), *Advances in behavior therapy* (pp. 121–127). New York: Academic Press.

Fichter, M. M., Wallace, C. J., Liberman, R. P., & Davis, J. R. (1976). Improving social interaction in a chronic psychotic using discriminated avoidance ("nagging"): Experimental analysis and generalization. *Journal of Applied Behavior Analysis, 9,* 337–386.

Fischer, J., & Nehs, R. (1978). Use of a commonly available chore to reduce a boy's rate of swearing. *Journal of Behavior Therapy and Experimental Psychiatry, 9,* 81–83.

Fixsen, D. L., Phillips, E. L., Phillips, E. A., & Wolf, M. M. (1976). The teaching-family model of group home treatment. In W. E. Craighead, A. E. Kazdin, & M. J. Mahoney (Eds.), *Behavior modification: Principles, issues, and applications* (pp. 310–320). Boston: Houghton Mifflin.

Fleischman, M. J. (1981). A replication of Patterson's "Intervention for boys with conduct problems." *Journal of Consulting and Clinical Psychology, 49,* 343–351.

Foley, F. W., Bedell, J. R., LaRocca, N. G., Scheinberg, L. C., & Reznikoff, M. (1987). Efficacy of stress-inoculation training in coping with multiple sclerosis. *Journal of Consulting and Clinical Psychology, 55,* 919–922.

Fordyce, W. E., Fowler, R. S., Lehmann, J. F., DeLateur, B. J., Sand, P. L., & Trieschmann, R. B. (1974). Operant conditioning in the treatment of chronic pain. *Archives of Physical Medicine and Rehabilitation, 54,* 399–408.

Forehand, R., Lautenschlager, G. J., Faust, J., & Graziano, W. G. (1986). Parent perceptions and parent-child interactions in clinic-referred children: A preliminary investigation of the effects of maternal depressive moods. *Behaviour Research and Therapy, 24,* 73–75.

Forehand, R., & McMahon, R. J. (1981). *Helping the noncompliant child: A clinician's guide to parent training.* New York: Guilford.

Forehand, R., Roberts, M. W., Doleys, D. M., Hobbs, S. A., & Resick, P. A. (1976). An examination of disciplinary procedures with children. *Journal of Experimental Child Psychology, 21,* 109–120.

Fowler, S. A., & Baer, D. M. (1981). "Do I have to be good all day?": The timing of delayed reinforcement as a factor in generalization. *Journal of Applied Behavior Analysis, 14,* 13–24.

Fowler, S. A., Dougherty, B. S., Kirby, K. C., & Kohler, F. W. (1986). Role reversals: An analysis of therapeutic effects achieved with disruptive boys during their appointments as peer monitors. *Journal of Applied Behavior Analysis, 19,* 437–444.

Fox, D. K., Hopkins, B. L., & Anger, W. K. (1987). The long-term effects of a token economy on safety performance in open-pit mining. *Journal of Applied Behavior Analysis, 20,* 215–224.

Fox, L. (1962). Effecting the use of efficient study habits. *Journal of Mathetics, 1,* 75–86.

Foxx, R. M. (1982). *Decreasing behaviors of severely retarded and autistic persons.* Champaign, IL: Research Press.

Foxx, R. M., & Azrin, N. H. (1972). Restitution: A method of eliminating aggressive-disruptive behavior of retarded and brain damaged patients. *Behaviour Research and Therapy, 10,* 15–27.

Foxx, R. M., & Bechtel, D. R. (1983). Overcorrection: A review and analysis. In S. Axelrod & J. Apsche (Eds.), *The effects of punishment on human behavior* (pp. 133–220). New York: Academic Press.

Foxx, R. M., & Hake, D. F. (1977). Gasoline conservation: A procedure for measuring and reducing the driving of college students. *Journal of Applied Behavior Analysis, 10,* 61–74.

Foxx, R. M., & Rubinoff, A. (1979). Behavioral treatment of caffeinism: Reducing excessive coffee drinking. *Journal of Applied Behavior Analysis, 12,* 335–344.

Foxx, R. M., & Shapiro, S. T. (1978). The time out ribbon: A nonexclusionary time-out procedure. *Journal of Applied Behavior Analysis, 11,* 125–136.

Frederiksen, L. W. (1975). Treatment of ruminative thinking by self-monitoring. *Journal of Behavior Therapy and Experimental Psychiatry, 6,* 258–259.

Frederiksen, L. W. (Ed.). (1982). *Handbook of organizational behavior management.* New York: Wiley.

Frederiksen, L. W., Jenkins, J. O., Foy, D. W., & Eisler, R. M. (1976). Social-skills training to modify abusive verbal outbursts in adults. *Journal of Applied Behavior Analysis, 9,* 117–125.

Friedling, C., & O'Leary, S. (1979). Effects of self-instructional training on second- and third-grade hyperactive children: A failure to replicate. *Journal of Applied Behavior Analysis, 12,* 211–219.

Friman, P. C., Finney, J. W., Glasscock, S. T., Weigel, J. W., & Christophersen, E. R. (1986). Testicular self-examination: Validation of a training strategy for early cancer detection. *Journal of Applied Behavior Analysis, 19,* 87–92.

Friman, P. C., & Hove, G. (1987). Apparent covariation between child habit disorders: Effects of successful treatment for thumb sucking on untargeted chronic hair pulling. *Journal of Applied Behavior Analysis, 20,* 421–426.

Furman, W., Geller, M., Simon, S. J., & Kelly, J. A. (1979). The use of a behavioral rehearsal procedure for teaching job interviewing skills to psychiatric patients. *Behavior Therapy, 10,* 157–167.

Gardner, W. I., Cole, C. L., Berry, D. L., & Nowinski, J. M. (1983). Reduction of disruptive behaviors in mentally retarded adults: A self-management approach. *Behavior Modification, 7,* 76–96.

Garfield, S. L., & Bergin, A. E. (Eds.). (1986). *Handbook of psychotherapy and behavior change: An empirical analysis* (3rd ed.). New York: Wiley.

Geller, E. S., Bruff, C. D., & Nimmer, J. G. (1985). "Flash for life": Community-based prompting for safety belt promotion. *Journal of Applied Behavior Analysis, 18,* 309–314.

Geller, E. S., Chaffee, J. L., & Ingram, R. E. (1975). Promoting paper recycling on a university campus. *Journal of Environmental Systems, 5,* 39–57.

Geller, E. S., Paterson, L., & Talbott, E. (1982). A behavioral analysis of incentive prompts for motivating seat belt use. *Journal of Applied Behavior Analysis, 15,* 403–415.

Geller, E. S., Winett, R. A., & Everett, P. B. (1982). *Preserving the environment: New strategies for behavior change.* Elmsford, NY: Pergamon Press.

Gesten, E. L., Rains, M., Rapkin, B. D., Weissberg, R. G., Flores de Apodaca, R., Cowen, E. L., & Bowen, G. (1982). Training children in social problem-solving competencies: A first and second look. *American Journal of Community Psychology, 10,* 95–115.

Gewirtz, J. L., & Baer, D. M. (1958). Deprivation and satiation of social reinforcers as drive conditions. *Journal of Abnormal and Social Psychology, 57,* 165–172.

Gillum, R. R., & Barsky, A. J. (1974). Diagnosis and management of patient noncompliance. *Journal of the American Medical Association, 12,* 1563–1567.

Glasgow, R. E., & Rosen, G. M. (1984). Self-help behavior therapy manuals: Recent developments and clinical usage. In C. M. Franks (Ed.), *New developments in behavior therapy: From research to clinical application* (pp. 525–570). New York: Haworth Press.

Glynn, E. L. (1970). Classroom applications of self-determined reinforcement. *Journal of Applied Behavior Analysis, 3,* 123–132.

Goetz, E. M., Holmberg, M. C., & LeBlanc, J. M. (1975). Differential reinforcement of other behavior and noncontingent reinforcement as control procedures during the modification of a preschooler's compliance. *Journal of Applied Behavior Analysis, 8,* 77–82.

Goldiamond, I. (1965). Self-control procedures in personal behavior problems. *Psychological Reports, 17,* 851–868.

Green, G. R., Linsk, N. L., & Pinkston, E. M. (1986). Modification of verbal behavior of the mentally impaired elderly by their spouses. *Journal of Applied Behavior Analysis, 19,* 329–336.

Green, R. B., Hardison, W. L., & Greene, B. F. (1984). Turning the table on advice programs for parents: Using placements to enhance family interaction at restaurants. *Journal of Applied Behavior Analysis, 17,* 497–508.

Greenwood, C. R., Delquadri, J. C., & Hall, R. V. (1984). Opportunity to respond and student academic performance. In W. L. Heward, T. E. Heron, D. S. Hill, & J. Trap-Porter (Eds.), *Focus on behavior analysis in education* (pp. 58–88). Columbus, OH: Merrill.

Greenwood, C. R., Dinwiddie, G., Bailey, V., Carta, J. J., Dorsey, D., Kohler, F. W., Nelson, C., Rotholz, D., & Schulte, D. (1987). Field replication of classwide peer tutoring. *Journal of Applied Behavior Analysis, 20,* 151–160.

Greenwood, C. R., & Hops, H. (1981). Group-oriented contingencies and peer behavior change. In P. S. Strain (Ed.), *The utilization of classroom peers as behavior change agents.* New York: Plenum.

Greenwood, C. R., Hops, H., Delquadri, J., & Guild, J. (1974). Group contingencies for group consequences in classroom management: A further analysis. *Journal of Applied Behavior Analysis, 7,* 413–425.

Greer, R. D., & Polirstok, S. R. (1982). Collateral gains and short-term maintenance in reading and on-task responses by inner-city adolescents as a function of their use of social reinforcement while tutoring. *Journal of Applied Behavior Analysis, 15,* 123–139.

Griffin, J. C., Locke, B. J., & Landers, W. F. (1975). Manipulation of potential punishment parameters in the treatment of self-injury. *Journal of Applied Behavior Analysis, 8,* 458.

Gross, A. M., & Drabman, R. S. (1982). Teaching self-recording, self-evaluation, and self-reward to nonclinic children and adolescents. In P. Karoly & F. H. Kanfer (Eds.), *Self-management and behavior change: From theory to practice.* Elmsford, NY: Pergamon Press.

Gross, A. M., & Ekstrand, M. (1983). Increasing and maintaining rates of teacher praise: A study using public posting and feedback fading. *Behavior Modification, 7,* 126–135.

Gross, A. M., & Wojnilower, D. A. (1984). Self-directed behavior change in children: Is it self-directed? *Behavior Therapy, 15,* 501–514.

Guidano, V. F., & Liotti, G. (1983). *Cognitive processes and emotional disorders: A structural approach to psychotherapy.* New York: Guilford.

Hackmann, A., & McLean, C. A. (1975). A comparison of flooding thought stopping in the treatment of obsessional neurosis. *Behaviour Research and Therapy, 13,* 263–269.

Hall, C. S., & Lindzey, G. (1978). *Theories of personality* (3rd ed.). New York: Wiley.

Hall, D. C., Adams, C. K., Stein, G. H., Stephenson, H. S., Goldstein, M. K., & Pennypacker, H. S. (1980). Improved detection of human breast lesions following experimental training. *Cancer, 46,* 408–414.

Hall, R. V., Axelrod, S., Foundopoulos, M., Shellman, J., Campbell, R. A., &

Cranston, S. (1971). The effective use of punishment to modify behavior in the classroom. *Educational Technology, 11,* 24–26.

Hall, R. V., Axelrod, S., Tyler, L., Grief, E., Jones, F. C., & Robertson, R. (1972). Modification of behavior problems in the home with a parent as observer and experimenter. *Journal of Applied Behavior Analysis, 5,* 53–64.

Hall, S. M., Cooper, J. L., Burmaster, S., & Polk, A. (1977). Contingency contracting as a therapeutic tool with methadone maintenance clients: Six single-subject studies. *Behavior Research and Therapy, 15,* 438–441.

Hallam, R. S., & Rachman, S. (1976). Current status of aversion therapy. In M. Hersen, R. M. Eisler, & P. M. Miller (Eds.), *Progress in behavior modification* (Vol. 2, pp. 179–222). New York: Academic Press.

Hancock v. Avery, 301 F. Supp. (M.D. Tenn. 1969).

Haney, J. I., & Jones, R. T. (1982). Programming maintenance as a major component of a community-centered preventive effort: Escape from fire. *Behavior Therapy, 13,* 47–62.

Haring, T. G., Kennedy, C. H., Adams, M. J., & Pitts-Conway, V. (1987). Teaching generalization of purchasing skills across community settings to autistic youth using videotape modeling. *Journal of Applied Behavior Analysis, 20,* 89–96.

Harris, K. R. (1986). Self-monitoring of attentional behavior versus self-monitoring of productivity: Effects on on-task behavior and academic response rate among learning-disabled children. *Journal of Applied Behavior Analysis, 19,* 417–424.

Harris, V. W., & Sherman, J. A. (1973). Use and analysis of the "good-behavior game" to reduce disruptive classroom behavior. *Journal of Applied Behavior Analysis, 6,* 405–417.

Hartmann, D. P. (1977). Considerations in the choice of interobserver reliability estimates. *Journal of Applied Behavior Analysis, 10,* 103–116.

Hartmann, D. P., & Hall, R. V. (1976). The changing criterion design. *Journal of Applied Behavior Analysis, 9,* 527–532.

Harvey, J. R., Karan, O. C., Bhargava, D., & Morehouse, N. (1978). Relaxation training and cognitive behavioral procedures to reduce violent temper outbursts in a moderately retarded woman. *Journal of Behavior Therapy and Experimental Psychiatry, 9,* 347–351.

Hauserman, N., & Lavin, P. (1977). Posthospitalization continuation treatment of anorexia nervosa. *Journal of Behavior Therapy and Experimental Psychiatry, 8,* 309–313.

Hawkins, R. P., & Dobes, R. W. (1975). Behavioral definitions in applied behavior analysis: Explicit or implicit. In B. C. Etzel, J. M. LeBlanc, & D. M. Baer (Eds.), *New developments in behavioral research: Theory, methods, and applications: In honor of Sidney W. Bijou.* Hillsdale, NJ: Lawrence Erlbaum Associates.

Hayes, S. C., Brownell, K. D., & Barlow, D. H. (1978). The use of self-administered covert sensitization in the treatment of exhibitionism and sadism. *Behavior Therapy, 9,* 283–289.

Hayes, S. C., & Nelson, R. O. (1986). Assessing the effects of therapeutic interventions. In R. O. Nelson & S. C. Hayes (Eds.), *Conceptual foundations of behavioral assessment* (pp. 430–460). New York: Guilford.

Hayes, S. C., Rosenfarb, I., Wulfert, E., Munt, E. D., Korn, Z., & Zettle, R. D. (1985). Self-reinforcement effects: An artifact of social standard setting? *Journal of Applied Behavior Analysis, 18,* 201–214.

Haynes, S. N., & Horn, W. F. (1982). Reactivity in behavioral observation: A methodological and conceptual critique. *Behavioral Assessment, 4,* 369–385.

Heaton, R. C., & Safer, D. J. (1982). Secondary school outcome following a junior high school behavioral program. *Behavior Therapy, 13,* 226–231.

Heckel, R. B., Wiggins, S. L., & Salzberg, H. C. (1962). Conditioning against silences in group therapy. *Journal of Clinical Psychology, 18,* 216–217.

Hegel, M. T., Ayllon, T., VanderPlate, C., & Spiro-Hawkins, H. (1986). A behavioral procedure for increasing compliance with self-exercise regimens in severely burn-injured patients. *Behaviour Research and Therapy, 24,* 521–528.

Herbert, E. W., Pinkston, E. M., Hayden, M., Sajwaj, T. E., Pinkston, S., Cordua, G., & Jackson, C. (1973). Adverse effects of differential parental attention. *Journal of Applied Behavior Analysis, 6,* 15–30.

Hermann, J. A., deMontes, A. I., Dominguez, B., Montes, F., & Hopkins, B. L. (1973). Effects of bonuses for punctuality on the tardiness of industrial workers. *Journal of Applied Behavior Analysis, 6,* 563–570.

Hineline, P. N. (1977). Negative reinforcement and avoidance. In W. K. Honig & J. E. R. Staddon (Eds.), *Handbook of operant behavior* (pp. 364–414). Englewood Cliffs, NJ: Prentice-Hall.

Hobbs, S. A., & Forehand, R. (1975). Effects of differential release from time out on children's deviant behavior. *Journal of Behavior Therapy and Experimental Psychiatry, 6,* 256–257.

Hobbs, S. A., & Forehand, R. (1977). Important parameters in the use of time out with children: A reexamination. *Journal of Behavior Therapy and Experimental Psychiatry, 8,* 365–370.

Hobbs, S. A., Forehand, R., & Murray, R. G. (1978). Effects of various durations of time out on the noncompliant behavior of children. *Behavior Therapy, 9,* 652–656.

Hoffman, M. L. (1960). Power assertion by the parent and its impact on the child. *Child Development, 31,* 129–143.

Holroyd, K. A. (1986). Recurrent headache. In K. A. Holroyd, & T. L. Creer (Eds.), *Self-management of chronic disease: Handbook of clinical interventions and research* (pp. 373–413). New York: Academic Press.

Holroyd, K. A., Andrasik, R., & Westbrook, T. (1977). Cognitive control of tension headache. *Cognitive Therapy and Research, 1,* 121–133.

Holroyd, K. A., & Creer, T. L. (Eds.). (1986). *Self-management of chronic disease: Handbook of clinical interventions and research.* New York: Academic Press.

Homme, L. E. (1965). Perspectives in psychology: XXIV. Control of coverants, the operants of the mind. *Psychological Record, 15,* 501–511.

Hopkins, B. L., Conrad, R. J., Dangel, R. F., Fitch, H. G., Smith, M. J., & Anger, W. K. (1986). Behavioral technology for reducing occupational exposures to styrene. *Journal of Applied Behavior Analysis, 19,* 3–12.

Horner, R. H., Albin, R. W., & Ralph, G. (1986). Generalization with precision: The role of negative teaching examples in the instruction of generalized grocery item selection. *Journal of the Association for Persons with Severe Handicaps, 11,* 300–308.

Horner, R. H., Bellamy, G. T., & Colvin, G. T. (1984). Responding in the presence of nontrained stimuli: Implications of generalization error patterns. *Journal of the Association for Persons with Severe Handicaps, 9,* 287–295.

Horner, R. H., Eberhard, J. M., & Sheehan, M. R. (1986). Teaching generalized table bussing: The importance of negative teaching examples. *Behavior Modification, 10,* 457–471.

Horner, R. H., & Keilitz, I. (1975). Training mentally retarded adolescents to brush their teeth. *Journal of Applied Behavior Analysis, 8,* 301–309.

Horner, R. H., Williams, J. A., & Knobbe, C. A. (1985). The effects of "opportunity to perform" on the maintenance of skills learned by high school students with severe handicaps. *Journal of the Association for Persons with Severe Handicaps, 10,* 172–175.

Hundert, J., & Bastone, D. (1978). A practical procedure to maintain pupils' accurate self-rating in a classroom token program. *Behavior Modification, 2,* 93–112.

Hutchinson, R. R. (1977). By-products of aversive control. In W. K. Honig & J. E. R. Staddon (Eds.), *Handbook of operant behavior* (pp. 415–431). Englewood Cliffs, NJ: Prentice-Hall.

Iwata, B. A. (1987). Negative reinforcement in applied behavior analysis: An emerging technology. *Journal of Applied Behavior Analysis, 20,* 361–378.

Iwata, B. A., & Becksfort, C. M. (1981). Behavioral research in preventive dentistry: Educational and contingency management approaches to the problem of patient compliance. *Journal of Applied Behavior Analysis, 14,* 111–120.

Jackson, D. A., & Wallace, R. F. (1974). The modification and generalization of voice loudness in a 15-year-old retarded girl. *Journal of Applied Behavior Analysis, 7,* 461–471.

Jackson, J. L., & Calhoun, K. S. (1977). Effects of two variable-ratio schedules of time out: Changes in target and nontarget behaviors. *Journal of Behavior Therapy and Experimental Psychiatry, 8,* 195–199.

Jacobs, H. E., Fairbanks, D., Poche, C. E., & Bailey, J. S. (1982). Multiple incentives in encouraging car pool information on a university campus. *Journal of Applied Behavior Analysis, 15,* 141–149.

James, J. E. (1981). Behavioral self-control of stuttering using time out from speaking. *Journal of Applied Behavior Analysis, 14,* 25–37.

James, S. D., & Egel, A. L. (1986). A direct prompting strategy for increasing reciprocal interactions between handicapped and nonhandicapped siblings. *Journal of Applied Behavior Analysis, 19,* 173–186.

Jason, L. A., & Liotta, R. (1982). Pedestrian jaywalking under facilitating and nonfacilitating conditions. *Journal of Applied Behavior Analysis, 15,* 469–473.

Jason, L. A., Neal, A. M., & Marinakis, G. (1985). Altering contingencies to facilitate compliance with traffic light systems. *Journal of Applied Behavior Analysis, 18,* 95–100.

Jay, S. M., Elliot, C. H., Katz, E., & Siegel, S. E. (1987). Cognitive-behavioral and pharmacologic interventions for children's distress during painful medical procedures. *Journal of Consulting and Clinical Psychology, 55,* 860–865.

Johnson, M. S., & Bailey, J. S. (1977). The modification of leisure behavior in a halfway house for retarded women. *Journal of Applied Behavior Analysis, 10,* 273–282.

Johnston, J. M., & Johnston, G. T. (1972). Modification of consonant speech-sound articulation in young children. *Journal of Applied Behavior Analysis, 5,* 233–246.

Jones, M. C. (1924). A laboratory study of fear: The case of Peter. *Pedagogical Seminary, 31,* 308–315.

Jones, R. R., Weinrott, M. R., & Howard, J. R. (1981, June). *The national evaluation of the teaching family model.* Final report to the National Institute of Mental Health, Center for Studies in Crime and Delinquency.

Jones, R. T., Kazdin, A. E., & Haney, J. I. (1981a). Social validation and training of emergency fire safety skills for potential injury prevention and life-saving. *Journal of Applied Behavior Analysis, 14,* 249–260.

Jones, R. T., Kazdin, A. E., & Haney, J. I. (1981b). A follow-up to training of emergency skills. *Behavior Therapy, 12,* 716–722.

Jones, R. T., Nelson, R. E., & Kazdin, A. E. (1977). The role of external variables in self-reinforcement: A review. *Behavior Modification, 1,* 147–178.

Kallman, W. H., Hersen, M., & O'Toole, D. H. (1975). The use of social reinforcement in a case of conversion reaction. *Behavior Therapy, 6,* 411–413.

Kandel, H. J., Ayllon, T., & Rosenbaum, M. S. (1977). Flooding or systematic exposure in the treatment of extreme social withdrawal in children. *Journal of Behavior Therapy and Experimental Psychiatry, 8,* 75–81.

Kanfer, F. H. (1977). The many faces of self-control, or behavior modification changes its focus. In R. B. Stuart (Ed.), *Behavioral self-management: Strategies, techniques, and outcomes* (pp. 1–48). New York: Brunner/Mazel.

Kanfer, F. H., Karoly, P., & Newman, A. (1975). Reduction of children's fear of the dark by competence-related and situational threat-related verbal cues. *Journal of Consulting and Clinical Psychology, 43,* 251–258.

Karasu, T. B. (1985). Personal communication, March 1, 1985.

Karoly, P. (1977). Behavioral self-management in children: Concepts, methods, issues, and directions. In M. Hersen, R. M. Eisler, & P. M. Miller (Eds.), *Progress in behavior modification* (Vol. 5, pp. 197–262). New York: Academic Press.

Karoly, P. (1982). Perspectives on self-management and behavior change. In P. Karoly & F. H. Kanfer (Eds.), *Self-management and behavior change: From theory to practice* (pp. 3–31). Elmsford, NY: Pergamon Press.

Karoly, P., & Kanfer, F. H. (Eds.). (1982). *Self-management and behavior change: From theory to practice.* Elmsford, NY: Pergamon Press.

Kazdin, A. E. (1971). The effect of response cost in suppressing behavior in a pre-psychotic retardate. *Journal of Behavior Therapy and Experimental Psychiatry, 2,* 137–140.

Kazdin, A. E. (1972). Response cost: The removal of conditioned reinforcers for therapeutic change. *Behavior Therapy, 3,* 533–546.

Kazdin, A. E. (1973a). Role of instructions and reinforcement in behavior changes in token reinforcement programs. *Journal of Educational Psychology, 64,* 63–71.

Kazdin, A. E. (1973b). The effect of vicarious reinforcement on attentive behavior in the classroom. *Journal of Applied Behavior Analysis, 6,* 71–78.

Kazdin, A. E. (1973c). The effect of response cost and aversive stimulation in suppressing punished and nonpunished speech disfluencies. *Behavior Therapy, 4,* 73–82.

Kazdin, A. E. (1974). Self-monitoring and behavior change. In M. J. Mahoney & C. E. Thoresen (Eds.), *Self-control: Power to the person* (pp. 218–246). Monterey, CA: Brooks/Cole.

Kazdin, A. E. (1977a). *The token economy: A review and evaluation.* New York: Plenum.

Kazdin, A. E. (1977b). Artifact, bias, and complexity of assessment: The ABC's of reliability. *Journal of Applied Behavior Analysis, 10,* 141–150.

Kazdin, A. E. (1977c). The influence of behavior preceding a reinforced response on behavior change in the classroom. *Journal of Applied Behavior Analysis, 10,* 299–310.

Kazdin, A. E. (1977d). Assessing the clinical or applied importance of behavior change through social validation. *Behavior Modification, 1,* 427–452.

Kazdin, A. E. (1977e). Vicarious reinforcement and direction of behavior change in the classroom. *Behavior Therapy, 8,* 57–63.

Kazdin, A. E. (1978). *History of behavior modification: Experimental foundations of contemporary research.* Baltimore: University Park Press.

Kazdin, A. E. (1979a). Vicarious reinforcement and punishment in operant programs for children. *Child Behavior Therapy, 1,* 13–36.

Kazdin, A. E. (1979b). Unobtrusive measures in behavioral assessment. *Journal of Applied Behavior Analysis, 12,* 713–724.

Kazdin, A. E. (1980a). *Research design in clinical psychology.* New York: Harper & Row.

Kazdin, A. E. (1980b). Acceptability of time out from reinforcement procedures for disruptive child behavior. *Behavior Therapy, 11,* 329–344.

Kazdin, A. E. (1980c). Acceptability of alternative treatments for deviant child behavior. *Journal of Applied Behavior Analysis, 13,* 259–273.

Kazdin, A. E. (1981a). Drawing valid inferences from case studies. *Journal of Consulting and Clinical Psychology, 49,* 183–192.

Kazdin, A. E. (1981b). Behavior modification in education: Contributions and limitations. *Developmental Review, 1,* 34–57.

Kazdin, A. E. (1981c). Acceptability of child treatment techniques: The influence of treatment efficacy and adverse side effects. *Behavior Therapy, 12,* 493–506.

Kazdin, A. E. (1982a). Symptom substitution, generalization, and response covariation: Implications for psychotherapy outcome. *Psychological Bulletin, 91,* 349–365.

Kazdin, A. E. (1982b). Observer effects: Reactivity of direct observation. *New Directions for Methodology of Social and Behavioral Science, 14,* 5–19.

Kazdin, A. E. (1982c). *Single-case research designs: Methods for clinical and applied settings*. New York: Oxford University Press.

Kazdin, A. E. (1982d). Current developments and research issues in cognitive-behavioral interventions. *School Psychology Review, 11*, 75–82.

Kazdin, A. E. (1983). Failure of persons to respond to the token economy. In E. B. Foa & P. M. G. Emmelkamp (Eds.), *Failures in behavior therapy* (pp. 335–354). New York: Wiley.

Kazdin, A. E. (1984). Covert modeling. In P. C. Kendall (Ed.), *Advances in cognitive-behavioral research and therapy* (Vol. 3, pp. 103–129). New York: Academic Press.

Kazdin, A. E. (1985a). Selection of target behaviors: The relationship of the treatment focus to clinical dysfunction. *Behavioral Assessment, 7*, 33–47.

Kazdin, A. E. (1985b). *Treatment of antisocial behavior in children and adolescents*. Chicago: Dorsey Press.

Kazdin, A. E. (1987a). *Conduct disorder in childhood and adolescence*. Newbury Park, CA: Sage.

Kazdin, A. E. (1987b). Treatment of antisocial behavior in children: Current status and future of directions. *Psychological Bulletin, 102*, 187–203.

Kazdin, A. E. (1988). *Child psychotherapy: Developing and identifying effective treatments*. Elmsford, NY: Pergamon Press.

Kazdin, A. E., & Cole, P. M. (1981). Attitudes and labeling biases toward behavior modification: The effects of labels, content, and jargon. *Behavior Therapy, 12*, 56–68.

Kazdin, A. E., Esveldt-Dawson, K., French, N. H., & Unis, A. S. (1987). Problem-solving skills training and relationship therapy in the treatment of antisocial child behavior. *Journal of Consulting and Clinical Psychology, 55*, 76–85.

Kazdin, A. E., French, N. H., & Sherick, R. B. (1981). Acceptability of alternative treatments for children: Evaluations by inpatient children, parents, and staff. *Journal of Consulting and Clinical Psychology, 49*, 900–907.

Kazdin, A. E., French, N. H., Unis, A. S., Esveldt-Dawson, K., & Sherick, R. B. (1983). Hopelessness, depression, and suicidal intent among psychiatrically disturbed inpatient children. *Journal of Consulting and Clinical Psychology, 51*, 504–510.

Kazdin, A. E., & Geesey, S. (1977). Simultaneous-treatment design comparisons of the effects of earning reinforcers for one's peers versus for oneself. *Behavior Therapy, 8*, 682–693.

Kazdin, A. E., & Hartmann, D. P. (1978). The simultaneous-treatment design. *Behavior Therapy, 9*, 912–922.

Kazdin, A. E., & Klock, J. (1973). The effect of nonverbal teacher approval on student attentive behavior. *Journal of Applied Behavior Analysis, 6*, 643–654.

Kazdin, A. E., & Mascitelli, S. (1980). The opportunity to earn oneself off a token system as a reinforcer for attentive behavior. *Behavior Therapy, 11*, 68–78.

Kazdin, A. E., & Moyer, W. (1976). Training teachers to use behavior modification. In S. Yen & R. W. McIntire (Eds.), *Training behavior modification* (pp. 171–200). Kalamazoo, MI: Behaviordelia.

Kazdin, A. E., & Polster, R. (1973). Intermittent token reinforcement and response maintenance in extinction. *Behavior Therapy, 4*, 386–391.

Kazdin, A. E., Silverman, N. A., & Sittler, J. L. (1975). The use of prompts to enhance vicarious effects of nonverbal approval. *Journal of Applied Behavior Analysis, 8,* 279–286.

Kazdin, A. E., & Smith, G. M. (1979). Covert conditioning: A review and evaluation. *Advances in Behaviour Research and Therapy, 2,* 57–98.

Kazdin, A. E., & Wilson, G. T. (1978). Criteria for evaluating psychotherapy. *Archives of General Psychiatry, 35,* 407–416.

Keep America Beautiful, Inc. (1968). *Who litters and why?* (Available from 99 Park Avenue, New York.)

Kelly, J. A., & Drabman, R. S. (1977). Overcorrection: An effective procedure that failed. *Journal of Clinical Child Psychology, 6,* 38–40.

Kendall, P. C., & Braswell, L. (1985). *Cognitive behavioral therapy for impulsive children.* New York: Guilford.

Kent, R. N., & Foster, S. L. (1977). Direct observational procedures: Methodological issues in naturalistic settings. In A. R. Ciminero, K. S. Calhoun, & H. E. Adams (Eds.), *Handbook of behavioral assessment.* New York: Wiley.

Kent, R. N., Kanowitz, J., O'Leary, K. D., & Cheiken, M. (1977). Observer reliability as a function of circumstances of assessment. *Journal of Applied Behavior Analysis, 10,* 317–324.

Kent, R. N., O'Leary, K. D., Diament, C., & Dietz, A. (1974). Expectation biases in observational evaluation of therapeutic change. *Journal of Consulting and Clinical Psychology, 42,* 774–780.

Kiecolt-Glaser, J. K., Glaser, R., Strain, E. C., Stout, J. C., Tarr, K. L., Holliday, J. E., & Speicher, C. E. (1986). Modulation of cellular immunity in medical students. *Journal of Behavioral Medicine, 9,* 5–21.

Kiecolt-Glaser, J. K., Glaser, R., Williger, D., Stout, J. C., Messick, G., Sheppard, S., Ricker, D., Romisher, S. C., Briner, W., Bonnell, G., & Donnerberg, R. (1985). Psychosocial enhancement of immunocompetence in a geriatric population. *Health Psychology, 4,* 25–41.

King, G. F., Armitage, S. G., & Tilton, J. R. (1960). A therapeutic approach to schizophrenics of extreme pathology: An operant-interpersonal method. *Journal of Abnormal and Social Psychology, 61,* 276–286.

Kinkade, K. (1973). *A Walden two experiment: The first five years of Twin Oaks Community.* New York: William Morrow.

Kirby, F. D., & Shields, F. (1972). Modification of arithmetic response rate and attending behavior in a seventh-grade student. *Journal of Applied Behavior Analysis, 5,* 79–84.

Kirigin, K. A., Braukmann, C. J., Atwater, J. D., & Wolf, M. M. (1982). An evaluation of teaching-family (Achievement Place) group homes for juvenile offenders. *Journal of Applied Behavior Analysis, 15,* 1–16.

Kirigin, K. A., Wolf, M. M., Braukmann, C. J., Fixsen, D. L., & Phillips, E. L. (1979). Achievement Place: A preliminary outcome evaluation. In J. S. Stumphauzer (Ed.), *Progress in behavior therapy with delinquents* (pp. 118–145). Springfield, IL: Charles C Thomas.

Koegel, R. L., O'Dell, M. C., & Koegel, L. K. (1987). A natural language teaching paradigm for nonverbal autistic children. *Journal of Autism and Developmental Disorders, 17,* 187–200.

Koegel, R. L., & Rincover, A. (1974). Treatment of psychotic children in a classroom environment: 1. Learning in a large group. *Journal of Applied Behavior Analysis, 7,* 45–59.

Kohlberg, L., Yaeger, H., & Hjerthuim, E. (1968). Private speech: Four studies and a review of theories. *Child Development, 39,* 691–736.

Konarski, E. A., Johnson, M. R., Crowell, C. R., & Whitman, T. L. (1981). An alternative approach to reinforcement for applied researchers: Response deprivation. *Behavior Therapy, 12,* 653–666.

Kushner, M. (1968). The operant control of intractable sneezing. In C. D. Spielberger, R. Fox, & B. Masterson (Eds.), *Contributions to general psychology.* New York: Ronald Press.

Lancioni, G. E. (1982). Normal children as tutors to teach social responses to withdrawn mentally retarded schoolmates: Training, maintenance, and generalization. *Journal of Applied Behavior Analysis, 15,* 17–40.

Lattal, K. A. (1969). Contingency management of toothbrushing behavior in a summer camp for children. *Journal of Applied Behavior Analysis, 2,* 195–198.

LeBlanc, J. M., Busby, K. H., & Thomson, C. L. (1974). The functions of time out for changing the aggressive behaviors of a preschool child: A multiple-baseline analysis. In R. Ulrich, T. Stachnik, & J. Mabry (Eds.), *Control of human behavior* (Vol. 3, pp. 358–364). Glenview, IL: Scott, Foresman.

Lennox, D. B., Miltenberger, R. G., & Donnelly, D. R. (1987). Response interruption and DRL for the reduction of rapid eating. *Journal of Applied Behavior Analysis, 20,* 279–284.

Liberman, R. P., Teigen, J., Patterson, R., & Baker, V. (1973). Reducing delusional speech in chronic, paranoid schizophrenics. *Journal of Applied Behavior Analysis, 6,* 57–64.

Lichstein, K. L. (1988). *Clinical relaxation strategies.* New York: Wiley.

Lindsay, W. R., & Stoffelmayr, B. E. (1976). A comparison of the differential effects of three different baseline conditions within an ABA_1B_1 experimental design. *Behaviour Research and Therapy, 14,* 169–173.

Lindsley, O. R. (1956). Operant conditioning methods applied to research in chronic schizophrenia. *Psychiatric Research Reports, 24,* 289–291.

Lindsley, O. R. (1960). Characteristics of the behavior of chronic psychotics as revealed by free-operant conditioning methods. *Diseases of the Nervous System* (Monograph Supplement), *21,* 66–78.

Linscheid, T. R., & Cunningham, C. E. (1977). A controlled demonstration of the effectiveness of electric shock in the elimination of chronic infant rumination. *Journal of Applied Behavior Analysis, 10,* 500.

Lochman, J. E., Burch, P. R., Curry, J. F., & Lampron, L. B. (1984). Treatment and generalization effects of cognitive-behavioral and goal-setting interventions with aggressive boys. *Journal of Consulting and Clinical Psychology, 52,* 915–916.

Locke, E. A., Cartledge, N., & Koeppel, J. (1968). Motivational effects of knowledge of results. *Psychological Bulletin, 70,* 474–485.

Lovaas, O. I. (1987). Behavioral treatment and normal educational/intellectual functioning in young autistic children. *Journal of Consulting and Clinical Psychology, 55,* 3–9.

Lovaas, O. I., Koegel, R., Simmons, J. Q., & Long, J. S. (1973). Some generalization and follow-up measures on autistic children in behavior therapy. *Journal of Applied Behavior Analysis, 6,* 131–166.

Lovaas, O. I., & Simmons, J. Q. (1969). Manipulation of self-destruction in three retarded children. *Journal of Applied Behavior Analysis, 2,* 143–157.

Lowe, K., & Lutzker, J. R. (1979). Increasing compliance to a medical regimen with a juvenile diabetic. *Behavior Therapy, 10,* 57–64.

Lowitz, G. H., & Suib, M. R. (1978). Generalized control of persistent thumbsucking by differential reinforcement of other behaviors. *Journal of Behavior Therapy and Experimental Psychiatry, 9,* 343–346.

Luce, S. C., Delquadri, J., & Hall, R. V. (1980). Contingent exercise: A mild but powerful procedure for suppressing inappropriate verbal and aggressive behavior. *Journal of Applied Behavior Analysis, 13,* 583–594.

Luce, S. C., & Hall, R. V. (1981). Contingent exercise: A procedure used with differential reinforcement to reduce bizarre verbal behavior. *Education and Treatment of Children, 4,* 309–327.

MacPherson, E. M., Candee, B. L., & Hohman, R. J. (1974). A comparison of three methods for eliminating disruptive lunchroom behavior. *Journal of Applied Behavior Analysis, 7,* 287–297.

Madsen, C. H., Becker, W. C., & Thomas, D. R. (1968). Rules, praise, and ignoring: Elements of elementary classroom control. *Journal of Applied Behavior Analysis, 1,* 139–150.

Madsen, C. H., Becker, W. C., Thomas, D. R., Koser, L., & Plager, E. (1970). An analysis of the reinforcing function of "sit down" commands. In R. K. Parker (Ed.), *Readings in educational psychology.* Boston, MA: Allyn & Bacon.

Mahoney, K., Van Wagenen, R. K., & Meyerson, L. (1971). Toilet training of normal and retarded children. *Journal of Applied Behavior Analysis, 4,* 173–181.

Maloney, D. M., Harper, T. M., Braukmann, C. J., Fixsen, D. L., Phillips. E. L., & Wolf, M. M. (1976). Teaching conversation-related skills to predelinquent girls. *Journal of Applied Behavior Analysis, 9,* 371.

Maloney, K. B., & Hopkins, B. L. (1973). The modification of sentence structure and its relationship to subjective judgments of creativity in writing. *Journal of Applied Behavior Analysis, 6,* 425–433.

Mank, D. M., & Horner, R. H. (1987). Self-recruited feedback: A cost-effective procedure for maintaining behavior. *Research in Developmental Disabilities, 8,* 91–112.

Mansdorf, I. J. (1977). Reinforcer isolation: An alternative to subject isolation in time out from positive reinforcement. *Journal of Behavior Therapy and Experimental Psychiatry, 8,* 391–393.

Marholin, D., II, & Gray, D. (1976). Effects of group response cost procedures on cash shortages in a small business. *Journal of Applied Behavior Analysis, 9,* 25–30.

Marholin, D., II, & Steinman, W. M. (1977). Stimulus control in the classroom as a function of the behavior reinforced. *Journal of Applied Behavior Analysis, 10,* 465–478.

Marholin, D., II, & Townsend, N. M. (1978). An experimental analysis of side effects and response maintenance of a modified overcorrection procedure: The case of a persistent twiddler. *Behavior Therapy, 9,* 383–390.

Marks, I. M. (1987). *Fears, phobias, and rituals.* New York: Oxford University Press.

Marshall, W. L., Presse, L., & Andrews, W. R. (1976). A self-administered program for public speaking anxiety. *Behaviour Research and Therapy, 14,* 33–40.

Martin, R. (1975). *Legal challenges to behavior modification: Trends in schools, corrections, and mental health.* Champaign, IL: Research Press.

Mash, E. J., & Johnson, C. (1983). Parental perceptions of child behavior problems, parenting self-esteem, and mothers' reported stress in younger and older hyperactive and normal children. *Journal of Consulting and Clinical Psychology, 51,* 86–99.

Matson, J. L., & Ollendick, T. H. (1977). Issues in toilet training normal children. *Behavior Therapy, 8,* 549–553.

Mayhew, G. L., & Harris, F. C. (1978). Some negative side effects of a punishment procedure for stereotyped behavior. *Journal of Behavior Therapy and Experimental Psychiatry, 9,* 245–251.

McClannahan, L. E., & Risley, T. R. (1975). Design of living environments for nursing-home residents: Increasing participation in recreation activities. *Journal of Applied Behavior Analysis, 8,* 261–268.

McGee, C. S., Kauffman, J. M., & Nussen, J. L. (1977). Children as therapeutic change agents: Reinforcement intervention paradigms. *Review of Educational Research, 47,* 451–477.

McLaughlin, T. F., Williams, R. L., Truhlicka, M., Cady, M., Ripple, B. J., & Eakins, D. (1983). Model implementation and classroom achievement in the Northern Cheyenne Behavior Analysis Follow-Through Project. *Child and Family Behavior Therapy, 4,* 103–111.

McMahon, R. J., & Forehand, R. (1978). Nonprescription behavior therapy: Effectiveness of a brochure in teaching mothers to correct their children's inappropriate mealtime behaviors. *Behavior Therapy, 9,* 814–820.

McNees, M. P., Egli, D. S., Marshall, D. S., Schnelle, R. S., Schnelle, J. F., & Risley, T. R. (1976). Shoplifting prevention: Providing information through signs. *Journal of Applied Behavior Analysis, 9,* 399–405.

McReynolds, W. T., & Church, A. (1973). Self-control study skills development and counseling approaches to the improvement of study behavior. *Behaviour Research and Therapy, 11,* 233–235.

Meichenbaum, D. H., & Cameron, R. (1983). Stress inoculation training: Toward a general paradigm for training coping skills. In D. H. Meichenbaum & M. E. Jeremko (Eds.), *Stress reduction and prevention.* New York: Plenum.

Miller, A. J., & Kratochwill, T. R. (1979). Reduction of frequent stomachache complaints by time out. *Behavior Therapy, 10,* 211–218.

Miller, P. M. (1972). The use of behavioral contracting in the treatment of alcoholism: A case report. *Behavior Therapy, 3,* 593–596.

Miller, W. R. (1977). Behavioral self-control training in the treatment of problem drinkers. In R. B. Stuart (Eds.), *Behavioral self-management: Strategies, techniques, and outcomes* (pp. 154–175). New York: Brunner/Mazel.

Minkin, N., Braukmann, C. J., Minkin, B. L., Timbers, G. D., Timbers, B. J., Fixsen, D. L., Phillips, E. L., & Wolf, M. M. (1976). The social validation and training of conversational skills. *Journal of Applied Behavior Analysis, 9,* 127–139.

Mirman, R. (1982). Performance management in sales organizations. In L. W. Frederiksen (Ed.), *Handbook of organizational behavior management* (pp. 427–475). New York: Wiley.

Mitchell, W. S., & Stoffelmayr, B. E. (1973). Application of the Premack principle to the behavioral control of extremely inactive schizophrenics. *Journal of Applied Behavior Analysis, 6,* 419–423.

Monti, P. M., McCrady, B. S., & Barlow, D. H. (1977). Effect of positive reinforcement, informational feedback, and contingency contracting on a bulimic anorexic female. *Behavior Therapy, 8,* 258–263.

Morin, C., Ladouceur, R., & Cloutier, R. (1982). Reinforcement procedure in the treatment of reluctant speech. *Journal of Behavior Therapy and Experimental Psychiatry, 13,* 145–147.

Morris, E. K., & Redd, W. H. (1975). Children's performance and social preference for positive, negative, and mixed adult-child interactions. *Child Development, 46,* 525–531.

Morse, W. H., & Kelleher, R. T. (1977). Determinants of reinforcement and punishment. In W. K. Honig & J. E. R. Staddon (Eds.), *Handbook of operant behavior* (pp. 174–200). Englewood Cliffs, NJ: Prentice-Hall.

Mowrer, O. H., & Mowrer, W. M. (1938). Enuresis: A method for its study and treatment. *American Journal of Orthopsychiatry, 8,* 436–459.

Mudford, O. C. (1987). Acceptability of a visual screening procedure for reducing stereotypy in mentally retarded children: Evaluation by New Zealand institutional staff. *Behavior Change, 4,* 4–13.

Murphy, H. A., Hutchison, J. M., & Bailey, J. S. (1983). Behavioral school psychology goes outdoors: The effect of organized games on playground aggression. *Journal of Applied Behavior Analysis, 16,* 29–36.

Neef, N. A., Iwata, B. A., & Page, T. J. (1978). Public transportation training: In vivo versus classroom instruction. *Journal of Applied Behavior Analysis, 11,* 331–344.

Neef, N. A., Parrish, J. M., Egel, A. L., & Sloan, M. E. (1986). Training respite care providers for families with handicapped children: Experimental analysis and validation of an instructional package. *Journal of Applied Behavior Analysis, 19,* 105–124.

Neisworth, J. T., & Moore, F. (1972). Operant treatment of asthmatic responding with the parent as therapist. *Behavior Therapy, 3,* 95–99.

Nelson, G., & Carson, P. (1988). Evaluation of a social problem-solving skills program for third- and fourth-grade students. *American Journal of Community Psychology, 16,* 79–99.

Nelson, R. O., & Hayes, S. C. (1981). Theoretical explanations for reactivity in self-monitoring. *Behavior Modification, 5,* 3–14.

Nelton, S. (1988, March). Motivating for success. *Nation's Business,* pp. 18–26.

New Tool: "Reinforcement" for good work. (1971, December 18). *Business Week,* pp. 76–77.

Nordyke, N. S., Baer, D. M., Etzel, B. C., & LeBlanc, J. M. (1977). Implications of the stereotyping and modification of sex role. *Journal of Applied Behavior Analysis, 10,* 553–557.

Novaco, R. W. (1979). The cognitive regulation of anger and stress. In P. C. Kendall & S. D. Hollon (Eds.), *Cognitive-behavioral interventions: Theory, research, and procedures* (pp. 241–285). New York: Academic Press.

Nunes, D. L., Murphy, R. J., & Ruprecht, M. L. (1977). Reducing self-injurious behavior of severely retarded individuals through withdrawal-of-reinforcement procedures. *Behavior Modification, 1,* 499–516.

O'Banion, D. R., & Whaley, D. L. (1981). *Behavior contracting: Arranging contingencies of reinforcement.* New York: Springer.

O'Brien, F., & Azrin, N. H. (1972). Developing proper mealtime behaviors of the institutionalized retarded. *Journal of Applied Behavior Analysis, 5,* 389–399.

O'Brien, F., Azrin, N. H., & Bugle, C. (1972). Training profoundly retarded children to stop crawling. *Journal of Applied Behavior Analysis, 5,* 131–137.

O'Brien, F., Bugle, C., & Azrin, N. H. (1972). Training and maintaining a retarded child's proper eating. *Journal of Applied Behavior Analysis, 5,* 67–72.

O'Brien, T. P., Riner, L. S., & Budd, K. S. (1983). The effects of a child's self-evaluation program on compliance with parental instructions in the home. *Journal of Applied Behavior Analysis, 16,* 69–79.

O'Leary, K. D., Kent, R. N., & Kanowitz, J. (1975). Shaping data collection congruent with experimental hypotheses. *Journal of Applied Behavior Analysis, 8,* 43–51.

O'Leary, K. D., & Wilson, G. T. (1987). *Behavior therapy: Application and outcome* (2nd ed.). Englewood Cliffs, NJ: Prentice-Hall.

Ollendick, T. H. (1981). Self-monitoring and self-administered overcorrection: The modification of nervous tics in children. *Behavior Modification, 5,* 75–84.

Ollendick, T. H., & Matson, J. L. (1978). Overcorrection: An overview. *Behavior Therapy, 9,* 830–842.

Ollendick, T. H., Shapiro, E. S., & Barrett, R. P. (1981). Reducing stereotypic behaviors: An analysis of treatment procedures using an alternating-treatments design. *Behavior Therapy, 12,* 570–577.

Osborne, J. G., & Powers, R. B. (1980). Controlling the litter problem. In G. L. Martin & J. G. Osborne (Eds.), *Helping in the community: Behavioral applications* (pp. 103–168). New York: Plenum.

Pace, G. M., Iwata, B. A., Edwards, G. L., & McCosh, K. C. (1986). Stimulus fading and transfer in the treatment of self-restraint and self-injurious behavior. *Journal of Applied Behavior Analysis, 19,* 381–389.

Page, T. J., Iwata, B. A., & Neef, N. A. (1976). Teaching pedestrian skills to retarded persons: Generalization from the classroom to the natural environment. *Journal of Applied Behavior Analysis, 9,* 433–444.

Paine, S. C., Hops, H., Walker, H. M., Greenwood, C. R., Fleischman, D. H., & Guild,

J. J. (1982). Repeated treatment effects: A study of maintaining behavior change in socially withdrawn children. *Behavior Modification, 6,* 171–199.

Parrish, J. M., Cataldo, M. F., Kolko, D. J., Neef, N. A., & Egel, A. L. (1986). Experimental analysis of response covariation among compliant and inappropriate behaviors. *Journal of Applied Behavior Analysis, 19,* 241–254.

Parsons, M. B., Schepis, M. M., Reid, D. H., McCarn, J. E., & Green, C. W. (1987). Expanding the impact of behavioral staff management: A large-scale, long-term application in school's serving severely handicapped persons. *Journal of Applied Behavior Analysis, 20,* 139–150.

Parsonson, B. S., & Baer, D. M. (1978). The analysis and presentation of graphic data. In T. R. Kratochwill (Ed.), *Single-subject research: Strategies for evaluating change* (pp. 101–165). New York: Academic Press.

Patterson, G. R. (1982). *Coercive family process.* Eugene, OR: Castalia.

Patterson, G. R., & Fleischman, M. J. (1979). Maintenance of treatment effects: Some considerations concerning family systems and follow-up data. *Behavior Therapy, 10,* 168–185.

Paul, G. L., & Lentz, R. J. (1977). *Psychosocial treatment of chronic mental patients: Milieu versus social learning program.* Cambridge, MA: Harvard University Press.

Peacock, R., Lyman, R. D., & Rickard, H. C. (1978). Correspondence between self-report and observer-report as a function of task difficulty. *Behavior Therapy, 9,* 578–583.

Peck, C. A., Apolloni, T., Cooke, T. P., & Raver, S. A. (1978). Teaching retarded preschoolers to initiate the free-play behavior of nonretarded classmates: Trained and generalized effects. *Journal of Special Education, 12,* 195–207.

Peck, C. A., Cooke, T. P., & Apolloni, T. (1981). Utilization of peer imitation in therapeutic and instructional contexts. In P. S. Strain (Ed.), *The utilization of classroom peers as behavior change agents* (pp. 69–99). New York: Plenum.

Pedalino, E., & Gamboa, V. U. (1974). Behavior modification and absenteeism: Intervention in one industrial setting. *Journal of Applied Psychology, 59,* 694–698.

Pertschuk, M. J., Edwards, N., & Pomerleau, O. F. (1978). A multiple-baseline approach to behavioral intervention in anorexia nervosa. *Behavior Therapy, 9,* 368–376.

Peterson, L. (1984). Teaching home safety and survival skills to latch-key children: A comparison of two manuals and methods. *Journal of Applied Behavior Analysis, 17,* 279–294.

Pfiffner, L. J., & O'Leary, S. G. (1987). The efficacy of all-positive management as a function of the prior use of negative consequences. *Journal of Applied Behavior Analysis, 20,* 265–271.

Phillips, E. L., Phillips, E. A., Fixsen, D. L., & Wolf, M. M. (1971). Achievement Place: Modification of the behaviors of predelinquent boys within a token economy. *Journal of Applied Behavior Analysis, 4,* 45–59.

Phillips, E. L., Phillips, E. A., Wolf, M. M., & Fixsen, D. L. (1973). Achievement Place: Development of the elected-manager system. *Journal of Applied Behavior Analysis, 6,* 541–561.

Piaget, J. (1928). *Judgment and reasoning of the child*. New York: Harcourt Brace Jovanovich.

Pigott, H. E., Fantuzzo, J. W., & Clement, P. W. (1986). The effects of reciprocal peer tutoring and group contingencies on the academic performance of elementary school children. *Journal of Applied Behavior Analysis, 19,* 93–98.

Pinkston, E. M., Reese, N. M., LeBlanc, J. M., & Baer, D. M. (1973). Independent control of a preschool child's aggression and peer interaction by contingent teacher attention. *Journal of Applied Behavior Analysis, 6,* 115–124.

Plummer, S., Baer, D. M., & LeBlanc, J. M. (1977). Functional considerations in the use of procedural time out and an effective alternative. *Journal of Applied Behavior Analysis, 10,* 689–705.

Poche, C., Brouwer, R., & Swearingen, M. (1981). Teaching self-protection to young children. *Journal of Applied Behavior Analysis, 14,* 169–176.

Poche, C., Yoder, P., & Miltenberger, R. (1988). Teaching self-protection to children using television techniques. *Journal of Applied Behavior Analysis, 21,* 253–261.

Poling, A., & Ryan, C. (1982). Differential-reinforcement-of-other-behavior schedules. *Behavior Modification, 6,* 3–21.

Porterfield, J. K., Herbert-Jackson, E., & Risley, T. R. (1976). Contingent observation: An effective and acceptable procedure for reducing disruptive behavior of young children in a group setting. *Journal of Applied Behavior Analysis, 9,* 55–64.

Powers, R. B., Osborne, J. G., & Anderson, E. G. (1973). Positive reinforcement of litter removal in the natural environment. *Journal of Applied Behavior Analysis, 6,* 579–586.

Praderas, K., & MacDonald, M. L. (1986). Telephone conversational skills training with socially isolated, impaired nursing home residents. *Journal of Applied Behavior Analysis, 19,* 337–348.

Premack, D. (1965). Reinforcement theory. In D. Levine (Ed.), *Nebraska symposium on motivation*. Lincoln: University of Nebraska Press.

Puder, R., Lacks, P., Bertelson, A. D., & Storandt, M. (1983). Short-term stimulus control treatment of insomnia in older adults. *Behavior Therapy, 14,* 424–429.

Rachman, S. (1977). The conditioning theory of fear-acquisition: A critical examination. *Behaviour Research and Therapy, 15,* 375–387.

Rapport, M. D., Murphy, H. A., & Bailey, J. S. (1982). Ritalin versus response cost in the control of hyperactive children: A within-subject comparison. *Journal of Applied Behavior Analysis, 15,* 205–216.

Redd, W. H., & Birnbrauer, J. S. (1969). Adults as discriminative stimuli for different reinforcement contingencies with retarded children. *Journal of Experimental Child Psychology, 7,* 440–447.

Redd, W. H., Morris, E. K., & Martin, J. A. (1975). Effects of positive and negative adult-child interactions on children's social preference. *Journal of Experimental Child Psychology, 19,* 153–164.

Reid, D. H., Luyben, P. L., Rawers, F. A., & Bailey, J. S. (1976). The effects of prompting and proximity of containers on newspaper recycling behavior. *Environment and Behavior, 8,* 471–482.

Reisinger, J. J. (1972). Treatment of "anxiety depression" via positive reinforcement and response cost. *Journal of Applied Behavior Analysis, 5,* 125–130.

Rekers, G. A. (1977). Atypical gender development and psychosocial adjustment. *Journal of Applied Behavior Analysis, 10,* 559–571.

Rekers, G. A., & Lovaas, O. I. (1974). Behavioral treatment of deviant sex role behaviors in a male child. *Journal of Applied Behavior Analysis, 7,* 173–190.

Rescorla, R. A. (1988). Pavlovian conditioning: It's not what you think it is. *American Psychologist, 43* 151–160.

Resick, P. A., Forehand, R., & McWhorter, A. Q. (1976). The effect of parental treatment with one child on an untreated sibling. *Behavior Therapy, 7,* 544–548.

Resick, P. A., Forehand, R., & Peed, S. (1974). Prestatement of contingencies: The effects on acquisition maintenance of behavior. *Behavior Therapy, 5,* 642–647.

Rilling, M. (1977). Stimulus control and inhibitory processes. In W. K. Honig & J. E. R. Staddon (Eds.), *Handbook of operant behavior* (pp. 432–480). Englewood Cliffs, NJ: Prentice-Hall.

Rincover, A. (1978). Sensory extinction: A procedure for eliminating self-stimulatory behavior in developmentally disabled children. *Journal of Abnormal Child Psychology, 6,* 299–310.

Riordan, M. M., Iwata, B. A., Finney, J. W., Wohl, M. K., & Stanley, A. E. (1984). Behavioral assessment and treatment of chronic food refusal in handicapped children. *Journal of Applied Behavior Analysis, 17,* 327–342.

Roberts, M. C., & Fanurik, D. (1986). Rewarding elementary school children for their use of safety belts. *Health Psychology, 5,* 185–196.

Roberts, M. W., Hatzenbuehler, L. C., & Bean, A. W. (1981). The effects of differential attention and time out on child noncompliance. *Behavior Therapy, 12,* 93–99.

Roberts, R. M., Nelson, R. O., & Olson, T. W. (1987). Self-instruction: An analysis of the differential effects of instruction and reinforcement. *Journal of Applied Behavior Analysis, 20,* 235–242.

Robertson, S. J., DeReus, D. M., & Drabman, R. S. (1976). Peer and college-student tutoring as reinforcement in a token economy. *Journal of Applied Behavior Analysis, 9,* 169–177.

Robertson, S. J., Simon, S. J., Pachman, J. S., & Drabman, R. S. (1979). Self-control and generalization procedures in a classroom of disruptive retarded children. *Child Behavior Therapy, 1,* 347–362.

Robin, A. L., Kent, R., O'Leary, K. D., Foster, S., & Prinz, R. (1977). An approach to teaching parents and adolescents problem-solving communication skills: A preliminary overview. *Behavior Therapy, 8,* 639–643.

Rollings, J. P., Baumeister, A. A., & Baumeister, A. A. (1977). The use of overcorrection procedures to eliminate the stereotyped behaviors of retarded individuals: An analysis of collateral behaviors and generalization of suppressive effects. *Behavior Modification, 1,* 29–46.

Rollins, H. A., McCandless, B. R., Thompson, M., & Braswell, W. R. (1974). Project Success Environment: An extended application of contingency management in inner-city schools. *Journal of Educational Psychology, 66,* 167–178.

Romanczyk, R. G., Kent, R. N., Diament, C., & O'Leary, K. D. (1973). Measuring the reliability of observational data: A reactive process. *Journal of Applied Behavior Analysis, 6,* 175–184.

Rosen, G. M., Glasgow, R. E., & Barrera, M., Jr. (1976). A controlled study to assess the clinical efficacy of totally self-administered systematic desensitization. *Journal of Consulting and Clinical Psychology, 44*, 208–217.

Rosen, G. M., Glasgow, R. E., & Barrera, M., Jr. (1977). A two-year follow-up on systematic desensitization with data pertaining to the external validity of laboratory fear assessment. *Journal of Consulting and Clinical Psychology, 45*, 1188–1189.

Rosen, H. S., & Rosen, L. A. (1983). Eliminating stealing: Use of stimulus control with an elementary student. *Behavior Modification, 7*, 56–63.

Rosenbaum, A., O'Leary, K. D., & Jacob, R. G. (1975). Behavioral intervention with hyperactive children: Group consequences as a supplement to individual contingencies. *Behavior Therapy, 6*, 315–323.

Rosenthal, T. L., & Bandura, A. (1978). Psychological modeling: Theory and practice. In S. L. Garfield & A. E. Bergin (Eds.), *Handbook of psychotherapy and behavior change: An empirical analysis* (2nd ed., pp. 621–658). New York: Wiley.

Rotter, J. B. (1954). *Social learning and clinical psychology*. Englewood Cliffs, NJ: Prentice-Hall.

Rowbury, T. G., Baer, A. M., & Baer, D. M. (1976). Interactions between teacher guidance and contingent access to play in developing preacademic skills of deviant preschool children. *Journal of Applied Behavior Analysis, 9*, 85–104.

Ruggles, T. R., & LeBlanc, J. M. (1982). Behavior analysis procedures in classroom teaching. In A. S. Bellack, M. Hersen, & A. E. Kazdin (Eds.), *International handbook of behavior modification and therapy* (pp. 959–996). New York: Plenum.

Rusch, F. R., & Kazdin, A. E. (1981). Toward a methodology of withdrawal designs for the assessment of response maintenance. *Journal of Applied Behavior Analysis, 14*, 131–140.

Russo, D. C., & Koegel, R. L. (1977). A method for integrating an autistic child into a normal public school classroom. *Journal of Applied Behavior Analysis, 10*, 579–590.

Russo, D. C., & Varni, J. W. (Eds.). (1982). *Behavior pediatrics: Research and practice*. New York: Plenum.

Safer, D. J., Heaton, R. C., & Parker, F. C. (1981). A behavioral program for disruptive junior high school students: Results and follow-up. *Journal of Abnormal Child Psychology, 9*, 483–494.

Saigh, P. A. (1986). In vitro flooding in the treatment of a 6-yr-old boy's post-traumatic stress disorder. *Behaviour Research and Therapy, 24*, 685–688.

Sajwaj, T., Libert, J., & Agras, W. S. (1974). Lemon juice therapy: The control of life-threatening rumination in a six-month-old infant. *Journal of Applied Behavior Analysis, 7*, 557–563.

Sajwaj, T., Twardosz, S., & Burke, M. (1972). Side effects of extinction procedures in a remedial preschool. *Journal of Applied Behavior Analysis, 5*, 163–175.

Salter, A. (1952). *The case against psychoanalysis*. New York: Henry Holt.

Sanders, M. R., & Glynn, T. (1977). Functional analysis of a program for training high- and low-preference peers to modify disruptive classroom behavior. *Journal of Applied Behavior Analysis, 10*, 503.

Sanders, M. R., & Glynn, T. (1981). Training parents in behavioral self-management:

An analysis of generalization and maintenance. *Journal of Applied Behavior Analysis, 14,* 223–237.

Sanson-Fisher, B., Seymour, F. W., Montgomery, W., & Stokes, T. F. (1978). Modifying delinquents' conversation using token reinforcement of self-recorded behavior. *Journal of Behavior Therapy and Experimental Psychiatry, 9,* 163–168.

Scheirer, M. A. (1981). *Program implementation: The organizational context.* Beverly Hills, CA: Sage.

Schepis, M. M., Reid, D. H., & Fitzgerald, J. R. (1987). Group instruction with profoundly retarded persons: Acquisition, generalization, and maintenance of a remunerative work skill. *Journal of Applied Behavior Analysis, 20,* 97–105.

Schnelle, J. F. (1974). A brief report on invalidity of parent evaluations of behavior change. *Journal of Applied Behavior Analysis, 7,* 341–343.

Schnelle, J. F., Kirchner, R. E., Macrae, J. W., McNees, M. P., Eck, R. H., Snodgrass, S., Casey, J. D., & Uselton, P. H. (1978). Police evaluation research: An experimental and cost-benefit analysis of a helicopter patrol in a high-crime area. *Journal of Applied Behavior Analysis, 11,* 11–21.

Schreibman, L. (1988). *Autism.* Newbury Park, CA: Sage.

Seaman, J. E., Greene, B. F., & Watson-Perczel, M. (1986). A behavioral system for assessing and training cardiopulmonary resuscitation skills among emergency medical technicians. *Journal of Applied Behavior Analysis, 19,* 125–136.

Seaver, W. B., & Patterson, A. H. (1976). Decreasing fuel oil consumption through feedback and social commendation. *Journal of Applied Behavior Analysis, 10,* 147–152.

Shafto, F., & Sulzbacher, S. (1977). Comparing treatment tactics with a hyperactive preschool child: Stimulant medication and programmed teacher intervention. *Journal of Applied Behavior Analysis, 10,* 13–20.

Shapiro, E. S., & Shapiro, S. (1985). Behavioral coaching in the development of skills in track. *Behavior Modification, 9,* 211–224.

Shure, M. B., & Spivack, G. (1982). Interpersonal problem solving in young children: A cognitive approach to prevention. *American Journal of Community Psychology, 10,* 341–356.

Singh, N. N., Dawson, M. J., & Manning, P. (1981). Effects of spaced responding DRL on the stereotyped behavior of profoundly retarded persons. *Journal of Applied Behavior Analysis, 14,* 521–526.

Singh, N. N., & Katz, R. C. (1985). On the modification of acceptability ratings for alternative child treatments. *Behavior Modification, 9,* 375–386.

Singh, N. N., Watson, J. E., & Winton, A. S. W. (1986). Treating self-injury: Water mist spray versus facial screening or forced arm exercise. *Journal of Applied Behavior Analysis, 19,* 403–410.

Skinner, B. F. (1938). *The behavior of organisms: An experimental analysis.* New York: Appleton-Century.

Skinner, B. F. (1948). *Walden two.* New York: Macmillan.

Skinner, B. F. (1953). *Science and human behavior.* New York: Macmillan.

Skinner, B. F. (1974). *About behaviorism.* New York: Knopf.

Smith, B. M., Schumaker, J. B., Schaeffer, J., & Sherman, J. A. (1982). Increasing participation and improving the quality of discussions in seventh-grade social studies classes. *Journal of Applied Behavior Analysis, 15,* 97–110.

Smith, L. K. C., & Fowler, S. A. (1984). Positive peer pressure: The effects of peer monitoring on children's disruptive behavior. *Journal of Applied Behavior Analysis, 17,* 213–227.

Snyder, J. J., & White, M. J. (1979). The use of cognitive self-instruction in the treatment of behaviorally disturbed adolescents. *Behavior Therapy, 10,* 227–235.

Solnick, J. V., Rincover, A., & Peterson, C. R. (1977). Some determinants of the reinforcing and punishing effects of time out. *Journal of Applied Behavior Analysis, 10,* 415–424.

Solomon, R. L., Kamin, L. J., & Wynne, L. C. (1953). Traumatic avoidance learning: The outcomes of several extinction procedures with dogs. *Journal of Abnormal and Social Psychology, 48,* 291–302.

Sowers-Hoag, K. M., Thyer, B. A., & Bailey, J. S. (1987). Promoting automobile safety belt use by young children. *Journal of Applied Behavioral Analysis, 20,* 133–138.

Spivack, G., Platt, J. J., & Shure, M. B. (1976). *The problem-solving approach to adjustment.* San Francisco: Jossey-Bass.

Spivack, G., & Shure, M. B. (1982). The cognition of social adjustment: Interpersonal cognitive problem-solving thinking. In B. B. Lahey & A. E. Kazdin (Eds.), *Advances in clinical child psychology* (Vol. 5, pp. 323–372). New York: Plenum.

Sprague, J. R., & Horner, R. H. (1984). The effects of single instance, multiple instance, and general case training on generalized vending machine use by moderately and severely handicapped students. *Journal of Applied Behavior Analysis, 17,* 273–278.

Spring, F. L., Sipich, J. F., Trimble, R. W., & Goechner, D. J. (1978). Effects of contingency and noncontingency contracts in the context of a self-control-oriented smoking modification program. *Behavior Therapy, 9,* 967–968.

Staats, A. W. (1975). *Social behaviorism.* Chicago: Dorsey Press.

Stokes, T. F., & Baer, D. M. (1976). Preschool peers as mutual generalization-facilitating agents. *Behavior Therapy, 7,* 549–556.

Stokes, T. F., & Baer, D. M. (1977). An implicit technology of generalization. *Journal of Applied Behavior Analysis, 10,* 349–367.

Stokes, T. F., Baer, D. M., & Jackson, R. L. (1974). Programming the generalization of a greeting response in four retarded children. *Journal of Applied Behavior Analysis, 7,* 599–610.

Stokes, T. F., & Osnes, P. G. (1986). Programming the generalization of children's social behavior. In P. S. Strain, M. J. Guralnick, & H. M. Walker (Eds.), *Children's social behavior: Development, assessment, and modification* (pp. 407–443). New York: Academic Press.

Strain, P. S. (Ed.). (1981). *The utilization of classroom peers as behavior change agents.* New York: Plenum.

Strain, P. S., Shores, R. E., & Kerr, M. M. (1976). An experimental analysis of "spillover" effects on the social interaction of behaviorally handicapped preschool children. *Journal of Applied Behavior Analysis, 9,* 31–40.

Strain, P. S., Shores, R. E., & Timm, M. A. (1977). Effects of peer social initiations on the behavior of withdrawn preschool children. *Journal of Applied Behavior Analysis, 10,* 289–298.

Strupp, H. H., & Hadley, S. W. (1977). A tripartite model of mental health and therapeutic outcomes. *American Psychologist, 32,* 187–196.

Stuart, R. B. (1970). *Trick or treatment: How and when psychotherapy fails.* Champaign, IL: Research Press.

Stuart, R. B. (1971). Behavioral contracting with the families of delinquents. *Journal of Behavior Therapy and Experimental Psychiatry, 2,* 1–11.

Stuart, R. B. (Ed.). (1982). *Adherence, compliance, and generalization in behavioral medicine.* New York: Brunner/Mazel.

Stuart, R. B., & Lott, L. A., Jr. (1972). Behavioral contracting with delinquents: A cautionary note. *Journal of Behavior Therapy and Experimental Psychiatry, 3,* 161–169.

Sulzer-Azaroff, B. (1982). Behavioral approaches to occupational health and safety. In L. W. Frederiksen (Ed.), *Handbook of organizational behavior management* (pp. 505–538). New York: Wiley.

Sulzer-Azaroff, B., & de Santamaria, C. (1980). Industrial safety hazard reduction through performance feedback. *Journal of Applied Behavior Analysis, 13,* 287–295.

Surwit, R. S., & Keefe, F. J. (1978). Frontalis EMG feedback training: An electronic panacea? *Behavior Therapy, 9,* 779–792.

Swain, J. J., Allard, G. B., & Holborn, S. W. (1982). The good toothbrushing game: A school-based dental hygiene program for increasing the toothbrushing effectiveness of children. *Journal of Applied Behavior Analysis, 15,* 171–176.

Switzer, E. B., Deal, T. E., & Bailey, J. S. (1977). The reduction of stealing in second graders using a group contingency. *Journal of Applied Behavior Analysis, 10,* 267–272.

Taplin, P. S., & Reid, J. B. (1973). Effects of instructional set and experimenter influence on observer reliability. *Child Development, 44,* 547–554.

Tertinger, D. A., Greene, B. F., & Lutzker, J. R. (1984). Home safety: Development and validation of one component of an ecobehavioral treatment program for abused and neglected children. *Journal of Applied Behavior Analysis, 17,* 159–174.

Thomas, J. D., Presland, I. E., Grant, M. D., & Glynn, T. L. (1978). Natural rates of teacher approval and disapproval in grade-seven classrooms. *Journal of Applied Behavior Analysis, 11,* 91–94.

Thompson, M., Braswell, W. R., Persons, S., Tucker, R., & Rollins, H. (1974). Contingency management in the schools: How often and how well does it work? *American Educational Research Journal, 11,* 19–28.

Timberlake, E. M. (1981). Child abuse and externalized aggression: Preventing a delinquent lifestyle. In R. J. Hunner & Y. E. Walker (Eds.), *Exploring the relationship between child abuse and delinquency* (pp. 43–51). Montclair, NJ: Allanheld, Osmun.

Timberlake, W., & Allison, J. (1974). Response deprivation: An empirical approach to instrumental performance. *Psychological Review, 81,* 146–164.

Tucker, D. J., & Berry, G. W. (1980). Teaching severely multihandicapped students to put on their own hearing aids. *Journal of Applied Behavior Analysis, 13,* 65–75.

Turk, D. C., Meichenbaum, D., & Genest, M. (1983). *Pain and behavioral medicine: A cognitive behavioral perspective.* New York: Guilford.

Turkewitz, H., O'Leary, K. D., & Ironsmith, M. (1975). Generalization and maintenance of appropriate behavior through self-control. *Journal of Consulting and Clinical Psychology, 43,* 557–583.

Twardosz, S., & Baer, D. M. (1973). Training two severely retarded adolescents to ask questions. *Journal of Applied Behavior Analysis, 6,* 655–661.

Upper, D. (1973). A "ticket" system for reducing ward rule violations on a token-economy program. *Journal of Behavior Therapy and Experimental Psychiatry, 4,* 137–140.

Upper, D., Lochman, J. E., & Aveni, C. A. (1977). Using contingency contracting to modify the problematic behaviors of foster home residents. *Behavior Modification, 1,* 405–416.

Urbain, E. S., & Kendall, P. C. (1980). Review of social-cognitive problem-solving interventions with children. *Psychological Bulletin, 88,* 109–143.

Van Houten, R. (1979). Social validation: The evolution of standards of competency for target behaviors. *Journal of Applied Behavior Analysis, 12,* 581–591.

Van Houten, R., Hill, S., & Parsons, M. (1975). An analysis of a performance feedback system: The effects of timing and feedback, public posting, and praise upon academic performance and peer interaction. *Journal of Applied Behavior Analysis, 8,* 449–457.

Van Houten, R., Malenfant, L., & Rolider, A. (1985). Increasing driver yielding and pedestrian signaling with prompting, feedback, and enforcement. *Journal of Applied Behavior Analysis, 18,* 103–110.

Van Houten, R., Nau, P. A., MacKenzie-Keating, S. E., Sameoto, D., & Colavecchia, B. (1982). An analysis of some variables influencing the effectiveness of reprimands. *Journal of Applied Behavior Analysis, 15,* 65–83.

Van Houten, R., Nau, P. A., & Marini, Z. (1980). An analysis of public posting in reducing speeding behavior on an urban highway. *Journal of Applied Behavior Analysis, 13,* 383–395.

Van Houten, R., & Rolider, A. (1988). Recreating the scene: An effective way to provide delayed punishment for inappropriate motor behavior. *Journal of Applied Behavior Analysis, 21,* 187–192.

Van Houten, R., Rolider, A., Nau, P. A., Friedman, R., Becker, M., Chalodovsky, I., & Scherer, M. (1985). Large-scale reductions in speeding and accidents in Canada and Israel: A behavioral ecological perspective. *Journal of Applied Behavior Analysis, 18,* 87–93.

Varni, J. W. (1981). Self-regulation techniques in the management of chronic arthritic pain in hemophilia. *Behavior Therapy, 12,* 185–194.

Wahler, R. G. (1975). Some structural aspects of deviant child behavior. *Journal of Applied Behavior Analysis, 8,* 27–42.

Wahler, R. G., Berland, R. M., & Coe, T. D. (1979). Generalization processes in child behavior change. In B. B. Lahey & A. E. Kazdin (Eds.), *Advances in clinical child psychology* (Vol. 2, pp. 36–69). New York: Plenum.

Wahler, R. G., & Fox, J. J. (1980). Solitary toy play and time out: A family treatment package for children with aggressive and oppositional behavior. *Journal of Applied Behavior Analysis, 13,* 23–29.

Walker, H. M., & Hops, H. (1976). Use of normative peer data as a standard for evaluating classroom treatment effects. *Journal of Applied Behavior Analysis, 9,* 158–168.

Walker, H. M., Hops, H., & Feigenbaum, E. (1976). Deviant classroom behavior as a function of combination of social and token reinforcement and cost contingency. *Behavior Therapy, 7,* 76–88.

Walker, H. M., Hops, H., & Greenwood, C. R. (1981). RECESS: Research and development of a behavior management package for remediating social aggression in the school setting. In P. S. Strain (Ed.), *The utilization of classroom peers as behavior change agents* (pp. 261–303). New York: Plenum.

Walker, H. M., Hops, H., & Johnson, S. M. (1975). Generalization and maintenance of classroom treatment effects. *Behavior Therapy, 6,* 188–200.

Warr, P. (1987). *Work, unemployment, and mental health.* New York: Oxford University Press.

Watson, J. B., & Rayner, R. (1920). Conditioned emotional reactions. *Journal of Experimental Psychology, 3,* 1–14.

Weissberg, R. P., & Gesten, E. L. (1982). Considerations for developing effective school-based social problem-solving (SPS) training programs. *School Psychology Review, 11,* 56–63.

Weissberg, R. P., Gesten, E. L., Carnike, C. L., Toro, P. A., Rapkin, B. D., Davidson, E., & Cowen, E. L. (1981). Social problem-solving skills training: A competence-building intervention with second- to fourth-grade children. *American Journal of Community Psychology, 9,* 411–423.

Wells, J. K., Howard, G. S., Nowlin, W. F., & Vargas, M. J. (1986). Presurgical anxiety and postsurgical pain and adjustment: Effects of a stress inoculation procedure. *Journal of Consulting and Clinical Psychology, 54,* 831–835.

White, L., & Tursky, D. (Eds.). (1982). *Clinical biofeedback: Efficacy and mechanisms.* New York: Guilford.

White, M. A. (1975). Natural rates of teacher approval and disapproval in the classroom. *Journal of Applied Behavior Analysis, 8,* 367–372.

Whitman, T. L., Mercurio, J. R., & Caponigri, V. (1970). Development of social responses in two severely retarded children. *Journal of Applied Behavior Analysis, 3,* 133–138.

Williams, C. D. (1959). The elimination of tantrum behaviors by extinction procedures. *Journal of Abnormal and Social Psychology, 59,* 269.

Williams, G. E., & Cuvo, A. J. (1986). Training apartment upkeep skills to rehabilitation clients: A comparison of task analytic strategies. *Journal of Applied Behavior Analysis, 19,* 39–52.

Wilson, D. D., Robertson, S. J., Herlong, L. H., & Haynes, S. N. (1979). Vicarious effects of time out in the modification of aggression in the classroom. *Behavior Modification, 3,* 97–111.

Wilson, G. T., Leaf, R. C., & Nathan, P. E. (1975). The aversive control of excessive alcohol consumption by chronic alcoholics in the laboratory setting. *Journal of Applied Behavior Analysis, 8,* 13–26.

Winett, R. A., & Winkler, R. C. (1972). Current behavior modification in the classroom: Be still, be quiet, be docile. *Journal of Applied Behavior Analysis, 5,* 499–504.

Winkler, R. C. (1971). The relevance of economic theory and technology of token-reinforcement systems. *Behaviour Research and Therapy, 9,* 81–88.

Winkler, R. C. (1977). What types of sex role behavior should behavior modifiers promote? *Journal of Applied Behavior Analysis, 10,* 549–552.

Wolf, M. M. (1978). Social validity: The case for subjective measurement, or how applied behavior analysis is finding its heart. *Journal of Applied Behavior Analysis, 11,* 203–214.

Wolfe, D. A. (1987). *Child abuse.* Newbury Park, CA: Sage.

Wolfe, D. A., Mendes, M. G., & Factor, D. (1984). A parent-administered program to reduce children's television viewing. *Journal of Applied Behavior Analysis, 17,* 267–272.

Wolpe, J. (1958). *Psychotherapy by reciprocal inhibition.* Stanford, CA: Stanford University Press.

Wong, S. E., Terranova, M. D., Bowen, L., Zarate, R., Massel, H. K., & Liberman, R. P. (1987). Providing independent recreational activities to reduce stereotypic vocalizations in chronic schizophrenics. *Journal of Applied Behavior Analysis, 20,* 77–82.

Wood, R., & Flynn, J. M. (1978). A self-evaluation token system versus an external evaluation token system alone in a residential setting with predelinquent youth. *Journal of Applied Behavior Analysis, 11,* 503–512.

Woolfolk, A. E., Woolfolk, R. L., & Wilson, G. T. (1977). A rose by another name . . . : Labeling bias and attitudes toward behavior modification. *Journal of Consulting and Clinical Psychology, 45,* 184–191.

Wright, D. G., Brown, R. A., & Andrews, M. E. (1978). Remission of chronic ruminative vomiting through a reversal of social contingencies. *Behaviour Research and Therapy, 16,* 134–136.

Wright, K. M., & Miltenberger, R. G. (1987). Awareness training in the treatment of head and facial tics. *Journal of Behavior Therapy and Experimental Psychiatry, 18,* 269–274.

Wyatt v. Stickney, 344 F. Supp., 373, 344 F. Supp. 387 (M.D. Ala. 1972); affirmed sub nom. Wyatt v. Aderholt, 503 F.2d 1305 (5th Cir. 1974).

Yates, A. J. (1980). *Biofeedback and the modification of behavior.* New York: Plenum.

Yeaton, W. H., & Bailey, J. S. (1978). Teaching pedestrian skills to young children using an instructional package: An analysis and one-year follow-up. *Journal of Behavior Analysis, 11,* 315–329.

Zeiss, R. A. (1978). Self-directed treatment for premature ejaculation. *Journal of Consulting and Clinical Psychology, 46,* 1234–1241.

Zivin, G. (Ed.). (1979). *The development of self-regulation through private speech.* New York: Wiley-Interscience.

Author Index

Subject Index